# The Role of
# TRAVEL AGENT
# in
# Managing Tourist Product

## By the Same Author

International Tourism Management

Tourism Development: Principles and Practices

Travel Tourism – An Industry Facilitator

The Business of Tourism: Concepts and Strategies

Tourism Management and Marketing

Tourism in India-History and Development

# The Role of
# TRAVEL AGENT
# in
# Managing Tourist Product

## A. K. Bhatia

**STERLING**

**STERLING PUBLISHERS (P) LTD.**
Regd. Office: A1/256 Safdarjung Enclave,
New Delhi-110029. Cin: U22110DL1964PTC211907
Phone: +91 82877 98380
e-mail: mail@sterlingpublishers.in
www.sterlingpublishers.in

The Role of TRAVEL AGENT in Managing Tourist Product
*Originally Published*
The Business of Travel Agency and Tour Operations Management.
© 2019, A. K. Bhatia
ISBN 978 93 86245 75 5
First Edition: 2012
Second Revised Edition: 2019

All rights are reserved. No part of this publication may be reproduced, stored in a retrieval system or transmitted, in any form or by any means, mechanical, photocopying, recording or otherwise, without prior written permission of the original publisher.

*Printed and Published in India by*

**Sterling Publishers Pvt. Ltd.,**
Plot No. 13, Ecotech-III, Greater Noida - 201306, U. P. India

## To My Loving Parents

Who lived a life of excellence with unwavering compassion and love for their family. Integrity an honour had been their hallmark.
Their life was a blessing, their memory a treasure. They are loved beyond words and missed beyond measure. We miss them in every moment of our lives – with deepest love, greatest pride and honour. Their absence is felt deeply in our hearts. We continue to seek their blessings and affection.

## To My Loving Wife

It has been almost four years that you left for heavenly abode and there has not been a single day that I have not missed your presence in my life. You may be gone from this world, but you are forever alive in my heart.

# Preface

Retail travel agents is the most important travel intermediary. They act as sales outlets for suppliers and wholesalers from whom they receive commission for any sales made. They also act as travel counselor, advising people as to when, where, and how to travel; as salesperson actively selling travel, and as assitant, making reservations in response to customer requests.

Travel retailing is the outcome of the urge of people to travel in an organised way. This essentially means using the services of retailers who are in a position to offer them a comparatively better price as they have entered into an agreement with the providers of these services to buy these in bulk and pass them on to the consumers on payment or credit. These services include transport, accommodation, sightseeing and several other ancillary services, which a prospective traveller wishes to buy and pay for accordingly.

The travel industry developed along certain well-defined lines as the worldwide demand on its services increased. The urge to travel became very intense over the years, resulting in widespread growth of travel agencies in the world. Most travellers wished to have their travel arrangements made in advance and to be relieved of the difficulties of coping with various pre-travel arrangements, of which they had limited knowledge.

In line with continuing shift in economic power to Asia, particularly to India and China the Asia-Pacific region will continue to lead world tourism growth in years to come.

The forecasts based on Asia Travel Monitor, part of the IPK International's World Travel Monitor as well as on interim inbound arrival data gathered by the UN World Tourism Organization (UNWTO) and the European Travel Commission (ETC), show that the Asia-Pacific region will be the fastest growing inbound and outbound tourism region in the world in the years to come.

International tourist arrivals in Asia-Pacific increased by more than 8% in 2018 after recording a rise of 7% in 2016-17. And in terms of outbound travel demand, a number of Asian markets are showing even more impressive growth. The top eight markets alone (Japan, China, South Korea, Taiwan, Singapore, India, Malaysia and Thailand) generate considerable tourist arrivals.

Regarding international tourism arrivals the figure has crossed 1.4 billion in the year 2018 according to the World Tourism Organisation.

The growth in the tourism industry being witnessed today, is a visible result of the great advancements in the technology which has changed social and economic fabric of people globally. Today, millions of people seem to enjoy the prospects of not only moving from one continent to another but within their own countries in a matter of hours.

The ever expanding tourism business resulting in the creation of millions of jobs presupposes the availability of trained manpower in the tourism sector. Maintaining high standards of professionalism in the industry is of paramount importance. As per the World Travel and Tourism Council (WTTC), employment opportunities in Travel and Tourism are expected to rise to over 60 million jobs in the year 2020, i.e., one in every 9.6 jobs. The industry is now ranked fifth in long term (10 years) growth and is expected to be the second largest employer in the world by the year 2020. On the other hand, the domestic tourism sector is expected to be the second largest employer globally by 2020.

The book is an effort to help upcoming professionals in the field of travel and tourism to acquire knowledge and skills in the area of managing the world's largest industry. The book will also be of help as a refresher programme to those already is the profession.

The book has been divided into thirteen chapters, each covering key areas of travel agency and tour operation business. All through, the approach has been to provide a simple and comprehensive outline of relevant areas.

The format of the book has been designed to assist the upcoming professionals pursuing systematic study of travel and tourism as a career, both at undergraduate as well as post graduate levels at colleges, training institutes, universities and management institutes.

Each of the chapters begins with chapter objectives. Appendices make the book more valuable, add interest and are an excellent support to the subject. The appendices include Hotel Industry Terms, Travel Trade Publications. International Tourism Periodicals, Travel Industry Journals and Periodicals. A list of Travel Research Journals, Education and Training in Travel and Tourism Institutes, International Organisations, Travel Related Publications of International Organizations and a Bibliography are also included. Later in the book, a comprehensive glossary of travel terms with special reference to Travel Agency and Tour operations has been added.

No single publication, however comprehensive, it may be, is sufficient to cover any subject in detail. Those who wish to make further detailed study of any particular topic will obviously have to undertake more reading.

Ex-Deputy Director General
Ministry of Tourism Government of India

*A.K. Bhatia*

# Acknowledgements

No published work is completely the work of the author or authors whose names are listed on the title page of the book. The unnamed authors as also research scholars and academicians of this book are legion as they are the ones who have done the pioneering work in explaining the complex tourism phenomenon in its various manifestations. In the first place my special thanks go to them from whom I have derived great inspiration. It is these pioneers who must be credited with whatever merit this book may have. My special thanks go first to them. On the other hand all the weaknesses and shortcomings of the book are solely the responsibility of the author.

Sincere thanks are extended to several international travel and tourism organisations and associations especially the UN World Tourism Organisation whose various reports and publications have immensely helped in shaping the present revised and enlarged version of the edition. The contributions of these organisations have been invaluable and for that I am deeply grateful.

My understanding of the complex subject of tourism and the knowledge have been influenced and shaped by my work in the Central Ministry of Tourism, Government of India. The manifold opportunities of work experience not only at the headquarters establishment but various overseas tourist-offices provided by the department proved to be quite invaluable in the writing of this book. I owe a debt of gratitude to my former Ministry of Tourism for providing me an opportunity to pursue a profession which I have always cherished.

My thanks and gratitude, as also appreciation, to all the professionals and organisations in the field as also eminent persons in the travel industry in Belgium, France, Switzerland and India, whose in-depth knowledge and experience proved to be of great value in explaining various facets of tourism. In addition, I am gratefull to Travel Industry, specially Travel Agents an their Associations who provided me with ample information as also guidelines which helped me a great deal in writing this book.

My sincere thanks to Sterling Publishers Limited for organising the entire manuscript of the book on computer and thereby publishing the same. Thanks are also due to Priyanka Sah and Mohammed. Firoz in helping to type the manuscript of the book.

Finally, my special thanks to my wife Kamla who is no more, for always encouraging me to continue in not only revising my publications but also writing new books. Both my late parents and my wife have always given their blessings.

*A.K. Bhatia*

# Contents

*Preface* v
*Acknowledgements* vii
*Abbreviations* xiii

1. **TRAVEL AGENCY HISTORICAL PERSPECTIVE** 1
   Retail Travel • Scope and Role of Retailers • Historical Perspective • Thomas Cook • Thomas Cook's European Tours • Competition with Railroads • Cook's Guided Tours • American Connection • Nile Tours • Hotel Coupons • Thomas Cook's Indian Connections • American Express Company • Cox and Kings • Types of Agencies • Consolidators • Travel Retailing and Product Sale • Definition of a Travel Agency • Types of Agency • Suburban Agency • Business House Agency • The Process of On-site Service Delivery Establishment corporate travel department • Implants • Departments in a Corporate Travel Agency • Travel Agency Skills And Competencies • Travel Agency Economics • The Future of Travel Agents • Tomorrow's Travel Agent • Travel and Technology.

2. **OPERATIONS OF A MODERN TRAVEL AGENCY** 19
   Organised Travel • Modern Travel Agencies • Travel Agency Operations • Travel Organisation • Individual Ordinary Trips • Knowledge About Air Schedules • International Ticketing Guides • Passenger Air Ticket • Sample of an E-Ticket • Settlement of Account • The Benefits of Insurance • General Details of Coverage • Conditions Applying To Insurance Policy • The Procedure to Claim Insurance • Miscellaneous Charge Order (MCO) • Prepaid Ticket Advise (PTA).

3. **TRAVEL ITINERARY** 39
   Principles of Itinerary Planning • Resources for Planning Travel Itineraries • Steps for Planning an Itinerary • Key points in Planning Itinerary • Mapping Itinerary • Resources for Planning Itinerary • Billing and Settlement Plan (BSP) • Benefits of BSP

4. **STARTING A TRAVEL AGENCY** 53
   • IATA-Controlled Approval • Additional Appointments • Basic Conventions • The Chicago Convention • The Bilateral Agreements • The Warsaw Convention • The IATA General Conditions of Carriage • Application Form for Recognition • Sale of a Tour • Steps on how to start a Traval Agency • NTO rules for recognition • Guidelines for approval/ recognition of Travel Agnecy/ Tour Operator • WATA Master key.

## 5. TOUR PACKAGING       71
Defining a Tour Operators • The Origins of the Packaged Tour • Growth in the Package Vacations • Mass Market Operators • Specialist Tour Operators • Domestic Operators • Incoming Operators • Types of Packaged Tours • Tour Operation Economics • Customised Tours and Excursions • Pricing a Tour • Control Over Tour Operating • Distributing the Product • Direct Marketing • Functions of Ground Tour Operator.

## 6. INBOUND TOUR MANAGEMENT       84
Introduction • Types of Inbound Travellers • The Major Markets of Inbound Tourists • Trends in Inbound Tourists • Inbound Itinerary • Itinerary Description • Transport • Accommodation • Steps to Itinerary Making • Some Sample Programmes for Inbound Tourists • Cost of an Itinerary • Cost Sheet • Cost Includes • Terms and Conditions • Optional Tours (Tour Extensions) • Inbound Tourism Products • The Inbound Tourist Products Available • Popular Inbound Destinations in India • Requirements of Inbound Tourists • Access to Information • Transport • Facilities • Events • Attractions • Language • Cultural Differences • Some Tips • Inhouse Operations • Field Operations

## 7. OUTBOUND TOUR MANAGEMENT       120
Introduction • The Major Markets for Outbound Tourism • Major Outbound Markets of Indians (Countrywise) • New Destinations: • Better Packages: • Safety and Security: • Handling Outbound Groups: • Reasons for Growth • Potential of Indian Outbound Market • Profile of Outbound Travellers • Outbound Tourist Data • European Introduction • European Jewels • The Best of Italy and France • Switzerland • Super Saver USA • Jewels of USA • Tour Pricing • Fixed Costs • Variable Costs • Tour Participant Estimation • Profit Mark-up • Travel Protection • Visas and Passports • Travel Documents • Service Inquiries after the Vacation • Holidays

## 8. SUPPLIER RELATIONSHIP IN TRAVEL INDUSTRY       144
Relationship with Air Travel Providers (Airlines) • Customer Centric • Relationship with Tourist Transport Suppliers • Private Bus Line Operators • Operators of Mass Transit Systems • Relationship with Accommodation Suppliers • Relationship between Travel Agents and Tour Operators • Proper Co-ordination • Importance of Agency-Suppliers Relationship • Challenges and Relationship

## 9. TRAVEL TRADE ASSOCIATIONS       155
• Forms of Travel Associations • Major International Travel Associations • Membership Criteria • The Aims of the Federation • ASTA History • The 1950s • The 1970s • The 1980s • Present Day Activities • Membership • ASTA World Travel Congress • ASTA Chapters • Structure of the Association • Mission Statement • Code of Conduct • Aims and Objectives of Tour Operators • Of Excursion Agents • For Hotels • For Airline Companies • For General Sales Agents (GSAs) • Of Agents Providing Travel Related Services • Of Courier Companies • Of Banks • Administrative Set-Up

## 10. TRANSPORT AND ACCOMMODATION SECTORS     180

Key Issues • Basic Component • Modes of Transport • Car Ownership • Introduction of Jets • Advances in Air Travel • Rapid Expansion in Europe • Factors Responsible for growth • High-Speed Trains • European High Speed Trains • Trains in USA • The Eurostar • Super-High Speed Trains • Deep Sea Travel • Holiday Sea Cruises • Fly Cruise • Cruise Market • Varied Activities Accommodation Segment • Hotel Accommodation • Forms of Hotel • Accommodation • International Hotels • Resort Hotels • Commercial Hotels • Residential Hotels • Floating Hotels • Airport Hotels • Hotel Reservation Checklist • Restaurant Services and Cuisines • Room Service • Meal Plans • Motels • Youth Hostel • Caravan and Camping Sites • Bed and Breakfast Establishments • Tourist Holiday Villages • Apartments •Farmhouses • Guesthouses • Bus Travel • Rail Travel • Euro Rail System • Railways in the System • Validity of the Pass • Different Products on Eurail • Child Discount • Senior Travellers • Youth Passes • 1st and 2nd class • Tour passes • Sleeping Accommodation • Reservation • Compulsory Seat Reservations • Refund • British Rail • Swiss Rail • Swiss Pass • Car Rentals • Car Rental Reservation Checklist • Sightseeing/Excursions/Tours • Hire of Private Car with Chauffeur • Land Arrangements • Selecting Accommodation • Selecting Sight Seeing Places at Destinations • Booking Flights • Computerised Travel Agency Systems • Hotel Reservation • Car Rental Reservation • Reserve the Car • Tour Package Reservation • Ferry Reservation • Diffrent modes of transport •

## 11. COMMUNICATION WITH THE CLIENT     223

The Issue • Customer Loyalty and Travel Agents • Some Ways to Increase Your Customers Loyalty • Definitions • Delivering Reliable Service • Maintaining Client Relationship • Client Complaint • Practical Tips for Handling Complaints • Communication Skills • Keys to Effective Listening • Communication Barriers • Ways to Better Communication • Communication Styles • Listening Skills • Body Language • Other Individual Examples • Language Usage • Interview Preparation • The Selection Process • Dressing for an Interview • Group Discussions • Important Tips for Group Discussion

## 12. TRAVEL TECHNOLOGY     239

Multiple Use of Technology • Trends in Industry (applicable to most countries) • Air Transportation • Reservation Systems • In-room Terminals • Internat usage • Rail Transportation • Surface Transportation • Car Rental Companies.

## 13. BUSINESS TRAVEL     248

Mice Tourism • Participation Advantages • Important Action Areas for Participation • Making a Choice • Major Findings • Marketing for New Products • International Tourism Borse (ITB) • ITB Survey • Range of Programmes • World Travel Market (WTM) • Database Driven Web-site • International Brussels Travel Fair (BTF) • Salon Mondial Du Tourism et Voyages (SMTV) • Feria International Tourismo (FITUR) • Travel Trade Workshop (TTW) • European Incentive and Business Travel and Meetings (EIBTM) • Swedish International Tourism and

Travel Fair (TUR) • Dutch Travel Trade Exhibition Tour • Computer Appointment Scheduling • Geographical Factors • The Structure of the Market • The Conference Bidding Process • International Congress and Convention Association (ICCA) • Membership • India Convention Promotion Bureau (ICPB) • Aims and Objectives • Membership • Incentive and Corporate Travel Segment • Effective Incentive Program • Incentive Programme Design and Implementation • Types of Incentive Programs • Online Programs • Incentive Rewards • Reasons for Offering Incentives • Types of Incentive Organisations • Profile of Incentive Winner • Main Users of Incentive Travel • Decision Making Process • Venue • Planning Team • Programme • Budget • Sponsorship • Promotion • Booking • At the Event • Post Event • Categories of Events • Event Planning • Steps to Planning an Event • Services of Event Management Company

# Abbreviations

| | |
|---|---|
| AAI | Airports Authority of India |
| ABTA | Association of British Travel Agents |
| ACI | Airport Council International |
| ACTE | Association of Corporate Travel Executives |
| AFTA | Australian Federation of Travel Agents |
| AI | Air India |
| AP | American Plan |
| ARC | Airline Reporting Corporation |
| ASTA | American Society of Travel Agents |
| ATC | Air Traffic Control |
| ATF | Aviation Turbine Fuel |
| ATME | Association of Travel Marketing Executives |
| ATTA | African Travel and Tourism Association |
| BITS | Internation Bureau of Social Tourism |
| BOP | Balance of Payment |
| BSP | Billing and Settlement Plan |
| CECTA | Central European Countries Travel Association |
| CLIA | Cruise Line International Association |
| CP | Continental Plan |
| CRM | Customer Ralationship Management |
| CRS | Computer Reservation System |
| DIT | Domestic Independent Tour |
| DRVS | German Travel Agents Association |
| EP | European Plan |
| ERAA | European Region Airline Association |
| ETA | Estimated Time of Arrival |
| ETC | European Travel Commission |
| E-TKT | Electronic Ticket |
| EU | European Union |
| FFP | Frequent Flyer Programme |
| FHRAI | Federation of Hotel and Restaurants Association of India |
| FIT | Free Independent Traveller |
| FIYTO | Federation of International Youth Travel Organisations |
| FSAV | Swiss Travel Agents Association |
| GDP | Gross Domestic Products |
| GDS | Global Distribution System |
| GIT | Group Inclusive Tour |
| GSA | General Sales Agent |
| GST | Goods and Services Tax |

| | |
|---|---|
| IACVB | International Association of Convention and Visitor Bureau |
| IATA | International Air Transport Association |
| ICCA | International Congress and Convention Association |
| ICCL | International Council of Cruise Lines |
| IFITT | International Federation for Information Technology and Tourism |
| IITTM | Indian Institute of Travel and Tourism Management |
| IT | Inclusive Tour |
| IT | Information Technology |
| ITB | International Tourism Bourse |
| ITSA | Interactive Travel Services Association |
| ITX | Inclusive Tour Excursion |
| IUTOO | International Union of Official Tourism Organisation |
| JATA | Japan Association of Travel Agents |
| LCC | Low Cost Carrier |
| MAP | Modified American Plan |
| MCO | Miscellaneous Charge Order |
| MICE | Meetings, Incentives, Conferences and Events |
| MIS | Management Information System |
| NBTA | National Business Travel Association |
| NTO | National Tourism Organisation |
| OAG | Official Airline Guide |
| OBT | Outbound Tourism |
| OTA | Open Travel Alliance |
| PATA | Pacific – Asia Travel Association |
| PATA | Pacific Area Travel Association |
| PAX | Passenger |
| PTA | Prepaid Ticket Advice |
| RAA | Regional Airline Association |
| SATH | Society for Accessible Travel and Hospitality |
| SITE | Society of Incentive and Travel Executives |
| SITE | The Society for Incentive Travel Executives |
| SLA | Service Level Agreement |
| SOP | Standard Operating Procedures |
| SRM | Supplier Relationship Management |
| SYTA | Student and Youth Travel Association |
| TA | Travel Agent |
| TAAI | Travel Agents Association of India |
| TAC | Travel Agent Commission |
| TTRA | Travel and Tourism Research Association |
| UFTAA | Universal Federation of Travel Agents Association |
| UN | United Nations |
| USTOA | United States Tour Operators' Association |
| VAT | Value Added Tax |
| VFR | Visiting Friends and Relations |
| VISA | Visitors Intention to Stay Aboard |
| WATA | World Association of Travel Agents |
| WTM | World Travel Market |
| WTO | World Tourism Organisation |
| WTTC | World Travel and Tourism Council |

# 1
# TRAVEL AGENCY HISTORICAL PERSPECTIVE

### Chapter Objectives

**After reading this chapter, the reader should be able to:**
- Know the historical perspective of the travel agency business
- The pioneering role of Thomas Cook- The First Agent
- Travel retailing and product sale
- Types of agencies
- Know the future of travel agencies
- To know travel retailing and product sale
- To understand travel agency economics
- To understand travel agency economics
- Travel agent and technology

## Introduction

Retail travel agents is the most important travel intermediary. They act as sales outlets for suppliers and wholesalers from whom they receive commission for any sales made. They also act as travel counsellor, advising people as to when, where, and how to travel; as salesperson actively selling travel, and as assistant, making reservations in response to customer requests.

## Travel Retailing

Travel retailing is the outcome of the urge of people to travel in an organised way. This essentially means using the services of retailers who are in a position to offer them a comparatively cheap price as they have entered into an agreement with the providers of these services to buy them in bulk and pass them on to the consumers on payment or credit. These services include transport, accommodation, sightseeing and several other ancillary services, which a prospective traveller wishes to buy and pay for accordingly.

The travel industry developed along certain well-defined lines as the worldwide demand on its services increased. The urge to travel became very intense over the years, resulting in widespread growth of travel agencies in the world. Most travellers wished to have their travel arrangements made in advance and to be relieved of the difficulties of coping with various pre-travel arrangements, of which they had limited knowledge.

Travel during those days was a very simple affair and did not require any major formalities to be completed before undertaking a trip. The rapid transport systems had not evolved resulting in travel only within the neighbouring cities and areas. With the development of different modes of transport, travel became more complicated and so did the functions of the travel agents. They were not only looking for the reservation of seats but were also negotiating with hotel companies for the booking of accommodation for their clients. In addition, the surface transport operators also became part of the wider travel business as they were required to transport passengers from place to place for sightseeing, in and around different tourist destinations.

## Historical Development

In 1841, Thomas Cook, a British Carpenter and Baptist missionary chartered a train to take people about 37 kilometers from Leicester to Loughborough to attend a temperance meeting. He is credited with being the first travel agent. Soon came trips to Europe and, in 1866, Cook organized and led a tour of the US Civil War battlefields, Niagara Falls, New York City, US and Toronto, Canada. In 1872, he escorted a group of travellers around the world. It is said that this trip inspired the Jules Verne book Around the World in 80 Days. In 1873, he introduced the "circular note", the forerunner of the present-day traveller's check. The notes were issued originally in denominations of GBP 5 and 10 and could be exchanged for local currency at prevailing exchange rates in any hotels that were part of the Cook system. This meant that people no longer had to travel with large amounts of cash on their person.

Cook's organised trips and tours were very popular and earned him much fame. The reason for Cook's success was his ability to arrange every detail of a tour in advance, from transportation and lodging to sight-seeing and meal service. His clients paid a lump sum for the entire trip. In this way travellers knew their exact itinerary and all the costs the trip would entail before their departure.

## Thomas Cook's European Tours

Cook's conquest of Europe began in 1862 when he made arrangements with Brighton and South Coast Railway for passenger traffic to the continent. His Paris excursions were the first true 'package tours' in that all the details of transport and accommodation were pre-arranged. In 1863 Cook visited Switzerland where his ideas were greeted with enthusiasm by hoteliers and railway proprietors. His next stop was Italy. Cook first made a personal survey of Turin, Milan, Florence and Genoa, to familiarise himself with their touristic attractions and facilities. In 1864 the first guided tour of Italy left England with applications far in excess of the available tickets.

Railroads were still a novelty and the concept of a round-trip fare hadn't been foreseen by the railroads. By putting together a package which included "eleven miles and back for a shilling, and children half-price," Cook brought excursions within the budget of common, ordinary citizens.

Until that time, only the wealthy and aristocratic travelled for pleasure; other folks travelled only out of necessity, as roads were hazardous, safety unsure, and accommodations rather rough.

For this first tour, Cook went to Liverpool beforehand and ensured that hotels and restaurants would provide the best possible service for his guests. He even wrote the first guidebook, "A Handbook of the Trip to Liverpool". Other trips followed, Cook's pioneering excursionists to Scotland were greeted with crowd-lined streets, brass bands and cannon fire because the tourist was still unusual enough to be an entertaining curiosity.

Cook was quick to see the possibilities for travel which the newly invented railways presented. He reacted speedily when the S.S. Great Britain ran aground in Dundrum Bay by organising an excursion to view the stranded ship in 1847. The Great Exhibition of 1851 brought him an excellent opportunity to expand his business and he seized it with relish. The service wasn't yet profitable, but he did make his name by persuading a great many people to visit the Exhibition with Cooks.

## Competition with Railroads

With the railroads trying to undermine him by undercutting his prices, Cook was forced to find more passengers than had at first calculated. He brought his son John Mason, 17, into the business to help and together they paraded though the streets of Sheffield, Leeds, Derby and Bradford with a band, making speeches about their trips to the Great Exhibition. They had also set up clubs so working men could pay small sums a week toward the total cost which included accommodation at the Ranclagh Club—bed and a hearty Victorian breakfast—for two shillings, and the fare was five shillings. Through their direct selling methods, Cook was able to take 165,000 people to the Exhibition.

## Cook's Guided Tours

Although Cook is believed to have been the first full-time travel agent, he was best known for organising deluxe tours for the world's wealthiest citizens. In 1895, Cook escorted a group of industrialists from England and America to the Paris Exhibition. One year later, he organised a "Grand Tour" of every major European country. Cook's tour groups travelled first-class on luxury ships and trains and enjoyed elegant accommodation in the best hotels in Europe. They were accompanied by a guide whose job was to ensure that all arrangements proceeded smoothly. Cook's clients included such luminaries as Thomas Edison and Samuel Clements, better known as Mark Twain. The term "Cook's tour" is still used today, usually in a humorous context, to refer to any informal guided tour.

Other Victorian entrepreneurs did not miss the opportunity to copy Cook and many rivals gave him keen competition. Over the years he took tourists to such varied places as the Paris Exhibition, a Grand Circular Tour of Antwerp, Brussels, Waterloo, Cologne, Frankfurt, Heidelberg, Baden Baden and Paris. In 1863 he led a tour to Paris and Switzerland and in 1864 to Italy. That year Cook claimed that he had one million clients and the business was stable enough for him to settle clients' bills, but he was not actually running inclusive tours yet. The following year Cook opened an office at Fleet Street which was run by his son, John Mason.

## American Connection

In 1865, Cook finally visited America. During the American Civil War Cook observed the vast North American continent, which was then virgin territory, untrampled due to the absence of the footfalls of British tourists. That year the very first group of European tourists set foot in America. Led by his son, they visited, among other places, New York, Washington, Niagara, Chicago, the Mammouth Caves of Kentucky and the rather gruesome, deserted battlefields of Virginia where they saw, "skulls, arms and legs all bleaching in the sun." The party travelled 10,500 miles in nine weeks.

## Nile Tours

During the famous Nile Tours, there were no hotels available. So in 1868 they travelled as a vast caravan, accompanied by 65 horses, 87 pack mules, tents, beds and field kitchens to prepare Victorian breakfasts of boiled eggs, followed by chicken and cutlets and seven-course dinners including wild boar and mutton. However, it was not all fun and games, Cook had to face certain problems with the tourists and was able to resolve these with tact and care.

No matter what the circumstances, Cook had a bevy of admirers. Oscar Wilde said of Cook, "They wire money like angels." Kipling found words of praise. Even Mark Twain gave Cook a mention in his writings. Cook's tours were not only for the middle classes, they also attracted the likes of the British Royal family, the Kaiser, the Czar, many European aristocrats, politicians, bishops, archbishops and others.

The inclusive tour, in which everything is paid for in advance, was a creation of Cook as well as the Circular Note, the forerunner of the traveller's cheque, which he created in 1873.

## Hotel Coupons

The 1860s also saw the introduction of Cook's railway and hotel coupons. Cook personally examined the system by travelling from Italy to Vienna, down the Danube into Hungary and from there into Switzerland. By the 1890s, 1,200 hotels throughout the world accepted his coupons. Starting in 1868 Cook arranged regular circular tours of Switzerland and northern Italy. These tours became extremely popular as hundreds of people travelled and enjoyed the trips. In fact these circular trips can be called the forerunners of the present day "inclusive trips".

## Thomas Cook's Indian Connections

Thomas Cook and Son had established their first official London office in 1865. John Mason Cook now joined his father as a permanent partner and took charge of the London office. From that year on, the history of Thomas Cook and Son was one of continuous expansion. In the year 1880 John Mason Cook left for India and established offices in Bombay (Mumbai) and Calcutta (Kolkata) and formed the Eastern Princes Department. In 1887 this department arranged the visits of Indian princes to Queen Victoria's jubilee celebrations. By the end of the century, taking advantage of nineteenth-century advances in transport technology, Thomas Cook and Son had effected a revolution in tourism. No longer the preserve of the rich and the aristocrats, tourism was now an industry. Armed with Cook's hotel and rail coupons, the tourist could demand uniform prices, standards of service and accommodation. This new standardisation had distinct advantages. It meant comfort and convenience and less need for decision making on the part of the individual tourist. The tourist was less likely to experience discomfort or embarrassment.

## AMERICAN EXPRESS COMPANY

The American Express Company also had its beginning in the year 1841. It is an interesting coincidence, that two of the world's largest travel companies are said to have their origins in the same year – 1841. While Thomas Cook persuaded a railway company to carry a trainload of passengers at very cheap fares that year, Henry Wells commenced his business in the USA at the same time. Henry Wells commenced his business initially as a shopper who later formed the well-known American company known as Well Fargo. The American Express Company, popularly known today as AMEX, is the world's second largest travel agency after Thomas Cook. Besides selling package tours, the company deals in traveller's cheques. The American Express Company is a major participant in international transactions, buying and selling huge amounts of foreign currency on each working day during the week.

The company has also introduced American Express credit cards. These credit cards are very popular internationally. The services one can buy through these cards are varied and include purchase of international air tickets, payment of hotel bills, among many others. The cards have wide acceptance throughout the world. The company also handles services for various types of insurance, including travel insurance.

## COX AND KINGS

Cox & Kings is another major company associated with the travel business. Although the company had its origin in the year 1758, earlier than Thomas Cook, the company's initial activities were associated with the handling of the affairs of British officers stationed overseas. The history of Cox and Kings stretches back to the appointment of Lord Ligonier as colonel to the First Foot Guards in the year 1757 and his appointment of Richard Cox as regimental agent to the Foot Guards. Cox and Kings' handling of the affairs of the officers stationed overseas was appreciated and by 1878 their appointment as agents and bankers had been extended to the Household Brigade, many of the infantry regiments, the Royal Artillery and the Royal Wagon Train. The company's responsibilities increased steadily, including serving prestigious ships of the Royal Navy, the Royal Flying Corps and by the year 1918, the newly formed Royal Air Force.

With the rapid expansion of the British Empire, Cox and Kings expanded from its base in London, to establish overseas offices. By the year 1918, Cox and Company had become an international corporation employing more than 4,500 people and had established offices in India. In the year 1922 the company merged with Henry S. King, a banking concern. In 1923 the banding business was sold to Lloyd's Bank and the

Cox and Kings branch, as the company is known today, was opened. The fully integrated company, Cox and Kings, today, has a comprehensive network of local agents offering a wide range of travel related services to their clients.

Much has changed since the year 1841 when Thomas Cook chartered a train to carry 570 travellers at a specially reduced fare from Leicester to Loughborough in England. Cook, who bought the railway tickets in bulk and resold them to members of his group, can be credited with being the first bona fide travel agent to work as a full-time professional.

However, neither Thomas Cook and Son nor American Express Company or Cox and Kings were retail agents, as the modern, complex distribution chains had not yet evolved in any trade, including travel and tourism.

The development of the transport system, especially jet travel, improved living standards, combined with reduction in working hours, are the root cause of today's upward surge in travel. Side by side with the rapid improvements in industry and technology, practically all aspects of life have become, more complex, particularly during the past half century. This is certainly the case in the travel industry in which, only a century ago, the job consisted almost entirely of arranging simple reservation for the travellers in some means of transport. Today the functions and duties of a person at the travel agency counters are vastly different and more interesting. He is now called upon to perform a variety of duties rather than just issue tickets and reserve seats in trains, and aeroplanes or book hotel accommodation. Travel today is no longer the privilege of a few, but is sought by millions. No longer does the travel agency exist for the sole purpose of selling tickets from one point to another. The scope of their functions has expanded greatly.

## TYPES OF TRAVEL AGENCY

Travel agencies can be broadly categorised in two ways:
i) Retail Travel Agency.
ii) Wholesale Travel Agency.

## Retail Travel Agency

A travel agency is a private retailer or public service that provides travel and tourism related services to the public on behalf of suppliers such as activities, airlines, car rentals, cruise lines, hotels, railways, travel insurance, and package tours. In addition to dealing with ordinary tourists, most travel agencies have a separate department devoted to making travel arrangements for business travellers; some travel agencies specialize in commercial and business travel only. There are also travel agencies that serve as general sales agents for foreign travel companies, allowing them to have offices in countries other than where their headquarters are located.

## Definition of a Travel Agency

Lavery (1992) defines a retail travel agency as a business that performs the following functions:
- Selling prepared package tours, preparing individual itineraries, personally escorted tours and group tours;
- Arranging transport; selling airline tickets, rail, coach and cruise trips and arranging car hire abroad;
- Arranging hotels, motels, sightseeing trips, music festivals, transfer of passengers between terminals and hotels;
- Handling and advising on many details involved in travel especially foreign travel such as travel and luggage insurance, medical insurance, travellers cheques, visa requirements and so on;
- Providing information and advise on airline, rail and coach schedules and fares; hotel rates; whether rooms have baths; whether their rates include local taxes. All of this information can take days of the intending tourist's time or weeks of endless phone calls and letters;
- Arranging reservations for special interest activities such as business travel, sporting holidays, religious travel, pilgrimage, etc.
- In the case of legitimate complaints from customers writing to the principal (tour operator or airline) to try and get a refund or a written statement or apology for any mishaps that may have occurred;
- Interpreting and advising clients of the many complex discounted fares offered by the airlines and to warn clients of 'overbooking'.

The travel agency therefore represents all the package tour companies, all the airlines and all the coach and rail operators who use his or her services. A good travel agent will be able to advise the potential traveller on a wide range of matters concerning his journey, accommodation and final destination (holiday resort). The agent must have a good knowledge of the product and should know what he or she is selling.

## Types of Agency

Travel agents can also be classified in various ways.
(i) According to their location
(ii) By the type of business in which they specialise.

City centre agencies are located in or close to the main business and shopping areas of cities or major towns. They are meant to catch business from those who visit and pass through these zones. Because the rent and other costs of these locations are high, they will need a substantial turnover or revenue to show a reasonable trading profit.

There are suburban agencies which serve the residents of dormitory suburbs. Located in the main shopping areas they sell holidays, usually inclusive and semi-inclusive package tours and independent travel facilities.

Because of the lower costs, a high level of turnover as required by city centre locations is not essential. However, the seasonality of the business requires them to get the most business they can during peak sales periods.

**Suburban Agency**

State, department or country town agencies serve the resident population and business community in their towns. Surveys have shown that a mix of holiday and business travel makes these agencies the more profitable ones. Their function is similar to that of city centre agencies and they are usually bigger than the average suburban agency. They too may have branches in other nearby towns.

To the above geographical classification of agencies can be added a classification based on the type of business in which they specialise. Agencies can be geared towards capturing the leisure or business market (and in some cases both).

**Business House Agency**

Business house agencies are intended primarily to serve the needs of industrial and commercial enterprises but they will also deal with personal holiday needs, particularly from the staff of their clients. They are most effective when employing direct marketing to potential client firms. This involves visits by appropriate agency staff to the travel decision-makers in the firms, with supporting direct mail shots, letters and telephone calls. For the casual holiday customer, the agency depends on its name and reputation being known for handling business travel efficiently. Usually their staff and office costs are higher than those of other types of agencies. Because of this it can put pressure on profit margins. In this sector of retail travel, competition is intensive, however rewards can be great.

An extension of the business house agency, is the in-plant or on-site or in-house agency, a department or division of a company set up to handle the travel requirements of the company's employees. The company's employees are the in-plant agency's main customers. A typical in-plant agency is located on the premises of a client company but is actually an extension or branch of an independent retail agency.

**On-site and Off-site Servicing**

An on-site travel location is an implant service provided at the corporate customers premises with an objective to ease, improve and control service delivery to the corporate travellers travelling on business. The concept relates to the practice of providing an on-location service to medium/large corporate customers. The concept is also termed as on onsite in-plant. A retail travel agency sells tourists products directly to the customers on the behalf of the products suppliers and in return get commissions. Some package tours are sold in two ways i.e., on a commission basis and on mark up the price.

When a travel agency sells a tour on the marked-up price it means that first, it markup the cost of the tour and then sell it at a higher rate. The markup price is the difference between retail price and wholesale cost.

According to Airlines Reporting Corporation (ARC) a retail travel agency is defined as a business that performs the following functions:
(i) quotes fares
(ii) rates
(iii) make reservations
(iv) arrange travel tickets and accommodation

(v) arrange travel insurance
(vi) arrange foreign currency
(vii) prepare documents and accepts payments.

According to SARC (1967), " retail travel agency business consists of the activities involved in selling tourism products/services directly to the tourists and performs normal functions such as issuing air tickets, making accommodation and transportation reservation, providing specialized services, and accepting and making payments."

The main source of the revenue for the travel agency is the commission received from the vendors. However, the rate of the commission differs from organization to organization and travel component to the travel component. A travel agency receives approx. 95% of their revenue from the commission, and the remaining 5% from consultancy services and others.

## Wholesale Travel Agency

These agencies are specialized in organizing package tours, which are marketed to the customers/tourists through the network of a retail travel agency or directly to the prospective clients ( if wholesale travel agency has a retail division). A wholesale travel agency purchases tourists product components in the bulk and designs tour package. Sometimes, a wholesale travel agency buys travel components from the vendor in bulk and resell them to another travel business originations.

Wholesale travel agencies assemble package holidays and sell them to the clients through retail travel agencies. A typical package tour includes – air tickets, accommodation, and something other services may also be included in it such as entertainment, sightseeing, and sports activities etc. These packages are referred to as 'package tours' most of these tours include the services of escorts but a few are sold to people who wish to travel independently.

## Consolidators

Travel consolidators or wholesalers are high volume sales companies that specialise in selling to niche markets. They may or may not offer various types of services, at a single point of access. These can be hotel reservations or flights or car-rentals. Sometimes the services are combined into vacation packages that include transfers to the location and lodging. These companies do not usually sell directly to the public, but act as wholesalers to retail travel agencies. Commonly, the sole purpose of consolidators is to sell to ethnic niches in the travel industry. Usually, no consolidator offers everything, they may only have contracted rates to specific destinations. Today, there are no domestic consolidators, with some exceptions for business class contracts.

## Airline consolidator

An airline consolidator is a wholesaler of airline tickets, sometimes described as a broker. Airlines make tickets available to consolidators at significant discounts and special conditions to those available to the general public. Consolidators seek to reach more niche markets, and are able to offer discounts and fare flexibility that is relevant to the target group.

# The Role of TRAVEL AGENT

Consolidators enter contracts with major carriers to sell at reduced prices to niche markets, the main benefit being that fares through consolidators will be lower than published rates available from the airlines themselves. Consolidators normally do not buy the seats in bulk for resale, they sell the available seats at contracted rates. Airlines normally preset the selling rates for these fares for sale to sub-agents and to end customers, thereby ensuring that the fares are not undercut. Consolidators most commonly operate in international markets. In domestic markets, they typically only offer business class and first class tickets. Tickets purchased through consolidators may have very different fare rules than published fares, and sometimes frequent flyer credits may not accrue.

Even though many consolidators are online, most consolidators still work only through retail travel agents. Many consolidators also act as host agencies for local travel agencies. Today many of the online OTA use consolidators to increase margins on sales since airlines do not pay commissions.

Travel agents are an integral part of the travel and tourism industry. Worldwide, a substantial percentage of all international travel and domestic travel is arranged by travel agents. The travel agent acts as a sales intermediary, an agent for airlines, railways, car rental companies and ferry operators. The agent also brokers tours and may package some for the agency's own account. The vital role of the travel agent in the modern world is summarised in the principles of *Professional Conduct and Ethics of the American Society of Travel Agents*, as follows:

"We live in a world in which travel has become both increasingly important and complex in its variety of modes and choices. Travellers are faced with a myriad of alternatives as to transportation, accommodation and other travel services. They must depend on travel agencies and others in the industry to guide them honestly and competently."

The travel agent's role is dissimilar to that of most other retailers, in that agents do not purchase a product for resale to their customers. Only when a customer has decided on a travel purchase, do agents approach their principals on their customer's behalf to make a purchase. The travel agent does not, therefore, carry 'stock' of travel products. This has two important implications for the business of travel distribution. First, the cost of setting up in business is comparatively small when compared to that of other retail businesses and second, agents are not seeking to dispose of products they have already purchased.

## Travel Agency Economics

If travel agencies have no stock how can they make money or even a profit? The answer to this is that they make their living through commission, so that the more they sell, the more commission they earn. Commission can vary, depending on the carrier, tour operator and accommodation concern or the insurance agency, paying for it.

Retail travel agents receive income in the form of commissions paid by suppliers and wholesalers. A commission is a percentage of the total sale. The traveller does not pay for the services of a travel agent when a booking is made by the agent.

## Commissions

In the past, the ATC regulated the percentage of commission paid by the airlines. Deregulation, however, has meant that airlines can pay different percentages of commissions to the agents they deal with. Suppliers can also pay overrides or bonuses for volume sales. A wholesaler may offer a graduated rate schedule to stimulate the retailer to sell more. As the number of bookings increase beyond certain points, the commission percentage increases. Often these overrides are retroactive, the higher percentage commission applies to earlier bookings within a given time frame. It may be, for example, that the basic commission for selling a package is 10 per cent. An override or incentive commission may be offered of 1 per cent for bookings over X amount; 2 per cent for bookings over X amount + X amount and 3 per cent over XXX, etc.

## Rebates

In order to attract customers, some agencies offer rebates for volume business to them. In this case an agency would split the commission received with the customer, which usually is a company doing a large volume business with the agency. While this is legal for domestic air travel, it is against the law to rebate international air travel. It is not uncommon for such rebating to go on, however. Almost 60 per cent of the average agency's income comes from commissions from selling some form of air travel.

Income from the cruise lines comprises, on average, 16 per cent of travel agency income, and travel agents book 95 per cent of all cruises sold in the around the world.

Commissions from hotels account for 11 per cent of agency income. Agents are responsible for 25 per cent of domestic and 85 per cent of international sales to hotels.

Car rental business accounts for 8 per cent of travel agency business, and approximately half of all car rental sales are made through travel agents.

Rail travel accounts for only 3 per cent of agency business nationwide. Just over one-third of rail ticket sales are made by retailers.

Commissions from package tours can run from 11 to 22 per cent. Retail travel agents account for 90 per cent of all package tour sales. Other income sources. It may however, be stated that the commissions given by various service providers vary from time to time and place to place.

Two additional sources of income for agencies are service charges and sales of travel- related products and services.

Over the past few years there has been some discussion among agents about levying a charge for services rendered to travellers. The argument is made that a "travel counsellor", in giving professional advice, should charge for that advice. Such a move, some feel, would help professionalize the industry. This argument has received some backing because low air fares have reduced the dollar amount of commission received. However, the public is not yet ready to pay for an agent making a reservation, but some agencies do charge for drawing up complicated itineraries and making trip cancellations.

There are travel-related services that some full-service agencies provide to increase their income. These include such things as personal, baggage and trip cancellation insurance, providing travellers checks and foreign currency, and taking passport photos.

## Travel Agency Skills and Competencies

According to Holloway (1994) owing to the extremely competitive nature of the retail travel business, two factors are of paramount importance if the agency is to succeed:

(i) Good management
(ii) Good service

Good management will ensure that costs are kept under control, that staff is motivated and that the agency goes out actively to seek business rather than wait for it to come through the door. Good service will ensure satisfied clients, help to build a regular clientele and encourage word of – mouth recommendation, which will increase the share of the local market for the agent.

In addition to product knowledge, the main skills that agency staff require will include:

(i) The ability to read data sources
(ii) to compute airline fares
(iii) to write E-tickets
(iv) to have sufficient knowledge of their customers and
(v) to be able to match customer needs with the products available.

Today there is also a growing need for staff who can competently operate computers, especially computer reservation systems (CRS).

The correct construction of airline fares and issue of airline tickets is a far more complex subject than might be apparent to the uninitiated, it entails a lengthy period of training coupled with a continuous exercise of these skills. A number of internationally recognised courses are available to provide these skills, e.g., IATA Fares and Ticketing.

However, airline CRSs increasingly include all the basic point-to-point air fares and the ticketing function is also widely computerised so that fare quotation and ticketing skills—are becoming less important for most staff than they once were.

An understanding of the principles underlying the construction of fares, however, can be helpful—for example, in explaining complex fares to customers and of course, there will be a continuous need for fare experts in the industry. The large travel agency chains have, in some cases, centralised this role, so that a handful of experts can quickly determine the lowest fares for a particular journey by air, on request from a member of their counter-staff at any of the company's branches.

## SETTING UP A TRAVEL AGENCY

The capital cost of setting up a retail travel agency is much less than for almost any other kind of retail business, because the agent requires relatively little in the form of stock. The agent is buying or leasing office space, viewing data systems with access to airlines and tour operators bookings and information services, telephones and office equipment. The stock in the form of brochures, tickets and related material is supplied by the tour operator (wholesaler) or carrier (airline, rail or coach company).

### Right Location

In opening a travel agency the most critical step is finding the right location. This is related to several factors such as:

(i) **Identifying** the market for the product and type of clientele it wishes to attract. The agency should be in such a neighbourhood that will require it to service clients who will wish to take foreign package holidays, cruises, special interest holidays, etc;

(ii) **Accessibility:** Although much of the travel agent's business is conducted over the telephone or using e-mail or via viewdata links, the agency must be visible and easily accessible to its customers. A ground-floor office in the main shopping and business district, with ample nearby parking is the ideal location;

(iii) **Ample investment capital:** Most airlines, for example, will not give commission on the sale of tickets until the agency receives appointments as an official agent for the International Air Transport Association (IATA). Approval or license can take some time to be obtained and an agency should have at least two years operating capital available before it can realistically begin to make a profit from its operations.

## Travel Agency Appointments

A travel agency obtains the bulk of its income from commission on the sale of its products and to collect commission it must be officially "appointed" as an agent for the airlines, transport companies and the tour operators (wholesalers).

To obtain an appointment, typically an agency will have to be open for business; be operated under the direction of a qualified manager; have a good credit rating and (to protect the financial interests of the public and the airlines) have its operations investigated and approved by a bonding company who will guarantee responsibility for the agency's commitments and sufficient funding to operate for one year without commission from the principal; and be actively involved in the production of travel.

Licensing requirements vary. In Austria, Belgium, Bulgaria, Italy and France travel agents need a government license. In Britain and elsewhere in Europe, in order to obtain commission on airline ticket sales, a travel agency must obtain a license from IATA. IATA insists that at least one employee has one or more years experience in international ticketing. Proof that the agency is actively promoting international air travel is also needed.

In order to obtain commission on package tours offered by the main tour operators the European Commission now insists under the European Package Tour Directive that prospective retailers must provide evidence of their financial stability and deposit a bond to protect the public in the event of that agency declaring bankruptcy.

Other travel services such as car hire companies and hotels do not need individual agency appointments but will pay commissions for any reservation or booking made by a travel agency that has been appointed as an official agent by the major travel and tourism organisations such as IATA.

## The Future of Travel Agents

The travel agent of the future undoubtedly will have ready access to more computerised information. He or she will be able to call up not only fares and alternate routes, but also weather forecasts around the world, current events at major destinations and snow conditions at ski areas. Instant information on available rooms at major hotels around the world will be possible by pressing the appropriate computer button.

The sales tools of travel agents will increase in sophistication. American Express's vision of the travel office of the future can be seen at the EPCOT Centre at Disney World. Two people may seat themselves before a console activated by touch and by responding to inquiries from the computer, they may zero in on the type of trip and destination they would like. Videotaped scenes of vacation destinations around the world can be called up for the viewers to observe.

Advances in home computer technology allow direct access to airline reservation systems, hotel accommodation and car rentals. The microcomputer and telephone modem can already access via the "internet" the computer systems of companies such as Holiday Inns, Avis-rent-a-car, United Airlines, British Airways and many more. Not only is it possible to make a reservation charged to a credit card but also, given enough advance notice, have the ticket sent to a home or business address.

The pace of change is frightening. CD-ROMs are replacing brochures; home shopping for holidays on digital interactive TV, (already well advanced in France) and in a local bank a fully automated travel kiosk featuring touch screen display and instant ticketing, all testify to the pace of change.

Frequent-flyer, frequent hotel and travel clubs are all infringing on the work of the travel agent. In 1981 American Airlines introduced the first frequent-flyer plan, since copied by many other airlines. The plans reward the frequent flyer (mostly persons flying for business purposes) for flying with the airline by offering the plan. Several airlines provide free hotel rooms. In 1993, Holiday Inns, began to offer a frequent-guest plan by which participants are awarded points each time they are guests at the hotel.

## Specialization

In Great Britain the trade association ABTA (or Association of British Travel Agents) predicts that more travel agencies will have to specialise or become part of chains or franchises if they are to survive. The trend toward travel conglomerates and huge travel companies that operate multiple offices in a number of cities seems inevitable. Vertical integration also seems likely; even now, hotel companies own travel agencies that feed business to hotels within the system. Government permitting, airlines are also likely to buy or create multi-office travel agencies.

The small independent travel agent, like the small restaurant owner, will probably always have a place, especially in small communities. The travel agency business will probably continue to include numerous small agencies that make only modest profits. The small independent agency will be competing against the larger, multi-officed agency that can develop its own tours and has the capital to invest in the best accounting and office equipment. The smaller agency is disadvantaged by being unable to negotiate prices and overrides with the suppliers.

The travel agent of the future will certainly be more sophisticated, will use up-to-the-minute marketing techniques, analyse products and emphasise those that are most profitable. Travel and education will help agents become better informed about specific destinations and the requirements of special market segments. Whatever happens, one can be sure that the job of the travel agent will continue to demand intelligence, reliability and a desire to serve the public.

## Adding value

In the past three decades, the business model of the travel agent has merely been to identify and focus on channels that have not been disrupted by new tech. When airline commissions disappeared, agents moved to taxi and hotel booking, and when they got disrupted, they set their eyes on package tours. But this is not likely to last long.

The best ways to survive disruption is by reinventing the model and adding value. The average traveller is beset with a number of problems - finding the right hotel, getting plugged in with internet in a new country, currency exchange, landing at a tourist spot in the wrong/crowded season, and so on.

While there are online startups that address each of these many issues, the average traveller doesn't recognize the need for these services until they are too late. A travel agent may however bring together all these different services under one roof. A tour package that includes all these value-added services to clients is likely to retain and grow their business.

TAs may also look at expanding their offering to include exotic and unexplored holiday destinations that are not part of the average holiday experience today. The idea is to create value that a traveller does not get with traditional OTAs and market that offering. The challenge here, however, is that if there is business potential to something, competition swoops in. Adding new value to offering thus needs to be a continuous process.

## Consulting

Travel agents get access to thousands of data points that a regular traveller is not exposed to. This provides them with a unique perspective on travelling. In Addition, the ability to access thousands or even millions of flight and travel related data, the agent can provide unique insights to travellers.

One app based startup, for instance, advises its users on the average wait time at each of the many attractions at destinations like Walt Disney World. The startup then uses this information to optimise the schedule for its users. As a travel agent, you may offer paid consultations on similar insights to your clients. Such data driven insights could help travellers know the optimal travel plan for their vacation, places to avoid, and also the best hotel to stay while on a holiday.

There are two challenges here for a travel consultant. Firstly, most agents cater to passengers outbound from their city to other parts of the country or the world. It may not be realistic for an agent to keep tab of insights from across the world. Secondly, travel agents house thousands of local data points that do not come in handy with a bulk of their clients who are outbound.

Many of modern travel agents are being equipped with technical systems that can consolidate insights from around the world. This makes it easy for the agent to consult their clients on questions specific to particular destinations or travel routes.

Travel Agent partnerships are emerging as one of the most effective ways to keep the industry alive. A growing number of travel agents today partner with fellow agents from other parts of the world to share and service each other. For instance, an agent from Mumbai may tie up with agents located in cities like Singapore, Kuala Lumpur or Hong Kong (China). Often times, cheap domestic flights and trains in these places may not be accessible or known to agents from other parts of the world. Having a local partner book for you can thus be more value-adding.

Another aspect of this partnership is data sharing. Consolidated data points from hundreds of travel agents could help each of these businesses derive meaningful insights that could help agents with their consulting.

## Travel Agents And Technology

The benefits of technology for travel agencies are no less profound. Today, travel agents know that to compete with the digitalization of consumer travel, they need to evolve the technology they use.

Streamlined travel management platforms allow agents to remove the guesswork involved in free online booking tools, and any traveller serious about finding the most convenient and economical way to get from A to B understands this. It's the responsibility of travel agencies to communicate this point clearly and with data-based evidence.

For corporate travellers, enlisting the help of an agent is an absolute must. It's no secret how complex business travel can be, especially when navigating unexpected changes to itineraries and strict corporate travel policies.

Being a reputed travel agency means providing exclusive and valuable services to their customers with proper online travel booking portals to help them reserve their preferred high esteem hotels, flights and holiday packages on their fingertips while maintaining the overall cost that gives them an edge over their possible competitors. By only executing these techniques to the fullest, a travel agency can sustain in the market with remarkable competition and think of increasing their sales.

Whether it is a travel company or any other business venture, keeping the customers happy is the top most priority that will lead to increased sales. However, many online travel booking portals are not adapting favourable travel technology and making any unique strategies to force their sales up. They focus only in maintaining their services of online booking of accommodations and travel means, which would be more than enough to attract new customers.

Below are some of the major points of sales for travel agents to sell their services:-

(i) *Developing a highly efficient online travel agent system:-* With the evolution in travel technology, developing an online travel booking system has become more innovative and exceptional. By appointing proper technology and highly knowledgeable travel experts, agent can create a unique and easy to use system that provides great comfort and convenience to the user to reserve rooms and flights as per their budget and predilections in real time.

(ii) *Maintaining front desk sales:-* Guests initial point of contact is hotel's front desk, which provides the first impression and increases or decreases the user expectations. A highly trained and educated front desk agent can easily attract the customer's awareness, whether on the phone or face to face interaction and increases their chances of possible sales by skilfully selling the property features and answering the questions of the guests with confidence.

(iii) *Highlighting services:-* Every customer looks for some uniqueness and have a recommendation for any services. Try not to be same as your competitors and look for ways to improve yourself better. Ask your customers to review your services and point out those areas where you can vary from your oppositions. Highlight those inclusions and establish a niche market to let the new customers be well aware of your services.

(iv) *Integrating with GDS and hotel APIs:-* You can provide best possible rates of esteem hotels, car rentals, flights and other excursions by having a travel booking software that is integrated with Global Distribution System (GDS) & hotel API's worldwide.

(v) *Value added offers:* One of the best way to increase your revenue is by providing value added offers such as complimentary meals or additional equipments on their bookings. Furthermore, private discounts and coupons can also be given to the customers on their online bookings.

(vi) *Engaging in social media* for promotion and offering exclusive packages to build unique travel products can also attract users' attention and increase further revenue of the company.

## Tomorrow's Travel Agents

The travel industry currently leads the world in Internet of Things spending, and the ramifications of this movement are still emerging.

However, it's clear that consumers will be empowered to achieve most of what agents can by themselves. They just won't be able to do so as accurately, as quickly, as economically or with as minuscule fuss as travel agents can.

The travel agencies of tomorrow must be armed with the most powerful travel management technology available. Other alternatives aren't viable, because after all, consumers who enlist their help expect more than a mutual searching of Sky scanner from the agent's desktop computer.

# 2
# OPERATIONS OF A MODERN TRAVEL AGENCY

**Chapter Objectives**

**After reading this chapter, the reader should be able to:**
- Understand broadly the functions of a modern travel agency.
- Analyse travel agency operations.
- Know the details of ticketing and issuance of the same.
- Learn about e-ticketing.
- Understand the meaning of Pre-paid Ticket Advice (PTA).
- Know about Miscellaneous Charge Order (MCO).
- Understand the importance of travel insurance.

Travel in the past used to be a simple affair. All the formalities existing today were absent. Besides, in the absence of various modes of transport, communication and also the motivation to travel, as it exists today were not there. It was only after transportation systems were developed, and the emergence of the urge to travel and to see different lands, that organised travel began to take a shape. Rising incomes as a result of industrialisation and urbanisation were another important factor that helped the growth and development of organised travel.

Travel retailing is the outcome of the urge of people to travel in an organised way. This essentially means using the services of retailers who are in a position to offer them a comparatively better price as they have entered into an agreement with the providers of these services to buy them in bulk and pass them on to transport, accommodation, sightseeing and several other ancillary services, for which a prospective traveller wishes to pay.

The development of organised travel as we know it today had its roots in the mid-nineteenth century and can be associated with a man known as Thomas Cook. Any discussion on sale and organisation of travel must make a reference to this pioneer. The history of the business of the present Thomas Cook Group Limited can be tracked back over 155 years to its founder Thomas Cook, who can not only be called the first organised travel agent in the world, but who could be said to have invented the travel and tourism business, as we know it today.

Much has changed since the year 1841 when Thomas Cook chartered a train to carry 570 travellers at a specially reduced fare from Leicester to Loughborough, in England. Cook, who bought the railway tickets in bulk and resold them to members of his group, can be credited with being the first bona fide travel agent to work as a full-time professional. However, neither Thomas Cook and Son nor American Express Company or Cox and Kings were then retail agents, as the modern complex distribution chain had not yet evolved in any trade, including travel.

Continuing development of the transport system, especially jet travel, improved living standards combined with reduction in working hours, are the root causes of today's upward surge in travel. Side by side with the rapid improvements in industry and technology, practically all aspects of life have become, more and more complex, particularly during the past half a century. This is certainly the case in the travel industry in which, only a century ago, the job consisted almost entirely of arranging a simple reservation for the travellers in some means of transport. Today, the functions and duties of a person at the travel agency counter are vastly different and more interesting. He is now called upon to perform a variety of duties rather than just issue tickets and reserve train or aeroplane seats or accommodation in a hotel. Travel today is no longer the privilege of the few, but is sought by millions. No longer does the travel agency exist only for the sole purpose of selling tickets from one point to another.

## Modern Travel Agency

The range and activities of a retail travel agent have increased manifold over the years. In the modern context the role of a travel agent is rather different from that of most of other retailers selling merchandise. The travel agent does not purchase travel with a view to reselling the same to has customers. It is only when a customer has finally decided on the purchase of travel that the agent approaches the principal on behalf of his customer. The retail travel agent unlike most other retailers does not carry an inventory or "stock" of travel products in his premises.

The main role of retail travel agents is to provide to their customers a convenient location for the "purchase" of various elements of travel like transport, accommodation and several other ancillary services associated with holiday and travel. Travel agents act as booking agents for holidays and travel, and disseminate information and give advice on such services. This role can be summed up as follows:

(i) to give advice to the potential tourists on the merits of alternate destinations, and
(ii) to make necessary arrangements for a chosen holiday which may involve booking of accommodation, transport or other relevant services associated with his travel.

A travel agent, in order to give advice to his potential customers on the merits of a destination, must possess knowledge, expertise and up-to-date information about that destination. Besides, a travel agent must have close contacts with providers of services, i.e., their principals from whom they purchase services for their customers. In other words, a retail travel agent is an intermediary providing a direct link between the customer and the suppliers of tourist services, i.e., airlines, transport companies, hotels, auto rental companies, etc. The retail agent is the one who acts on behalf of the principal, i.e., the original provider of tourist service such as an airline company, hotel company, shipping company, insurance company, railways or a tour operator. An agent sells the principal's services and is rewarded with a commission.

## TRAVEL AGENCY OPERATIONS

The scope and range of travel agency operations would depend on the size of an agency. If the company is large in size, the range of activities will be more comprehensive. In this case the agency will have specialised departments, each having to perform different functions. To deal with the subject of a travel agency, the best method of approach is, perhaps, to consider the functions of a travel agency. These may be broadly classified as follows:

### (a) Provision of Travel Information (Information Resource)

One of the primary functions of a retail travel agent from the point of view of the tourists or the general public is to provide necessary information about travel. This information is provided at a convenient location where the intending tourists may ask certain questions and seek clarifications about their proposed travel. This is a very specialised job and the person behind the counter should be a specialist with excellent knowledge of various alternate travel plans. He should be in a position to give up-to-date and accurate information regarding various services and general information about travel, etc.

The presentation to potential customers must be forceful and exciting variations must continually be devised to help sell tours. A good travel agent is something of a personal counsellor who knows all the details about the travel and also the needs and interests of the intending traveller. Communication plays a key role in dissemination of any type of information. The person behind the travel counter should be able to communicate with the customer in his language, the knowledge of foreign languages is an essential perquisite for personnel working in a travel agency.

### (b) Preparation of Itineraries (Programme Planning)

Tourists itineraries are a composition of a series of operations that are a result of the study of the market. A tourist journey is characterised by an itinerary using various means of transport to link one locality with another. Preparation of different types of itineraries is another important function of a travel agency. A travel agent gives advice to intending travellers on the type of programmes which they may choose for their holidays or business travel. The study and the realisation of their itineraries call for a perfect organisation (technical and administrative) as also knowledge of the desires of the public for a holiday and the propensity to receive tourists by the receiving localities.

### (c) Travel Facilitation

Tourists need information about what is available at the destination in order to get the most from the leisure holiday or a business trip. The travel agents who handle tourists for various destinations must have complete travel information to facilitate their clients to visit a particular country. The information to be provided does not relate only to travel but on variety of topics like local transport, sites and destinations, fairs and festivals, cultural aspects of the country, accommodation available, medical facilities, entertainment, eating places, etc.

A tourist seeking the help of a travel agent for planning his trip to a particular destination would require information on the following areas:

(i) Mode of travel to the destination
(ii) Travel within the destination
(iii) Travel advisories, like visa regulations and health precautions
(iv) Custom formalities
(v) Currency and exchange
(vi) Departure formalities

While within the destination the potential tourist will be particularly interested in the following aspects:

(i) Climate
(ii) Clothing
(iii) Cultural Aspects
(iv) Tipping
(v) Time Conversions
(vi) Electricity
(vii) Business hours and public holidays
(viii) Banking
(ix) Photography
(x) Worship
(xi) Medical facilities
(xii) Emergencies
(xiii) Entertainment
(xiv) Shopping

### (d) Planning and Costing Tours

Once the contracts and arrangements have been entered into, there comes the task of planning and costing tours, both for inclusive programmes and to meet individual requirements. This job is intensely interesting and at the same time challenging. The job calls for a great deal of initiative and drive, for travel to those places included in the itineraries. This is essentially a job for a meticulously minded person and calls for considerable training and ability. Many agencies, with the cooperation of airlines and other transportation companies, take the opportunity of arranging educational tours for such staff to destinations with which they deal.

Many large agencies have experts who are authorities on particular countries and in addition to a general programme, many will issue separate programmes dealing with holiday offer territories. Separate programmes dealing with holiday offers based on specific forms of transportation, e.g., air, road or sea, may also be prepared. Programmes also have to be prepared to cover different seasons of the year.

Publicity is an important part of the programme. Having spent considerable time and money on preparing all that goes into the issue of a programme, publicity must feature considerably in the activities of a travel agency and more so if the agency happens to be a large one. The majority of large travel agencies have their own publicity departments under the management of an expert in the publicity field.

## (e) Provision of Foreign Currencies

Providing foreign currencies to intending travellers is another specialised activity of a travel agency. Some of the larger travel agencies deal exclusively in the provision of foreign currencies, traveller's cheques, etc. This is an important facility for intending travellers as it saves them a lot of time and energy in avoiding visits to regular banking channels.

## (f) Insurance

Insurance, both for personal accident risks and of baggage, is yet another important activity of the travel agency. Some of the larger travel agents maintain sizeable shipping and forwarding departments, aimed at assisting the traveller to transport personal effects and baggage to any part of the world with minimum inconvenience.

## Travel Organisation

Organised travel by a travel agency can be of two types, i.e.,
  (i) single client, and
  (ii) group client.

In order to effect the journey, the following main elements in both types of travel need to be considered:
  (i) Study of the journey
  (ii) Estimate of expenditure
  (iii) Execution of the journey
  (iv) Presentation of accounts

## Individual Ordinary Trips

The following steps are involved in organising individual or ordinary trips:
- The client turns to the travel agent to organise for him a particular journey (cultural, natural business, religious, etc.).

- The agency from this angle will examine as to what will be involved, e.g. scope of the journey, when the journey is to take place, various services needed and the accessories required.
- Based on the above evaluation and other elements in his possession, the travel agent will suggest itinerary and will then communicate to the client the estimated maximum cost for the client's approval.
- The travel agent will then compile the definite estimates, a total of a series of costs added up, e.g., transport, accommodation, services such as those of guides, operative costs such as (postage, telex, telefax, e-mail, telephones, etc.).
- The travel agent will then present a document in duplicate of the amount of money to be paid, by the customer. The client returns one of the debit (in anticipation). The deposit normally is about 25 per cent of the total cost.
- Once the client's approval has been obtained, the travel agent's operation department executes the journey.
- The 'operation' department's task now is to book the transport and various other services for the established dates. After the booking confirmation has been received, the travel agent issues the vouchers.
- The travel agent prepares the 'tourist itinerary' which will accompany the client through the entire journey. It will be an indicator of the tickets to be used, the hotels and other services booked and will include vouchers, etc. Normally the itinerary is made in triplicate: one for the client, another for the agency and the third for the hotelier or those who will provide the required services paid by means of vouchers.
- The last formality is the delivery to the client of the vouchers, confirmed tickets and the technical itinerary.
- When the group is particularly large, e.g., for sports, etc., the travel agent needs to take extra care by way of informing public authorities for purposes of security, etc.

Travel agents in a highly developed market cover all the above activities and range of services. The range of activities of a travel agent in any country depends upon the extent of the economic development of that country, the travel patterns of the population, countries and high incomes resulting in availability of disposable incomes for holidays, taking more holidays as compared to earlier times. The services of travel agents are increasingly utilized in developed countries. In some of the advanced countries like the Canada, Germany and Japan a very large percentage of tourists are utilising the services of travel agents.

## TICKETING

Selling tickets to clients using different modes of transport like air, rail and sea is yet another important function of a travel agency. This calls for a thorough knowledge of schedules of various modes of transport. Air carriers, railways and steamship companies have hundreds of schedules and the person behind the counter should be conversant with all these. Ticketing is, however, not an easy job as the range and diversity of international airfares is very complex and varied. Change in international, as also in the local air schedules and additions of new flights from time to time, makes the job of the travel agent a constant challenge. An up-to-date knowledge about various schedules of air companies, steamship companies and railways is very essential.

The computerised reservation system has in the recent years rather revolutionised the reservation system, both for air and rail seats, and also rooms in a hotel. Many large travel agencies are using this system. This system comprises a computer network that can be used by the travel agent to reserve an air or rail accommodation and also accommodation in a hotel. Through a wide network, confirmation of reservations is available in a matter of seconds.

"Ticket" generally constitutes the final step of the sale of service of a carrier. It represents the contract of carriage finalised between the carrier and the client to the passenger. It is a very important document and, therefore, it is necessary that this document is completed with the utmost care. The staff of the airlines as well as that of the travel agency have to recognise the importance of this document as any incorrect entries or endorsement in a passenger ticket may result in serious problems leading to passenger inconvenience. It may also result in substantial financial as well as business loss for the travel agent.

Ticketing, especially airline ticketing, however, is not an easy job to handle as the range and diversity of international air fares is very complex and varied. There are hundreds of different types of fare combinations available all over the world and understanding these requires a thorough study. Frequent changes in international and local air schedules and addition of new flights from time to time make the job of a travel agent one of constant challenge.

## Knowledge About Air Schedules

Knowledge about air schedules is the key to ticketing, without which it is not possible to issue a ticket. Each airline issues air schedules (timetables) which provide most accurate and up-to-date information about air schedules relating to their airlines. Normally these schedules are issued twice a year – in summer and winter. However, it is difficult and cumbersome for a travel agent to refer to different timetables when he is making a schedule which uses the services of more than one carrier. Therefore, the travel agent must refer to a comprehensive guide which contains individual schedules of all airlines.

## International Ticketing Guides

The two most important international ticketing guides used in air passenger transportation worldwide are:
(a) ABC World Airways Guide
(b) Official Airlines Guide (OAG)

Both these international air passenger transportation guides have worldwide acceptance and are used extensively. In fact, without these guides, it would be extremely difficult for a travel agent to function smoothly. A travel agent has to be thoroughly conversant with the contents and use of the these guides. Out of the above two guides, the ABC Guide is extensively used in Europe, Africa and Asia, whereas the OAG is normally used in North, Central and South American regions. The ABC World Airways Guide is published every month.

## Passenger Air Ticket

Every carrier issues its own tickets which bear its name, emblem and colour. On each coupon of the ticket, the airline's name appears in full. The ticket is individually numbered. The 3-digit identification or code number of the carrier precedes the ticket number. Each ticket contains the following coupons:

(i) Audit coupon
(ii) Flight coupon
(iii) Agent coupon
(iv) Passenger coupon

**Audit Coupon:** Meant for the accounts department of the issuing airline. This is detached at the time of issuance of the ticket and attached to the sales report.

**Flight Coupon:** This coupon gives the flight information and status, and is valid for travel between the points specified in the relevant boxes.

**Agent Coupon:** This coupon is meant for the agency records and is detached at the time of issuance of the ticket by the agency.

**Passenger Coupon:** This is a passenger's copy and contains details of the trip. The coupon also serves as receipt for money paid by the passenger.

A standard international air passenger ticket contains four flight coupons all of which, with the exception of the last one, are carbon-backed. Each of the boxes of a ticket is to be completed by the agent by strictly adhering to the rules specified in a IATA Ticketing Handbook. This handbook gives detailed instructions for the issuance and the reissuance of interline passengers tickets. The instructions given in the handbook are based on the IATA Traffic Conference Resolutions relating to tickets and ticketing procedures.

## E-TICKETING

Most of the airlines have now stopped issuing paper tickets, instead e-tickets are issued to the passengers. The e-ticket is used in exactly the same way as a paper ticket but instead of processing a paper document, all the information relating to a passenger's itinerary, fare, class, taxes, endorsements, baggage, etc., are stored as an electronic record in the database of the airline issuing the ticket. The e-ticket does not have coupons as it in a paper ticket.

The e-ticket can be sent to the passenger by email through a SMS or by post, on confirmation of the passenger's booking.

The passenger can access his/her booking details at any time on airline's website or at an airport check-in desk/kiosk using his/her booking reference, the PNR, which is a series of six letters and numbers (ALFA-NUMERIC) that uniquely identifies their booking, and the passenger's last name.

## Airline ticket

E-tickets in the airline industry were devised in about 1994, and have now largely replaced the older multi-layered paper ticketing systems. Since 1 June 2008, it has been mandatory for IATA members to use e-ticketing. Where paper tickets are still available, some airlines charge a fee for issuing paper tickets.

When a reservation is confirmed, the airline keeps a record of the booking in its computer reservations system. Customers can print out or may be provided with a copy of a e-ticket itinerary receipt which contains the record locator or reservation number and the e-ticket number. It is possible to print multiple copies of an e-ticket itinerary receipt.

Besides providing itinerary details, an e-ticket itinerary receipt also contains:
- An official ticket number (including the airline's 3-digit ticketing code, 4-digit form number, a 6-digit serial number, and sometimes a check digit).
- Carriage terms and conditions, (or at least a reference to them)
- Fare and tax details, including fare calculation details and some additional data such as tour codes. The exact cost might not be stated, but a "fare basis" code will always identify the fare used.
- A short summary of fare restrictions, usually specifying only whether change or refund are permitted but not the penalties to which they are subject.
- Form of payment.
- Issuing office.
- Baggage allowance.

## E-ticket (electronic ticket)

An e-ticket (electronic ticket) is a paperless electronic document used for ticketing passengers, particularly in the commercial airline industry. Virtually all major airlines now use this method of ticketing.

When a customer books a flight by telephone or using the Web, the details of the reservation are stored in a computer. The customer can request that a hardcopy confirmation be sent by postal mail, but it is not needed at the check-in desk. A confirmation number is assigned to the passenger, along with the flight number(s), date(s), departure location(s), and destination location(s). When checking in at the airport, the passenger simply presents positive identification. Then necessary boarding passes are issued, and the passenger can check luggage and proceed through security to the gate area. The principal advantage of e-ticketing is the fact that it reduces booking expense by eliminating the need for printing and mailing paper documents. Another advantage is that it eliminates the possibility of critical documents getting lost in the mail or being sent to the wrong address.

### The Benefits of an e-ticket:
- As all the booking details are stored securely in the airline's booking system an e-ticket cannot be lost or stolen.
- It is easy and simple to read an e-ticket receipt by email.
- The airline sends a copy of the receipt immediately after the ticket is issued.

- If the passenger books his/her ticket on the phone and doesn't have an email address, the agency or the airline will send an e-ticket receipt to the passenger by post, or send the PNR as a SMS to the passenger's mobile phone.
- The ticket itinerary can be emailed to friends and family or can be printed any number of times.
- Travel agents can refund tickets in a more timely manner without the need for the customer to be present.
- Can avoid waste of time sending PTA'S as (SOTO) ticket can be issued instantly and mailed to the passenger regardless of where the passenger resides.
- As the coupons are held electronically the travel agent can make changes, exchange or reissue the ticket any number of times as per the requirements of the passenger, taking into account the penalties levied by the airline for the same.
- Audit coupons are saved electronically. The coupons are saved in the server of the issuing airline and by the CRS company. BSP downloads the information from the airline's database for preparing the fortnightly billing which is sent to the IATA-BSP agents for remittance.
- Physical stock need not be maintained as electronic tickets can be replenished. The stock of these tickets is loaded on a fortnightly basis by the airlines and the agents through the CRS companies.

Pax must show his/her Photo ID such as passport together with the e-ticket while checking-in at a airport

## The E-TKT has the following coupons:

The audit coupon—maintained in the airline's data base.
The agent's coupon—maintained in the system by the travel agency.
The passenger receipt—sent to the passenger as proof of payment.
The e-ticket itinerary—used for check-in at the airport (with Pax Photo ID).

## SAMPLE OF AN E-TICKET

ELECTRONIC TICKET

PASSENGER ITINERARY RECEIPT

ABC TRAVELS  
G123  
112, NUNGAMBAKKAM ROAD  

CHENNAI 600 034  
IATA : 143456 45660  
TELEPHONE: 42671172, 42282763  

DATE: 25 FEBRUARY 2009  
AGENT: 4712  
NAME: RAGHAVANS/ KRISHNASWAMIMR  
FQTV: 231981341  

ISSUING AIRLINE : EMIRATES  
TICKET NUMBER : ETKT 176 3304262143  
BOOKING REF: AMADEUS: YPTI6T, AIRLINE: EK/DTGPEJ

| FROM/TO | FLIGHT | CL | DATE | DEP | FARE BASIS | NVB | NVA | BAG ST |
|---|---|---|---|---|---|---|---|---|
| CHENNAI<br>TERMINAL:1 | EK 0543 | U | 14MAR | 0330 | UPX1YIN1 | 14MAR | 14MAR | 2PC OK |
| DUBAI<br>TERMINAL:3 | | | | | ARRIVAL TIME: 0620 | | | |
| DUBAI<br>TERMINAL:3 | EK 0201 | U | 14MAR | 0830 | UPX1YIN1 | 14MAR | 14MAR | 2PC OK |
| NEW YORK JFK<br>TERMINAL:4 | | | | | ARRIVAL TIME: 1415 | | | |
| NEW YORK JFK<br>TERMINAL:4 | EK 0202 | U | 09SEP | 2300 | UPX1YIN1 | 09SEP | 09SEP | 2PC OK |
| DUBAI<br>TERMINAL:3 | | | | | ARRIVAL TIME: 1945 | | | |
| DUBAI<br>TERMINAL:3 | EK 0542 | U | 10SEP | 2125 | UPX1YIN1 | 10SEP | 10SEP | 2PC OK |
| CHENNAI<br>TERMINAL:1 | | | | | ARRIVAL TIME: 0300 | | | |

AT CHECK-IN, PLEASE SHOW A PHOTO IDENTIFICATION AND THE DOCUMENT YOU GAVE FOR REFERENCE AT THE TIME OF RESERVATION

ENDORSEMENTS  : VALID ON EK ONLY/NON-ENDOPENALTY FOR DTE CHNGE APLY

PAYMENT        : CASH

FARE CALCULATION : MAA EK X/DXB EK NYC405.87EK X/DXB EK
         MAA405.87NUC811.74END
  ROE49.264000XT277YC810US810US252XA352XY126AY226XF
  JFK4.5

| AIR FARE | : INR | 39990 | | |
|---|---|---|---|---|
| TAX | : INR | 300YR | 225WO | 2853XT |
| TOTAL | : INR | 43368 | | |

**NOTICE**
CARRIAGE AND OTHER SERVICES PROVIDED BY THE CARRIER ARE SUBJECT TO CONDITIONS OF CARRIAGE, WHICH ARE HEREBY INCORPORATED BY REFERENCE. THESE CONDITIONS MAY BE OBTAINED FROM THE ISSUING CARRIER.

THE ITINERARY/RECEIPT CONSTITUTES THE 'PASSENGER TICKET' FOR THE PURPOSES OF ARTICLE 3 OF THE WARSAW CONVENTION, EXCEPT WHERE THE CARRIER DELIVERS TO THE PASSENGER ANOTHER DOCUMENT COMPLYING WITH THE REQUIREMENTS OF ARTICLE 3.

**NOTICE**
IF THE PASSENGER'S JOURNEY INVOLVES AN ULTIMATE DESTINATION OR STOP IN A COUNTRY OTHER THAN THE COUNTRY OF DEPARTURE THE WARSAW CONVENTION MAY BE APPLICABLE AND THE CONVENTION GOVERNS AND IN MOST CASES LIMITS THE LIABILITY OF CARRIERS FOR DEATH OR PERSONAL INJURY AND IN RESPECT OF LOSS OF OR DAMAGE TO BAGGAGE. SEE ALSO NOTICES HEADED 'ADVICE TO INTERNATIONAL PASSENGERS ON LIMITATION OF LIABILITY' AND 'NOTICE OF BAGGAGE LIABILITY LIMITATIONS'.

### Settlement of Account

Linked with the function of ticketing and reservation of accommodation in a hotel, is the settlement of accounts of the clients. Accountancy plays an important part and is one of the major duties to be performed by the travel agency. Dealing with the settlement of accounts in all parts of the world calls for a thorough knowledge of foreign currencies, their cross-values and, above all, the intricacies of exchange control regulations, which vary from country to country.

### Miscellaneous charges order

In addition to the cost of an international air ticket, there are several other services related to air travel but not covered by an air ticket. These miscellaneous services which a passenger might require include charges for excess baggage, car rental, surface accommodation, land arrangements for inclusive tours, etc. The travel agent has to collect money for all these services from his client in addition to the cost related to air travel. For covering money for miscellaneous services, a travel agent issues a Miscellaneous Charge Order (MCO). The MCO may contain up to four exchange coupons in addition to the audit coupon, agent's coupon and passenger's coupon issued with the air ticket.

A miscellaneous charges order (MCO) is an accountable IATA document, similar to an old-style airline ticket, used to process the payment of travel arrangements. They are issued by airlines, but normally pay for services other than airfares. A MCO may be used to purchase most services offered by airlines, hotels and tour operators.

## Coupons

In common with older airline tickets, MCOs had a number of passenger coupons, as well as valueless coupons for the agency's records and the airlines' interline clearing house.

There were two main types of MCO, those with a specific value for each coupon, and those with the residual value moving to the next coupon. These were often used where the cost of a service would not be known in advance – such as paying for excess baggage.

Typically the passengers' copies on the second type would not show any value, allowing payment for inclusive tours without the services' prices being known to the passenger.

## MCO issue

Travel agency MCOs were printed blank without airline information, and were endorsed to the airline providing the service (or its local agent if the airline was not represented locally). Like tickets, they were valid for a maximum of one year unless otherwise endorsed for a shorter time.

## Future usage

As most MCOs are now issued electronically like e-tickets, they are sometimes referred to as vMCOs (virtual Miscellaneous Charges Order) MCO's are being phased out and replaced with Electronic Miscellaneous Documents.

The MCO has a validity of one year from the date of its issue and is not transferable. For each of the miscellaneous service and honouring party, a separate exchange coupon is to be issued. MCO is an important document and is as valuable as a bank cheque. It is, therefore, to be completed with the utmost care to avoid any cancellations. An alteration or overwriting on it results in its automatic cancellation. An MCO is issued only for a particular service. An MCO, issued for a specified transportation, can only be accepted by the firm to a carrier (agency, hotel, car rental, etc.) on whom it has been drawn. Exchange coupons presented without the corresponding passenger coupons are not accepted.

## The Prepaid Ticket Advice (PTA)

The prepaid ticket advice, commonly known in travel parlance as PTA, is a document in the form of a telex, special form or MCO asking the carrier to issue a ticket in favour of a person who starts his journey in a place other than from where the payment of such a journey was made. In other words, a person undertaking a journey does not pay for it himself but is being paid by someone else and at another place. The PTA issued may cover the fare and taxes for transportation, prepayment of excess baggage charges and such other related services, in connection with the prepayment of specified transportation. It may also cover provision of a cash advance to cover expenses en-route in connection with the prepayment of a specified air transportation.

The Prepaid Ticket Advice (PTA) is an authorization permitting the issuance of a ticket at a location other than the point of payment. It can involve domestic or international reservations. A PTA is used for prepayment of tickets, baggage charges, and incidental expenses directly related to the transportation covered by the Prepaid Ticket Advice. When a PTA is entered and processed through an airline on-line reservations system it is referred to as an automated PTA. Worldspan automated PTA system processing is designed to handle prepaid tickets within the Worldspan system. The PTA is contained within the associated PNR. There are seven PTA fields that can be entered into a PNR. Any addition, change, or deletion made to the PTA field is recorded in the history of the PNR. As PNRs containing PTAs are completed or purged from the system, the complete PNR with all historical data is copied to microfiche. PTA refund request must be initiated through the hosted airline PTA desk in the local reservations office. If the PTA is refundable, the prepaid desk can issue a refund card or a refund letter. This card or letter along with a Ticket Refund Notice (ATC Form 895), is the only acceptable refund documentation which will be accepted by the airlines. Once a PTA ticket has been issued to the traveller, unless restricted by the purchaser, the ticket can be exchanged like any other ticket.

The arrangement for issuance of PTA is that the carrier will send a request through a message to its representative closest to the passenger's point of departure, who in turn will contact the passenger and issue the requested document. In the transaction of PTA the persons/agencies involved include the SPONSOR (the person who pays for the ticket issued), the AGENCY issuing the PTA (the agency sends the request and the payment to the carrier's representative located in its country, and the PASSENGER, the person who will actually be travelling with the ticket issued).

Generally, PTAs are issued for international transportation commencing in a country other than that in which a passenger resides. In other words, these are issued in a foreign country, the method of the fare calculation therefore to be used is that which applies to payments for tickets in a country other than that in which the ticket is issued and/or in which the journey begins. There are strict conditions imposed by both the carriers and interested governments for the issue of PTAs by travel agencies. These, however, vary from one carrier or government to another.

## Transportation

Transportation will be included from a particular destination to the country to be visited and also the local transportation while in the country. The local transportation will include different modes of travel like air, railways, surface transport, taxis and motoring. It is important for travel agents to provide all the necessary information on all the modes of transport within the country, which may include the schedules of both domestic air carriers and railways, especially to major tourist centres. As far as rail travel is concerned it is important for a travel agent to give detailed information about the tourist trains on different railways. In addition information about rail passes, for the foreigners, is to be given. The procedure for booking and reservation is also to be explained to the tourists.

As far as the surface transport is concerned the information on sight-seeing tours conducted by both State Tourism Corporation and Private Charter Bus Operators would be of great help to the tourists. In addition the information and procedures about rent-a-car may also be given to those who are interested in driving within the country on their own.

## Accommodation

Wide range of accommodation in the form of hotels and also supplementary accommodation catering to every budget and preference must be available with the travel agency. Information about the major private sector hotel chains with centralised reservation system offering a variety of options must be readily available with them. Information about the public sector hotels, range of services, location and prices should be available with the travel agents.

## Communication

Every tourist visiting a country, away from home would like to be in touch with people back home. In this world of Information Technology a tourist would definitely like to know the procedures and modes of communication from the destination to his home country. The information on telephone services both landline and mobile and the procedure required to be completed to obtain the equipment must be known to the travel agents. Information about Internet and telex services would also form a part of the tourist information.

The tourist would also be like to be in touch with the news of his country through the medium of newspapers and magazines. They would certainly like to know the availability of these in the country, which they visit as tourists. Today, a large number of newspapers and magazines from different countries are available at the newsstands. It is important for a travel agent to provide the information about the availability in different cities and towns, the tourists are planning to visit.

## Health and Emergencies

A tourist may require information concerning pharmacists, in case they require some medications. The pharmacists are located all over the country, even in the smallest towns. In some big cities, some pharmacists are open round the clock. The contact address of these, along with opening and closing time must be available with the travel agent. In addition, it is also necessary for the travel agent to have information about medical services, which may include hospitals, nursing homes and emergency services.

### Shopping

Shopping is one of the major attractions for tourists visiting a destination. In fact considerable amount of tourist expenditure is spent on shopping in the local markets and bazaars. Every tourist would like to buy some souvenirs to remind him of the visit and he may like to buy local handicrafts to present to his relations, colleagues and friends. Places selling handicrafts of all types are an inevitable first stop for the shoppers. Their incredible variety is itself a statement of the diversity of a destination and its remarkably varied and attractive artistic traditions.

It is important for a travel agent to be able to give all kinds of information about shopping which may include shopping outlets, opening and closing hours and close days. The travel agents should also have detailed information about popular markets and especially the shops selling handicrafts, like carpets, textiles, gems and jewellery, marble inlay work and papier-mâché items with intricate designs. Special mention must be made of the government run Cottage Industries Emporium, State Cottage Industries Emporium located in the metros and two-tier cities and towns.

### Cultural Activities

A large majority of tourists while visiting different countries are interested in the cultural activities of that country. The destination's numerous artistic and archeological treasures are displayed in museums located in all major towns and at several historical sites. In addition the destinations have a large number of art galleries in all big cities, where paintings can be purchased. There will be many who are interested in classical musical, dance performances and festivals, it is therefore important for the travel agent to be able to give detailed information to those interested in the cultural activities when they visit a destination. Also, a large number of festivals and cultural events are celebrated in various destinations. There is almost always some colourful event to see. The travel agents must have all the information about the festivals taking place in different parts of the destination.

### Liaison with Providers of Services

Before any form of travel can be sold over the counter to a customer, contracts have to be entered into with the providers of various services. These include transportation companies, hotel proprietors, the providers of surface transport like motor cars or coaches for transfer to and from hotels and for sightseeing, etc., and also for general servicing requirements. In the case of a large agency with worldwide branches, the liaison work involves a great deal of coordination with the principals.

### Provision of Foreign Currencies

Provisions of foreign currencies to intending travellers is another specialised activity of a travel agency. Some of the larger travel agencies deal exclusively in the provision of foreign currencies, traveller's cheques, etc., this is an important facility to intending travellers as it saves them a lot of time and energy in avoiding visits to regular banking channels.

## Travel insurance

Travel insurance is insurance that is intended to cover medical expenses, trip cancellation, lost luggage, flight accident and other losses incurred while travelling, either internationally or domestically.

Travel insurance can usually be arranged at the time of the booking of a trip to cover exactly the duration of that trip, or a "multi-trip" policy can cover an unlimited number of trips within a set time frame. Some policies offer lower and higher medical-expense options; the higher ones are chiefly for countries that have high medical costs, such as the United States.

Some credit card issuers offer automatic travel insurance if travel arrangements are paid for using their credit cards, but these policies are generic and particular care must be taken to take into account personal requirements. There are many travel insurance policies available in the market place, but care must be taken of what events are covered by each policy, and what exclusions, exceptions and limits apply, besides other issues.

### Why Insurance:

The idea of buying a package of travel, accommodation and perhaps some ancillary services such as entertainment became established in Western Europe in the 1960s. By 1970, tour operation had become a full-fledged part of tourism. Its growth was spectacular.

It succeeded in reducing the real price of travel abroad, in doing this; it brought holidays abroad to a segment of the market not reached by conventional methods of taking a holiday.

Today in most countries which are generators of tourism, tour operation is the dominating describes the feature of the holiday market.

An inclusive tour is a package of transport and accommodation and perhaps some other services which are sold as a single holiday for a single all-inclusive price. The popular term, 'package holiday' nature of a tour more accurately than the term 'inclusive tour'.

The original demand for inclusive arrangements came from the convenience of buying a single travel product.

In today's world, travel especially overseas travel has taken great strides. Millions of people are travelling overseas from places of their residence to various destinations. In fact, there has been a vertical increase in the number of people travelling in the world. People travel for various reasons which may include leisure and holiday, visiting friends and relatives, on business, attending conferences and conventions, etc. While in a foreign country away from home travellers are exposed to many health related problems.

At times the traveller may even require a doctor's attention, hospitalisation, or a simple treatment for common diseases. The medical treatment overseas is extremely expensive and a traveller will not be in a position to cover the cost. However, if a traveller takes a travel insurance cover, he can make a smooth ride in case of any problems in terms of paying off the expenses through the insurance cover. These days travellers are taking the insurance cover to avoid any risks. In addition many countries insist on travel insurance cover before they grant a visa to the traveller.

## The Benefits

When a passenger buys an insurance cover, the need is to cover safety, security and medical contingencies. The travel agent should convince the passenger to take an insurance cover as it is advantage to the passenger in the hour of need. The vaccines do not protect against accidents and all health problems. The most frequent problem a passenger faces is dehydration, though the problem is not a serious one, it requires immediate treatment, since it upsets the whole itinerary of the passenger. The effect of such a problem can last a few weeks, causing discomfort, so a visit to a doctor becomes very essential, and a doctor's requirements or the cost of the treatment may be very high. To avoid such situations a passenger is advised to take a travel insurance cover to help tackle such problems. Apart from health, policies are made for covering lost baggage, any financial failure of the service providers and other misfortunes, etc.

The travel insurance policy can be bought from insurance companies, clinics, banks, specialist shops, and directly through insurance companies. The policies vary as per the time period and the rules of different countries. There are different levels of coverage and will vary from policy to policy. When travel insurance is purchased, a certificate is issued which states the details of the coverage and the policy number. The passenger is always advised to carry the original with him/her and leave a photocopy with the people at home.

A travel insurance policy generally covers the following:
- Medical and other related expenses
- Personal liability
- Cancellation, curtailment, missed departures
- Hi-jacking
- Travel trade indemnity
- Legal expenses
- Death and permanent disablements
- Luggage, personal effects and travel documents

## General Details of Coverage Include:

(i) Medical and other related expenses – covers medical and dental charges, repatriation and search and rescue. There can be many exclusions, which can be found in the policy document.

(ii) Personal liability – the coverage is against injury, damage to people or property.

(iii) Cancellation, curtailment, missed departures – protection against the need to delay or cancel travel arrangements due to illness or death of the policy holder, travelling companion, or family member etc. If a student has to delay a holiday due to the need to retake an examination, then this may also be covered.

(iv) Hi-jacking and travel trade indemnity – protection against the travel agent or the company becoming bankrupt.
(v) Legal expenses – cover all legal expenses as mentioned in the policy.
(vi) Death and permanent disablements – the cover is given for accidental death and personal accidents. The normal coverage does not apply to the accidents caused or connected with any hazardous sports. Clients may have to pay for hazardous sports like horse riding, rafting, trekking, white-water canoeing, etc. Some sports are covered under normal insurance policies. The insurers define them dangerous, i.e. deep sea diving, ballooning, parachuting and bungee jumping.
(vii) Luggage, personal effects – loss of passports, luggage, ticket and travel documents. Luggage delay is also covered. The amount of claim is limited for loss of personal effects. Some policies do not cover large amount of cash.

## Conditions Applying To Insurance Policy

The conditions vary from policy to policy but there are some common conditions:

(i) Travel insurance is mandatory for all passengers above 60 years of age.
(ii) Policy holders must take necessary steps to prevent accidents, loss or damage.
(iii) The claims must be made within a month or 28 days after the date of the event.
(iv) All claims must be submitted in writing to the insurer where the policy was purchased. Few companies allow medical claims to be settled at local offices.
(v) The policy covers amounts in excess of the minimum specified.
(vi) If luggage, money or passport is lost or stolen, a police notification in written has to be obtained.
(vii) If an airline or other carrier loses luggage, a report of irregularity is to be completed and authorised by the carrier or handling agent whether the loss is temporary or otherwise.
(viii) The proof of ownership must be submitted for claiming lost articles.
(ix) Most of the policies do not cover any consequences of war.
(x) The coverage for HIV or other related illness, including AIDS is not provided.
(xi) Where repatriation is required, a doctor's certificate is required to support the necessity of return home.

The agent must be familiar with the information contained within the insurance policy, the products covered, the claim procedure, etc., and should be able to explain the same to the client.

## The procedure to Claim Insurance

It is important to check the name of the policy holder, address, policy no., period of coverage, start and end dates covered by the policy. The client should be guided about the source to obtain the policy booklet. The client should be advised to go through the claims procedure in detail.

Care should be taken to ensure:
(i) Claims are be made in writing with all details
(ii) Receipts, bills, official valuations or estimates are enclosed
(iii) A police report is to be made for claims on theft or loss
(iv) Reservations proof is given for claiming cancellation
(v) Written confirmation is given about when and how the delay of transportation has occurred.
(vi) Policy number is quoted in all the correspondence

# 3
# TRAVEL ITINERARY

### Chapter Objectives

**After reading this chapter the reader should be able to:**
- Understand the basics of travel itinerary.
- Know the basic principals of making an itinerary.
- Identify various resources for planning travel itineraries.
- Understand Billing and Settlement Plan (BSP).
- Know the steps of itinerary planning.
- Know the benefits of (BSP).

Tourist itinerary is a composition of a series of operations that are a result of the study of the market. A tourist journey is characterised by an itinerary using various means of transport to link one locality with another. Preparation of different types of itineraries is another important function of a travel agency. Programmes, which clients may choose for their holiday or business travel. The study and the realisation of the itineraries call for a perfect organisation (technical and administrative) and also the knowledge of the desires of the public for a holiday and the propensity to receive tourists by the receiving localities.

A travel itinerary is a schedule of events relating to planned travel, generally including destinations to be visited at specified times and means of transportation to move between those destinations. For example, both the plan of a business trip and the route of a road trip, or the proposed outline of one, would be travel itineraries.

The construction of a travel itinerary may be assisted by the use of travel literature, including travel journals and diaries, a guide book containing information for visitors or tourists about the destination, or a trip planner website dedicated to helping the users plan their trips. Typically a travel itinerary is prepared by a travel agent who assists one in conducting their travel for business or leisure. Most commonly a travel agent provides a list of pre-planned travel itineraries to a traveller, who can then pick one that they're most satisfied with. However, with the advent of the internet, online maps, navigation, online trip planners and easier access to travel information in general, travellers, especially the younger ones prefer a more do-it-yourself approach to travel planning.

**Travel itinerary**

A travel itinerary might serve different purposes for different kinds of travellers. A typical business traveller's itinerary might include information about meetings, events and contacts with some time for leisure travel, while a leisure traveller's itinerary would predominantly include destinations, points of interest and transportation means.

"Itinerary is the step by step representation of the entire tour program; clearly indicating the program schedule along with other details like sector, sightseeing and transport etc. to the guests".

A good itinerary will save, time and money, apart from making the trip hassle free and a pleasant experience. It will give the framework for figuring out how many rail or road days will be required and where one can go by car, how much time it takes to see sights – and get to them as well as the cost. A good itinerary will consider all ground realities like actual transportation time during local sight-seeing and in heavy metropolitan traffic. It will help save time for locating accommodation close to the client's sightseeing that fits his budget as well. It will avoid making the trip uninteresting because of too many monuments in a row, standing in long lines or too much unexpected time getting to places.

## Principles of Itinerary Planning

Planning itineraries is an essential function for a professional travel agent and is an effective way to gain client trust. Once you have planned an effective itinerary for a client and the trip runs smoothly and according to plan, the client will be more likely to refer to you in future. Happy clients are also more likely to refer to you to their friends and business associates, thereby generating additional revenue.

When planning itineraries, it is helpful to follow some basic guidelines that can be broken down into five categories:

(i) Pace
(ii) Interest
(iii) Details
(iv) Energy
(v) Routing

**PACE:** Pacing refers to how quickly or slowly an itinerary moves. Providing a comfortable pace for clients is essential to their enjoyment of the trip. While it is frequently important to keep the itinerary moving, setting a pace that is too rapid can overburden clients and decrease their enjoyment. A client's age and health should also be considered when determining pace. Generally younger and healthier clients can move at a faster pace, but this is not always true, and each client should be considered on an individual basis. Finally, any disabilities need to be evaluated when determining an itinerary's pace. A good rule of thumb for determining pace for self-driving clients is not to exceed 120 miles per day. Also, allowing for rest stops and sightseeing along the way can improve the client's enjoyment of the trip.

**INTERESTS:** One very significant way to add value to your client's trip is to match his or her interests with corresponding activities and attractions along the way. To do this effectively, you must talk to your clients and listen carefully to the types of activities and the manner in which they describe their interests. It is helpful to provide a balance by planning some variety into the trip. To do this, you can schedule a mix of recreational activities educational activities and "frivolous activities" into the basic itinerary. Determining and matching interests takes practice and destination expertise, but the extra effort it takes to practice and learn will be rewarded in the form of client satisfaction.

**DETAILS:** No matter how clever an itinerary you put together for your client, if you do not pay attention to the details, the itinerary may be a failure. Details include checking to make sure attractions on your itinerary are open when your client arrives, reconfirming all ground handlers and transport and even checking with your clients to make sure they have made all necessary preparations including taking their passports and filling all essential prescriptions. Paying attention to detail may seem tedious, but imagine how embarrassing it would be to schedule a client's visit to the Louvre in Paris on Tuesday, only to learn that the museum is closed on that day.

**ROUTING:** It is important as a travel agent to plan both an interesting and efficient routing for your client. Ideally the route should be both scenic and practical. Whenever possible, avoid backtracking, doubling back or routing a client in circles. This is particularly important when routing corporate clients because you will need to build the routing around the individual's business appointments. It is important to listen carefully to clients' plans and help them access if the plan is realistic within the framework of geography.

Time spent on careful and detailed planning of an itinerary is never wasted. You might have to plan a route that includes places unfamiliar to you, or take into consideration the fact that certain passengers may not travel via some countries, whilst yet others will want to reach their destination by a specific time. All these special aspects have to be borne in mind in order to produce the most practical itinerary in accordance with the passenger's desires.

**ENERGY:** Finally, matching the energy level of the client with the energy level and intensity of the itinerary is another way to ensure the overall success of the trip. When considering this aspect, it is important to take note of how much walking certain destinations require, whether or not the client is travelling alone or with a family that includes small children and what type of travel experience the client is looking for. A traveller in search of a quiet beach vacation may not appreciate four scheduled activities per day. Get a sense of your client's energy level, listen to what they tell you they want, and then match the itinerary based on your observations and experience.

### Key Points in Planning an Itinerary

When planning the itinerary for a passenger, always remember to observe the following steps:
- Establish the places the passenger wishes to visit.
- Establish the order in which the passenger wishes to visit them.
- Link the cities in such a way as to avoid doubling back and zigzagging, (unless absolutely necessary) while at the same time meeting any special request made by the passenger.
- Take account of the political situation, geographical limitations and the practicality of the transport options.
- Ascertain that convenient air/sea/rail or road connections exist and, where possible, choose the quickest.
- Give preference, wherever possible, to itineraries with the lowest fares. Detours often raise the price.
- Plan the itinerary methodically, using a form.
- Be prepared to provide alternatives in case the passenger changes his or her mind or, when unexpected circumstances arise which will prevent the itinerary proceeding as originally planned. Initial notes and calculations can often help in this regard and should therefore always be retained.

## Mapping Itinerary

a) *Collect the important information for trip:*

Flight numbers, hotels, car rentals, and restaurant reservations are all key pieces of information to manage and maintain. You may also want to include directions to your hotel, the car rental company are using, as well as directions to the airport for your return flight. If you will be using airport transportation to get to hotel, include information about fees and hours of operation.

b) *Make a list-*

It's helpful to list all of the things to do on your trip. Even if it's more than you think you can manage, create a list of everything you'd like to do. Research local events, holidays, and observances of the places you're travelling to as well. You may be able to witness or experience a cultural event that other travellers don't get to experience.[1]

Be conscious of the amount of time you will spend at each stop. Certain destinations, like the Museum of Modern Art, can be an all-day endeavour.

If you're travelling with one or more people, be sure to get feedback and ideas for destinations.

c) *Map stops-*

Match stops to specific locations on a map and note their locations. Try and map them sequentially to efficiently use your travel time. You'll most likely be travelling from adjacent cities as you travel. For each activity, estimate the length of time it will take to get to there, and how long you will be there.

Be sure have local maps for the areas you will be exploring. It is also helpful to obtain schedules for bus and train services and numbers for local taxis. Make sure that the maps are up-to-date. Cities and other areas change often. A road that existed 10 years ago may no longer exist today.

d) *Create a budget-*

Do want a trip with days spent at four star restaurants and nights spent in five star hotels? Or are you more interested in finding local favourites and rustic B&Bs? Your vacation is as expensive (or inexpensive) as you want it to be. It ultimately comes down to what you can afford.

A spreadsheet program like Microsoft Excel can help create an organized and portable budget and itinerary.

Alternatively, consider using a budgeting app or website. The downside is that this may not be as portable, especially if you don't have Wi-Fi access.

e) *Stay flexible-*

Don't hesitate to give yourself a free day or two. can use this free day to explore, or take some time off to rest. Ultimately itinerary is a guide to keep you on track while visiting. If you miss a reservation, it isn't the end of the world. Consider asking around about a local favourite to eat at, find a local market, or see if there's a museum or oddity nearby.

Consider having some back-up plans. For example, if you make a reservation, have a few other places to eat at in mind, just in case you miss it. Never lose sight of the fact that your trip is supposed to be an enjoyable and fulfilling experience.

## Organizing Itinerary

Record information. Record your check in times, confirmation numbers, hotel names, and any other information you might need on hand. Don't worry about organizing this information yet. In the meantime, focus on accumulating and documenting as much helpful information as you can think of. Organize travel information. Try and condense your travel information into a single document for easy access while travelling. Keep a printed copy or type the details of your itinerary into a word processing document. Use an online travel itinerary template. This will give you a basic set-up, so all have to do is fill in the blanks. Consider downloading a travel app to keep organized during your trip.

If you are travelling out of the country, include the address, telephone number, and directions to country's embassy or consulate if applicable. may want to save a list of addresses of family and friends, so can send them postcards from the destinations you will visit.

## Account for Responsibilities

Even if will only be gone for a weekend, it's a good idea to make sure that everything at home will be in order and accounted for. If you have pets, plants, or will need mail checked for an extended amount of time, ensure that a friend or family member will be there to do so. This will ultimately offer peace of mind so can relax and fully enjoy vacation.

## Resources for Planning Travel Itineraries

The various resources necessary to help in the process are:

(a) **Thorough Understanding of Travel Geography:** The best way to gain knowledge of travel itineraries is to travel to the destination yourself. Unfortunately, there is simply no way to visit every possible destination that the clients might request. Therefore, following resources may be considered:

(b) **Familiarisation with your Clients Feedback:** Follow up with your current clients and find out how their trips were. Feedback, both positive and negative, can be a valuable source of information. Consider developing a database of clients and making notes about their experience in the database. This type of follow-up will not only give valuable information about the destinations and itineraries that are planned, but it will also help build rapport and establish client loyalty and trust.

(c) **Consulting Travel Guidebooks:** Libraries and bookstores carry large numbers of travel guidebooks. Many of these guidebooks are quite helpful to travel agents. Some guides to consider are Michelin, Fielding, Fodor, Frommer, Birnbaum and the Blue Guides.

(d) **Information from National and Regional Tourist Board:** Governmental tourist boards and offices offer a tremendous variety of useful information for the travel agent. One is able to gather information about the history, culture, geography, transport system, lodging, museums, special events and local currency. Many of these boards will send the professional brochures, posters, and videos etc. that can be used as part of the sales process.

(e) **Consulting Periodicals:** Subscribe or utilize local libraries to locate appropriate travel articles. There are dozens of excellent publications, including Conde Nast traveller, National Geographic, Travel and Leisure and Travel holidays. In addition, there are a number of excellent speciality magazines that focus on a particular aspect of travel such as scuba diving, skiing or boating.

(f) **Referring to Speciality Journals:** There are a variety of professional speciality journals that may be of help. Topics include anything from art to zoos and often have statistics useful for the travel industry. For example, *Museum News* published an entire issue devoted to cultural tourism.

(g) **Information from Travel Industry Organisations:** Industry organisations are extremely useful sources of information to the professional travel agent. Examples of these include CLIA (Cruise Line International Association) ASTA, ARTA, ICTA, and Travel and Tourism Research Association, Adventure Travel Society, Ecotourism Society, Dive travel Industries Association and the Finishing Travel Industry Association.

(h) **Travel Industry Journals:** Publications including Travel weekly, travel Agent and Travel Age are designed specifically for the professional travel agent. Consider subscribing to one or more of these trade publications.

(i) **Consulting Confidential Tariffs:** Many tour and ground operators offer publications for specific destinations and countries that describe land services, rates for accommodations, sightseeing and excursions, transfers, meals and other items.

(j) **Referring to Internet:** Perhaps two of the greatest technological advances for the travel agent are personal computers and the Internet. Changes in the travel industry are occurring rapidly and an ability to keep abreast of these changes is essential to the effectiveness as a travel agent. There is a variety of excellent computer CD-ROMs that contain volumes of information about geography and myriad travel issues and destinations. The Internet is also becoming an essential source of information to the professional travel agent. Not only can a wealth of information be obtained through the Internet, but it is now possible to take "virtual" tours of just about any destination in the world.

(k) **Understanding Client's Comfort Level:**
- The travel agent must keep reminding the clients that they can visit that destination again many times and not to stress over trying to see everything on their first trip. Enjoy what they are able to do and realise that the things they miss this time can be done the next time or the time after. A big mistake people make is to try to cram too much into a trip. Don't view a trip as a once-in-a-lifetime event! That mentality puts a lot of pressure on a traveller to do and see everything.
- More important is just to relax and enjoy. After the first trip you learn so much that your knowledge would be an advantage to make your next trip even better, and to see all the stuff you missed the first time.
- Figure out what you need to be comfortable, and then take all the steps necessary to care for yourself and make sure that you have arranged for whatever makes you comfortable. If you love small boutique hotels, stay in them! If a long series of flights with plane changes in the middle is an ordeal for you, book a break in the middle of the journey.
- Don't visit a tourist place that doesn't interest you intensely because it is a "must see". If it is not YOUR must see, it's a waste of valuable vacation time. Do enough research to learn what is available, but don't spend all day at an art museum if what you really want to do is taste wine or search for ceramics! It is supposed to be fun, not a school trip.
- Go with an open mind. Nowadays there is so much available information on destinations. People have preferences and will express their opinion to friends and relatives and others. Don't let that influence you! If you want to see an Opera, go see an Opera. If you enjoy shopping, go and spend quality time in good market places of the destination.

## The Role of TRAVEL AGENT

- Don't just head for the popular tourist destinations. Seek out roads less travelled. Search for that spirit of a traveller and an adventurer within you to try out different places and different cuisines. Something that you are not able to experience in your resident country or city.

## Steps in Planning an Itinerary

Following steps needs to be taken for planning an itinerary:

Make sure you book the right trains/ships/buses for the right date- For independent travel you'll often have to put the trip together yourself, booking each leg of the journey separately via a different agency or website, and it pays to make sure you get it right.

To plan a budget — Travellers often ask a question about the cost of the total trip. Obviously before working out the total cost of the trip the travel professional needs to ask the client about the duration of the trip, type of hotel accommodation required, as also the tours, which he may like to take. Additional information is required to be ascertained from the tourist, including stopover, meals etc. Or a 10 day trip, travelling 2nd class, staying in hostels and living on snacks? The possibilities are endless, and they are all your decision. The best and only way to work out costs is to sketch out an itinerary and a budget and adjust what the traveller wants and can afford.

To see if you're happy with how long you get in key places — Many people want to stop everywhere and see everything, but haven't thought through how long they'll actually get in each place after allowing for travelling time. Again, plan it out, and if necessary adjust your plans.

### Example of an itinerary

The table below is just an example. This is just to demonstrate how to plan a trip, not a real suggested itinerary. This example is for a Trans-Siberian trip. However, the techniques can be applicable for any type of journey, simple or complex.

Then add one-off items to the bottom of your table:

| A | B | C | D | E | F | G |
|---|---|---|---|---|---|---|
| Date | Day | Activity or journey | Fares (£) | Hotels (£) | Food etc. (£) | Others (£) |
| 28 August | Monday | London depart 12:39 Brussels arrive 16:10, Eurostar. | 59 | | | |
| | | Brussels depart 17:25 Cologne arrive 19:45, Thalys. | 25 | 0 | 20 | |
| | | Cologne depart 22:28 by sleeper to Moscow. | 170 | | | |

| Date | Day | Activity | | | | |
|---|---|---|---|---|---|---|
| 29 August | Tuesday | On board sleeper via Warsaw. | 0 | 0 | 10 | |
| 30 August | Wednesday | Arrive Moscow 10:59. Day in Moscow | 0 | 40 | 20 | |
| 31 August | Thursday | Day in Moscow | 0 | 40 | 20 | 10, entrance fees |
| 1 September | Friday | Day in Moscow. Depart Moscow 23:00 by train to Irkutsk | 150 | 0 | 20 | |
| 2 September | Saturday | On train in Siberia. | 0 | 0 | 10 | |
| 3 September | Sunday | On train in Siberia. | 0 | 0 | 10 | |
| 4 September | Monday | On train in Siberia. | 0 | 0 | 10 | |
| 5 September | Tuesday | Arrive Irkutsk 04:30 (08:30 local time). Day in Irkutsk. | 0 | 30 | 20 | |
| 6 September | Wednesday | Day in Irkutsk. Day tour to Lake Baikal. | 0 | 30 | 20 | 20, Baikal day tour |
| 7 September | Thursday | Depart Irkutsk 15:00 by sleeper for Ulan Bator | 60 | 0 | 20 | |
| 8 September | Friday | On train in Siberia. | 0 | 30 | 10 | |
| 9 September | Saturday | Arrive Ulan Bator 06:00. Day in UB | 0 | 30 | 20 | |
| 10 September | Sunday | Day in UB. Day tour. | 0 | 30 | 20 | 15, day tour |
| 11 September | Monday | Depart UB 09:30 for Beijing by sleeper train | 80 | 0 | 10 | |
| 12 September | Tuesday | Arrive Beijing 15:00 | 0 | 40 | 20 | |
| 13 September | Wednesday | Day in Beijing. See Forbidden City. | 0 | 40 | 20 | 10, entrance fees |
| 14 September | Thursday | Day in Beijing. Day tour to Great Wall. | 0 | 40 | 20 | 25, Great Wall tour |
| 15 September | Friday | Flight Beijing-London: Beijing depart 21:30. | 420 | 0 | 20 | 20, Taxi to airport |

| One-off items: | Cost (£): |
|---|---|
| Guidebooks | 35 |
| Belarus transit visa | 10 |
| Russian visa | 40 |
| Mongolian visa | 30 |
| Chinese visa | 30 |
| Travel insurance | 45 |

Column A shows the date. If the client needs to pre-book any part of his itinerary, he can now book it for the right date.

Column B shows the days of the week. If the client needs to take a train or ferry that only runs on certain days of the week, he can see that he has got the day right.

Column C shows a rough idea of what client might do that day. He can see how long he gets in major stops, and can adjust the itinerary if he thinks it is not long enough. It can be for planning purposes only - he does not have to stick to it rigidly once he is travelling.

Column D shows likely train, bus or ferry costs. He uses rough estimates if he is not 100% sure.

Column E shows likely hotel costs. The hotel cost is zero when the client is on a sleeper train. He also allows a higher budget in an expensive western city than he would in a cheaper city. If the client knows where he want to stay, he enters the actual cost, otherwise he use a rough estimate.

Column F is for daily spending on food, local transport, normal museum entrance fees and so on. Some people try and plan a whole trip using a flat 'budget per day' which never changes, but the client adjusts the amount he budgeted for, depending on whether he is on a train or in a city, in a western city or a third world city, likely to want a restaurant meal or is happy with snacks and so on.

## BILLING AND SETTLEMENT PLAN (BSP):

BSP is a system designed to simplify - airlines receive one settlement covering all agents - and assist the selling, reporting and remitting procedures and improve financial control and cash flow. IATA members and non-IATA members can join. The electronic distribution of billing reports and generation of ADMs/ACMs via the BSPlink results in fewer resources required and a centralized and neutral system enables increased financial and accelerated quality controls

A billing and settlement plan (BSP) (also known as "Bank Settlement Plan") is an electronic billing system designed to facilitate the flow of data and funds between travel agencies and airlines. The advantage of such an intermediary organization is that instead of each travel agency having an individual relationship with each airline, all of the information is consolidated through the BSP.

BSP's are organized on a local basis, usually one per country. However, there are some BSP's which cover more than one country (for example the Nordics). The International Air Transport Association states that at the close of 2009, there were 86 BSP's covering more than 160 countries worldwide, while at the close of 2011, there were 88 BSPs, covering 176 countries and territories serving about 400 airlines, with gross sales processed amounting to USD 249 billion.

Travel agents are usually required to be accredited by either Airlines Reporting Corporation (ARC), when they are located in the US, or BSP outside of the US, in order to issue airline reservations through GDS.

BSP is a system designed to facilitate and simplify the selling, reporting and remitting procedures of IATA Accredited Passenger Sales Agents, as well as improve financial control and cash flow for BSP Airlines.

Billing and settlement plan in other words means the method of providing and issuing Standard Traffic Documents and of accounting and settling accounts between Member-Airlines and approved agents described in the applicable resolution and adopted as a Billing & Settlement plan for any particular country or group of countries in accordance with the applicable resolution.

## Agent:

A Passenger Sales Agent who has been duly authorized to report under BSP rules.

## BSP Airline:

An air carrier operating scheduled passenger services that has been admitted to participate in the Billing and Settlement Plan.

## BSP Area:

The country or groups of countries in which a Billing and Settlement Plan operates.

## Billing Data:

The data on which the Processing Centre must produce billing to the agents, according to the data submitted by the means of the Sales Committee.

## Billing Period:

The time-span comprising one or more reporting periods for which a billing period is rendered. The BSP committee sets the duration.

## Carrier Identification Plate (CIP):

A plate supplied by the BSP airline to an agent, for use in the issue of standard traffic Documents (STD's) under BSP.

## Cancelled:

It is used in connection with a Traffic Document, which has been spoilt or is not suitable for sale, whether or not validated with an airline CIP. All coupons must be boldly marked across with the word "Cancelled".

## Check Digit:

A device that mathematically tests the accuracy of a series of digits. In BSP, it is used for STD numbers.

## Clearing Bank:

The bank or other organisation appointed under a Billing and Settlement Plan to perform the following function: to receive remittances from agents to settle the money due to airlines and reporting timely receipt of agent remittance. It can take over the functions of the processing centres in some BSPs.

### Direct Debit:
A system of payment where agents authorise the clearing bank to debit their accounts for the amounts they owe on the remittance date.

### Hand of Tape (HOT):
A Magnetic tape containing all the data raised from the tickets and other documents in a sale transmittal and produced in accordance with the specifications published under the authority of the BSP committee.

### Notice of irregularity:
A warning letter sent to an agent to inform him that some failure has been detected on his part in matters such as reporting or remittance. Accumulation of four instances or so results in DEFAULT action being taken, where the agent's approval by IATA is reviewed.

### Passenger Agency Conference (PA CONF):
The conferences established pursuant to the provision for the conduct of IATA traffic conference to take action on matters relating to the relationship between airline and recognized IATA Passenger sales agents.

### Plan Management:
The Department of IATA responsible to the agency administrator for the administrative management and development of the Billing and Settlement plan in the different countries/areas where it is applicable. "The local representative of the Plan Management is the BSP Manager".

### Processing Centre (EDP):
The entity appointed under a Billing and Settlements Plan to receive sales transmittals from agents to extract and process data there, to render billing to agents and to notify the clearing bank and the BSP Airlines of the amounts due by agents.

### Remittance Date:
The clearing bank's close of business, on the latest date by which the agents remittance must reach the clearing bank. The date is established by the BSP committee on the BSP panel's recommendation, within the limits of the Sales Agency Rules of the area.

### Remittance Period:
That time-span between two remittance dates. It must not be shorter than one billing period, but may cover more than one billing period.

## Reporting Period:
The last date of the reporting period, or the date when the sales transmittal for the period must be prepared.

## Reporting Date:
The time-span covered by a sales transmittal. Its length is recommended by the Feasibility-Study-Panel to the BSP-Panel and must be endorsed by the BSP-Committee.

## Sale Agency Rules:
IATA resolution 800 or 808, as applicable in the BSP area concerned.

## Sales Transmittal:
The agents lists, for a reporting period, of all STDs and SAFs used, accompanied by the audit coupons of all STDs reported and other relevant administrative forms/supporting documentation. STD serial numbers of SAFs are entered on an Agency Sales Transmittal form. All documentations are transmitted electronically. It is mandatory that a "No Sales" report must be followed when applicable.

## Standard Administrative Forms (SAF):
Accountable forms originated by airlines of agents for adjusting sales transaction and other forms to substantial sales or to prepare sales transmittals.

## Standard Traffic Documents (STDs):
Are standard passenger tickets and MPDs supplied to agents for issue to customers under the BSP. Such documents may be issued manually, mechanically or electronically for air passenger transportation on the lines that a carrier has authorised. They do not bear any airlines identification until after validation by the agent.

## Steering Panel:
A panel, which, in accordance with the instruction and directions of the Billing and Settlement plan committee, is charged with the implementation and certain supervisory aspects of a Billing and Settlement Plan.

## Submission Date:
The processing centres close of business on the day when the sales transmittal must be in the possession of the processing centre.

## Unit Transportation Processed:
A transaction going through the processing centre, consisting of one or more documents related to the passenger's trip or an accounting adjustment for the trip.

### Void:

Unused coupons of properly validated tickets. The letter VOID should be printed in the relevant areas of the passenger tickets and the voided coupons detached prior to handing the ticket over to the passenger.

### Payment Processing:

Since the physical stock of manual tickets has been completely phased out from the industry, the BSP in collaboration with the various CRS companies manage the stock adding procedure through the system. This process is called capping. Since physical stock adding is no more required the control on tickets issued is done electronically through the data stored in the airline's and the CRS'S companies database. The agent coupon which is saved electronically forms the basis for payment generation.

The BSP follows certain set procedures for processing the bill of payment, agency credit notes, agency debit notes and incentives offered by airlines.

In India all airlines including domestic airlines participate in BSP

The Accounting Period for which the bill is generated is on a fortnightly basis.

Following are the documents involved in the process of payment.

- Sales transmittal form
- Main billing statement
- Agency discrepancy report
- Supplementary billing statement
- Check for payment

## Benefits of a BSP

### Simplification

- Agents issue one sales report and remit one amount to a central point
- Airlines receive one settlement covering all agents
- Simplifies and reduces work through the use of electronic ticketing on behalf of all BSP Airlines
- Agents' sales are reported electronically

### Savings

- Less resources required for billing and collection
- Electronic distribution of billing reports and generation of debit/credit memos (ADMs/ACMs)

### Enhanced Control

- Increased financial control thanks to centralization and grouping
- Consolidated document flow, permitting accelerated quality controls
- Overall process monitoring by a neutral body

# 4
# STARTING A TRAVEL AGENCY

## Chapter Objectives

**After reading this chapter the reader should be able to:**
- How to start travel agency.
- Explain the need for approval of a travel agency.
- Understand IATA controlled approval.
- Know about various international regulations like the Chicago convention, Bilateral agreement, the Warsaw contention and IATA general conditions of travel.
- Know about travel information in the WATA Master Key.
- NTO rules for recognition.
- Guidelines for approval for travel agent, tour operator.

Travel agents are the market place intermediaries responsible for selling the services of airlines worldwide, considering the role and importance of air transport, which is at the heart of travel and tourism. Selling its services becomes the key motivation for engaging in the travel agency business. Therefore, the importance of approval for a travel agency is essential to enable it to sell the services of airlines and other service providers.

For setting up a travel agency business there are however, no legal requirements. In some countries, however, governments exercise some kind of a licensing control over agencies. Most principals license the sale of their services through the issue of an agency contract, or agency agreement. In the absence of such a contract or an agreement, a travel agency will not get any commission from selling the services on behalf of the principal. The income of a travel agent is derived only from commission that he receives from the principal after selling their services.

A license is required by a travel agency for a commission to be payable on the sale of services of air carriers who are members of the International Air Transport Association. Domestic air services are, however, exempted from this. Most airlines want to sell their services worldwide but cannot do so on their own as it is not economically viable for them to set up extensive network of sales offices in every city of the world. It is the travel agents who are the market place intermediaries who make the sale of the services of the airlines possible worldwide through their own network.

## Steps On How To Start A Travel Agency

### (i) Find Your Niche

Find out your niche market which is an important aspect. One of the mistakes many new travel agency business owners make is they want to sell everything. In that way, they are inviting hard competition from everywhere. That is not a wise thing to do for a startup as it may be lacking in experience and resources. When you pinpoint a particular segment of the market, you reduce the competition since not many operators are active in it. A niche market is the one that very few have explored thus far. There is always a good potential for growth in it.

What could be a niche for a travel agency? To find it out, you need to do a comprehensive research. Know what the emerging new travel needs are that very few agencies are able to meet. As very few competitors are active in that niche, your agency can grow fast.

For example, if you research the market, you may come to know that some newly married couples prefer going backpacking. They do not want to spend their honeymoon days in a conventional way. Instead, they look for trekking destinations. If you find that not many travel agencies are providing special travel packages to such couples, you can start doing so. That may be your niche. But do an extensive research.

### (ii) Make An Effective Business Plan

An effective business plan keeps you on the right track. It guides you in making your endeavour to run the agency successfully. But the business plan is not about setting the goals randomly and having a rough idea of what you will be doing. It is much more than that. You should, in fact, prepare a detailed plan. Your business plan must include some key points. It should be based on your market analysis and sales strategies. Make sure to mention your funding requirements and financial projections. Your business description should be precise in the plan to you have a clear picture of your business goals.

Certain additional points in the plan should also be considered. The plan must state the resources available to you to start a travel agency. Do not forget to determine your goals and objective of the business. At the same time, you should identify any constraints that you might face in operating the company. The plan should mention your strategy to remove the hurdles.

### iii) Branding Exercise

Branding is important for all types of businesses including your travel agency. Branding is all about creating a perception of your company and the products or services it sells.

One of the effective ways to build a positive perception is to create high-quality visuals such as an impressive logo design. Design other items such as brochures, business cards etc. Make sure that colours and typefaces in all the visuals are the same for brand consistency. If you are able to convey your brand message successfully through these items, customers will think positively about your services.

### iv) Legal Laws

You should thoroughly research the laws for travel agencies in your state. An easier way to find out these laws is to contact a host agency which will let you know about the registration process and the licensing.

Another thing to note here is that you must obtain a trademark for your business. Your logo is the trademark of your agency. But, after you create a logo, get it legally registered with the concerned authority.

### v) Requirements for Funds

When you start a travel agency, make sure that you have a funding strategy in place. You may be starting the agency on a small scale or from home; still, it needs a constant flow of money to meet various expenses. If you want to work from home, probably your family members can support.

But if you need a proper office and staff as well as online and offline marketing, you may be applying for a bank loan. Remember that you will need a lot of funds for marketing and create different promotional material. For example, businesses need professional website designs, which require dedicated funds.

### vi) Convenient Location

The success of your agency will depend a lot on its location. Here, one of the key things to consider is the foot traffic. Choose a location where people gather frequently and your signboard is visible to the crowds from a good distance. People get a good impression of a business if it is located in a nice area that has facilities such as car parking.

If you cannot afford an expensive location, settle for the next best convenient location. Remember that if your agency is at a good site, it is helpful in building a trustworthy brand image of a business. Additionally, your office should be big enough to accommodate your growing numbers of employees. It should be suitable for future expansion.

### vii) Promotional Plans

One of the conditions for growth of a business is that it is promoted aggressively across different platforms. Since not many people know your new agency very well, you need to launch an aggressive promotion campaign to target customers. They should know that your little company exists.

Consider all means of marketing and advertisements for making people aware of your agency. You can start giving ads in local newspapers either use display advertising platform or distribute leaflets to people. Keep brochures about your business in your office so that clients can pick them up easily. You should set aside a budget for online and offline advertisements at the local level. You should create a lot of marketing materials such as brochures etc. It would be good that you get the services of a professional graphic designer. The designer understands how to use colours etc. elements to convey a brand message of your travel agency.

### (viii) Using Social Media

Modern day businesses need to build a good presence on different social channels. This is because most people have social media accounts or channels such as Twitter and Facebook to exchange their thoughts on an issue. Your agency can find potential clients or customers on these channels. First of all, create your dedicated social media page for different channels. Make sure that the page design looks unique and impressive. It should stand out from the pages of your business rivals. Then, post content regarding your travel business regularly. Inform people about the latest price cuttings from our agency or any other feature you added for the customers.

### (ix) Building Customer Relationship

No business can thrive without paying attention without building a rapport with customers. Your travel agency must take steps to build up relationships with various individual customers who have used your agency or are likely to use in near future. Make sure that you train your staff on how to treat your guests while they are enjoying their vacations. Your local cooks, tour guides, and drivers all staff should be aware of the value of treating your customers well.

Make sure that you train your staff on how to treat your guests while they are enjoying their vacations. Your local cooks, tour guides, and drivers all staff should be aware of the value of treating your customers well.

If customers come with complaints offline or on your website, address them and resolve their issues right away. To build a solid customer relationship, you should create videos to answer your customers' travel related queries and send emails to them. In fact, you will need many graphic design ideas to create materials that help you to be in touch with customers.

### (x) Involve Partners

You simply can't run a travel agency without having something to sell. After all, you need to sell tickets, packages etc things to the potential travellers. Where do you get these from? Obviously, you will have to approach a few established travel companies for the permission to sell their packages from your agency. You need to sell their attractive offers to make money. But to get their nod is not easy.

The well-established operators will ask many questions about your startup travel agency. Most importantly, they would like to know what

percentage commission your agency will charge. Therefore, have a competitive percentage in mind.
Remember that your new agency may not be in a position to demand an outrageous commission. Consider also that you need the big operator more than they require you. Surely, in the early phase of your business, keep your commission and other demands low.

Another point to mention here is that you should be able to earn the respect and trust of your partners. Once the big travel companies have faith in your ability to sell, they may consider your demand for a better commission. First, build your brand image by earning your partner's' trust. Maintain a good reputation of your agency by resolving the travel related issues of your customers. You should also think of building partnerships with agencies who offer online graphic design services. You will need their services to create marketing materials regularly.

### (xi) Optimize Travel Website

Your online travel agency must be visible to the potential customers when they type keywords to find similar agencies on the web. This is called search engine optimization of a website. If the site does not appear on the top search results, most customers will not bother to find more sites. They will simply click on the top ranking sites.

Therefore, optimize your travel website so that it ranks higher. However, a first requisite for optimization is that your website design is perfect. This means that the site should have keywords inserted at the right places in your web content. Make a strong content marketing strategy that will help you build your audience.

### (xii) Achievable Goals

Many travel agents set high goals in their enthusiasm for making huge money instantly. But most of them end up achieving very little of the set goals. This leads to building up of frustration.

Experts suggest that the agents should set realistic sales target and keep it lower when they start a travel agency. First, consider your expenses, costs, expenses, and personal salary. After setting aside this amount, any money you get additionally will be your earnings from sales. So, find out your sales target.

### (xiii) Seizing an Opportunities

Some agents have this tendency of waiting for the sales opportunities. These are the agents who do not want to come out of their comfort zone. They wait for the conditions to improve and ultimately miss their sales goals by a long margin.

Rather than waiting for the clients to enter your agency's door, a better way is to approach them. You should be doing everything to contact your potential clients. Whenever you get the opportunity, seize it with both hands.

## IATA-Controlled Approval

As IATA travel makes up a substantial proportion of a total sale of a travel agency turnover, it is important for the travel agent who wishes to offer his clients the full range of travel services to obtain the necessary IATA approval or appointment.

The travel agency approval of IATA is controlled by its agency Administration Board. This Board is made up of a number of IATA members operating from a particular country. Before approval is granted by the IATA, a travel agency has to fulfil certain conditions.

The most important condition is the demonstration by an agency of its financial soundness or financial standing. It has to prove that it has sufficient finances to settle the accounts of various airlines whose business it is handling.

Another condition, which an agency has to fulfil, is to ensure the suitability and security of its premises. The premises of a travel agency are to be centrally located preferably, in the centre of the town, in a commercial district having proper security. The security aspect is very important, as the agency has to keep the ticket stock of various airlines companies, which is quite expensive.

Proficiency of the staff of a travel agency is another important aspect, which is considered by the IATA before giving an approval. The staff has to be professionally trained in the handling of airlines business. IATA in association with UFTAA conducts the International Travel Agents Training Programme to meet the growing demand for professionally trained manpower for the travel industry. The IATA-UFTAA training programme operates under the authority of the Passenger Agency Training Board. IATA's Agency Training Services (ATS) located in Geneva (Switzerland) is responsible for the general administration of the programme.

In the field, the training programme is administered by a Local Coordinator who is responsible for the promotion of the training courses, the distribution of the training materials and the organisation of the examinations. The Local Coordinator is provided by the local IATA agency services, the National Airlines or the National Travel Agents Association in a particular country.

The IATA-UFTAA training courses have been designed primarily for travel professionals who work in IATA accredited travel agencies and whose main task is to sell international air transportation on behalf of IATA member airlines. The agents' staff can demonstrate proficiency by completing an IATA/UFTAA (passenger) training course.

The applicant's ability to generate new business is another requirement to be taken into consideration by the IATA before considering an applicant for approval. This is to ensure that an agent is capable of generating new business in the market and has sufficient contacts to do so.

To sum up, any travel agency, in order to get IATA approval for selling the services of IATA airlines worldwide, has to ensure the following:

- Financial standing
- Suitability of the premises

- Security for control of ticket stock
- Proficiency of the staff
- Ability to generate new business

After considering the above aspects and if the IATA's Agency Administration Board is satisfied, necessary IATA approval is accorded to an agency. Once approved, a Passenger Sales Agreement is issued and a numeric ticket validation code is provided which will be stamped on all tickets issued by that IATA-approved agent.

IATA approval enables the agent to do business on behalf of all IATA members. It enables the agent to sell the services of all IATA member airlines throughout the world. The entire process of getting IATA approval can be quite time-consuming and lengthy and in the meantime agents applying for IATA approval are expected to generate business without getting any commissions.

## Additional Appointments

In addition to the IATA approval, which is basic for a travel agency, there are certain other approvals/recognitions required for running a travel agency. These approvals, however, will depend on the extent of activities and range of services, which a particular agency would like to offer to its clients. For instance, in order to make commissionable sales on the services of railways, domestic airlines services and other principals such as car hire companies, shipping and cruise services, necessary approval is to be obtained, these approvals will enable travel agents to sell services on behalf of these principals with remuneration.

In case a travel agency is an IATA-approved agent, or a member of the National Travel Agents Association, obtaining approvals or most of other principals becomes largely a formality.

## International Regulations

For a travel agent, it is essential to know the general framework within which commercial international air services function. The general framework explains the different types of traffic rights exercised by the scheduled carriers and describes the arrangements that exist between governments on the subject. The general framework also defines the board principles, which govern the liabilities of airlines to their passengers and to air cargo shippers in case of death, injury or loss of baggage.

## Basic Conventions

There are certain basic conventions and bilateral agreements regulating international air transport. Air transport regulations are the result of a number of international agreements between countries dating back over many years. Some of the important agreements are:
(i) The Chicago Convention
(ii) Bilateral Agreement
(iii) The Warsaw Convention
(iv) The IATA General Conditions of Carriage

## The Chicago Convention

The Chicago convention, which is a basic convention regulating international air transport, was held in the year 1944 in which eighty governments were represented. Today all countries active in international air transport are parties to this Convention. The Convention governs relations between states on both technical and commercial subjects concerning air transport. This convention was also responsible for the establishment of the International Civil Aviation Organisation (ICAO) which establishes standards and practices to facilitate international air navigation and develops laws to govern international air transport. Although the Convention does not itself grant rights to operate international air services, it makes provisions for the manner in which such rights may be granted.

The Chicago Convention also makes a distinction between "scheduled" and "non-scheduled" services. Scheduled international services may be operated by an agreement between the two countries. Several such agreements known as Bilateral Agreements or Bilateral have been entered into between countries. Regarding "non-scheduled", the Chicago Convention states that each country may impose such conditions and regulations as it may consider desirable.

## The Bilateral Agreements

Under the Bilateral Agreements scheduled carriers are designated by each state. The agreements specify the rights that each designated carrier will enjoy in the other country. The most important part of the bilateral agreements specify the cities, which may be served by the designated carriers. These rights (including the right to overfly through a country or make stops due to technical reasons only in another country) are known as Six Freedoms of the Air. These are explained as follows:

First Freedom: The right of an airline of a country to fly across the territory of another country without landing.

Second Freedom: The right of an airline of a country to land in the territory of another country for non-traffic purposes like for refuelling aircraft.

Third Freedom: The right of an airline of a country to off-load passengers, mail or freight from an aircraft from which those passengers, mail or freight originated-the home country of the airline.

Fourth Freedom: The right of an airline of a country to pick up, in another country passengers, mail and cargo destined for the home country of the airline.

Fifth Freedom: The right of an airline of a country to carry passengers, mails and cargo from a point of origin in a foreign country to a point of destination in another foreign country.

Sixth Freedom: A term sometimes refers to the type of fifth freedom traffic in which passengers, mail and cargo, are carried from a point of origin on a foreign country to a point of destination in another foreign country via the home country of the airline.

The above traffic can only be exercised by countries if specifically permitted in the bilateral agreements. Besides, a special authorisation is required not only in the bilateral between the two countries but also in the bilateral between the country of the designated carrier and each of the countries where the intermediaries point or point beyond is situated.

## The Warsaw Convention

The Warsaw Convention, concluded in the year 1929, first established common agreement on the extent of the liability of the airlines in the event of death or injury of its passengers and for delay, damage or loss to passenger baggage. The Convention had several additions and amendments since it was concluded in the year 1929.

The broad principle underlining the Warsaw Convention, is that the carrier is liable to the passengers, shipper or consignee unless it can prove that it has taken all necessary precautions to avoid damage. The Convention prescribes liability limits in the event of death of or injury to a passenger, and of loss, damage or delay of baggage and cargo. For baggage and cargo the liability limit is related to the weight of the concerned baggage or cargo.

## The IATA General Conditions of Carriage

The Warsaw Convention does not deal with all aspects of the legal relationship between the airlines and the passengers. Specific contractual provisions not governed by the convention concerning liability are, however, printed on the passenger tickets issued by individual airline companies. These are printed under the title "conditions of contract". These conditions do not cover all aspects because of the limited space available on the passenger ticket. More detailed provisions concerning carriage of the airline concerned and are specifically applicable to transportation on that particular airline services need not to be taken care of. Standard General Conditions of Carriage as developed by the IATA Legal Committee have been adopted by a large number of IOATA member airlines.

## NTO RULES FOR RECOGNITION

The Ministry of Tourism, Govt. of India has a scheme whereby any travel agent can get a recognition as an approved travel agency. The aims and objectives of the scheme for recognising travel agency are to promote tourism in India. This is a voluntary scheme opened to all bonafide travel agencies in the country. According to the Ministry of Tourism, a travel agency is one to make arrangement of tickets for travel by air, rail, ship and for passport and VISA, etc. It may also arrange accommodation, tours, entertainment and other tourism related services.

Before a recognition is accorded, the travel agency must fulfil the following conditions:
1. The application for a grant of recognition is to be given in the prescribed form and submitted in duplicate.
2. The travel agency must have a minimum paid-up capital duly supported by the latest audited balance sheets/Charted Accountant's Certificate.

3. The travel agency should be approved by the International Air Transport Association (IATA) or the General Sales Agent (GSA) of an IATA member airline.
4. The minimum office space where the Travel Agency has to establish a business should be 250 sq. feet. Besides, the office may be located in neat & clean surroundings and equipped with a telephone, fax and Computer Reservation System (CRS), etc. The office must be located preferably on the ground floor or first floor, if situated in a residential area with sufficient space for reception and easy access to washroom facilities.
5. The travel agency should be under the charge of a full-time member who is professionally trained, experienced in matters relating to ticketing, transport, accommodation facilities, currency, customs regulations and other Travel and Tourism related services. In addition, greater emphasis may be given to effective communication skills, knowledge of foreign languages other than English.
6. There should be a minimum of four qualified staff out of which at least two should have Diploma/Degree in Travel and Tourism from a recognized University (IITTM) or Institution approved by AICTE. The academic qualification may be relaxed in case of exceptionally experienced personnel in airlines, shipping transport, PR agencies, hotel and other corporate bodies and those who have worked for at least three years with IATA/UFTAA agencies.
7. The Travel Agencies have been in operation for a period of one year after IATA approval at the time of filling the application.
8. The Travel Agency should be an income tax assessee and must have filled income tax returns for the current assessment year.

After necessary inspection and fulfilment of conditions as stipulated by the Ministry of Tourism, necessary recognition is granted to an agency. Initially the recognition as a travel agency is granted for a period of three years and renewal is granted for five years on an application made by the travel agency along with the prescribed fee. The travel agency will be required to pay a non-refundable one-time fee while applying for recognition. The fee is to be made payable to an accounts officer, Ministry of Tourism in the form of bank draft.

Recognition is to be granted to the Headquarter office of the travel agency. Branch offices will be approved along with Headquarter Office. Branch office can also be approved subsequently provided the particulars of these are submitted to Ministry of Tourism and accepted by it.

The decision of the Govt. of India in the matter of recognition is to be final. However, the Govt. of India, may in their discretion refuse to recognise any firm or withdraw/withhold, at any time, recognition already granted with the approval of the competent authority. However, before such a decision is taken, necessary show-cause notice would be issued and the reply considered on merit. This will be done as a last resort and circumstances in which withdrawal is resorted to would also be brought out.

## GUIDELINES AND PROCEDURE FOR THE APPROVAL OF TRAVEL AGENCY AND TOUR OPERATOR BY GOVERNMENT OF INDIA, MINISTRY OF TOURISM

**Introduction**

Over the years, the function and activities of travel/tour companies have increased drastically. Now, almost all travel companies are operating at local as well as international levels. Technically and practically a travel/tour company need to be approved and recognized by the airlines, railways, hotels/resorts department of tourism (Dot)(Govt. of India) and Dot (state govt. for small scale companies), ministry of external affairs, RBI (Reserve Bank of India), IATA, TAAI, Cruises, car rental companies and other organizations. However, the most important approval and recognition in this context is in form of Department of Tourism.

### Approval/Recognition of Department of Tourism (DOT):

The aims and objectives of the recognition are to promote tourism in India. It is a voluntary scheme open to all bonefide travel agencies and tour operators' enterprises. The travel companies which are granted recognition or entitled to such incentives and constituencies as may be granted by govt. from time to time.

### Rule for the travel agency:

The following are the main rules prescribed by the DOT for the approval of travel agencies:

1) Application shall be in the prescribed form and shall be addressed to the director of tourism, ministry of tourism, govt. of India New Delhi.
2) The company has functioned successfully for at least one year.
3) Have minimum paid of capital.
4) Have an IATA license of GSA (general service agent) of IATA member airlines.
5) Has been approved by RBI to book foreign tourist.
6) Approved by ministry of external affairs to handle document, passports, visas and such another items.
7) Income taxes assess.
8) Registered under the local; shops and establishments.
9) Good professional reputation, at least one or two staff members should be from IATA and Dot recognized tourism educational institutional.
10) Recognized by airlines.
11) Approved by railways.
12) Prescribed fees for recognition.
13) A travel agency must attach the audited annual report.

The applications form prescribed by DOT.

Contents
1) Name and address……………………………………………..
2) Year of establishment…………………………………………..
3) Nature of business and year of commencement…………………..
4) Types of business form………………………………………..
5) Name and address of directors/partner………………………….
6) Staff employed………………………………………………..

i) Qualification..........................................................................
ii) Salary/wages structure.............................................................
iii) Experience..........................................................................
iv) Length of service..................................................................
7) Name of bankers....................................................................
8) Name of auditors...................................................................
9) Auditor's financial statement....................................................
10) Copy of income Tax no..........................................................
11) Auditor's financial statement..................................................
12) Letters of approval from IATA.................................................
13) Membership of professional travel trade organization such as IATA/ TAAI/IATO/WTO/ASTA/PATA /etc...........................
14) Sales turnover during last five years........................................
15) Steps taken to promote tourist traffic in the country................
16) Any other steps/activities......................................................

### Rules for Recognition of tour operator by DOT

The main rules are:
1) Application shall be in the prescribed form.
2) Minimum paid be capital as prescribed by the organization.
3) Minimum turnover should be 5 lacks.
4) Good professional reputation and trained staff in various segment of travel industry.
5) Operation for minimum one year.
6) Income taxes assess.
7) Approved from IATO.
8) Maintained ethical standards of tourism business.
9) Approved for RBI, ministry of external affairs.
10) At least two or three staff members from IATO/DOT recognized tourism and training institute.
11) Sound financial position.
12) Recognized by the railway and airlines.
13) Should employ only approved guides,.
14) Should have contributed towards the promotion and development of tourism.
15) Good location.

### Application form for tour operators:

1) Name and address of tour company...........................................
2) Year of registration................................................................
3) Nature of business and year of commencement of business........
4) Name and address of directors/partner.....................................
5) Staff employed.....................................................................
6) Qualification........................................................................
7) Salary/wages structure..........................................................
8) Name of bankers...................................................................
9) Name of auditors..................................................................
10) Auditor's financial statement..................................................

11) Copy of income tax return..................................................................
12) Member of international and domestic tourism organizations...............
13) Turn over..................................................................................................
14) Volume of tourist traffic handles..............................................................
15) No. of conferences and convention handled..........................................
16) No. of package tours handled during the last year.................................
17) No. of incentive tour handle....................................................................
18) Steps taken to promote tourism..............................................................
19) Any other activities..................................................................................

## GOVERNMENT OF INDIA MINISTRY OF TOURISM

GUIDELINES FOR RECOGNITION / RENEWAL OR EXTENSION AS AN APPROVED TRAVEL AGENT / AGENCY (TA)

[Revised with effect from 18 July 2011]

The aims and objectives of the scheme for recognition of Travel Agent / Agency (TA) are to encourage quality standard and service in this category so as to promote tourism in India. This is a voluntary scheme open to all bonafide travel agencies to bring them in organized sector.

Definition: A Travel Agent / Agency (TA) is the one who makes arrangements of tickets for travel by air, rail, ship, passport, visa, etc. It may also arrange accommodation, tours, entertainment and other tourism related services.

The application for approval shall be submitted online through etravel tradeapproval.nic.in.

1. The following conditions must be fulfilled by the TA for grant of recognition/ renewal or extension by MOT:-
    i) The application for grant of recognition / renewal or extension shall be in the prescribed form and submitted in duplicate along with the required documents.
    ii) TA should have a minimum Paid up Capital (Capital employed) of Rs. 3.00 lakh for rest of India and Rs. 50, 000/- for the agencies located in the North – Eastern region, remote and rural areas duly supported by the latest audited Balance Sheet / firm's Statutory Auditor's certificate.
    iii) TA should be approved by International Air Transport Association (IATA) or should be General Sales Agent (GSA) / Passenger Sales Agent (PSA) of an IATA member Airlines.
    iv) TA should have been in operation for a minimum period of one year before the date of application.
    v) The minimum office space should be at least 150 sq. ft for rest of India and 100 sq. ft for hilly areas which are above 1000 meters from sea level. Besides, the office may be located in neat and clean surrounding and equipped with telephone, fax and computer reservation system etc. There should be sufficient space for reception and easy access to toilet facilities.
    vi) TA should be under the charge of the Owner or a full time member

who is adequately trained, experienced in matters regarding ticketing, itineraries, transport, accommodation facilities, currency, customs regulations and tourism and travel related services. Besides this, greater emphasis may be given to effective communication skills, knowledge of foreign languages, other than English.

There should be a minimum of four qualified staff out of which at least one should have Diploma / Degree in Tourism & Travel Management from a recognized University, IITTM or an institution approved by AICTE. The owner of the firm would be included as one of the qualified employees.

The academic qualifications may be relaxed in case of the other two staff members who are exceptionally experienced personnel in Airlines, Shipping, Transport and PR agencies, Hotel and other Corporate Bodies and those who have worked for three years with IATA / UFTA agencies and also those who have two years experience with MOT approved Travel Agencies.

For the Travel Agents / Agencies located in the North – Eastern region, remote and rural areas, there should be a minimum of two staff out of which one should be a qualified employee with a Diploma / Degree in Tourism & Travel Management from a recognized University, IITTM or an institution approved by AICTE. The owner of the firm would be included as one of the qualified employees.

vi) TA should be an income-tax assessee and should have filed Income Tax Return for the current assessment year.

viii) For the monuments protected under the Ancient Monuments and Archaeological Sites & Remains Act, 1958 (24 of 1958), the TAs should deploy / engage the services of Regional Level Tourist Guides trained and licensed by Ministry of Tourism, Government of India or other guides authorized by the Government of India or under orders of the Hon'ble Court(s). For other monuments and destinations, the guides authorized under the orders of the appropriate authority, if any, of the concerned monument / destination should be deployed / engaged by TAs.

ix) For outsourcing any of the services relating to tourists, the TA(s) shall use approved specialized agencies in the specific field of activity.

2. TA would be required to pay a non-refundable fee of Rs. 3, 000/- while applying for the recognition and renewal of Head Office as well as each Branch Office. The fee would be made payable to the Pay & Accounts Officer, Ministry of Tourism in the form of online payment.

3. The TA should adhere to the tenets of the Code of Conduct for "Safe & Honourable Tourism".

4. The recognition / renewal would be granted to the Head Office of the TA. The Branch Offices of TA would be approved along with the Head Office or subsequently, provided the particulars of the Branch Offices are submitted to MOT for recognition and concerned RD for renewal or extension and accepted by it.

5. The TA so granted recognition / renewal or extension shall be entitled to

such incentives and concessions as may be granted by the Government from time to time and shall abide by the terms and conditions of recognition as prescribed from time to time by the MOT,GOI.
6. TA would have to report action taken by them in their Annual Report which shall be kept with them & shown to the Committee(s) at the time of renewal.
7. Even though the scheme of granting approval of recognition / renewal or extension to TA is voluntary, in nature, there is a need to have a pro - active role of MOT and Travel Trade to ensure that more and more Travel Agencies seek approval and then service the tourists. There is also a need to educate the stakeholders as well as consumers against the potential risk of availing services through the unapproved TA(s).
8. It shall be mandatory for an approved TA to prominently display the Certificate of approval of recognition / renewal or extension given by MOT in the office by pasting it on a board or in a picture frame so that it is visible to a potential tourist.
9. The decision of MOT, GOI in the matter of recognition / renewal or extension shall be final. However, MOT may in their discretion refuse to recognize / renew or extend any firm or withdraw / withhold at any time recognition / renewal or extension already granted with the approval of the Competent Authority. Before such a decision is taken, necessary Show Cause Notice would invariably be issued and the reply considered on merit. This would be done after careful consideration and generally as a last resort. Circumstances in which withdrawal is effected would also be indicated.

## WATA MASTER KEY

Updated and published yearly, the WATA Master-Key is a selectively comprehensive source of travel information. Individual agency tariffs given in the publication represent the selling tool for members, incoming and outgoing services. Along with the tariffs the Master-Key gives a country description sheet containing a wealth of useful background information of a destination. In addition, the Master-Key also gives detailed information about some hotels located in important cities and tourist centres together with prevalent confidential tariffs and other relevant information for travel agencies.

The WATA Master-Key is valuable reference material for travel agents. Its presentation makes it easy for the users to extract the information they need. The guidelines as enumerated in the Master-Key are as follows:

## Sale of a Tour

It should first be determined whether the client who wants to book a tour prefers to:

Join an escorted tour, or choose a FIT, combining leisure and activity according to his individual tastes and interests.

## FIT - Relations with Client

If client wants a "tailor made" tour, let him make the suggestions, without imposing your own views, on the following points:

### a) Itinerary

Determine the cities to be visited.
Number of days (overnights) in each place.
Mode of transportation between cities.
Establish a rough time schedule, taking into consideration the time at his disposal.
For a leisurely trip it may be justified to convince the client to leave out some places which he can visit another time.

### b) Transportation

Air transport should be used when time is limited and for long distances. Surface transportation should be recommended for shorter distances.
For trains, determine whether advance reservation is necessary. Indicate stations where trains are to be changed. Buses should be recommended in some countries, as this usually allows additional sightseeing.

### c) Hotel Accommodation

Category of Hotels: Examine with the client which category of hotel he wants to stay at – Deluxe, First Class, Standard or Economy class. It is preferable that he is accommodated in a maximum rate room; however, if he must consider the cost, then rather suggest a lower grade hotel with the best available room.

Type of Rooms: Examine whether the client wishes a special room on a special floor, with or without bath/shower, sea view, outside or inside, etc., draw his attention to the fact that in high season a room with a bath may be difficult to obtain in some places. In some cases a double room for single occupancy can be suggested, a single room often being small or not well situated. If your client insists on having a particular room, he may have to pay a supplement.

Meals: Ask the client whether he wants to have accommodation in a bed and breakfast, demipension or full pension basis. If accommodation is on a bed and breakfast basis, keep in mind that in certain resorts or hotels demi or full pension is compulsory.

Check-in Time: Remind the client that check in time at hotels is usually after 12 noon. Immediate occupancy on early morning arrivals can only be secured if the room is reserved for the previous night. If your client leaves late in the evening you may propose to him that he pay for an additional night.

During periods of festivals, fairs or congresses, hotel space may not be available, rendering it necessary for your client to change the dates in those places; cabled hotel confirmation should, therefore, be suggested.

## d) Transfers

The need of transfers upon arrival or departure results from the fact that it is often difficult to find one's way at airports, piers or stations with which one is not familiar.

Transfers by agencies include interpreters meeting and assistance, accompanying clients (unless otherwise specified), porterage and transportation of 2 pieces of hand luggage per person between airport, station, bus or air terminal and hotels or vice versa, as well as tip to drivers, but it does not include the tip to the hotel porter. Type of vehicle varies according to cities, generally by private car or taxi/cab. Airport transfers are naturally more expensive, but also the most convenient ones.

When opting for transfer from the city air terminal, your client must know that there will be no assistance at the airport that he will have to tip for baggage at the airport and pay for the bus between the airport and the city terminal.

Bus Arrival: Certain bus companies stop at the major hotels to drop or collect clients, the disadvantage of this being the clients' dependence on time schedules and waiting for his turn to be dropped off.

## e) Sightseeing/Excursions/Tours

The advantage of arranging sightseeing in advance is that the client does not have to waste his time, queuing up at the local agency. Also, a balance can be established in advance between leisure time and sightseeing as well as for tours of the city and countryside.

**Motor Coach Tours:** Apart form the economic viewpoint, there is the advantage of meeting other travellers, but clients have to arrange their own transportation to meeting points, as pick-up is very seldom done on motorcoach tours.

**Private Car Tours:** The client is picked up at the hotel, has the choice of the time of departure and can stop wherever he likes, but this is the most expensive solution. In some places there are regular private car tours or else sightseeing can be done on a seat-in-car basis.

**Hire of Private Car with Chauffeur**

**City Hire**: must be recommended to deluxe clients, whose time is limited between trains, boats or planes or who already know the city and want to see only special places or go shopping. Since very often the chauffeur cannot act as a guide, a private guide will be needed for sightseeing.

**Touring Hire:** if a private car is used for travelling from one city to another, local guides in each place will be sufficient. Distance covered daily should not exceed 250 km. The client's attention has to be drawn to the fact that he will have to pay for empty run of car (return to point of departure). The full daily basis charge is due, even if the vehicle is picked up in the evening.

**Motor Launch Tours/Boats Trips:** The same applies for motor coach tours. Deluxe clients will be picked up at the hotel by a private car and driven to the embarkation pier.

**Self-driven cars** can also be provided when clients fill the necessary conditions and, if wanted, a local guide can be placed.

### f) Musical Festival, Theatre and Concert Tickets

Clients must be told that advance reservation is necessary. Confirmation of requested tickets cannot be guaranteed and tickets are not refundable unless they can be resold.

## Quotations

### a) Land Arrangements

On the basis of all details furnished by the clients, it will enable you to make an estimate of the land arrangements.

### b) Transatlantic/Pacific Transportation

To the land arrangements, the cost of flight/boat tickets for Transatlantic/Pacific transportation has to be added.

### c) Cost Price

Items (a) and (b) above give the cost price.

### d) Selling Price

In order to obtain the selling price you have to add the handling fees or mark-up, as well as margin safeguarding any possible increase.

## Suggested Itinerary

A suggested itinerary should be drafted of what has been agreed upon with your client and submitted to him, together with the final price. The accompanying letter should clearly specify what is included in the price:

Price and type of land arrangements.

Price and class of air/sea/rail tickets, indicating that they are subject to change without notice.

The agency's conditions regarding handling charge, cancellation fees, possible deposits request, etc.

It should also point out what is NOT included, such as cost of passport, visa, gratuities, tips to hotels porters, beverages, laundry, taxes (government, landing, embarkation charges).

# 5
# TOUR PACKAGING

### Chapter Objectives
**After reading this chapter the reader should be able to:**
- To know origin of the package tour.
- Define what a package tour is.
- Identify types of different tour operators.
- Understand planning a package tour.
- Explain pricing of a tour.
- Understand why it is important to have control over tour operating.
- To Know the Functions of Tour Operator.
- To Know the Functions of Ground Tour Operator.

An organization, firm or company who buys individual travel components, separately from their suppliers and combines them into a package tour, which is sold with their own price tag to the public directly or through middlemen, is called a Tour Operator. More precise tour operators are primarily responsible for delivering and performing the services specified in a given package tour. They can provide these services themselves as some have their own cars and coaches, hotels and other travel related services or can obtain these from the other suppliers. That is why they are called manufacturers of tourism products. Tour operators are sometimes called as wholesalers but this is partially true because a wholesaler buys goods and services in bulk at his own account to prepare a tour package and then retails it through the travel agencies or directly to clients. However, a tour operator who has his own one or more tourists products components, formulates a new tourists product for example 'inclusive tours.'

Tour operators generally offer a variety of package tours to cater to the needs of different kinds of travellers.

## Definitions

Poyther (1993) defines, "tour operator is one who has the responsibility of putting the tour ingredients together, marketing it, making reservations and handling actual operation."

Holloway (1992) stated that tour operations undertake a distinct function in the tourism industry, they purchase separate elements of tourism products/services and combine them into a package tour which they sell directly or indirectly to the tourists.

Today, tour operators have become highly competitive. They endeavour to achieve a high volume of turnover, and maximum International and domestic market share by effectively operating. Moreover, the success of many developed and developing nations as tourists destinations depend heavily on a tour operator's ability to attract tourists, development and promotion of tourism plant, diversification of tourism product and their social responsibilities to develop a remote and backward area. Tour operators undertake a distinct function in the tourism industry.

Tour operators are sometimes referred to as tour wholesalers. This is because they purchase services in bulk, e.g., flights seats, hotel rooms etc., which they package into a series of individual tourism products. By buying in bulk the tour operator can often secure considerable discounts from suppliers, which could not normally be matched by the customer buying direct. Tour operators are therefore able to assemble and present to the customer a range of products, which are both convenient to purchase and competitively priced.

Tour operators provide vital service for the tourism industry. They provide, for example a means by which hoteliers or airlines can off-load surplus capacity. Tour operators can guarantee a fixed level of income throughout the season. Service providers are also in the enviable situation of having another company selling and marketing their wares for them.

Tour operators consequently generate a large amount of revenue for the tourism industry. Although worldwide, there are many tour operators, some very large companies are dominating the industry. This is particularly the case in Europe. Most of the sales volumes are generated by these companies. They can deal easily and are in a strong position when negotiating with tourist suppliers such as airlines. They are therefore in a position to offer their clients low prices.

## The Origins of the Packaged Tour

In 1841, Thomas Cook, a British carpenter and Baptist missionary, arranged transportation for 570 rail passengers travelling to a Temperance Convention. Cook chartered a train from Loughborough to Leicester, where the Temperance Society was to meet. He printed brochures advertising "tea and buns" and brass band music on the 10-mile journey. The cost was one shilling, or about 10 pence in today's currency. On July 5, the charter train steamed out to Loughborough on schedule, the first of many organised tours for which Cook would later become famous.

Although Cook is believed to have been the first full-time travel agent, he was best known for organising deluxe tours for the world's wealthiest citizens. In 1895, Cook escorted a group of industrialists from England and America to the Paris Exhibition. One year later, he organised a "Grand Tour" of every major European country. Cook's tour groups travelled first-class on luxury ships and trains and enjoyed elegant accommodation in the best hotels in Europe. They were accompanied by a guide whose job was to ensure that all arrangements proceeded smoothly. Cook's clients included such luminaries as Thomas Edison and Samuel Clements, better known as Mark Twain. The term "Cook's tour: is still used today, usually in a humorous context, to refer to any informal guided tour.

The reason for Cook's success was his ability to arrange every detail of a tour in advance, from transportation and lodging to sigh-seeing and meal service. His clients paid a lump sum for the entire trip. In this way travellers knew before they departed, their exact itinerary and all the costs the trip would entail. Cook's prepackaged trips inspired other people in the travel industry to organise similar tours to all parts of the globe. In Europe, such trips continued to be arranged for only the wealthiest travellers, but in the US, tours for common citizens also became popular.

## Increase in the Package Vacations

The Industrial Revolution improved the standard of living of working-class people throughout Western Europe, resulting in a large increase in travel by the early 1900s, package vacations had become an important part of the tourism industry, prompting the construction of luxury ships, trains and hotels. Most of the big cruise ships and famous luxury trains of the early twentieth century depended on revenues from tour groups to continue operating. A typical package vacation of the 1930s took travellers across the Atlantic Ocean on a luxury liner such as the Queen Mary or the Mauritania to Europe, where passengers boarded a deluxe train for a long-distance tour of all the western European capitals.

Subsequently the tour operator's role expanded considerably when wide-bodied jet aircrafts were introduced and required more people than ever to fill those airline seats and the hotel rooms built to accommodate the airline passengers. In addition, as people learned that tour packages were generally cheaper than if the individual tourists put together and paid for the various parts separately, the consumer demand for these packages increased.

## Types of Tour Operators

Following are basically the seven categories of Tour Operators:

Tour Operators
- Mass Market Tour Operators
- Specialist Tour Operators
- Domestic Tour Operators
- Incoming Tour Operators
- Inbound Tour Operators
- Outbound Tour Operators
- Ground Tour Operators

### a. Mass Market Tour Operators

These tend to concentrate on mass-market destinations, they frequently divide their operations into different markets (e.g. ski holidays, city breaks, summer sun, winter sun, etc). many own their own airlines. Examples: Thomson in Great Britain, TUI and NUR in Germany, Kuoni in Switzerland.

### b. Specialist Tour Operators

These can be grouped into a number of distinct categories. A tour operator can be a specialist in that, he only features one particular country; he only uses one particular type of accommodation, e.g., camping holidays;

he utilises one particular type of transportation medium, eg. shipping; or he caters for holidaymakers with a specific interest, e.g., safari operators or golf operators.

### c. Domestic Operators

These operators are not only concerned with carrying traffic out of a country but also exist to organise package holidays domestically. That is, to a country in which the tourists reside.

Domestic tour operators are those who assemble, combine tourist components into inclusive tours and sell it to the domestic travellers. In general, these tour operators provide travel services within the tourist's native country.

The domestic tour operators operate within the boundary of the home country and offer package tour to the travellers viz. Domestic inclusive tours or independent tours.

### d. Incoming Operators

Companies specialising in handling incoming foreign holidaymakers, e.g., British visitors to Poland. Some of these companies are merely ground handling agents, their role is limited to organising hotel accommodation on behalf of an overseas tour operator, or greeting incoming visitors and transferring them to their hotels. Other companies, however, will offer a comprehensive range of services, which may include negotiating contracts with hotels, organising study tours, providing dinner or theatre arrangements.
Types of Tour Operators
Tour operators are basically categories into four types. These are categories on the basis of their nature of the business and their operations.

### e. Inbound Tour Operators

Also known as incoming tour operators. Technically, the operators who receive guests, clients/tourists and handle arrangements in the host country are called inbound tour operators. For example, a group of American Tourists is coming through TCI Ltd. to India and the company makes arrangements and handles the group in India then TCI is called an inbound tour operator.

Incidentally, the inbound traffic to the country for the last two decades has been decreasing. Essentially the tour operators need to adopt innovative marketing strategies and should introduce a special interest tour to cater the special needs of Japanese, Americans, French and British people.

### f. Outbound Tour Operators

Tour operator who promote tours for foreign destinations, maybe business tour or leisure tour is called outbound tour operators. For example a group of American tourists going to a trip of India and Thomas Cook handle arrangement in America like as ticket reservation, hotel booking etc. then Thomas Cook is called Outbound Tour operators in the context of America.

### g. Ground Operators/Destination Management Companies

These are commonly known as handling agencies and their main function is to organize tour arrangements for incoming tourists on the behalf of overseas operators. Let us take the case of India as a destination that – has a varied culture. When a tour operator himself promotes beach holidays, wildlife holidays, adventure tours, heritage tours at the different places, the difficulty arises. It is the ground operator then who by handling the incoming travellers in the same season but at different places ensures that the entire operation is according to the package tours or agreements.

Sometime when a handling agency is at a prominent tourist place i.e., Mumbai and it has to make arrangements to Bangalore, then it contracts (If it has no office of its own) with a local operator (known as excursion agent) to handle the arrangement on his behalf.

## Reasons for Ground Operators?

The tour operation companies do not have close contact with suppliers, governments, destinations and so on. It leaves no choice with the companies but to appoint handling agencies at the destinations. The main reasons are:
- Introduction of new products to promote an exotic destination.
- Lack of regulations.
- Lack of personal contract.
- Communications problem.
- The company does not have its own branch.

Recognizing the very fact that the reputation, performance, and profitability of tour company in its own market largely depends on the efficiency and effectiveness of ground operators, it is necessary for the company to consider following factors before the selection of a handling agency.
- Business size
- Qualified and Professional staff
- Period in the business
- Operation area
- Market share

## Functions of Ground Tour Operators

Over the years of functions and activities of the destination, companies have changed drastically to cope with the changing environment of the tourism industry. In fact, today's destination companies have become more professional and are bound to provide personalized travel services to the tourists. The following functions are performed by ground tours operators:
1. Land arrangement
2. Contract and Negotiation with other vendors
3. Handling of Arrival and departure procedure
4. Planning and organizing local package tour
5. Tourists Escorting
6. Provision of market information
7. Costing and pricing package tour

If we see the working of the travel agencies and tour operators in the industry we find that most of the organizations are performing different types of activities like the retail travel agency, wholesale travel agency, and tour operators.

# The Role of TRAVEL AGENT

Over the last three decades, the pattern and structure of travel agencies have changed to meet tough challenges in the international market. Today, small-scale agencies are finding the travel industry increasingly difficult to manage.

## Functions of Tour Operator

A tour operator is an organization, firms or a person who is responsible for the actual arrangement of transport and accommodation facilities in any tour or vacations. They are also responsible for operating and providing vacation through contracting, booking and packaging together of the various components of the tour such as hotel, transportation, meals, guides, optional tours and sometimes flights.

A tour operator is like a service provider, providing the most convenient option for tourists to stay, visit, as well as leave from the city. A tour operator owns a high volume of travel services across carriers, services, and accommodation. Following are the most important functions of the tour operators.

### (i) Planning a Tour

The most important functions of the tour operators are planning a tour. Tour operators plan a tour and make tour itinerary which contains the identification of the origin, destination and all the stopping point in a traveller's tours. A prospective tour operator also gives advice to intending tourists in various types of tour programmes, which they may choose for their leisure or commercial travel.

### (ii) Making Tour Package

Tour operator buys individual travel components, separately from there suppliers and combines them into a package tour. Tour operators make tour package by assembling various travel components into a final product that is called tour package which is sold to tourist with own price tag. Making tour packages is also an important function of Tour Operator.

### (iii) Arranging a Tour

Tour operators make tour package and also arrange a tour according to tourist demands. Tour operators arrange the tour package and various tourists activities to provide the best experience to tourists/traveller.

### (iv) Travel Information

Whatever the size of tour operators, it has to provided necessary travel information to the tourists. This task is difficult and very complicated. A tour operator must give up-to-date, accurate and timely information regarding destinations, modes of travel, accommodation, sightseeing, immigration, health and security rules as also various permits required to travel in a particular area etc.

### (v) Reservation

This is a very important function of all type tour operators and travel agencies. Tour operator makes all the reservation by making linkages with accommodation sector, transport sector and other entertainment organizations to reserve rooms, and seats in cultural programmes and transportation.

## (vi) Travel Management

Tour operators manage tour from beginning to the end. A tour operator has the responsibility to look after the finer details of a vacation or tour such as hotel, accommodation, meals, conveyance etc. Tour operators provide travel guide, escorting services and arrange all travel related needs and wants.

## (vii) Evaluate the Option Available

Tour operators evaluate all available options to provide a unique or unforgettable travel experience to tourists during their journey. Tour operators evaluate the various options available for a tour package and provide best of them to tourists.

## (viii) Promotion

Tour Operators makes tour packages and promote them into various tourists markets at domestic as well international level. Tour operators promote a travel destination to attract a large group of tourists at domestic as well as international level. In the promotion of tourist destination, tour operators play a key role. Travel agencies or tour operators are called as image builder of a country being promoted and marks ted .

## (ix) Sales and Marketing

Tour operators do sales and marketing of tourist products. They buy individual travel components, separately and combine them into a tour package, which is sold with their own price tag to the public directly. Tour operators do marketing of tourist destinations and tourism product to attracts the attention of the tourists/travellers.

## Importance of Tour Operators

Tours operators play a key role in the tourism sector. They create tourist product, promote them an finally sell these to tourist.

Tour operators provide the best and competitive price to the tourist. Tour operators they negotiate with suppliers of tourism product such as hotels, airlines and provide the best possible price to the tourist. They buy tourist product in bulk and get huge discounts from suppliers. So that they provide tourist products at affordable price.

Tour operators organized a tour in the best way. They personalize and make sure each and every component of the tour is well-taken care. Tour operators provide best travel experience during a tour.

Tour operators provide immediate support system at host country as well as foreign land. When tourists travel to a foreign land and things get uncertain, maybe its a health or loss of documents and need to return back or change of travel plan. A qualified tour operator takes care of all these unavoidable events with efficiency.

## Difference between Travel Agent and Tour Operator

- A travel agent is a person who has a full knowledge of tourist product – destinations, modes of travel, climate, accommodation and other areas of the service sector. He acts on the behalf of the product providers/principals and in return get a commission.

- Tour operator is an organization, firm or company who buys individual travel components, separately from their suppliers and combines them into a package tour, which is sold with their own price tag to the public directly or through middlemen.
- Tour operators are like wholesalers and travel agents are the retailers. A tour operator makes the package holidays up and the travel agents sell them on.
- Tour operator takes up the bulk of the responsibilities and his fee is obviously much higher than a travel agent.
- A tour operator has the responsibilities to look after the finer details of a vacation or tour such as hotel, accommodation, meals, conveyance etc.

## Types of Packaged Tours

Package tours are of three types:
(i) Independent
(ii) Hosted
(iii) Escorted

**Independent package tours,** are designed for clients whose desire is to travel independently. Most such tours consist of airfare, hotel accommodation and either airport transfers or a car rental. In some cases, airfare may not be included, or may be offered separately. An independent tour provides travellers with considerable freedom in planning their activities. The total package cost varies depending on the type of tour, the selection of hotel, the departure date and optional activities. An independent package tour provides travellers with the cost benefits of a package vacation with a maximum amount of free time.

With independent package tours add-on components, called tour supplements, also affect the price. For example, clients might elect to include a sight-seeing bus tour, a boat ride, or a scuba-diving trip in their tour package.

**A hosted tour** is a package tour that utilises the services of a representative, called a host, at each destination. The tour representative is available at specified times every day to provide travel advice and assistance. A typical hosted tour may involve several stops or a single destination. Hosted tours provide travellers with the advantages of a pre-arranged trip and the services of a personal adviser at their destination.

As an example, assume a retired couple purchases a hosted tour to London, Amsterdam and Paris. As with an independent tour, each hosted tour includes round-trip airfare, hotel, accommodation and airport transfers. However, when the clients arrive in London, they are greeted at the airport by an English tour host, who assists them with claiming their baggage and making their way to their hotel. After checking in, the clients are on their own until their next scheduled departure. However, their tour host is available to offer advice about local attractions and entertainment, book a car rental or bus tour, or recommend a restaurant. When the travellers arrive at their other destinations, Amsterdam and Paris, a different host greets them at each airport.

**An escorted tour** includes the services of a qualified tour manager, or escort. The clients travel together in manageable groups and may be accompanied by their escort on the whole or part of the itinerary. Escorted tours are especially popular with travellers who are planning to visit a foreign country for the first time. The escort's job is to provide comprehensive assistance to the group, from airport check-in to hotel room assignments. Escorted tours provide travellers with a maximum level of pre-arrangement and personal assistance in a package vacation.

Most package tours have two basic rates: double and single. The double rate applies if two people are booked together in the same reservation and will share the same accommodation. The rate applies for each traveller. In some cases, a reduced rate is offered for a third or fourth traveller sharing the same accommodation.

The single rate applies to unaccompanied travellers who do not wish to share their accommodation. The single rate is usually higher than the double rate for the same accommodation. The reason for this discrepancy is that hotel rooms are usually priced on the basis of double occupancy. If a room will be occupied by one person, a higher rate is applied to offset the loss of revenue from not having two people occupy the room. On some tours, a discount rate is available for single travellers who are willing to share accommodation with another traveller of the same sex. If a package tour does not have a single rate, an add-on charge called a single room supplement is applied to unaccompanied travellers. In some cases, unaccompanied travellers are required both to pay a single supplement and to share a room with another unaccompanied traveller.

## Tour Operation Economics

While the financial rewards of establishing a tour operating business can be great, the risks are high especially with small companies. These risks include:

- Operators growing too fast, over-borrowing to finance the expansion and in some cases lacking the management expertise to operate larger companies;
- Making insufficient profit to survive, in the face of intense competition which drove down prices; and
- Being hit by external problems such as, rises in the price of fuel, political unrest in some of the destination countries and economic recession at home.

The tour operating business is characterised by its ease of entry. It is not difficult to open a tour operating business, as it requires very little cash to start up. Although there sometimes are government or industry constraints on what constitutes a tour and how long it may last, the wholesaler needs only to abide by airline and/or government constraints on pricing, advertising, bonding and commissions. The operator contracts with airlines, hotels and other for a specified number of seats and hotel rooms on which a deposit may be required. This deposit is recovered by the operator fairly rapidly from the deposits paid by customers who buy the package.

The balance of the customer's price is paid before the trip begins, but the operator does not pay the supplier (such a hotels) the balance owed them until after the trip is over. During this period the operator has the use of these funds, known as positive cash flow. Operators run into trouble when the cash flow funds, known as positive cash flow from one tour is used to finance their deposits to suppliers on the next one. A rule of thumb is that a tour wholesaler will make money only if more than 85% of the packages are sold; that is, 85% is the break-even point.

## Customised Tours and Excursions

A customised tour is an independent tour designed to meet the specific need of an individual client. Here every detail of a traveller's itinerary from departure to return may be planned in advance. Designing such tours requires considerable research and takes much time. They are also expensive. However, many clients still prefer custom tours, hoping to combine the benefits of a tour with maximum flexibility.

### Planning a Tour Package

One problem that tour operators have is that it can require as much as eighteen months from the start of putting a package together until it is over. During this lead time the operator must do market research, including analysing the results of past tours, in order to develop any new destinations and services, and decide on each particular tour's specifications.

About a year ahead of the tour, ground services (hotels and other aspects of the tour) and transport commitment must be made. Subsequently, pricing decisions for the ultimate tour must also be made. Over the next few months brochures must be prepared, a reservation system established and arrangements made with the travel agencies who will actually handle the tour sales. Once this is done, the brochures must be distributed and any other advertising (newspaper, radio, television) planned. Before the tour actually begins, this cycle of events will have already begun again for the following year's business.

One of the problems that operators have is that as much as a year ahead of a tour, contracts will have been signed committing the wholesaler to pay stipulated prices to foreign suppliers in their local currencies. The operator receives his payment in the currency of the country where the tour is marketed. An unfavourable change in currency exchange rates thus could quickly erode the wholesaler's profit. On the other hand, a favourable exchange could substantially increase his profits.

## Pricing a Tour

It is vital for any company to price its product correctly. Prices must be right for the market and sufficient to cover overheads and provide a satisfactory level of profit.

The prices vary according to season (and hence reflect the level of demand) and tend to be set by the market leader. The cost of an inclusive tour reflects:

- Transportation costs (calculated over the course of a season to take into account seasonal variation in demand)

- Accommodation
- Ground handling arrangements
- Airport/port taxes
- Value added tax
- Gratuities, porterage
- A small fee to cover price rises
- Mark-up (approx 25% of cost price)

(This covers agency commission, marketing costs, head office administration costs and profit.)

The typical cost structure of an inclusive tour would be:

| | |
|---|---|
| Transportation | - 45% (as a percentage of overall cost) |
| Accommodation | - 37% (as a percentage of overall cost) |
| Other services at destination | - 3% (as a percentage of overall cost) |
| Head office overheads | - 5% (as a percentage of overall cost) |
| Travel agency commission | - 10% (as a percentage of overall cost) |

On entering a new market it may be that the principal objective is to penetrate and obtain a targeted share of the market in the first year of operating, and this may be achieved by reducing or even forgoing profits during the first year, and/or by reducing the per capita contribution to corporate costs. Indeed, to some destinations the operator may introduce loss pricing policies, subsidising the cost of this policy from other more profitable routes in order to get a foothold in the market to the new destination.

In some other cases it may be necessary to discount tours in order to clear surplus capacity. However, the technique can also be used to encourage members of the public to book early.

In some cases, comparatively small operating margins tour operators are always looking for additional sources of revenue. These can come from:

- The sales of excursion at the destination
- Duty free sales on board flights
- Car hire
- Interests received on deposits and final payments invested
- Foreign currency speculation
- The sale of insurance policies
- The imposition of high cancellation charges – that exceed any costs borne by the operator.

## Control Over Tour Operating

A lack of control over members of the industry, and one or two spectacular collapses have led to suggestions that the work of tour operators should be more strictly monitored. This concern was shared by the European Commission who in 1991 launched the EC Directive on Package Travel. This requires:

- All tours to be licensed;

- A public protection fund to be set up, protecting the consumer and creditors in the advent of a tour operator going into liquidation;
- Tour operators to be required to observe certain minimum standards in brochure descriptions;
- Travel agents to become responsible, not only for the information contained in brochures they stock, but also for providing necessary advice to clients on booking (e.g., health requirements, passport and visa requirements, insurance needs, etc.)
- Restriction on surcharges and changes to bookings.

What does appear clear is that the additional burden of responsibility placed on tour operators will inevitably lead to an increase on cost for consumers, as operators attempt to cover themselves against any threat of legislation. Operators now become responsible for any negligence on the part of their suppliers overseas, or failure of their suppliers to provide any services for which he has booked. Some estimates put the added cost to consumers of this legislation at a some percentage increase in the basic cost of a package.

## Distributing the Product

Basically, the tour operator has to choose between two alternative methods of selling their tour programmes through:
- Retail travel agents,
- Direct to the public

Larger operators whose product is of universal appeal and whose market is national in scope will expect to sell the bulk of their holidays through the retail trade, although many will be glad to receive the occasional booking direct from the customer, since this will enable them to retain the commission normally paid to the agent. While operators may be keen to increase the volume of bookings coming to them direct, they must also avoid generating any fear among the agents themselves that they are in any way attempting to 'poach' the business away from the retail trade, as agents may switch their loyalty to other operators if they suspect this is the case.

Few operators now deal indiscriminately with all retail agents. The cost of servicing the less productive agents is often greater than the revenue they produce – they must not only be provided with expensive free brochures, but also receive regular mailing to update their information, and be supported by sales material and even, in some cases, visits from sales representatives of the operator. The operators must therefore decide whether to vary the support they offer to different agents, or to dispense with the services of some agents altogether.

## Direct Marketing

In another development in tour operating, a handful of larger tour operators have chosen deliberately to market their product direct to the public, a strategy that directly booked holidays, by cutting out the agents' commission. This would represent a saving to the customers. However, while isolated bargains were certainly on offer, many holidays were cheaper, and sometimes more expensive, than similar packages booked through an agent. The reasons for this are not hard to understand: while travel agency commissions are saved, huge budgets are required to inform and promote to the mass public.

The company had to invest millions in heavy advertising in the media, and similar high costs were borne by the need to have a large reservations staff and multiple telephone computer lines to answer enquiries from the public. These costs are, of course, fixed, while commissions are only paid to agents when the latter achieves a sale.

# 6
# INBOUND TOUR MANAGEMENT

## Chapter Objectives

**After reading this chapter the reader should be able to:**
- Understand the meaning of inbound tour management and differentiate it from an outbound tour.
- Analyse trends in inbound tourists.
- Describe the elements of an inbound itinerary.
- Discuss sample programmes for inbound tourists in India.
- Know how the inbound groups are to be handled.
- Prepare itineraries of important destinations.
- Types of Inbound Travellers.
- Major markets of Inbound Tourists.

Inbound tourists are considered in relation to a given country's residents visiting another country on a foreign passport and the main purpose of visit is other than the exercise of an activity remunerated from within the country or establishment of residence in the country. The main purpose of this type of tourist can be classified under one of the following headings:

Leisure (recreation, holiday, study, religion and sport);

Business (family, mission, meeting).

The following are the major aspects which need to be considered for inbound tours:

- Type of inbound travellers
- Hotel operations and reservations
- Destinations to be selected
- Itineraries in the destination

- Important tourist circuits

The travel manager responsible for inbound tours must be fully conversant with all the above aspects in order to be able to handle inbound tours effectively and profitably.

## Types of Inbound Travellers

### (i) Leisure Traveller

A person travelling for relaxation or personal satisfaction as per some personal interest. A leisure traveller can be alone or with a family. It can be organised or unorganised when it comes to domestic travel. Outbound is mostly organised and especially planned well in case of families or people travelling together.

### (ii) Business Travellers/Corporate Travellers -

Are persons or a group travelling for meetings, incentives, conferences, exhibitions or any other corporate event and seeking a travel agent's assistance in planning, arranging and coordinating the same. Corporate clients today are looking to suppliers who are experts in their business and who have in-depth domain knowledge and expertise. When addressing such clients you need to first decide what is your area of specialisation and what value, in terms of knowledge and processes, you bring to your client. Increasingly you have suppliers who are focusing on a niche – corporate travel, meetings and incentives, leisure tours, sports tours, retail travel, etc.

## Most visited destinations by international tourist arrivals

In 2018, there were 1.4 billion international tourist arrivals worldwide, with a growth of 5%. as compared to 2018. The top 10 international tourism destinations in 2018 were.

| Rank | Destination | International tourist arrivals (2018) | International tourist arrivals (2016) | Change (2016 to 2017) (%) | Change (2015 to 2016) (%) |
|---|---|---|---|---|---|
| 1 | France | 86.9 million | 82.7 million | 5.1 | 2.1 |
| 2 | Spain | 83 million | 75.6 million | 8.6 | 10.5 |
| 3 | USA | 80 million | 75.6 million | - | 2.1 |
| 4 | China | 63 million | 59.3 million | 2.5 | 4.2 |
| 5 | Italy | 62 million | 52.4 million | 11.2 | 3.2 |
| 6 | Mexico | 41 million | 35.1 million | 12.0 | 9.3 |
| 7 | UK | 36 million | 35.8 million | 5.1 | 4.0 |
| 8 | Turkey | 46 million | 30.3 million | 24.1 | 23.3 |
| 9 | Germany | 39 million | 35.6 million | 5.2 | 1.8 |
| 10 | Thailand | 38 million | 32.6 million | 8.6 | 8.9 |

**Source:** World Tourism Organisation.

## TABLE 1

**Inbound Tourism: Foreign Tourist Arrivals (FTAs), Arrivals of Non-Resident Indians (NRIs) and International Tourist Arrivals (ITAs) 2000-2017 (till June)**

| Year | FTAs in India (in million) | Percentage (%) change over previous year | NRIs arrivals in India (in million) | Percentage (%) change over the previous year | International Tourist Arrivals in India (in million) | Percentage (%) change over the previous year |
|---|---|---|---|---|---|---|
| 2000 | 2.65 | 6.7 | - | - | - | - |
| 2001 | 2.54 | -4.2 | - | - | - | - |
| 2002 | 2.38 | -6 | - | - | - | - |
| 2003 | 2.73 | 14.3 | - | - | - | - |
| 2004 | 3.46 | 26.8 | - | - | - | - |
| 2005 | 3.92 | 13.3 | - | - | - | - |
| 2006 | 4.45 | 13.5 | - | - | - | - |
| 2007 | 5.08 | 14.3 | - | - | - | - |
| 2008 | 5.28 | 4 | - | - | - | - |
| 2009 | 5.17 | -2.2 | - | - | - | - |
| 2010 | 5.78 | 11.8 | - | - | - | - |
| 2011 | 6.31 | 9.2 | - | - | - | - |
| 2012 | 6.58 | 4.3 | - | - | - | - |
| 2013 | 6.97 | 5.9 | - | - | - | - |
| 2014 | 7.68 | 10.2 | 5.43 | - | 13.11 | - |
| 2015 | 8.03 | 4.5 | 5.26 | -3.15 | 13.29 | 1.4 |
| 2016 | 8.80 | 9.7 | 5.77 | 9.67 | 14.57 | 9.6 |
| 2017(P) (Jan-Jun) | 4.89 | 17.2@ | - | - | - | - |

(P) Provisional, @ Growth rate over Jan-Jun, 2016
Source: (i) Bureau of Immigration, Govt. of India, for 2000-2016
    (ii) Ministry of Tourism, Govt. of India, for Jan-June, 2017

## TABLE 2
### Month-wise Foreign Tourist Arrivals in India, Jan 2015 – Jun 2017

| Month | 2015 | 2016 | 2017(P) | Percentage (%) Change | |
|---|---|---|---|---|---|
| | | | | 2016/15 | 2017/16 |
| January | 790854 | 844533 | 983413 | 6.8 | 16.4% |
| February | 761007 | 848782 | 956337 | 11.5 | 12.7% |
| March | 729154 | 809107 | 904888 | 11.0 | 11.8% |
| April | 541551 | 592004 | 740275 | 9.3 | 25.0% |
| May | 509869 | 527466 | 630438 | 3.5 | 19.5% |
| June | 512341 | 546972 | 669989 | 6.8 | 22.5% |
| July | 628323 | 733834 | | 16.8 | |
| August | 599478 | 652111 | | 8.8 | |
| September | 542600 | 608177 | | 12.1 | |
| October | 683286 | 741770 | | 8.6 | |
| November | 815947 | 878280 | | 7.6 | |
| December | 912723 | 1021375 | | 11.9 | |
| Total | 8027133 | 8804411 | | 9.7 | |
| Sub-total (Jan-June) | 3844776 | 4168864 | 4885340 | 8.4@ | 17.2@ |

P: Provisional, @ Growth rate over January-June of previous year
Source: (i) Bureau of Immigration, Govt. of India, for 2015 & 2016
    (ii) Ministry of Tourism, Govt. of India for 2017

## TABLE 3
### Share of India in International Tourist Arrivals (ITAs) in World and Asia & the Pacific Region, 2000 - 2016

| Year | ITAs (in million) | | | Percentage (%) share and rank of India in World | | Percentage (%) share and rank of India in Asia and the Pacific | |
|---|---|---|---|---|---|---|---|
| | World | Asia and the Pacific | India | % Share | Rank | % Share | Rank |
| 2000 | 683.3 | 109.3 | 2.65 | 0.39 | 50th | 2.42 | 11th |
| 2001 | 683.4 | 114.5 | 2.54 | 0.37 | 51st | 2.22 | 12th |
| 2002 | 703.2 | 123.4 | 2.38 | 0.34 | 54th | 1.93 | 12th |
| 2003 | 691.0 | 111.9 | 2.73 | 0.39 | 51st | 2.44 | 11th |
| 2004 | 762.0 | 143.4 | 3.46 | 0.45 | 44th | 2.41 | 11th |
| 2005 | 803.4 | 154.6 | 3.92 | 0.49 | 43rd | 2.53 | 11th |
| 2006 | 846.0 | 166.0 | 4.45 | 0.53 | 44th | 2.68 | 11th |
| 2007 | 894.0 | 182.0 | 5.08 | 0.57 | 41st | 2.79 | 11th |
| 2008 | 917.0 | 184.1 | 5.28 | 0.58 | 41st | 2.87 | 11th |
| 2009 | 883.0 | 181.1 | 5.17 | 0.59 | 41st | 2.85 | 11th |
| 2010 | 948.0 | 204.9 | 5.78 | 0.61 | 42nd | 2.82 | 11th |
| 2011 | 994.0 | 218.5 | 6.31 | 0.63 | 38th | 2.89 | 9th |
| 2012 | 1039.0 | 233.6 | 6.58 | 0.63 | 41st | 2.82 | 11th |
| 2013 | 1087.0 | 249.7 | 6.97 | 0.64 | 41st | 2.79 | 11th |
| 2014 | 1134.0 | 264.3 | 13.11 | 1.15 | 24th | 4.86 | 8th |
| 2015 | 1184.0 | 278.6 | 13.28 | 1.12 | 24th | 4.67 | 7th |
| 2016 | 1235.0 | 308.7 | 14.57 | 1.18 | 25th | 4.72 | 8th |

Source: UNWTO Barometers of June 2010, January 2011, April 2014, August 2015, May 2016 and July 2017 and Tourism Highlights 2011 and 2012.
Note: Figures of ITAs in India, and accordingly the percentage share and rank, has increased for the years 2014, 2015 and 2015 due to inclusion of NRIs arrival data

## TABLE 5
### Top 10 Source Countries for Foreign Tourist Arrivals (FTAs) in India in 2016

| S. No | Source Country | FTAs | Percentage (%) Share |
|---|---|---|---|
| 1 | Bangladesh | 1380409 | 15.68 |
| 2 | United States | 1296939 | 14.73 |
| 3 | United Kingdom | 941883 | 10.70 |
| 4 | Canada | 317239 | 3.60 |
| 5 | Malaysia | 301961 | 3.43 |
| 6 | Sri Lanka | 297418 | 3.38 |
| 7 | Australia | 293625 | 3.33 |
| 8 | Germany | 265928 | 3.02 |
| 9 | China | 251313 | 2.85 |
| 10 | France | 238707 | 2.71 |
| | Total top 10 Countries | 5585422 | 63.44 |
| | Others | 3218989 | 36.56 |
| | G.Total | 8804411 | 100.00 |

Source: Bureau of Immigration, Govt. of India

### TABLE 6
**Share of Top 10 Countries of the World and India in International Tourist Arrivals in 2016**

| Rank | Country | International Tourist Arrivals (in million) | Percentage (%) Share |
|---|---|---|---|
| 1 | France | 82.6 | 6.7 |
| 2 | USA @ | 75.6 | 6.1 |
| 3 | Spain | 75.6 | 6.1 |
| 4 | China | 59.3 | 4.8 |
| 5 | Italy | 52.4 | 4.2 |
| 6 | UK | 35.8 | 2.9 |
| 7 | Germany | 35.6 | 2.9 |
| 8 | Mexico | 35.0 | 2.8 |
| 9 | Thailand | 32.6 | 2.6 |
| 10 | Turkey@ | 30.9 | 2.5 |
| | Total of Top 10 countries | 408.9 | 41.6 |
| | India | 14.6 | 1.2 |
| | Others | 705.0 | 57.2 |
| | World Total | 1235.0 | 100 |

Source: UNWTO Barometer June 2017 and Bureau of Immigration (BOI)
@: Country's respective website.

## THE MAJOR MARKETS OF INBOUND TOURISTS

### Trends in Inbound Tourists

The above statistics show that the inflow of tourists was predominantly from countries like UK, U.S.A, Germany, France, etc., and also from Asian countries like Sri Lanka, Japan, Malaysia, China etc.

Statistics on number of foreign tourist arrivals recorded by Government of India (monthwise)

### United Kingdom

United Kingdom remained on top of the tourist generating countries for India. The maximum number of arrivals are recorded during the winter months from October to December and January to March. A large majority of tourists from United Kingdom visit India for the purposes of tourism and leisure, followed by business. The most predominant age group of visitors from UK is 45-54 years followed by 35-44 years and 55-64 years.

### United States of America

USA continues to be the second largest market for India. The dominant age group among Americans is 45-54 years followed by 35-44 years. The maximum number of tourist arrival are during October to December, followed by January to March. A large majority of US nationals visit India for tourism and leisure purposes, followed by business.

### Canada

Canada occupies the third position in tourist generating countries for India. The predominant age group is 35-44 years followed by 45-54 years. The period from October to December is the most popular period for Canadians to travel to India followed by January to March. From Canada also a large majority visits India for tourism and leisure purposes, followed by business.

## France

France occupies the fourth position among the tourist generating countries. The age group of 45-54 years accounts for one third of the total arrivals followed by age group of 34-44 years and 55-64 years. For the French the period from January to March and October to December is the most popular period for visiting India. Majority of the French visit India for the purpose of tourism and leisure followed by business.

## Germany

Germany occupies the fifth position among the tourist generating countries for India and has potential of elevating to the third position in the near future. The age group 35-44 years dominated the arrivals followed by 45-54 years age group. The maximum number of Germans visited India during the period from January to March followed by October to December. A large majority of German nationals visited India for tourism and leisure purposes, followed by business.

## Sri Lanka

Sri Lanka occupies the sixth position amongst tourist generating countries for India. The most favoured destination for Sri Lankans in India are the states in South India followed by Maharashtra (Mumbai). The most dominant age group is 25-44 years followed by 45-54 years. A large majority of the Sri Lankan visits India for tourism and leisure travels, followed by business.

## Japan

Japan is one of the most important tourist generating markets in the East for India. The dominant age group of the tourists was 25-44 years. The maximum number of Japanese tourists arrive in India during the period from January to March followed by October to December. A large majority of Japanese nationals visit India for tourism and leisure purposes, followed by business. The percentage of business travellers from Japan, however, is highest as compared to inbound visitors from any other country.

## Malaysia

The tourist traffic from Malaysia is also increasing quite rapidly. The dominant age group is between 35-54 years. The maximum number of tourists who visit India from Malaysia come during the period from October to December followed by January to March. A large majority visits India for tourism and leisure purposes, followed by business.

## Italy

Italy is also one of the important tourist generating markets for India. The age group, which dominates the arrivals, is between 35 and 54 years. The maximum number of tourist arrivals from Italy is from October to

December followed by January to March. A large majority of tourists visits India for tourism and leisure purpose, followed by business

Some other important countries from where we have inbound tourists are:
Australia
Singapore
Netherlands
Spain
Korea (South)
Malaysia

## Inbound Itinerary

A good itinerary will save both, time and money apart from making the trip hassle-free and a pleasant experience. It will give the framework for figuring out how many rail or road days are needed and where all you can get around by car, how much time it takes to see the sights – and to get them as well as how much they cost. A good itinerary will consider all the ground realities like actual transportation time during local sight seeing and in heavy metropolitan traffic. It will help save time for locating accommodation close to the sight seeing and that fits the budget as well. It will avoid making the trip too boring because of too many monuments in a row, standing in long lines or too much unexpected time getting to places.

## Things to remember

### (i) Customised

An itinerary has to be made as per the customer type i.e. inbound/ domestic/ corporate/school groups etc. (for example, sight seeing places and mode of transport chosen can be different for a school and an inbound group.)For this purpose it is very essential for the tour planner to not only have good knowledge of the destination, sightseeing places, inter and intra connectivity modes but also have very good understanding of the customers and their needs.

### (ii) Itinerary Description

Description of the itinerary can vary from very short to a detailed one, depending upon the client it is offered to and the stage at which it is offered. For example, a website itinerary can be short and precise as compared to when it is offered to customer where it can be moderately detailed in order to make it interesting and appealing. Alterations are possible at any stage in the itinerary, to customise it according to the needs of the customers. A more descriptive version giving details about sight seeing places, places visited and the properties used during the programme can be given as in-flight reading material to the inbound guests.

### (iii) Transport

The mode of transport has to be chosen carefully keeping the following points in mind.
a. Time available for the entire tour
b. Budget of the traveller

c. Type of traveller i.e., senior executives or front level executives
d. As a substitute to overnight hotel stay (hotel stay at a destination can be substituted with a comfortable train journey, bringing down the cost element)

## (iv) Accommodation

Accommodation has to be chosen carefully considering:
a. Primary interest of the travellers; (for example in case of a cultural tour, preferably heritage properties must be chosen.)
b. Budget of the traveller.
c. Type of traveller i.e., senior executives or front level executives.
d. Location of the hotel i.e., centrally located, down town, near airport or away from the city in green environs, etc. The purpose of the visit and duration of stay.

Sightseeing places must reflect the basic interest of the client as it should neither be too tiring nor should it be over-relaxed.

**Steps to Itinerary Making**

Following or the major steps to be taken into consideration when planning an Itinerary:
(i) Select destinations as per details collected from your customers. Details of the major interests of the travellers, age group, time of the year, duration of their visit, and budget would be helpful.
(ii) Route itinerary considering the arrival and departure point of guests into the country. Use maps and details given in guide books and on the internet for correct routing.
(iii) Select sightseeing places and entertainment options carefully at each place. Consider any participation in local festivals or other special events. Consider any holidays or closing days of particular sightseeing places. Think how much of rest is required after a particular road journey or how much time would be reasonably good at a particular sightseeing or shopping place. Take help of local handling agents in order to receive precise information.
(iv) Select the most appropriate mode of connectivity between various destinations considering the above details.
(v) Add value in terms of some evening entertainment, or surprise birthday/ anniversary celebrations during the tour.
(vi) Add specialities of the destination visited – add memorable moments to their tour.

**Some Sample Programmes for Inbound Tourists**

There could be several possibilities concerning various itineraries, which could be prepared for inbound tourists who have an interest in seeing different aspects of a country's tourist products. Considering the size and geographical elements of the country, India is considered to have multi-dimensional tourist products, which may interest various categories of people interested in different segments. For those who have an interest in cultural tourism there are programmes/itineraries, which may take the inbound tourists to places of tourist interest associated with cultural tourism.

## North India

15 Days

**Delhi – Varanasi – Agra – Gwalior – Udaipur – Delhi**

**Day 1 & 2.** Depart from Europe: Fly from your departure city in Europe to India.

**Day 3.** Arrive in Delhi: Arrive in Delhi and transfer to the hotel for 2 nights. Afternoon free to rest after your flight.

**Day 4.** Delhi: Visit New Delhi, the capital city and a 'Jewel in the Crown' with its buildings - many of which were designed by Sir Edwin Lutyens - the Qutab Minar and Emperor Humayun's tomb. The historic capital of the Mughal and British rulers is a fascinating blend of the old and the new. In the afternoon see the famous Red Fort – once the most opulent fort in the Mughal Empire - the Jama Masjid (mosque), Raj Ghat and Old Delhi's bazaar.

**Day 5.** To Varanasi: Fly to Varanasi, the holiest of Hindu cities situated on the sacred River Ganges and a centre of philosophy and religion. Just outside the city is Sarnath, where Buddha preached his first sermon. Visit the Sarnath museum where the ancient Sarnath monastery's treasures are displayed. Stay at the hotel for 1 night.

**Day 6.** To Agra: Early morning boat ride along the 'ghats', the steps that lead down to the river, to see the gathered faithful, ritually cleansing themselves of their sins. In the afternoon, fly to Agra, once the capital of the Mughal empire and the home of the Taj Mahal. Transfer to the hotel for 3 nights.

**Day 7.** Agra: Morning visit to the Taj Mahal, Shah Jahan's monument of eternal love to his bride Mumtaz Mahal. Also visit the massive complex of the Agra Fort with its many palaces. In the afternoon, visit the tomb of Itimad-ud-Dualah or the tomb of the great emperor Akbar, at Sikandra. A second visit to the Taj Mahal in the soft light of the setting sun is also well worth the while.

**Day 8.** Gwalior is known for its massive fort built atop sheer cliffs rising out of the plains. Within the walls lie Jain statues, Rajput palaces, 9th century Hindu temples and a Victorian school. Travel to Gwalior by train and, on arrival, drive to the royal guesthouse, for lunch. After lunch, sightseeing will commence followed by a return to Agra.

**Day 9.** To Jaipur: Transfer by road to Jaipur, stopping en route at Fatehpur Sikhri, the deserted red sandstone city which Akbar built as his capital in the 16th century and abandoned just 15 years later. In Jaipur, stay for 3 nights at the hotel.

**Day 10.** Jaipur: Jaipur is known as the 'Pink City' for its many pink-coloured sandstone buildings in the walled city. See the City Palace, the Jantar Mantar observatory and the 'Palace of the Winds'. In earlier times, the ladies of the court would stand behind the sandstone screen to see and not be seen. The afternoon is at leisure.

**Day 11.** Jaipur: The highlight of the morning is a ride on elephant back to the ancient capital of Amber, perched on a hill and surrounded by a 20-kilometer long wall. In the afternoon visit the colourful and friendly bazaars of Jaipur.

**Day 12.** To Udaipur: The princely state of Mewar is known for its lakes, palaces and gardens. Fly to Udaipur and stay at the hotel for 2 nights. En route to the hotel you visit the vast City Palace. In the afternoon visit the private royal gardens and other sites of interest.

**Day 13.** Udaipur: The full day is at leisure. Optional excursions are available to the nearby hill top forts and temples.

**Day 14.** To Delhi: Morning you fly back to Delhi, bidding farewell to the magical city of Udaipur. A room has been reserved at the hotel up until the time of your departure for the airport late at night. The afternoon is free for final shopping.

**Day 15.** To Europe; Early morning flight to Europe.

## South India

19 Days

Mumbai - Hyderabad - Bangalore - Mysore - Chennai - Madurai - Thekkady - Kochi - Goa - Mumbai

**Day 1 & 2.** Depart from USA: Fly from your departure city in USA to India.

**Day 3.** Mumbai: Arrive in Mumbai where you stay at the hotel. In the afternoon you explore this bustling metropolis, India's commercial capital. See the Marine Drive, Malabar Hill and the Gateway of India.

**Day 4.** To Hyderabad: Travel to Elephanta Island by motor launch, visiting its 7th century rock-cut temples. The afternoon is free to explore Mumbai, before your evening flight to Hyderabad where you will stay at a hotel on Banjara Hills for 2 nights.

**Day 5.** Hyderabad: Hyderabad became famous as the capital of the fabulously wealthy Nizam of Hyderabad. Visit the impressive and strategically placed Goloconda Fort. Also visit the Charminar Gate and the thriving Mecca Masjid. Hyderabad's market was reputed to be the finest in India and it retains much of its old charm.

**Day 6.** To Bangalore: early morning, fly south to Bangalore and check in at the hotel. Known as the Garden City, Bangalore is situated 1,000 meters above sea level. It is famous for its botanical gardens, racetrack, polo fields and distinctive style of architecture. Afternoon is free to explore on your own.

**Day 7.** To Mysore: Drive from Bangalore to Mysore, stopping at Srirangapatnam, where the legendary warrior Tipu Sultan built a summer palace. In Mysore, visit the Maharajah's Palace, Chamundi Hill and the Statue of Nandi, the sacred bull of Shiva. Stay at the hotel.

**Day 8.** To Chennai: Morning for leisure before taking the Shatabdi Express to Chennai, arriving in the evening. Chennai was the chief British settlement under Clive and provided the base for British expansion in India. It has soaring Gothic monuments along the palm-fringed esplanade. Stay at the hotel for 3 nights.

**Day 9.** Chennai: This day will be spent exploring some of India's oldest monuments which are situated here: Fort St. George built in 1653 and the garrison church of St. Mary's which is the oldest Anglican church in India. The afternoon is for leisure.

**Day 10.** Chennai: Drive south to Kanchipuram, one of the seven sacred cities of India. It has a spectacular temple complex with many gopurams (cupolas). After lunch at the hotel drive down to the famous shore temples at Mahabalipuram which date from the 7th century and were the work of the sculptors of the Pallav dynasty.

**Day 11.** To Madurai: Fly to the temple town of Madurai, stay at the hotel for one night.

**Day 12.** To Thekkady: Morning tour of this famous town, which boasts of the magnificent Meenakshi Temple, remaining till today a 'living' temple. Afternoon drive to Thekkady which is located in the cool of the Cardamom Hills, a beautiful area of plantations growing pepper and coffee. Stay 2 nights at the village in Thekkady.

**Day 13.** Thekkady: An excursion to Periyar Wildlife Reserve, famous for its herds of wild elephant and spectacular birdlife.

**Day 14.** To Kochi: Morning drive via Kottayam for lunch at Vembanad Lake. After lunch travel to Alleppey by boat along the famous 'backwaters'. These are a series of lagoons and waterways surrounded by a profusion of tropical vegetation. They cover thousands of acres adjacent to the Kerala coast where riverside village life can be observed all along the route. On arrival in Alleppey you will be met and driven to Kochi where you stay at the hotel on Willingdon Island for 2 nights.

**Day 15.** Kochi: Known as the 'Venice of the East', Kochi is a town characterised by its colonial influences and many canals. Morning visit to the Portuguese church of St. Francis, the Jewish Synagogue of 1568 and the Matancherry Palace, built by the Portuguese and renovated by the Dutch. In the late afternoon, cruise on the Pathira Manal along South India's most beautiful water route and watch the sunset from on board. Dinner will be served on board and you return to the hotel later in the evening.

**Day 16.** To Goa: A Portuguese colony until 1961, Goa is an oasis of palm-fringed beaches, whitewashed churches and Mediterranean style houses. You arrive in the morning by plane from Kochi and transfer to the hotel.

**Day 17.** Goa: A morning excursion brings you to Old Goa, the former capital of the state, where you visit the Se Cathedral in the abandoned city. The afternoon is free to relax on Goa's famous beaches.

**Day 18.** To Mumbai: After a morning of leisure, an early afternoon flight to Mumbai, where a room will be at your disposal at the hotel until departure for the airport late at night.

**Day 19.** To USA: Early morning flight from Mumbai to the USA.

## Golden Triangle Delhi, Agra, Jaipur, Delhi

6 Days

**Day 1:** Arrive New Delhi: Early morning, on arrival at IGI Intl. Airport at New Delhi, meet, greet and transfer to Hotel Imperial in the heart of the City. Enjoy full day sight seeing of the political hub of India. Post breakfast visit Qutub Tomb (Qutub Minar) and take a trip to British landmarks such as India Gate, President's House and Govt. Secretariat. Afternoon sightseeing tour of Old Delhi's Mughal monuments like Jama Masjid and Red Fort and also the option to enjoy the Light and Sound show at Red Fort. Overnight in Delhi.

**Day 02:** Delhi – Agra: Today by road move from Delhi to Agra (203 kms/ 5 hrs). During the later half of the day visit the Agra Fort and the famous "Taj Mahal", an enchanting monument to love, built by the Mughal Emperor Shah Jahan for his beloved wife Mumtaz Mahal after her death in 1631.

**Day 03:** Agra – Jaipur (235 kms/5.5 hrs): On the way visit the town of Fatehpur Sikri. The town built by Emperor Akbar contains many grand monuments but was abandoned after his death. Arrive in the Pink City (Jaipur), check into the hotel and rest. Evening at disposal.

**Day 04:** Jaipur: A tour of the Pink City (Jaipur) built in the 1727 A.D. to visit Hawa Mahal - palace of winds, City Palace, and Jantar Mantar, an 18th century observatory. Also enjoy shopping in the markets of Jaipur. Enjoy an evening of typical Rajputana traditions and cuisines at "Chokhi Dhani", a hub of Rajasthani culture and hospitality.

**Day 05:** Jaipur-Delhi (258 kms/6 hrs): Morning visit to the stunning white marble and red sandstone structure at a height, "Amer Fort". Post lunch depart for Delhi by road. Overnight in Delhi.

**Day 06:** Delhi to onward destination: Morning visit symbol of ancient art and architecture; a famous place of worship in Delhi; Akshardham Temple followed by unique shopping experience in the bylanes of Chandni Chowk and late evening board flight to onward destination.

## Cost of an Itinerary

COST is the end result of COSTING. It includes all the expenses that the tour operator is willing to include in the cost along with his own profit margins.

The cost will depend upon:
- Duration of the tour
- Type of transport (connectivity between destinations, transfers and sight seeing)
- Number of travellers travelling together
- Category of hotels required (as per suggested budget)
- Type of rooms required
- Types of service required at hotels - meal plan
- Excursions and sight seeing requirements
- Time of the year

- Guides, escort allowances and expenses
- Any other permit and permission requirements

In order to avoid any errors it is preferred that the costing is done systematically. For this purpose a cost sheet is used. Costing is done as per the itinerary.

**B- Breakfast, L- Lunch, D- Dinner**

| S.No/Day | Sector | Accommodation based on respective meal plan | Additional Meals (i.e. meals other then those taken in hotels) | SRS (Single Room Supplement) | | Transportation | | | Miscelleneous |
|---|---|---|---|---|---|---|---|---|---|
| | | | | Sgl | Dbl | Transport (From One Destination to another destination) | Transfers | Sight seeing | |
| 1. | Delhi | B L D | | | | | | | Guides, Escort, Entrances, Games Rides, Taxes, Tips, Refreshments, Surcharges, Permits etc. |
| | | | | | | | | | |
| 2 | Delhi Agra | B L D | | | | | | | |
| | | | | | | | | | |
| 3 | Agra Jaipur | B L D | | | | | | | |
| | | | | | | | | | |
| 4 | Jaipur | B L D | | | | | | | |
| | | | | | | | | | |
| 5 | Jaipur Delhi | B L D | | | | | | | |
| | | | | | | | | | |
| 6 | Delhi | B L D | | | | | | | |

## Inbound Tour Management

## COST SHEET

In the above example, the entire transportation i.e., transport from one destination to another, transfers and sightseeing is taken care of by a single coach operator therefore the consolidated all inclusive cost for a Dlx Coach for the entire tour (Delhi Intl Airport to Delhi Intl Airport) can be obtained from one single supplier and there is no need to deal with separate handling agents or different transport suppliers at different destinations.

All costs must be calculated on per person basis. In case of accommodation the net per person is calculated on twin share.

INR and USD components are calculated separately and ultimately total INR component is converted into USD to arrive at final USD amount.

After calculating all the occurring costs and supplier taxes we can add a mark up in the form of certain percentage on net calculated cost as per above cost sheet.

Some tour operators avoid calculating net supplier costs and consider published costs while costing thereby protecting their margins in published costs itself.

Once all the costs have been calculated including margins on the basis of either of above mentioned arrangements the final COST is presented along with itinerary that looks like the e.g.

"{COST: USD 2300 p.p. on twin share}"

Above cost is based on twin share and doesn't explain any alternative cost for a single person. To easily calculate the cost for a person staying single i.e., using a single room we calculate single room supplement for each destination for every night and sum up all SRS for all nights to provide final SRS for the entire itinerary.

SRS (Single Room Supplement) – "Is that additional amount that a person pays for staying single instead of staying in a double room on twin sharing basis".

i.e., SRS = [EPAI* Cost of single room – ½ (EPAI Cost of Double room)]

EPAI*= European Plan All Inclusive (Luxury Tax Included)

Question: In a hotel in Manali the cost of Sgl room is Rs. 2000 and the cost of a dbl room is Rs. 2800. Luxury tax on the room is 10%. If 3 adults stayed in this hotel for 3 nights and 4 days then what would be the SRS?
Answer:

Dbl Room = INR 2800 + Tax10% = INR 3080

Sgl Room = INR 2000 + Tax 10% = INR 2200

SRS = [EPAI* Cost of single room – ½ (EPAI Cost of Double room)]

SRS = 2200 – ½ (3080) = INR 660 X 3 nights = INR 1980 p.p.

That means;

If the holiday costs INR 4620 p.p. on twin sharing

The same holiday would cost INR 4620 + INR 1980 p.p. on single occupancy.

## COST INCLUDES

Tour Operator clearly states everything that has been included in the cost or in other words all tangibles and intangibles that his customer would be getting against this cost.

## COST EXCLUDES

The tour operator clearly states all tangibles and intangibles that are not included in the mentioned amount. For example, it can be travel insurance or a particular meal or in general any cost of a personal nature like shopping, phone calls, personal medications or any expense due to any unexpected circumstances/natural calamity, etc.

## TERMS AND CONDITIONS

A very important section mentioning all other details that the traveller needs to know. Details like;
Booking terms and conditions
Cancellation terms and conditions
Child policy
Foreign exchange policy
Vaccination details
Details about properties where guests are staying
Any other general notes

## OPTIONAL TOURS (TOUR EXTENSIONS)

Optional tours are offered in order to extend the stay of travellers once they are already on the tour. They are also called extensions.

### Inbound Tourism Products

Following are some of the important tourist products which are popular amongst foreign tourists visiting India
- Wellness tourism,
- Domestic tourism
- Monsoon tourism
- Rural tourism
- Medical tourism
- Spa tourism
- Adventure tourism
- Nature/eco friendly packages
- Luxury train packages
- Wedding tourism
- Golf tourism
- MICE
- Heritage tourism
- Caravan tourism

### The Inbound Tourist Products Available

Across the country are scattered a host of various tourism options. The various Indian states and their capital cities emanate a unique distinctive feature. Each city in India reflects its uniqueness reflecting, the past heritage and modern products.

## Popular Inbound Destinations in India

## DELHI

Delhi, the political capital of India, is a major tourist attraction. The city has a rich cultural and historical past. Located on the banks of the river Yamuna, this city presents some of the architectural wonders of the yester years. Some of the important landmarks are:
- Jama Masjid
- Red Fort
- Qutab Minar
- Humayun's Tomb
- India Gate
- Jantar Mantar
- Purana Qila
- Akshardham
- Bahai Lotus Temple
- Dilli Haat
- Hauz Khas
- Pragati Maidan

## MUMBAI

Mumbai is another one of the tourist cities of India, which exudes glitz, glamour, glitter and gold. Set along the Arabian Sea, this land of dreams and opportunities offers many tourist attractions.

Being one of the major port cities of India and a trade hub since the British reign in India, the city has a lot to offer to the tourists with its colonial buildings that reflect the glory and brilliance of Victorian architecture. The main tourist attractions of the city comprise the beaches and the important landmarks. Mumbai City is well connected by air, rail and roadways from almost all the important cities in India. The accommodation options offered in Mumbai vary from three star budget hotels to luxurious five star hotels and therefore keep a traveller off the tension of finding good accommodation. Some of the important landmarks are:
- Gateway of India
- Bandra
- Elephanta Caves
- Nariman Point
- Chowpatty Beach
- Juhu Beach
- Marine Drive

## KOLKATA

Kolkata, another of the tourist cities of India, exudes a character of culture, education and warmth. This city is known as the City of Joy, has the following places of interest to be explored:
- Victoria Memorial

- Botanical Gardens
- Indian Museum
- National Library of India
- Academy of Fine Arts
- Howrah Bridge

## CHENNAI

Chennai is set along the Bay of Bengal in Southern India. This capital city of Tamil Nadu is again a major centre for art and culture. The city has the following places of tourist interest:

- Fort St.George
- Vivekanandar Illam
- Santhome Catheral Basilica
- Theosophical Society
- Elliots beach and Ashta Lakshmi Temple
- Guindy National Park
- Birla Planetarium

Several other tourist places in India include Agra, Bangalore, Thiruvanathapuram, Amristar, Varanasi, Hyderabad, Pune, Gwalior, etc. Apart from the important cities in India, the other places of tourist visit can be divided into:

- Monuments and Temples
- Wildlife Tourism

Five thousand years of Indian history have given us the treasure of thousands of monuments across the country, monuments belonging to Hindus, Buddhists, Muslims and Christians. The monuments of India narrate the tales of valour and courage of the Indian rulers.

Monuments in India form the great heritage of India and they are evidence of India's historical past. These monuments reflects the culture and the heritage of yore. Tourists visit India in order to spectate the miraculous beauty of Indian monuments.

## HANDLING THE INBOUND GROUPS

Inbound tour operators commence their action even before the group arrives into the country. The general group handling is listed out in sequence for a better understanding:

### A. Pre-Arrival Checks

- Reconfirm all land arrangements for the tour package
- Reconfirm the list of passengers with the customer's full name and details
- Reconfirm the availability of tour guides
- Discussion of the entire tour program with the respective tour guide.
- Reconfirm the special requests of the guests especially –lunch, drinks, escorts, entertainment show tickets.

- Reconfirm the rooming list with the hotel(s)

## B. Post Arrival services:
- Meet and assist services
- Transfers
- Introduction of the guide
- Welcome drink and check in at the hotel
- Discussion on the day's plan
- Travel information and entire itinerary discussion
- Foreign exchange requirements
- Health information
- Passport and visa queries
- Complaint handling
- Shopping information
- Additional tours and details on charges
- Additional services other than the services included in the tour package.

## C. Other Key Services

**Meet and assist service**
- Meet and assist service will be provided for the group on request as a part of the inbound tour service. Normally such services invite additional charges and are included in the tour package.
- Arrival passengers are met at the aircraft gate and guided to the ground transportation area, such services commence from inside the airport premises. Depending on the size of the groups one or more battery operated cars will be used.
- An example of where meet and assist service may be utilised is a couple travelling with many young children; a non-English speaking group; or a group of elderly guests not requiring a wheelchair.
- Staff normally assists the group or guests in completing the passport formalities, baggage collection, customs and accompanies them to the ground transportation area or the parking area.

## D. Transfers
- Transporting the guests from the port of arrival to the place of stay is called a transfer.
- Depending on the requirements of the group this service may or may not be included in the package, as this service invites additional charges. The cost is included in the package.
- Personalised Cars or a bus will be offered for service depending on the group size. Normally large buses with a/c and baggage hold are provided for such services.

### E. Introduction of the guide

- Not all groups request for guide services, as this service invites additional costs. Groups which have requested for guide service will meet the guide at the airport or in the bus, during transfer to the hotel. The guide gives his/her introduction and provides a warm welcome to the tourists.
- Normally no additional information will be shared as the guests are tired and not receptive.

### F. Check-in:

- Inbound tourists check-in at the hotel with the help of the guide, tour manger or inbound tour executive. The rooming list prepared earlier helps the guide to go through the process quickly.
- Discussion of the day's plan
- Once the check-in procedure is complete, the guests are given time to refresh and relax, the guide or the tour manager meets them during dinner or latter in the day to discuss the plan.

### G. The tour manager/guide

- Normally in an escorted tour the tour guide/escort has a detailed discussion of the entire plan with the group to ensure all the guests have clarity regarding the entire program.
- To ensure smooth operation of the tour, pre-planning is essential. Flawless operations require proper coordination and commitment to operations. A team of well trained staff is a necessity. Staff should be trained in customer handling, crisis management, complaint handling etc.

## Requirements of Inbound Tourists

Many foreign tourist visiting countries on inbound travel would have general needs when it comes to enjoying a holiday, short breaks or a day visit in a country. The needs are summarised in the figure below:

## Access to Information
Access to information prior to taking a trip and while in a destination, is vital to encourage inbound tourists to visit and get the most out of their stay. The supply of tourist information is normally provided by the government nominated bodies as also by providers of travel services.

The internet is becoming the most popular source of information for tourists. It is particularly useful for finding information on events, activities booking accommodation, etc.

## Transport
Tourists need transport services and facilities that are convenient, safe, frequent and reliable and offer good value for money. This holds true when visitors are on leisure, business or visiting friends and relatives. The travellers need a good network of routes and gateway airports plus efficient transit facilities.

## Facilities
Different types of tourists look for specific facilities when on trips. Business travellers often have specific needs, for example, speedy check-ins and check-out at hotels, electronic tickets and internet facilities in the hotel in order to save time.

A young traveller will look for youth discount passes for travel, cheap accommodation and good and inexpensive food and entertainment.

## Events
Festivals and events are an excellent way to learn about an area and have some fun. Events take place both in urban and rural areas, helping to spread the benefits of tourism across the country.

## Attractions
Visitors from overseas are drawn to a country's unique heritage, monuments, temples, historic sites, landscape, etc.

## Language:
For most of the tourists visiting India, China, Japan or any other country where the local language is unknown, makes language interpretation a particular need for most inbound tourists. For example a group of French tourists visiting India may need a language interpreter as they are unaware of the languages spoken in India and their knowledge of English is not very sound.

A person's stay can be made much more enjoyable by offering a range of facilities like:
- Signposting in many languages
- Multilingual menus
- A tour guide who speaks more than one language
- Multilingual audio guides at attractions

- Leaflets and brochures in a range of languages
- Tourist information offices with staff who are multilingual

### Cultural differences

Visitors from overseas may have different customs. Without an understanding of the local customs and practices, the visitor may unknowingly offend people.

Overseas visitors may follow different religious codes, eat a variety of food and drink and use different gestures while greeting people. The staff should have the knowledge to understand the cultural differences and respond as per the situation.

## INBOUND TOURS TO INDIA

There could be several possibilities concerning various itineraries, which could be prepared for the inbound tourists who have an interest in seeing different aspects of the country's tourist products. Considering the size and geographical elements of the country, India is considered to have multi-dimensional tourist products, which may interest various categories of the people interested in different segments. For those who have an interest in cultural tourism there are programmes/itineraries, which may take the inbound tourists to places of tourist interest associated with cultural tourism.

For those having an interest in Leisure holidays, the country has beautiful beaches along the coastline, which stretches more than 7,000 kilometers. Several itineraries are available to places of tourist interest associated with beaches and islands. Similarly, there are itineraries, which may interest adventure tourists, tourists who have an interest in health and also sports.

Some of the popular tourist circuits in India are as follows:

### (i) Heritage Circuits

Delhi – Agra – Gwalior – Shivpuri – Orchha – Khajuraho
Delhi – Jaipur – Agra – Khajuraho – Varanasi

### (ii) Forts and Palaces:

Delhi – Mandawa – Bikaner – Jaisalmer – Jodhpur – Bundi – Udaipur – Pushkar – Jaipur – Agra – Delhi

Mumbai – Goa – Belgaum – Badami – Hospet – Hassan – Madikeri – Mysore – Bengaluru

### (iii) Buddhist Circuits

Delhi – Jaipur – Agra – Varanasi – Sarnath – Bodh Gaya – Rajgir – Nalanda – Vaishali – Kushinagar – Lumbini – Kapilvastu – Sravasti – Balrampur – Lucknow – Delhi

Delhi – Agra – Varanasi – Sarnath – Kushinagar – Bodh Gaya – Vaishali – Sanchi

### (iv) Temple Circuit

- Kanchipuram – Madurai – Tiruchirapalli – Kanyakumari

# Inbound Tour Management

- Delhi – Jaipur – Jodhpur – Jaisalmer – Bikaner – Delhi **Desert Triangle**

In the following pages, are details of various packages for the inbound tourists which have been prepared by one of the leading travel agencies in Great Britain. These packages will give comprehensive details of some of the few programmes available in India. The programs have been appropriately titled to motivate the clients. For instance programme 1 titled "Indian Experience" is a 9-day classical tour covering Delhi – Agra – Jaipur – Delhi. From day one, which is a departure day from USA to India till the ninth day with departure from India to USA, each of the day's details have been worked out. The clients can also take an extension of one week's holiday to Goa to relax on a beach or go to look for a tiger at one of the several game parks. Most of the tour operators offer extension programmes beyond the planned itineraries. A client has initially to pay a printed price for a basic programme and an additional price in case he takes an extension. The brochure gives both the departure and return dates of the programme.

**Programme I-II** entitled "Splendours of the North" covers a two week programme covering in addition to Delhi-Agra-Jaipur, places like Varanasi, Gwalior and Udaipur.

**Programme III** is a special programme of 18 days entitled "Forts and Palaces". This programme has been specially put together for those clients who have interest in arts and architecture covering forts and palaces.

**Programme IV** is twin destination programme covering both India and Nepal. A 22 days programme takes clients first to Nepal and then to India. Titled as "Classical Journey" it covers places associated with religion, culture, legends and mysteries. Travelling at a leisurely pace, a tourist can absorb the splendid sights and savour the unique flavour on both Nepal and India.

**Programme V** is again a special interest programme for those interested in nature and wildlife. An 18-day programme takes a client through rich, tropical jungles, extensive grasslands and temperate forests of India, which are reserves of wildlife and some of the world's most stunning national parks.

**Programme VI** is a 19-day programme to South India entitled "Southern Trader" covering the golden beaches and temples in the region.

**Programme VII** is a 17-day tour entitled "Culinary Feast" covering both North and South India and tailor made for those who have interest in Indian cuisine.

Similarly **Programme VIII** again is a twin destination programme covering India and the Maldives. A special interest programme of 16 days cover the finest beaches in the Southern coast and also the Maldives discovered by the Arabs, Greeks, Romans, Portuguese, Dutch, French and British traders. A sample of the brochure may be seen in the following pages.

# PROGRAMME – I
**Indian Experience**

### 9 days: Delhi - Agra - Jaipur - Delhi

**Day 1 and 2.** Depart from USA: Fly from your departure city in the USA to India.

**Day 3. Delhi.** Arrive in Delhi and transfer to the hotel. The rest of the morning is at leisure. In the afternoon there will be a brief tour to the sights of New Delhi. You will see its many monuments and buildings designed by Lutyens, including India Gate and the President's house.

**Day 4.** To Agra: In the morning you will visit the sights of Old Delhi, the Red Fort, the Jama Masjid-India's largest mosque-and the Chandni Chowk bazaar. Early in the afternoon you will set off for Agra arriving in time for dinner, and stay at the hotel for 2 nights.

**Day 5.** Agra: The morning will begin with a visit to Agra Fort, a massive complex with exquisite marble work, a testament to the power of successive Mughal emperors. You will then be taken to the incomparable Taj Mahal, seen as a magnificent expression of Emperor Shah Jahan's undying love. In the afternoon there will be a visit to the tomb of Itimad-ud-Daulah, known to be the forerunner of the Taj Mahal, and later you may wish to return to the Taj Mahal to see it in the soft light of the setting sun.

**Day 6:** To Jaipur: You drive to Jaipur via Fatehpur Sikri, the once prosperous capital of the Mughal Empire. Built by emperor Akbar, Fatehpur Sikri remains in near perfect condition, as a reminder of the architectural wealth and power of one of the India's most famous empires. You will stay at the hotel.

**Day 7:** Jaipur: In the morning you visit Amber where the ascent to the ancient capital is made by gaily caparisoned elephants. The fort has a variety of places within its winding 20-kilometer walls, including the unusual Chamber of Mirrors. Enroute to Amber you will see the palace of the Winds in the morning sun. The afternoon tour allows time to explore the city Palace, still home of Jaipur's royal family, and the site of the Jantar Mantar or astrological observatory where India's impressive scientific heritage can be appreciated.

**Day 8:** To Delhi: You leave the romantic "Pink City" of Jaipur, departing from golden deserts of Rajasthan to the imperial grandeur of Delhi. You return to the hotel where a room has been reserved for you until the departure for the airport late in the night.

**Day 9.** To USA: Early morning flight from Delhi to USA.

Note: You may want to spend an additional week relaxing on one of India's most famous beaches in Goa or go in search of the elusive tiger at one of India's game reserves.

## PROGRAMME - II

**15 Days, Delhi – Varanasi – Agra – Gwalior – Udaipur – Delhi**

**Day 1 and 2.** Depart from USA: Fly from your departure city in the USA to India.

**Day 3. Arrive in Delhi:** Arrive in Delhi and transfer to the hotel for 2 nights. Afternoon free to rest after your flight.

**Day 4. Delhi:** Visit New Delhi, the capital city and a 'Jewel in the Crown' with its buildings - many of which were designed by Sir Edwin Lutyens. Also visit the Qutab Minar and Emperor Humayun's tomb. The historic capital of the Mughal and British rulers is a fascinating blend of the old and the new. In the afternoon see the famous Red Fort – once the most opulent fort for the Mughal Empire - the Jama Masjid (mosque), Raj Ghat and Old Delhi's bazaar.

**Day 5. To Varanasi:** Fly to Varanasi, the holiest of Hindu cities situated on the sacred River Ganges and a centre of philosophy and religion. Just outside the city is Sarnath, where Buddha preached his first sermon. Visit the Sarnath museum where the ancient Sarnath monastery's treasures are displayed. Stay at the hotel for 1 night.

**Day 6. To Agra:** Early morning boat ride along the 'ghats', the steps that lead down to the river, to see the gathered faithful, ritually cleansing themselves of their sins. In the afternoon, fly to Agra, once the capital of the Mughal empire and the home of the Taj Mahal. Transfer to the hotel for 3 nights.

**Day 7. Agra:** Morning visit to the Taj Mahal, Shah Jahan's monument of eternal love to his wife Mumtaz Mahal. Also visit the massive complex of Agra Fort with its many palaces. In the afternoon, visit the tomb of Itimad-ud-Dualah or the tomb of the great, emperor, Akbar, at Sikandra. A second visit to the Taj Mahal in the soft light of the setting sun is also well worthwhile.

**Day 8.** Gwalior is known for its massive fort, built atop sheer cliffs rising out of the plains. Within the walls lie Jain statues, Rajput palaces, 9th century Hindu temples and a Victorian school. Travel to Gwalior by train and, on arrival, drive to the royal guest house, for lunch. After lunch, sightseeing will commence followed by return to Agra.

**Day 9. To Jaipur:** Transfer by road to Jaipur, stopping en route at Fatehpur Sikri, the deserted red sandstone city which Akbar built as his capital in the 16th century and abandoned just 15 years later. In Jaipur, stay for 3 nights at the hotel.

**Day 10. Jaipur:** Jaipur is known as the 'Pink City' for its many pink-coloured sandstone buildings in the walled city. See the City Palace, the Jantar Mantar observatory and the 'Palace of the Winds'. In earlier times, the ladies of the court would stand behind the sandstone screen to see and not be seen. The afternoon is at leisure.

**Day 11. Jaipur:** The highlight of the morning is a ride on elephant back to the ancient capital of Amber, perched on a hill and surrounded by a 20 kilometer long wall. In the afternoon visit the colourful and friendly bazaars of Jaipur.

**Day 12. To Udaipur:** The princely state of Mewar is known for its lakes, palaces and gardens. Fly to Udaipur and stay at the hotel for 2 nights. En route to the hotel you visit the vast City Palace. In the afternoon, visit the private royal gardens and other sites of interest.

**Day 13.** Udaipur: The full day is at leisure. Optional excursions are available to the nearby hill top forts and temples.

**Day 14.** To Delhi: Morning you fly back to Delhi, bidding farewell to the magical city of Udaipur. A room has been reserved at the hotel up until the time of your departure for the airport late night. The afternoon is free for final shopping.

**Day 15.** To USA; early morning flight to the USA.

## PROGRAMME – III

**Forts & Palaces**

**18 Days: Delhi – Agra – Jaipur – Khimsar – Jaisalmer – Jodhpur – Udaipur – Delhi**

**Day 1 and 2.** Depart from USA: Fly from your departure city in the USA to India.

**Day 3.** Arrive in Delhi: Arrive in Delhi and transfer to the hotel for 2 nights. The rest of the afternoon is at leisure.

**Day 4.** Delhi: In the morning, visit the sights of New Delhi, the city built by the British with its many monuments and buildings designed by Lutyens. You will see the India Gate, the President's house as well as the Pre-Mughal monuments and the tomb of Emperor Humayun. In the afternoon, visit the Red Fort, the Jama Masjid – India's Largest mosque – Raj Ghat and the Chandni Chowk bazaar.

**Day 5.** To Agra: Early morning, board one of India's most modern trains, the Shatabdi Express, to Agra. Stay at the hotel for a night. After breakfast visit the vast Agra Fort. The afternoon is free and you may wish to visit the tomb of Itimad-ud-Daluah, often refferd to as 'Baby Taj'. Visit the Taj Mahal, the marble memorial of an emperor's undying love and see it in the most perfect of lights, the light of the setting sun in the late afternoon.

**Day 6.** To Jaipur: Drive to the land of the Rajputs and its capital, Jaipur. Spend 2 nights at the hotel. En route visit emperor Akbar's deserted capital city of Fatehpur Skri, built in 1571, abandoned 15 years later, which has remained unchanged for over 400 years.

**Day 7.** To Jaipur: After breakfast, visit Amber Fort, pausing en route to see the 'Palace of Winds'. Hawa Mahal. Arriving at Amber, ascend to the fort on an elephant and visit the myriad marble palaces. After lunch, visit the City Palace and the Jantar Mantar astronomical observatory.

**Day 8.** To Khimsar: Morning visit to the small village of Khimsar. Afternoon free. (accommodation will most likely be in picturesque Rajasthani tents.)

**Day 9.** Khimsar: Arrive at the medieval desert town of Nagpur, with a fine 11th century fort and a mosque built by the great Mughal emperor, Akbar. Return in the afternoon.

**Day 10.** To Jaisalmer: Following the sun, drive west into the heart of the Thar desert to Jaisalmer, a perfect example of a walled, desert city. Spend 2 nights at the hotel.

**Day 11.** Jaisalmer: Morning walk to the hilltop fort, through the maze of narrow streets dotted with Jain temples and havelis (ornately decorated mansions). After lunch an excursion to the sand-dunes at Sam and the opportunity to take a short camel ride.

**Day 12.** To Jodhpur: Drive east, to the edge of the desert before arriving at the ancient and imposing fort city of Jodhpur. Spend 2 nights at the hotel.

**Day 13.** Jodhpur: A morning tour of this ancient desert city takes you to the magnificient Meherangarh Fort. With its many palaces which serve as a constant reminder of the city's glorious past and the doomed romantic chivalry of the Rajput warriors. The afternoon is free.

**Day 14.** To Udaipur: Continue your journey south to the oasis city of Udaipur. En route, visit the Jain temples of Ranakpur and have a light lunch at the Castle. Continuing on through the Aravalli Hills, arrive at the Lake Palace in time for dinner and spend 3 nights here.

**Day 15.** Udaipur: A short tour of Jagdish Temple and the City Palace. The afternoon is free to relax in your luxurious surroundings or perhaps take a short cruise on Lake Pichola.

**Day 16.** Udaipur: Leisure for optional sightseeing in the area.

**Day 17.** To Delhi: Morning flight to Delhi. A room will be at your disposal at the hotel until you depart for the airport at late night.

**Day 18.** To USA: Early morning flight from Delhi to the USA.

## PROGRAMME – IV

**Classical Journey**

**India and Nepal**

22 Days: Delhi – Kathmandu – Temple Tiger – Varanasi – Khajuraho – Agra – Jaipur – Udaipur – Aurangabad – Mumbai

**Day 1 & 2.** Depart from USA: Fly from your departure city in the USA to India.

**Day 3:** Arrive in Delhi: Arrive in Delhi. After immigration clearance and baggage collection you will be met by a representative and transferred to the hotel for 2 nights. The historic capital of the Mughal and British rulers is a fascinating blend of the old and the new. In the afternoon, see the famous Red Fort, the Jama Masjid and Old Delhi's bazaar. In the evening meet your fellow North American travellers at a cocktail reception.

**Day 4:** Delhi – Kathmandu: The sights of New Delhi include the buildings of the British Raj, many designed by Sir Edwin Lutyens. Morning visit to the Qutab Minar and Emperor Humayun's tomb. In the evening board a 2-hour flight to the Mountain Kingdom of Nepal. Upon arrival transfer to the hotel.

**Day 5:** Royal Chitwan Park Temple Tiger: In the morning visit Pashupatinath which is dedicated to the Lord Shiva and continue to the airport for a short flight south to Bharatpur. From the airport, drive through the traditional Tharu villages before crossing the Narayani River by boat and arriving at Temple Tiger, your jungle home for the next 2 nights. In the late afternoon go on your first game viewing.

**Day 6:** Temple Tiger: The full day is spent in the pursuit of Chitwan's wildlife, both on elephant back and by jeep. Here you will look for the Indian rhinoceros and the Bengal Tiger in addition to hundreds of species of birds and smaller mammals.

**Day 7:** To Kathmandu: In the morning fly back to Kathmandu hotel. In the afternoon, explore the streets of Kathmandu, full of wooden pagodas, temples and Buddhist stupas. See Durbar Square and the Swayambhunath shrine. In the evening you meet the British members of your group at a special welcome dinner.

**Day 8:** Kathmandu: Early morning drive to the picturesque little village of Nagarkot to see the sunrise over Everest and the Himalayas. Return via Bhagdon, one of the three ancient capitals of Nepal. See the five-storyed Nyatapola Pagoda, the Golden Gate and the Palace of Fifty-five windows. The afternoon is free.

**Day 9.** To Varanasi: Fly to Varansi, the holiest of Hindu cities, situated on the sacred River Ganges. Transfer to the hotel for a night.

**Day 10.** To Khajuraho: Early morning boat ride along the 'ghats', the stone steps which lead down to the river, to see the gathered faithful, ritually cleansing themselves of their sins. After breakfast at your hotel, visit the important Buddhist centres of Sarnath before your flight to Khajuraho in the afternoon. Stay at the hotel for a night.

**Day 11.** To Agra: Morning visit to the Chandela dynasty temples, famous for their spectacular sculptures and erotic carvings. In the afternoon fly to Agra. Transfer to the hotel for 2 nights.

**Day 12.** Agra: Morning visit to the Taj Mahal-Shah Jahan's monument of the eternbal love- and Agra Fort with its many palaces and halls. In the afternoon there is an optional visit either to the tomb of Itimad-ud-Daulah or to Emperor Akbar's tomb at Sikandra.

**Day 13.** To Jaipur: Transfer by road to Jaipur, stopping en route at Fatehpur Sikri, the deserted red sandstone city which Akbar built as his capital in the 16th century. In Jaipur stay at the hotel for 2 nights.

**Day 14.** Jaipur: Morning drive out to the ancient capital, and magnificent fort at Amber on elephant back. After lunch explore Jaipur itself which is known as the 'Pink City'. See the City Palace, the Jantar Mantar observatory and the 'Palace of the Winds'.

**Day 15.** To Udaipur: Early morning flight to Udaipur. Stay at the hotel for 3 nights. En route to the hotel visit the vast City Palace. Afternoon, visit the private royal gardens.

**Day 16.** Udaipur: At leisure. Optional excursions available to the nearby hilltop forts and temples such as Chittorgarh or Eklingi.

**Day 17.** Udaipur: Drive out to visit the Jain temple at Ranakpur, one of the most impressive Jain temples in India. Return in the evening.

**Day 18.** To Aurangabad: Fly to Aurangabad, the most southerly and the last of the Mughal capitals. In the afternoon visit the Ellora cave temples, rock-hewn shrines of Hindu, Jain and Buddhist art. Stay at the hotel for 2 nights.

**Day 19.** Aurangabad: The Ajanta caves were discovered by a British Army patrol in the 19th century. The Buddhist sculptures and frescoes representing everyday secular and religious life are a thousand years old.

**Day 20.** To Mumbai: Fly to Mumbai, the wealthiest and one of the most cosmopolitan of Indian cities. Transfer to hotel until the time of departure.

**Day 21.** Mumbai: Visit the sights of Mumbai: the Gateway of India, the Prince of Wales Museum, Marine Drive and Malabar Hill. Afternoon free to explore, relax, shop.

**Day 22.** To USA: Early morning flight from Mumbai to the USA.

## PROGRAMME – V

### Jungle Odyssey

18 Days: Delhi – Corbett – Ranthambore – Bharatpur – Agra – Bandhavgarh – Khajuraho – Delhi

**Day 1 & 2.** Depart from USA: Fly from your USA departure city to India.

**Day 3.** Delhi: Arrive in Delhi and transfer to the hotel for a night.

**Day 4.** To Corbett National Park: After breakfast, set off into the foothills of the Himalaya and the Corbett National park. Spend 4 nights at the luxurious Tiger Tops Corbett Lodge. The park is set in the undulating Shiwalik foothills of the Himalayas with the Ramganga river flowing through it. Thicky forested, it provides cover for a vast amount of diverse game.

**Day 5,6,&7:** Game viewing in Corbett the next three days are dedicated to bird-watching and sighting animals, both in and outside the park. In this region, together with the elephant, leopard, hog deer and gharial, to name but a few animals, there is an extraordinary array of birdlife with over 520 known species.

**Day 8.** To Delhi: Drive back to Delhi, across the rich farmland of the Gangetic plain. Stay overnight at the hotel.

**Day 9.** To Ranthambore: An early morning flight brings you to Jaipur from where you continue to Ranthambore by road. Formerly the private hunting grounds of the Maharajas of Jaipur, this park has always boasted of an abundance of many species of game, including tiger, leopard, marsh crocodile, jungle cats and sloth bear. Spend 2 nights at the Lodge. Evening game drive.

**Day 10.** Ranthambore: Early morning and evening game drives, exploring the area by jeep and beginning your search for the elusive tiger and its prey. After the morning game drive, visit the ancient fort in the heart of the park.

**Day 11.** To Bharatpur: Early morning drive to Bharatpur and spend 2 nights at the Bharatpur Forest Lodge/Saras Lodge. Evening bird-watching down in the wetlands.

**Day 12.** Bharatpur: Bharatpur is one of the finest bird sanctuaries in Asia with a huge variety of birds, both migratory and resident, including duck, storks, waders and birds of prey. Watch birds of prey in the early morning. During daytime, relax at your lodge before returning to watch the birds coming in to roost later in the afternoon.

**Day 13.** To Agra: Leisurely start for the incomparable ancient capital of Agra. En route visit the exquisitely preserved city of Fatehpur Sikri. This deserted red sandstone city was built by Mughal emperor Akbar in the 16th century. Arrive in Agra and spend a night at the hotel. In the soft light of the setting sun visit the world's greatest monument to love, the Taj Mahal, built by Shah Jahan as a memorial to his beloved wife, Mumtaz.

**Day 14.** To Bandhavgarh: A morning flight brings you to Khajuraho from where you continue your journey through Madhya Pradesh by road to Bandhavgarh National Park. Spend 3 nights at the Bandhavgarh Jungle Camp.

**Days 15 and 16.** Game viewing in Bandhavgarh: Bandhavgarh was formerly the Rewa Maharaja's hunting preserve and was declared a national park in 1968. incorporated in 1994 into project Tiger, it has long been famous for tigers, leopards, deer, gaur, various species of monkeys and a wide variety of birds. Over half the area is covered by sal forest and towards the north there are large stretches of bamboo and grassland. Two days will be spent game viewing in the early mornings and evenings with the daytime being free for further explorations.

**Day 17.** To Khajuraho/Delhi: Drive to Khajuraho where, time permitting, you explore the decorative and unique temples for which the town is famous. After lunch, fly to Delhi and transfer to the hotel where a room will be at your disposal until your departure for the airport late at night.

**Day 18.** To USA: Early morning flight from Delhi to the USA.

## PROGRAMME – VI

**Southern Trader**

**19 Days: Mumbai – Hydearabad – Bangaluru – Mysore – Chennai – Madurai – Thekkady – Kochi – Goa – Bombay**

**Day 1 and 2.** Depart from USA: Fly from your departure city in the USA to India.

**Day 3.** Mumbai: Arrive in Bombay where you stay at the hotel. In the afternoon, you explore this bustling metropolis, India's commercial capital. See the Marine drive, Malabar Hill and the Gateway of India.

**Day 4.** To Hyderabad: Travel to Elephanta Island by motor launch, visiting its 7th century rock-cut temples. The afternoon is free to explore Bombay, before your evening flight to Hyderabad where you will stay at the hotel on Banjara Hill for 2 nights.

**Day 5.** Hyderabad: Hyderabad became famous as the capital of the fabulously wealthy Nizam of Hyderabad. Visit the impressive and strategically placed Goloconda fort. Also visit the Charminar and the thriving Mecca Masjid. Hyderabad's market was reputed to be the finest in India and it retains much of its old charm.

**Day 6.** To Bangaluru: early morning, fly south to Bangaluru and check in at the hotel. Known as the Garden city, Bangaluru is situated at 1,000 metres above sea level. It is famous for its botanical gardens, race track, polo fields and distinctive style of architecture. The afternoon is free to explore on your own.

**Day 7.** To Mysore: Drive from Bangaluru to Mysore, stopping at Srirangapatnam, where the legendary warrior Tipu Sultan built a summer palace. In Mysore, visit the Maharajah's Palace, Chamundi Hill and the Statue of Nandi, the sacred bull of Shiva. Stay at the hotel.

**Day 8.** To Chennai: Morning for leisure before taking the Shatabdi express to Chennai, arriving in the evening. Chennai was the chief British settlement under Clive and provided the base for British expansion in India. It has soaring Gothic monuments along the palm-fringed esplanade. Stay at the hotel for 3 nights.

**Day 9.** Chennai: Some of India's oldest monuments which are situated here: Fort St. George built in 1653 and the garrison church of St. Mary's which is the oldest Anglican church in India. The afternoon is for leisure.

**Day 10.** Chennai: Drive south to Kanchipuram, one of the seven sacred cities of India. It has a spectacular temple complex with many gopurams (cupolas). After lunch at the hotel drive down to the famous shore temples at Mahabalipuram which date from the 7th Century and were the work of the sculptors of the Pallava dynasty.

**Day 11.** To Madurai: Fly to the temple town of Madurai, stay at the hotel for one night.

**Day 12.** To Thekkady: Morning tour of this famous town which boasts of the magnificient Meenakshi Temple, is even today a 'living' temple. Afternoon drive to Thekkady which is located in the cool of the Cardamom Hills, a beautiful area of tranquil winding roads, tea gardens, rubber estates and plantations growing pepper and coffee. Stay 2 nights at the village in Thekkady.

**Day 13.** Thekkady: Excursion to Periyar wildlife Reserve, famous for its herds of wild elephant and spectacular birdlife.

**Day 14.** To Kochi: Morning drive via Kottayam for lunch at Vembanad lake. After lunch travel to Allappey by boat along the famous 'backwaters'. These are a series of lagoons and waterways surrounded by a profusion of tropical vegetation. They cover thousands of acres adjacent to the Kerala coast where riverside village life can be observed all along the route. On arrival in Alleppey you will be met and driven to Kochi where you stay at the hotel on Willington Island for 2 nights.

**Day 15.** Kochi: Known as the 'Venice of the East', Kochi is a town characterised by its colonial influences and many canals. Morning visit to the Portuguese church of St. Francis, the Jewish Synagogue of 1568 and the Matancherry Palace, built by the Portuguese and renovated by the Dutch. In the late afternoon, cruise on the Pathiramanal along South India's most beautiful water route and watch the sunset from on board. Dinner will be served on board and you return to the hotel later in the evening.

**Day 16.** To Goa: A Portuguese colony until 1961, Goa has Mediterranean style houses. You arrive in the morning by plane from Kochi and transfer to the hotel.

**Day 17.** Goa: A morning excursion brings you to Old Goa, the former capital of the State, where you visit the Se Cathedral in the abandoned city. The afternoon is free to relax on Goa's famous beaches.

**Day 18.** To Bombay: After a morning of leisure, an early afternoon flight to Bombay, where a room will be at your disposal at the hotel until departure for the airport late at night.

**Day 19.** To USA: Early morning flight from Bombay to the USA.

## PROGRAMME – VII

**A Culinary Feast**

**17 Days; Delhi – Lucknow – Kolkata – Hyderabad – Mumbai – Goa – Mumbai**

**Day 1 and 2.** Depart from USA: Fly from your departure city in USA to India.

**Day 3.** Delhi: Arrive in Delhi and transfer to the hotel for 2 nights. Afternoon for leisure.

**Day 4.** Delhi: Morning visit to New Delhi, the capital city and a 'Jewel in the Crown' with its imperial British buildings, many of thich were designed by Sir Edwin Lutyens, the Qutab Minar and the Emperor Humayun's tomb. In the afternoon see the famous Red Fort, once the most opulent fort of the Mughal Empire, the Jama Masjid mosque, Raj Ghat, Old Delhi's bazaars and the thriving spice market. Dinner will be at the open-air Hauz Khas village.

**Day 5.** To Lucknow: Morning excursion to a private residence for demonstration of authentic Mughalai cooking, followed by lunch with your host. Late afternoon flight to Lucknow where you spend 2 nights at the hotel. Lucknawi delicacies for dinner at a special restaurant.

**Day 6.** Lucknow: Visit the elegant city. Visit the great Bara Imambara, Hussainabad Imambara with its golden dome and the Residency, the centrepiece of one of the most dramatic sieges of all time. Finish with a visit to the marketplaces which are the pulse and nerve centre of city life, selling an enormous array of delicious local foods. Special Avadhi dinner.

**Day 7.** To Kolkata: Morning cooking demonstration and afternoon for leisure before you take an evening flight to Calcutta. Spend 2 nights at the hotel.

**Day 8.** Kolkata: Early morning visit to the flower market by Howrah bridge followed by a visit to what is considered to be one of the India's finest botanical gardens, set amid lakes and lawns, sprawled along the west bank of the Hoogly. Travel to the gardens in the traditional way, by ferry. Evening drinks will be hosted at the much renowned Tollygune Club followed by a traditional Bengali dinner at the hotel.

**Day 9.** To Hyderabad: Morning tour of this remarkable city, visiting the Victoria Memorial. Afternoon flight to Hyderabad where you spend 2 nights at the hotel.

**Day 10.** Hyderabad: Hyderabad became famous as the capital of the fabulously wealthy Nizam of Hyderabad. Visit the impressive and strategically placed Golconda Fort, Charminar, the thriving Mecca Masjid and the market which was reputed to be the finest in India. Return to Golconda Fort in the evening for a stunning light-and- sound show in the ramparts followed by a special Hyderabadi dinner where you will sample some of the many specialties of the city's cuisine.

**Day 11.** To Mumbai: Morning flight to Mumbai, where you spend 2 nights at the hotel. In the afternoon, explore this bustling metropolis. See the Marine Drive, Malabar Hill and the Gateway of India. In the afternoon a demonstration of Indian cooking will be organised by the legendary chefs of the Grand Hotel.

**Day 12.** Mumbai: Morning visit to Crawford Market and the Punjabi Family Curry and Spice markets. Afternoon for leisure. Dinner will be hosted at a private home with a typical, tempting, local, cuisine.

**Day 13.** To Goa: Late morning flight to Goa where you spend 3 nights at the hotel. Evening cocktails at Sunset Point followed by a poolside barbecue, serving local and seafood specialities.

**Day 14.** Goa: A Portuguese colony until 1961, the city of Old Goa still retains strong Portuguese influences which you explore today, including the Se Cathedral. Later, visit local Fenni (Goan wine) production site and farmers market in Mapusa. Dinner will be at Case Portuguese on Baga Beach, with a specially prepared local menu.

**Day 15.** Goa: Full day for leisure, relaxing on Goa's exquisite beaches followed by a cooking demonstration in a private home where a typical Goan dinner will be served.

**Day 16.** To Mumbai: Return to Mumbai where a room will be at your disposal at the hotel until the time of your departure for the airport late at night.

**Day 17.** To USA: Early morning flight from Mumbai to USA.

## PROGRAMME – VIII

**East Meets West**

**16 Days: Mumbai – Goa – Kochi – Thiruvananthapuram – the Maldives**

**Day 1 and 2.** Depart from USA: Fly from your departure city in the USA to India.

**Day 3.** Mumbai/Goa: Arrive in Mumbai and transfer to the hotel for relaxation before an afternoon flight to Goa. Spend 4 nights at the hotel.

**Day 4.** Goa: Morning for leisure, relaxing on Goa's famous beaches. Afternoon, introduction to the Malabar Coast with a walk around the hotel's own Portuguese fort remains.

**Day 5.** Goa: Morning cruise up the Mandovi River to Old Goa for a look around the Cathedral of St. Catherine da Se, and many other churches, convents and basilicas surviving amidst the ruins of this grand 16th Century Portuguese city. Lunch at a typical Goan Restaurant with an opportunity to stroll around the present capital, Panaji. En route to the hotel, visit an Old Goan mansion.

**Day 6.** Goa: Morning visit to the wetland, up river to see the crocodiles and a good variety of local and migratory birds. Afternoon for leisure.

**Day 7.** To Kochi: Early morning flight to Kochi, the Venice of the East and stay 3 nights at the hotel on Willington Island. Afternoon, introduction to Kerala and its spice traders followed by a sunset cruise to the mouth of the harbour.

**Day 8.** Kochi: Morning visit to Matancherry to see India's oldest synagogue, Jew town and the Dutch Palace, followed by visits to India's first European church, St. Francis' Church at Fort Kochi and a fine merchant's home. Afternoon for leisure before visiting a private home in Ernakulam (Kochi's twin city) to see a demonstration of some of Kerals's magnificent dance and martial arts traditions and ayurvedic exercise and cures. Dinner will be served at a private residence.

**Day 9.** Kochi: Morning drive down to Allepey for a cruise through the backwaters of Kerala, along canals bordered by mango trees, village, paddy fields, where life is lived both beside and on the water. Lunch on the shores of Vembanad Lake, before returning to Allepey where you visit a small coir factory before returning to Kochi.

**Day 10.** To Thiruvananthapuram: Morning drive south through lush Kerala to Thiruvananthapuram, the hilly and spacious capital of Kerala, arriving in time to visit the Napier Museum in the Botanical Gardens and see the Padmanabhaswamy Temple (closed for entry to non-Hindus). Stay a night in Kovalam at the hotel.

### Tour Manager providing quality service

Only those who really provide good customer service have a hope of surviving in the business. Customer satisfaction is achieved not only to give them value for money, but also to get repeat business and good publicity.

# Inbound Tour Management

It must be remembered that each of your customers would like to feel feel special and making each one feel different is all that is required to retain the satisfied customer, as also get new business.

- Always acknowledge clients when you meet them. Smile and mean it
- Address clients courteously
- Look them in the eye when you speak
- Use their name whenever possible

**Key Points to Remember**

- Acquiring complete product knowledge
- Managing linkages with service suppliers
- Costing the package
- Managing business correspondence
- Controlling vouchers
- Briefing and counselling
- Planning and scheduling pick-ups and transfers
- Feedback assessments/analysis

**Inhouse Operations**

## Inbound

**1. Supervising Pickup Transfer and Hotel Check-ins**

- Transfer
- Flight number
- Name list
- Details of transport voucher
- Hotels name and address, rooming list and hotel voucher
- Greetings/Sign board, individual tourist placard giving name, country, coming from or company he/she represents.

**Field Operations**

## While receiving clients at airport, you need to have the following material ready

- Badge
- Uniform as prescribed
- Greeting board
- Name list
- Clipboard and pin, mobile phone or phone card or coins
- Tips or vouchers for porters
- Transport vouchers
- Hotel vouchers
- Welcome packs gifts
- Hotel registration cards and
- Your SMILE

## Identify your passenger

- Greet them
- Name of passenger

- Place arrived from
- Easily identifiable point
- Ensure this announcement is in the language the passenger speaks

### During the transfer give some basic information such as:
- The local time at that point of time
- Explain the local currency and where money can be changed
- Weather/climate and
- Explain the next event on their programme.

### After their long journey, avoid the temptation to talk non-stop as your clients are tired.
- You may, however, give some general information about the route if you find the time is right.
- Now your clients are on their way to their rooms, but your job is still not over.
- You must ensure that you have a copy of the rooming list with room numbers on it.

### Check List
- Check rooming list with hotel
- Call airline for – ETA
- Be in good time
- Check whereabouts of vehicle
- Help with porters and tip wherever necessary
- Ensure all passengers and bags are present before moving off
- State journey time and kilometers/miles
- Comment on route
- Collect air tickets/e-tickets for reconfirmation of onward sector
- On arrival go ahead to reception
- Activate porters
- See all clients to rooms (smile)
- Wait till all is quiet and
- Depart

### Departure Transfer
- Brief clients in writing and in advance
- Brief hotel and porters to be ready
- Be at hotel early
- Ask reception if everyone has paid extra
- Gather up clients, phone rooms of those who do not appear
- Each client to confirm their bags
- Remind clients to

- Pay extra
- Return keys
- Empty safe deposits and
- Have passports and tickets in hand luggage
- Load passengers
- Depart for airport
- Drive as close as possible to check-in-area.
- Before leaving wish them a safe and happy journey home and that they will come back again.
- Sound as if you mean it
- While saying goodbye some passengers may offer small gifts/tips. Thank for these but NEVER solicit them.
- Assist with getting porters/trolleys.
- Assist with check in procedures/airport tax paying, etc.
- Escort to security and passport control

When all have gone inside you can leave but not before the plane has departed. If there is a delay before the clients have gone inside you are still responsible for them.

# 7
# OUTBOUND TOUR MANAGEMENT

> **Chapter Objectives**
>
> After reading this chapter the reader should be able to:
> - Understand the nature and meaning of an outbound tour.
> - Know about major outbound markets.
> - Identify the requirements of outbound tourists.
> - Understand handling of outbound tourists.
> - Know the reasons for growth in outbound traffic.
> - Identify the most popular outbound destinations in Europe and USA.
> - Learn about terms and conditions of tour.
> - Profile of outbound tourists.
> - Learn about tour costing and presentation.

Outbound tourism involves residents of a particular country travelling to another country. Vacationing abroad is known as outbound tourism.

The various marketing and promotional activities undertaken by the tourism boards have made a significant impact on the local market. Singapore tourism board, Malaysian tourism board, Finland tourism board, BTA Swiss Tourism and many others etc., have seen a remarkable improvement in their markets, due to their promotional efforts undertaken in India.

Apart form the major metro cities, people from the second tier and third tier cities have started travelling in large numbers. Many tour operators are offering packages at affordable prices because of the stiff competition they face in the local market, which is cited as another good reason for outbound tourism to grow in India.

Change in the way airlines have marketed their product, by promoting cheaper airfares has made air travel abroad more affordable along with flexible pay patterns, and banks coming forward to offer loans for vacationing.

Both the private and the public sector banks have tied up with many reputed tour operators to provide these facilities for the customers with easy EMI patterns, pay later facilities. This has increased the buyers of tour packages.

The Indian government has relaxed certain rules and increased its facilities in issuing passports for the Indian citizens. The visa formality for various countries has been relaxed as also visa on arrival, to increase the tourist inflow to their countries. The upper limit for foreign exchange for travel abroad has been revised by RBI, all this has contributed to the boost of outbound travel in India.

## The Major Markets for Outbound Tourism

Indians' destination preferences are highly influenced by factors like the internet, friends and relatives, Bollywood movies, location of the corporate head quarters, etc. According to the Indian tourism department the statistics shows that Indians travelled in large numbers to Singapore due to its proximity and popularity among Indians as the most preferred destination outbound.

Tourism boards of various countries are now targeting India as one of their most potential future markets. Various countries like Taiwan, U.S.A, China, Singapore, Gulf, Malaysia are receiving an increased number of tourists

Volume of outbound tourist from our country:

## (COUNTRYWISE) MAJOR OUTBOUND MARKETS VISITED BY THE INDIANS

**TABLE 4.1.1**
**NUMBER OF INDIAN NATIONALS' DEPARTURES FROM INDIA, 1991 TO 2017**

| Year | No. of Indian Nationals' departures from India | Percentage change over the previous year |
|---|---|---|
| 1991 | 1942707 | -14.8 |
| 1992 | 2161301 | 11.3 |
| 1993 | 2733304 | 26.5 |
| 1994 | 2734830 | 0.1 |
| 1995 | 3056360 | 11.8 |
| 1996 | 3463783 | 13.3 |
| 1997 | 3725820 | 7.6 |
| 1998 | 3810908 | 2.3 |
| 1999 | 4114820 | 8.0 |
| 2000 | 4415513 | 7.3 |
| 2001 | 4564477 | 3.4 |
| 2002 | 4940244 | 8.2 |
| 2003 | 5350896 | 8.3 |
| 2004 | 6212809 | 16.1 |
| 2005 | 7184501 | 15.6 |
| 2006 | 8339614 | 16.1 |
| 2007 | 9783232 | 17.3 |
| 2008 | 10867999 | 11.1 |
| 2009 | 11066072 | 1.8 |
| 2010 | 12988001 | 17.4 |
| 2011 | 13994002 | 7.7 |
| 2012 | 14924755 | 6.7 |
| 2013 | 16626316 | 11.4 |
| 2014 | 18332319 | 10.3 |
| 2015 | 20376307 | 11.1 |
| 2016 | 21871995 | 7.3 |
| 2017 | 23942957 | 9.5 |

*Source: Bureau of Immigration, India*

### TABLE 4.3.1
### PORT-WISE DEPARTURES OF INDIAN NATIONALS' DEPARTURES FROM INDIA, 2010 - 2017

| S. No. | Port/ Land Check post | 2010 | 2011 | 2012 | 2013 | 2014 | 2015 | 2016 | 2017 | % Share in 2017 |
|---|---|---|---|---|---|---|---|---|---|---|
| 1 | Delhi (Airport) | 2621535 | 3009762 | 3226344 | 3517589 | 3494923 | 4092035 | 4475300 | 5119669 | 21.38 |
| 2 | Mumbai (Airport) | 3031822 | 3264653 | 3501739 | 3734176 | 4146539 | 4474820 | 4692109 | 5097038 | 21.29 |
| 3 | Cochin (Airport) | 1022233 | 1098333 | 1205315 | 1390833 | 1610742 | 1960220 | 2190681 | 2215214 | 9.25 |
| 4 | Chennai (Airport) | 1450521 | 1540106 | 1620314 | 1730503 | 1803368 | 1900570 | 1999412 | 2078070 | 8.68 |
| 5 | Hyderabad (Airport) | 740350 | 777540 | 810903 | 925401 | 1068658 | 1274431 | 1313670 | 1395090 | 5.83 |
| 6 | Calicut (Airport) | 904130 | 970961 | 986463 | 1112297 | 1178769 | 1106353 | 1110940 | 1353560 | 5.65 |
| 7 | Bengaluru (Airport) | 664083 | 746051 | 810108 | 852591 | 953558 | 1143585 | 1240313 | 1353255 | 5.65 |
| 8 | Trivandrum (Airport) | 751861 | 677998 | 739698 | 854564 | 924216 | 1013203 | 1037257 | 1095913 | 4.58 |
| 9 | Kolkata (Airport) | 411210 | 453682 | 502802 | 562907 | 591621 | 712522 | 752497 | 832156 | 3.48 |
| 10 | Trichy (Airport) | 205750 | 248384 | 267968 | 321083 | 417346 | 455323 | 463888 | 532504 | 2.22 |
| 11 | Others | 1184506 | 1206532 | 1253101 | 1624372 | 1842579 | 2243245 | 2595928 | 2870488 | 11.99 |
| | Total | 12988001 | 13994002 | 14924755 | 16626316 | 18332319 | 20376307 | 21871995 | 23942957 | 100.00 |
| | % Share of Top 3 | 51.40 | 52.69 | 53.16 | 51.98 | 52.11 | 51.66 | 51.93 | 51.92 | - |
| | % Share of Top 10 | 90.88 | 91.38 | 91.60 | 90.23 | 89.95 | 88.99 | 88.13 | 88.01 | - |

Source:- Bureau of Immigration

## Statistics of Outbound Indians

The outbound tourism market in India indicates a strong preference for holidaying abroad, 76% of vacation seekers propose to visit an international destination.

**Requirements of Outbound tourists**

### DOCUMENTATION:

**Passport**

Acquiring a passport is much easier and faster nowadays, the government of India has taken many steps to simplify the process of acquiring a passport by opening many regional offices, online application and tracking facility, tatkaal passport, etc. The document is issued from 28 locations across the country and 160 Indian missions abroad. The time taken to issue an ordinary Indian passport has been reduced from 60 days to 30 days. The convenience of acquiring a passport has encouraged many Indians to apply and obtain a passport.

## Visa
The information of visa processing was never clear, the passenger were always doubtful about the procedure and documentation of visa papers. Today many countries are posting their requirements on their websites.

Many facilitating services and staff are available to assist the passenger to process the visa correctly. South East Asian countries and a few African countries have relaxed their visa rules in order to promote tourism. This is another significant reason why outbound tourism has improved in India. Many countries have allowed tourists the facility of visa on arrival.

## Better connectivity:
Many airlines are now operating into India, they have better connectivity directly or through code share or alliances. This has reduced the waiting time of the passenger en-route on transits.

## New destinations:
The Indian market is looking for newer destinations like Greece and Turkey, the outbound tourism today is very competitive and has to offer the well read customer options of a varied nature. Identification of new places to visit has increased the interest among the tourists.

## Better packages:
Cheaper packages, more options, increased services both pre and post sales is another requirement for an outbound passenger.

## Safety and security:
One of the most import aspects for an outbound tourist is his safety and security.

The common problems faced by tourists concerning safety issues are:
- Theft
- Sickness
- Unexpected political unrest
- Racism
- Frisking, this leads to unnecessary mental agony, etc.

An outbound tourist should be aware of all such risks and prepare and plan for a safe holiday abroad.

Proper planning ensures good quality.
The quality deliverance of a product depends on the following:
- Through product knowledge
- Knowledge of countries involved
- Flexible packages
- Personalised services
- Experience in handling groups
- Positive attitude

## Handling Outbound Groups:

- People handling skills
- Good language

Group handling techniques differ, depending on the size of the group. Smaller groups would require more personalised services and attention on every little aspect of the package. Larger groups demand more planning and meticulous coordination of the various activities. Such groups will be in touch with the tour operator throughout the tour, either through the tour manager or through the group leader.

## Reasons for Growth

The liberalisation of the economy gave birth to increased business opportunities in India both within the country and internationally. The growth of various corporates required executives to travel frequently, which gave birth to corporate travel. Increased global business, better employment, increased disposable income made holidaying possible for a middle class Indian. Outbound tourism increased in India due to various factors like change in the customer's attitude, people believed in earning and splurging their money on merry activities unlike in the yesteryears. The attitude of the society is slowly undergoing a change with advent of the internet and media.

Internet and media increased global exposure of the common man leading to awareness about the world and various facilities available.

With the implementation of Open Sky Policy in India, the number of airlines operating within and to other countries increased. Many European and American carriers started operating into India.

India was viewed as one of the most potential markets for various businesses. The potential Indian market invited many investors and multinational corporate business firms got a footing in India and this indirectly contributed to the need for travel inland and outbound, hospitality and related services.

India's outbound market has been growing rapidly over the past few years. If we look at the numbers the market has grown from about 3 million seven years ago to plus 9 million in the year 2010. Several tour operators advertise package tours to various destinations and there has been intense competition amongst them to get a share of the outbound tour market. Although European package tours continue to be extremely popular but lately South East Asia has emerged as the top outbound tour market.

The potential of outbound tour markets is very high and more and more foreign countries are setting up their representative offices in India to lure Indians to visit their countries. In the past few years a large number of countries from Europe and south East Asia have set-up their marketing and promotional offices in India.

### India-Outbound Market

The India outbound market refers to the travellers exiting India. In other words, tourist outflow from India to other countries comprises the outbound travel segment. As stated above the Indian outbound market has grown slowly but steadily over the past few years. This steady growth was seen as a result of increasing spending power of the middle-income groups as well as availability of more leisure time. The higher standards of living in the vast middle-income group of population has resulted in a big flow of Indian travellers exploring the world as tourists.

The concept of travelling just for "going" to a place has caught up travellers from India and many attractive, economical tour packages are made available to the travelling public. Intra-regional travel as between SARC countries and between the countries of South Asia, is on the rise and at times affordable as well. Travelling abroad seems to be the order of the day and in upper class social circles, it is like a fashion.

## Potential of Indian Outbound Market

The order of most preferred countries as a destination is as follows;
- Europe and North America
- United Kingdom
- Canada
- France
- Germany
- Italy
- Switzerland
- South East Asian regions (Malaysia, Singapore)

In this category the most popular destination are Singapore, Malaysia, Thailand, Hong Kong and Australia.

## Profile of Outbound Travellers

Over the years the face of Indian Outbound tourism has changed a lot. Earlier there were Reserve Bank of India (RBI) restriction in foreign exchange, which posed an obstacle to outbound tourist travel. Only people in the higher income bracket used to travel abroad for business

**Main reason for outbound travel:**
- Business
- Holidays
- VFR- Visiting friends and relatives
- Attending conferences and conventions

**Accommodation used most often while travelling abroad.**
- 3 star and budget hotels are the most preferred form of accommodation.
- Staying with friends and relatives, especially for those who are travelling to USA, UK and Australia.

**Period of Travel**
- The last month of the school vacation is the most popular moth for travelling abroad. USA seems to be chosen destination during this month (May) followed by UK and Australia.
- June, also a month of school and college vacation is the second favourite time for travelling abroad. Australia is the favoured destination for this month followed by USA.
- December and January are the other months for travelling abroad. Favoured destinations in these months are Hong Kong followed by Singapore, Malaysia and UK.

## Outbound Tourist Data

The compilation of outbound tourist statistics is done through Embarkation Cards. The total count of port-wise departures by Indian Nationals for visiting other countries is being compiled through this card. However, other details like purpose, destination of visit, duration of visit, etc., are not compiled from the Embarkation Card. From the data available concerning port-wise departure of Indian nationals going abroad, it is observed that Mumbai and Delhi International airports, are the most important departure ports for outbound tours. This is followed by Chennai, Trivandrum and Kochi, and Hyderabad airports.

### Major Outbound Destinations

The important outbound destinations being promoted by the tour operators are as follows:

**Brussels, Amsterdam and Paris**

**Day 1:** London-Brussels, Belgium.

Leave early in the morning from your London hotel and head through the lush English countryside to the Channel port, where you board a ferry for the continent. Here the tour director and luxury coach meet you and continue to Brussels.

**Day 2.** Brussels-Windmills of Kinderdijk, Holland, Amsterdam area.

Brussels, the modern centre of the European Union, still has its old world charm. Enjoy the sights of this fantastic city on an optional city sightseeing tour with a local guide. Leave Belgium past Antwerp into Holland for a stop to see the 19 windmills of Kinderdijk. Next, bypass the great port of Rotterdam before reaching the Amsterdam area for an overnight stay.

**Day 3.** Amsterdam.

A whole day to explore this colourful and fascinating city. Start the day with an included visit to a diamond factory to watch the cutting and polishing of precious stones. Included sightseeing features a drive with a local guide pointing out the city's highlights and finally a canal cruise to see the town from the water.

**Day 4.** Amsterdam area-Paris, France

Retrace your route at first, then cross into Flanders and drive across the farmland and cornfields of the Ile de France to Paris for an overnight stay.

**Day 5.** Paris

A day to get the feel of this magnificent city. The included sightseeing excursion starts with many of the best-known Parisian sights: La Sorbonne, Boulevard St. Germain, the Eiffel Tower, the Opera, the Champs Elysees and the Rue de Rivoli. Make the most of your time and visit the great Palace of Versailles on the optional excursion or join the optional Eiffel Tower and Seine cruise.

**Day 6.** Paris-London, England

A last look at Paris as your coach heads north to the coast, where you board your Channel ferry. Return to London through Kent for an evening arrival.

## European Introduction

**Day 1. London-Brussels, Belgium**

Leave in the early morning from your London joining hotel and head through the lush English countryside to the Channel port, where you board your ferry for the Continent. Here your tour director and a comfortable coach wait to take you to Brussels for an overnight stay.

**Day 2.** Brussels – Black Forest Area, Germany.

Brussels, the modern centre of the European Union, still has old-world charm. Enjoy the sights, including the Grand Place and the Mannekin Pis on your morning orientation drive. Later travel south via Heidelberg for a stop, then through the delightful scenery of the Black Forest for an overnight stay.

**Day 3.** Black Forest – Lake Titisee – Rhine falls – Liechtenstein – Lake Lucerne, Switzerland.

Today's itinerary is studded with quite a few highlights. Travel into the heart of the Black Forest for a stop to admire the small but lovely Lake Titisee. Further south into Switzerland to see the tiny but hugely wealthy principality of Liechtenstein, for a stop in its capital, Vaduz. By evening you'll be in the Lake Lucerne area for an overnight stay.

**Day 4.** Lucerne.

Your sightseeing takes you to the impressive city walls, a covered wooden bridge, ornate patrician houses lining cobblestone streets, and the Lion Monument. Don't miss the boat trip on the lake. A grand selection of optional activities completes the day: a cable car ride to the 10,000-foot summit of Mount Titlis, a typical folklore evening, and, of course, time to shop for that Swiss watch.

**Day 5.** Lake Lucerne – Interlaken – Lausanne

Start the day by driving over the scenic Brunig Pass to Brienz and its sparkling lake. After some sightseeing in beautiful Interlaken, continue to Gruyere, where you stop awhile. On to lake Geneva for a guided visit to Chillon Castle right on its shores. Overnight on Lausanne.

**Day 6.** Lausanne – Paris, France.

Travel through Burgundy to pretty Beaune, then on the expressway northwards to Paris. Tonight's optional cabaret show is a must.

**Day 7.** Paris.

Included sightseeing with a local expert of many of the best-known Parisian sights: La Sorbonne, Arc de Triomphe, Opera, Madeleine, the Eiffel Tower, the Pyramid near the Louvre, the Invalides, and Champs Elysees. Optional excursions are also available to the Palace and Gardens of Versailles and, to celebrate the success of your tour, a French farewell dinner might be just the ticket.

**Day 8.** Paris – London, England

Relax and let the countryside whiz by on the road north to the coast, where you board your Channel ferry. Return to London through Kent for an evening arrival.

## European Jewels

**Day 1.** London Amsterdam Area, Holland.

Leave early in the morning from your London joining hotel and head through the lush English countryside to the Channel port, where you board your ferry for the continent. Here you meet your tour director and join your luxury coach for the drive to the Amsterdam area.

**Day 2.** Amsterdam Area – the Rhineland, Germany.

A morning to enjoy Holland's busy metropolis. After you included visit to a famous diamond centre, it's time for morning sightseeing with a local guide pointing out the city highlights; finally a canal cruise to see Amsterdam at water level. In the afternoon travel southwards to reach the Rhineland for an overnight stay.

**Day 3.** Rhineland – Romantic Road – Munich.

Start the day with a scenic drive along the shores of the Rhine or opt for a Rhine cruise. Admire the pretty villages; the castles perched high above the river, and the numerous terraced vineyards. Next, a drive along the Romantic Road, through towns and villages protected by medieval tower gates and battlements, with squares of half-timbered houses and richly decorated fountains. Stop awhile in Rothenburg. Overnight in Munich.

**Day 4.** Munich – Innsbruck, Austria – Venice Area, Italy.

A fast drive from Munich to Austria for a stop in the capital of the Tyrol, Innsbruck. In the afternoon drive over the Brenner Pass into the Dolomites for a stop in the world famous resort of Cortina, before the descent into the Piave Valley to the Venice area.

**Day 5.** Morning in Venice-Florence Area.

The included tour starts with a boat ride and is followed by highlights such as a visit to St. Mark's Basilica and a chance to watch Ventian glass blowers fashion their delicate objects as they did centuries ago. Southwards into the hilly Tuscan countryside to reach the Florence area for overnight. End the day by joining the optional Tuscan dinner in a typical restaurant.

**Day 6.** Florence.

This Renaissance gem and City of the Medicis will keep you enthralled for a whole day. Traffic is banned in part of the historic centre, so visitors can wander at leisure and admire the city's timeless beauty in relative peace and quiet. Don't miss out on the included walking tour with a local guide that features most of the city highlights. You will see the Piazza Santa Croce; the beautiful Piazza Signoria; the Palazzo Vecchio and its courtyard; the Loggia dei Lanzi; and, to top it all, the Piazza del Duomo and it's cathedral with the Giotto Campanile, and the magnificent East Door of the Baptistry known as the "Gate to Paradise."

**Day 7.** Florence Area – Lake Lucerne, Switzerland.

Across the Lombardy Plain this morning to Italian Switzerland's subtropical resort of Lugano. Here you take a break to stroll along the lakeside promenade, before climbing towards the St. Gotthard tunnel. Emerge on the German-speaking side of Switzerland and then descend into the gentle landscape around Lake Lucerne. Time to enjoy an optional Swiss Folklore evening.

**Day 8.** Lake Lucerne-Paris, France.

This morning join an optional boat trip. Then visit a green pastures and attractive chalets with rustic timbering and luxuriant flowers. Then into France, on the fast and comfortable highway, past some of its most famous vineyards, to Paris. Arrive in time to enjoy an optional cabaret show.

**Day 9.** Paris.

Included sightseeing with a local expert of many of the best-known Parisian sights; La Sorbonne, Arc de Triomphe, Opera, Madeleine, the Eiffel tower, the Pyramid near the Louvres, Invalides and Champs Elysees. (Itinerary and sights may be altered due to newly enforced traffic and parking regulations). Optional excursions are also available to the Palace and Gardens of Versailles and, to celebrate the success of your tour, a French farewell dinner might be just the ticket.

**Day 10.** Paris-London, England.

Relax and let the countryside whiz by on the road north to the coast, where you board your Channel ferry. Return to London through Kent for and evening arrival.

### The Best Of Italy & France

11 Days

**Day 1.** Arrival in Rome, Italy.

Time to rest or start exploring the Eternal City. At 6 p.m. meet your tour director and travelling companions and leave the hotel for a special welcome dinner with in one of Rome's lively restaurants.

**Day 2.** Rome.

Sightseeing with your local guide starts with a visit to the Vatican Museum and Sistine Chapel, world famous for Michelangelo's ceiling paintings and The Last Judgment. Continue to monumental St. Peter's Square and Basilica. Cross the Tiber and visit the Colosseum and the Roman Forum, where Roman Legions marched in Triumph. Then time for independent activities and exciting optional excursion possibilities.

**Day 3.** Rome – Assisi – Venice.

Morning break in peaceful Assisi. Visit the massive 13th-century Sistine of St. Francis built above the saint's grave. A kaleidoscope of Italian landscapes parades past the coach windows on the way to the Adriatic coast and across the Po Delta to Venice. Why not join an optional dinner Venetian-style tonight?

**Day 4.** Venice.

Start morning sightseeing in style by Private Boat to meet your local guide. Highlights of your walking tour, are St. Mark's Square and the Byzantine Basilica, the lavish Doges' Palace, and the Bridge of Sighs.

Also watch skilled glass blowers fashion their delicate objects in an age old traditional manner. Then enjoy Venice at your own pace or join an optional cruise to Burano Island.

**Day 5.** Venice – Ferrara – Florence.

First stop this morning in Ferrara. Stroll past the imposing Este Castle and visit the marble Cathedral before continuing through the wooded Apennine Mountains into Tuscany to Florence, cradle of the Renaissance. Time to wander on your own at whim or to check out the enticing shops with Florentine leather goods and gold jewellery. You may want to join one of the exciting evenings optional.

**Day 6.** Florence.

A local guide takes you on a walking tour through the heart of Florence. See the magnificent Cathedral, Giotto's Bell Tower, the Baptistry's heavy bronze "Gate of Paradise," and the sculpture-studded Signoria square. Top it off with admiring Michelangelo's celebrated David in the Academy of Fine Arts. Afternoon at leisure.

**Day 7.** Florence-Pisa-Nice, France.

Focus on Pisa this morning for pictures of its amazing Leaning Tower, 180 feet high and 12 feet out of the perpendicular. Then a scenic drive past a string of Italian and French Riviera resorts towards the principality of Monaco. Here, leave the highway for the panoramic Moyenne Corniche. Before arriving in Nice, visit one of the Perfume Factories for which the area is famous. An optional outing is available tonight to Monte Carlo.

**Day 8.** Nice. Excursion to Cannes and St. Paul de Vence.

Follow the glittering shores of the Cote d'Azur to Cannes of film festival fame. Turn inland to visit the picturesque hilltop town of St. Paul de Vence. Then spend the afternoon in the blue Mediterranean or stroll along the elegant Promenade des Anglais.

**Day 9.** Nice-Marseilles-Paris.

A scenic drive along the comfortable highway to Marseilles, where you board the high-speed "TGV" train to Paris. Tonight an optional possibility to try out the one of Paris' fine restaurants and to explore the City of Light!

**Day 10.** Paris.

Discover the world's capital of chic and style with a local guide and admire its most famous sights: the Opera, Arc de Triomphe, Champs-Elysees, Notre Dame Cathedral, and more. For a bird's eye view take the elevator to the second floor of Paris' most famous landmark, the Eiffel Tower. An optional excursion to the lavish baroque of Versailles is available. Tonight a lively cabaret show might just be the ticket.

**Day 11.**

The vacation ends with breakfast in the morning.

# SWITZERLAND

8 Days

**Day 1.** Arrival in Zurich, Switzerland.

Time to rest or to discover Zurich's attractive historic centre and lakeside promenade. At 6 p.m. meet your travelling companions for a welcome drink hosted by your tour director.

**Day 2.** Zurich – Liechtenstein – St. Moritz.

First an orientation about Zurich, Switzerland's centre of banking and commerce. Then, east along Lake Zurich and Lake Walen to the tiny principality of Liechtenstein. After a break in Vaduz ascend the Rhine Valley into the mountainous Grisons, a canton where three of the country's four languages are spoken. The 7,504-foot Julier Pass, an important Alpine road since Roman times, leads to the Engadine. This valley is considered by many as the most beautiful mountain area in the world with deep-blue lakes, airy larch forests that turn golden in the fall, mountain peaks exceeding 12,000 feet, and quaint villages with massive white stone houses in the characteristic Grisons style. Afternoon at leisure in ritzy St. Mortiz.

**Day 3.** St. Moritz – Lugano.

A gradual change of scenery as you descend towards the enchanting shores of the Italian Lake Como and continue on to the southern tip of Switzerland. The vegetation south of the Alps is Mediterranean, chestnut groves, vineyards, olive and fig trees make you forget that earlier today you were within walking distance of glaciers. Afternoon arrival in the popular subtropical resort town of Lugano allows time for shopping under the arcades of Via Nassa, an espresso on flower-festooned Piazza Riforma, or a stroll along the lake with a magnificent view of the Swiss Alps.

**Day 4.** Lugano – Stresa, Italy – Zermatt.

From Lake Lugano to the Italian shore of Lake Maggiore for a break in elegant Stresa. Weather permitting, an optional boat ride to the enchanting Isol Bella can be arranged. On over the Lofty Simplon pass into the Swiss Valais, an area renowned for its excellent wines and Great Mountain resorts. To reach the most famous of them, leave the coach behind in Tasch and board a mountain train, climbing the last few miles up to Zermatt, a picturesque cluster of rustic chalets beneath the Matterhorn.

**Day 5.** Zermatt – Gruyere.

Morning at leisure. A suggestion: ride Europe's highest rack railway to 10,272-foot Gornergrat for a breathtaking panoramic view of the Alps. In the afternoon motor through the vineyards and apricot groves of the lower Rhone Valley to the shores of Lake Geneva. Here visit Chillon Castle, the 12th-century water fortress immortalised by the poet Lord Byron, before continuing to your hotel in the Gruyere region.

**Day 6.** Gruyere-Berne-Lucerne.

Travel along an excellent highway along some of the country's best farmlands to its stately capital, Berne. Sightseeing with a local guide starts at the popular Bear Pit and then focuses on the monumental Federal Palace and the beautifully preserved medieval Old Town. Witness the hourly parade of painted figures at the Clock Tower and take your pictures of ornate, flower-adorned fountains. After lunch, continue east through the verdant diary country of Emmental. On the way visit a cheese factory to learn how one of Switzerland's prime exports is made. Tonight you are in picture book Lucerne.

**Day 7.** Lucerne.

On your walking tour this morning, admire Thorwaldsen's Lion Monument; the ornate patrician houses of the walled Old Town, then cross the famous covered Chapel Bridge to the Jesuit Church. Afterwards shop for watches and choose from our optional activities: climb a mountain by cable car; take a cruise on the fjord-like lake; sign up for a folklore party with yodeling and alphorn blowing for a first-hand impression of Alpine merrymaking and a fitting goodbye to Switzerland.

**Day 8.** Lucerne – Zurich.

Home bound flight, morning transfer to Zurich airport where the vacation ends. Extra nights are available in Zurich, not Lucerne.

## SUPER SAVER USA

**Day 01.** Mumbai – New York.

Depart by Lufthansa for New York. Arrive New York and check into Hotel Pennsylvania. Later visit the Empire State Building. Enjoy the Indian dinner.

**Day 02.** New York – Washington.

After breakfast check out of the hotel and proceed for a city tour of New York including the Statue of Liberty, enjoy the Indian lunch. Later proceed to the station to board the Amtrak to Washington. On arrival transfer to Hotel Howard Johnson or a similar hotel.

**Day 03.** Washington – Orlando

After breakfast, check out of the hotel and proceed for a city tour of Washington. Later proceed to the airport to board your flight to Orlando. On arrival check into Hotel Hampton Inn or a similar hotel. Later, proceed for dinner.

**Day 04.** Orlando (Disney World's Magic Kingdom)

After breakfast, full day visit to Disney World's magic Kingdom. Evening enjoy the Indian dinner.

**Day 05.** Orlando (Epcot Centre)

After breakfast proceed for a full day at Epcot Centre.

**Day 06.** Orlando (Sea World)- Las Vegas.

After breakfast, check out of the hotel and proceed to Sea World. Afternoon board your flight for Las Vegas. Arrive Las Vegas and check into Hotel Excalibur or a similar hotel.

**Day 07.** Las Vegas – Los Angeles.

After breakfast, day free for personal activities at Las Vegas, try your luck at one of the casinos. Later in the evening proceed to the airport to board your flight for Los Angeles. On arrival at Los Angeles check into Hotel Holiday Inn or a similar hotel.

**Day 08.** Los Angeles – New York

After breakfast, check out of the hotel. Proceed to the Universal studios. Later enjoy your Indian dinner and proceed to the airport to board your flight for New York.

**Day 09.** New York – Frankfurt.

Arrival New York early morning. Late evening depart by Lufthansa for India.

**Day 10** Frankfurt – Mumbai.

## JEWELS OF USA

**Day 01.** Mumbai – New York

Depart by flight for New York. On arrival at John F. Kennedy airport, your tour director will meet you after you have completed the immigration and customs. Later transfer to your Hotel Pennsylvania or a similar hotel. Take an exciting ride on the Beast. Later proceed to Ground Zero of the World Trade Center.

Enjoy a spectacular view of Manhattan, from this classy restaurant. Enjoy the dinner at Top of the World restaurant. Later return to the hotel.

**Day 02.** New York – Washington.

After breakfast proceed for a city tour of New York, which will include New York's most celebrated skyscraper – The Empire State Building. Later visit The Statue of Liberty, holding her torch aloft. This includes the ferry ride to Liberty Island. Proceed to Penn Station for a unique experience on the American railway – Amtrak. On arrival at Union Station, check into Hotel Howard Johnson or a similar hotel. Indian dinner will be served at the restaurant.

**Day 03.** Washington – Buffalo – Niagara Falls.

After breakfast, a city tour of Washington. The first stop will be at the Abraham Lincoln Memorial and then a brief stop outside the White House. Later the Capital Building, and then to the National Air and Space Museum. Enjoy the lunch. Fly to Buffalo. Check into Hotel Travel Lodge Falls View or a similar hotel.

**Day 04.** Niagara Falls – Toronto – Niagara Falls.

After an American breakfast, proceed to Niagara Falls and view it from the American side and the Canadian Side (Canadian Visa required). Enjoy the thrilling and damp boat ride on The Maid of the Mist, which will take you very close to the Falls. (Maid of the Mist will be subject to operations. In case the Maid of the Mist is not operational, you will enjoy the Scenic Tunnel for which you require a Canadian visa). Later we will proceed to Toronto in Canada (you need to be in possession of Canadian visa). At Toronto you will have a panoramic city tour, which will include the C.N. Tower. Enjoy the delicious Indian lunch at the restaurant. Later return to Niagara. Enjoy the breathtaking view of the illuminated Niagara Falls.

(Passengers require a multiple entry U.S. visa and a Canadian visa in order to take the tour to Toronto. Those not in the possession of the above visas will return to the hotel and have a free day).

**Day 05.** Buffalo – Orlando.

After breakfast take a helicopter ride (subject to weather conditions) over Niagara Falls. Later proceed to the airport to board your flight for Orlando. On arrival at Orlando, check into Hotel Hampton Inn or a similar hotel. Enjoy the dinner.

**Day 06.** Orlando (Walt Disney World's Magic kingdom)

After breakfast leave for Walt Disney World's Magic Kingdom. Evening return to the hotel. Enjoy the Indian dinner at the restaurant.

**Day 07.** Orlando (Epcot Centre)

After breakfast proceed to Epcot Centre the experimental Prototype Community of Tomorrow – is the high tech counterpart of Magic Kingdom. On return enjoy the Indian dinner at the restaurant.

**Day 08.** Orlando – Sea World – Animal Kingdom.

After breakfast proceed to Sea World which is one of the world's largest Marine Parks. Later proceed to Animal kingdom – Disney's newest theme park. Evening enjoy dinner at Planet Hollywood.

**Day 09.** Orlando – (Ballooning/ Belz/ Sterling Casino Lines)

You all must have read 'Around the world in 80 days', and always wanted to try out flying in a hot air balloon. Here you have a chance (subject to weather conditions.) Raj has always tried to give its valued clients something unique. Today you will be up early. Our program begins at 6 am with a pre-flight briefing. We then board our vehicles and head off to one of our 25 launch sites depending on the wind direction. All passengers are invited to join in the inflation process as your balloon comes to life. We will fly for about half an hour. Your pilot will point out all the spectacular sites of our area. Your breakfast today shall be a boxed breakfast. Later return to the hotel. You have time to visit America's largest factory outlet Belz. You will need to make your own way to the Belz factory outlet. Belz Factory outlet World is the largest non-anchored factory outlet centre of its kind in the country with 700,000 sq. ft. and over four strip centres. Belz Factory Outlet World, Orlando has a population of over 32 million tourists per year. Talk about huge, this place is incredible. Just about every manufacturer you could dream of is here, offering you fantastic discounts on popular brands. Not just one or two stores, but 155 factory outlets all in one place, which makes it America's largest factory outlet centre. Raj offers you special discount vouchers.

Later in the evening welcome to Florida's finest and largest, casino, ship, the Sterling Casino Line, 75000 sq ft of Las Vegas style gaming and excitement. Located at Port Canaveral just 45 minutes form Orlando on the Space Coast, Sterling Casino Lines truly brings Las Vegas to Florida with this world-class ship! You'll enjoy 5 hours of Las Vegas style gaming and excitement. Experience the luxurious feel of an ambience of a full size Cruise Ship, with 4 Casinos, 1000 of the 'Loosest Slots' in the world, Las Vegas style entertainment and dancing, free Ambassador Club membership, 5 cocktail lounges, 50 table games.

Enjoy the deli-style buffet with unlimited coffee and soda. (Only passengers above the age of 21 years are permitted on board the cruise. Those below the stipulated age have to stay back at the hotel. The meal is on board the cruise. Passengers staying back will need to make their own arrangement for dinner). Late night return to the hotel

**Day 10.** Orlando – New York- Frankfurt

Today after breakfast we depart by flight for New York to connect to the flight for India.

Day 11. Frankfurt – Mumbai

**Tour Costing and presentation**

Tour costing and presentation is crucial for both inbound as well as outbound tourists.

It is important to understand components of tour pricing such as fixed and variable cost, unit price of costing, participant estimation and cost plus pricing. The details of tour cost worksheet and how to calculate the total net cost of a tour are explained as follows:

Providing an existing tour for the client while generating a profit for the travel professional is one of the most challenging aspects of the tour business. How do you provide value to the client, yet make a necessary profit? The answer lies in a methodical approach to tour pricing. There are many ways to price a tour, but ultimately most, if not all, are based on an analysis of fixed and variable costs, client volume, and profit margins.

**Tour Pricing**

Fixed costs can be defined as all the expenses that will remain the same regardless of how many clients take the tour. Examples of fixed costs include the expense of developing and mailing brochures and promotional materials, advertising, staff and escort salaries, and chartered transportation such as motor coaches. The last example, motor coaches, can be used to illustrate fixed costs. For example, the cost of a motor coach is the same whether it is filled with 45 tour participants or is occupied by only one. In other words, if the motor coach costs $500 USD for the day, that cost remains the same, regardless of how many tour participants occupy the coach. Obviously, a tour is more cost effective for the operator when the motor coach is filled to capacity.

**Fixed Costs**

Even independent tours, without transportation and escort fees, will still have some fixed costs. These would include promotional mailings, advertising, and costs for any entertainers or events during the tour, and in certain cases blocks of tickets purchased as promotional items. One advantage of independent tours, from the tour operator's perspective, is that they generally have fewer and lower fixed costs than other types of tours. Lower fixed costs generally mean less financial risk for the tour operator, which may be significant if the operator is small or new to the business of tour operations. In other words, due to their inflexible nature, higher fixed costs mean additional financial risk to tour operators, and bear consideration when planning and costing tours.

## Variable Costs

The other key expense components in tour operations are variable costs. Variable costs can be defined as all expenses that change in direct proportion to the number of clients taking the tours. They are sometimes also referred to as direct costs. Examples of variable costs for tours include meal expenses, accommodation (if they were not purchased as a block), promotional items that are given away to tour participants, and any other cost that is calculated per person or per room. Some hotel weekend packages pay a commission to the travel agent who makes the reservation for the client. The commission expenses paid by the tour wholesaler vary according to the number of clients the agent books for the weekend package. Therefore, in this case, the commission is also a variable cost.

A tour wholesaler and anyone else who produces a tour will encounter numerous variable costs. Some of these costs are as follows:
- Hotel room rates
- Airfares
- Meals
- Gratuities and other service charges
- Attraction admission fees and other entrance fees
- Local tours
- Taxes

The key to understanding variable costs is to realise that the cost is directly tied to the number of participants.

## Tour Participant Estimation

Once you have identified and quantified all the fixed and variable costs for the tour, you will need to estimate the total number of tour participants. This can be quite challenging because there is no way of knowing for certain how many participants will actually take a tour until final payments for the tour have been received. Unfortunately, you can't plan a tour after you have the confirmations. In order to calculate the tour cost per person, you must make some guesses about the number of participants.

One way to do this is to develop a best case, worst case, and average case scenario for the number of participants. The best case scenario means that the tour is filled to maximum capacity. The worst case scenario means that the tour has only a minimum number of participants. The average case scenario is a tour that has a medium or realistic number of participants. Calculating these scenarios takes experience, but it is an important business skill to develop as a tour operator.

The safest method is to use the worst case scenario, or the minimum number of tour participants expected. This is the method recommended by many tour operators because planning for the worst case scenario means that you will probably be pleasantly surprised. Another method favoured by some operators is to take the medium or realistic scenario and then reduce this number by 25 to 30 percent.

## Total Net Tour Cost

The next step is to calculate the total net cost of the tour. In order to make this calculation you must add all the fixed costs to the variable costs, based on the estimated number of participants. Expressed as an equation, the calculation would be as follows:

**Net Tour Cost** = Total Fixed Costs + (Variable Costs X Number of Participants)

The net tour cost is an extremely important figure because it tells you how much it will cost you, the tour operator, to run a tour without making any profit. In other words, it tells you how much it will cost to cover all the expenses associated with operating the tour.

## Profit Mark-up

Now that you have arrived at an estimated net cost for the tour, it is time to calculate the profit mark-up. Tour operators calculate profit mark-up in many different ways. Two of the most common methods are unit price costing and cost plus pricing.

**Unit Price Costing:** This method takes all the fixed and variable costs for the tour and adds a price mark-up to each item in the tour. Unit price costing is preferred by many tour operators because it allows for detailed profit analysis and control.

**Cost Plus Pricing:** This method takes all the fixed and variable costs as a unit and adds a percentage price mark-up for the entire tour. This costing method is used commonly for incentive tour groups and affinity tours.

## Tour Costing Sheets

Although tour costing is by no means a simple process, working out tour cost calculations on a tour cost worksheet can help simplify the process. A tour cost worksheet is an analytical tool designed to assist you with all the calculations necessary to arrive at a properly priced tour. Using the worksheet will ensure that you do not forget key items when computing tour costs. The following is an example of a tour cost worksheet. Experience will help you add or eliminate items, but the core concept will remain the same.

## TOUR COST WORKSHEET

Name of Tour:
Tour Dates:
Tour Operator:
Fixed Costs (Group)
Chartered Transportation:
Sightseeing:
Tolls:
Admissions:
Local Guides:
Transfers:

Promotion:
Communication:
Brochures:
Driver Gratuities:
Speaker Fees:
Programme Fees:
Administrative:
Miscellaneous:
Total Fixed Costs (Group):
Fixed Costs (Tour Director)
Transportation to Tour:
Transportation on Tour:
Hotel Rooms:
Airport Taxes:
Transfers:
Meals, Taxes and Gratuities:
Sightseeing Admissions:
Baggage Gratuities:
Wages:
Passports/Visas:
Vaccinations:
Currency Conversion:
Insurance:
Per Diem Allowance:
Miscellaneous:
Total Fixed Costs (Tour Director):
Variable Costs (per person)
Air Fare Basis:
Surcharges:
Airport Taxes:
Transfers:
Meals:
Meal Taxes & Gratuities:
Sightseeing:
Admissions:
Hotel Rooms:
Baggage Gratuities:
State VAT Taxes:

Service Charges:

Insurance:

Postage:

Single Room Supplement:

The Tour Cost Worksheet is meant as an example only. Factors affecting individual tours will vary by operator and place of operation. The basic ideas, however, will be similar for all tours.

## TERMS AND CONDITIONS

For every outbound package tour, tour operators specify terms and conditions for the tour. These terms and conditions are printed in the tour brochures of a tour operator and refer to several important issues as part of the entire tour programme from the beginning till the end. It is important for a client buying a tour package to go through these terms and conditions carefully and in case he has any doubts the same may be discussed with the organisation before he finally decides to buy a package tour.

Most of the terms and conditions as are mentioned in the tour operators brochure are common to all tour operators and refer to the areas like payment, cancellation, special assistance requirements, price guarantee, visa and passport, travel document, safety, etc. Listed below are some of the important terms and conditions as have been mentioned in one of the tour brochures of an outbound tour operator.

Following are the terms and conditions as mentioned in the tour brochure of a tour operator:

### (i) How to Make your Reservation

Just ask your travel agent to contact us with your requests and we will give immediate answers and booking options on the vacation(s) offered to you. All reservations must be made through your local travel agent.

### (ii) Deposit and Final Payment

A non-refundable, non-transferable deposit of per person, per vacation, is required for us to reserve space for you. Your payment is not considered made until it is received by tour operators. Final payment is due 45 days prior to commencement of services, if we do not receive final payment by this date, we reserve the right to cancel the reservation. In the case of billing errors, we reserve the right to re-invoice with correct pricing. Bookings within 45 days of departure require full payment at time of confirmation of space.

Acceptance on the vacation is subject to presentation of the Travel Certificate.

## Cancellation and Cancellation fees

If the tour operator receives a cancellation more than 45 days prior to commencement of services, the non-refundable deposit will be retained. For cancellations received within 45 days of commencement of services the following per person cancellation fees apply:

45-22 days prior to commencement of services: 20% of total price

21-8 days prior to commencement of services: 30% of total price

7-1 days prior to commencement of services: 50% of total price

On departure day and later: 100% of total price

Higher cancellation fees apply for vacations with an overnight train and cruise:

65-47 days prior to commencement of services: 50% of total price

46 days or less prior to commencement of services: 100% of total price

Cancellation fees may also apply to any additional services, including accommodations, independently supplied services and optional excursions, reserved prior to, during and after the vacation.

The tour operator reserves the right to cancel or re-schedule any vacation departure. If cancellation is made prior to departure, the only responsibility of the tour operator will be to refund the passenger the amount he has received for the reservation. He will try to re-book the same vacation with a different departure date, or a similar vacation. The tour operator cannot assume responsibility for any additional costs or any fees relating to the issuance and/or cancellation of air tickets or other travel arrangements not made through the tour operator.

## Travel Protection

The above cancellation charges will be applied in all cases. The tour operator would urge you to take adequate travel protection, including cover against cancellation, as recommended by your travel agent.

## Revision Fees

A fees of per transaction will be charged for any alteration or revision made to a reservation. Airline penalties on vacations with internal air flights may also apply. A change to traveller name, vacation date or vacation itinerary within 45 days of commencement of services (65 days on vacations with an overnight train or cruise vacation) will be treated as a cancellation and new reservation; standard cancellation fees will apply.

## Participation

As you are travelling with a group of international travellers on vacations listed in these brochures, you are expected to conduct yourself in a manner that is not offensive to others or disruptive to the group and are expected to conduct yourself in a manner that is appropriate for group travel. For the benefit of everyone on your vacation, the tour operator reserves the right to accept or reject any person as a vacation participant, and to remove from the vacation any participant whose conduct is deemed incompatible with the interests of the other participants.

## Travellers who Need Special Assistance:

The tour operator will make reasonable attempts to accommodate the special needs of disabled travellers, but is not responsible in the event he is unable to do so, nor is he responsible for any denial of services by carriers, hotels, restaurants, or other independent suppliers. Most transportation services, including the tourist motorcoach, are not equipped with wheelchair ramps. The tour operators regret that they cannot provide individual assistance to a vacation participant for walking, dining, getting on and off motor coaches and other vehicles, or other personal needs. A qualified and physically able companion must accompany travellers who need such assistance, and must assume total responsibility for the handicapped participant's well being.

## Young Travellers
Travellers who are less than 18 years old on the departure date must be accompanied by an adult. Children receive a 10% discount on the land price. Tour operators do not accept children who are less than eight years old. For special requirements regarding airline tickets for children, contact your airline directly.

Due to heightened security, many countries have adopted practices to prevent international abduction of children. If a child is travelling with adults other than the parents or with only one parent, it is recommended that a notarized letter be written by the parents or non-travelling parent granting authorization to travel, including the dates of travel. We suggest that you also contact the appropriate consulate and airlines because they may have additional requirements.

## Smoking
Smoking is not allowed on transportation that is exclusively provided by the tour operator.

## Price Guarantee
All vacation prices are based on rates (including foreign exchange rates) known at the time of printing and expected to be in effect at the time of departure. Prices are subject to increase without notice if such rates change prior to departure. The current price will be confirmed at the time of the reservation. However, once the tour operator has received your deposit for any vacation departing in a particular year, that land price is guaranteed, and any subsequent land cost increases are at our expense, not including surcharges and any government tax increases.

Vacation prices are per person, based on two persons sharing a room. Single room supplements and triple room reduction are listed where applicable.

## Visas and Passports
A valid national passport is needed for all vacations and, as the various countries all have their own formalities, it is imperative that you check with your travel agent, the visa requirements to enter the countries of vacation, you have chosen. Local consulates will also be in a position to

give advice. You are responsible for obtaining and payment for all visas and entry documents, and for meeting all health and other requirements and any documents required by laws, regulations, orders and/or requirements of the countries to be visited. Multiple-entry visas are required for some vacations. All passengers travelling internationally are required to have a passport. Most countries require that the passport be valid for at least six (6) months beyond the conclusion of your trip.

Passengers are responsible for getting their own visas and must ensure that they can obtain these visas before entering into a booking commitment with us.

### Accommodations

The accommodation listed in these brochures is intended to be used on all departures; however, if a change becomes necessary for any reason, the accommodations substituted will be equivalent in standard to those shown. Every effort is made to reserve only twin-bedded rooms. It may occasionally happen that an accommodation provides some double-bedded rooms instead. These rooms will be allocated to couples where possible. Triple-room configuration is at the discretion of individual hotels.

Note that accommodation check-in times vary worldwide.

### Private Bath and Single Rooms

In exceptional cases, where private bath or single rooms as reserved by us, are not available, refunds will be made by the tour director or local host. Claims made in this respect cannot be accepted after the vacation is complete.

### Baggage Allowance

Porterage for one suitcase is included in the vacation price. Airport porterage at the beginning and end of the vacation is not included. Due to limited coach capacity, this single bag should have dimensions not exceeding 30"x21"x11" and weight not exceeding 50 lbs. (22Kg) or less if your air carrier has stricter weight/dimension limitation. Tour operators recommend you consult your air carrier and even according to destination, as they are becoming more restrictive. The tour operators are not responsible for additional fees imposed by air carriers. Regulations within most airports require that travellers handle their own luggage through customs.

A carry-on bag should not exceed the dimensions specified by airlines. For safety reasons, a wheeled carry-on bag is not suitable as hand luggage on motor coaches and min-buses. No responsibility is accepted for loss of or damage to baggage of any of the vacation participant's belongings. Baggage insurance is recommended.

### Travel Documents

Travel documents are sent to your travel agent approximately two to three weeks prior to departure from your home country, provided full payment has been received.

## Not Included in the Vacation Price
International air transportation tax; agriculture tax; any other taxes; security fee; airport taxes and fees; port taxes; passports; visas and vaccinations; tips to your tour or cruise director, tour cost, tour driver, local city guides, ships' crew; gratuities on ferries, trains and cruise ships; laundry; telephone; mini bar; alcohol, beverages and food are not on the regular table d'hote menu (these extra items will be billed to you before leaving the hotel, shop or restaurant); optional excursions; porterage at airports; travel protection; excess baggage fees; all other items of personal nature.

## Refund
Note that any request for refunds is subject to the terms and conditions of the brochure; no refund can be made for used services of less than 48 consecutive hours, for unused transportation where group activity tickets are involved, or for voluntary modification made by the traveller.

## Service Inquiries after the Vacation
If after returning from your vacation, you wish to inquire about any services provided, please ensure that all correspondence relating to these services is received by the tour operator, within 60 days of the tour completion date. This will enable the tour operators to make timely investigation.

## Holidays
During local or national holidays, certain facilities such as museums and restaurants, sightseeing tours and shopping may be limited or not available. Alternatives will be offered whenever possible.

Most of the medium and big tour operating companies specify the the above terms and conditions in their brochure with some modifications from time to time.

# 8
# SUPPLIER RELATIONSHIP IN TRAVEL INDUSTRY

> **Chapter Objectives**
>
> After reading this chapter the reader should be able to:
> - Understand the importance of agency-supplier relationship.
> - Discuss the relationship of agent with airlines, accommodation suppliers, tour operators and tourist transport operators.
> - Understand the challenges in this relationship.

**Trusted Travel Management System**

What exactly is a supplier relationship in the travel industry? It's an ongoing, dedicated relationship between a travel agency and a vendor. Whether it's air, cars, hotels or tour operators, supplier relationships help travellers ensure they have the best travel contracts, vendor support and so much more.

To improve their overall level of service delivery to both leisure and corporate customers, it is very important for travel agencies, to know and understand, the level of their relationship with their suppliers.

The travel industry made of principal-agency relationship has served well over the last 80 years. In the beginning travel agents were just intermediaries, remunerated by airlines and other travel suppliers to distribute their products. These small businesses have come under pressure recently because of changing factors as follows:

(i) Technological
(ii) Competitive environment
(iii) Customer profiles
(iv) Changes in tourism fashions
(v) Internet penetration in various markets
(vi) Changes in market trends
(vii) Information and awareness
(viii) Increase to standard of living and also income

The modern travel industry is characterised by small businesses and the service providers. Today a very different world is emerging where agents are emerging as "Travel Management Companies". The first loyalty of travel agents today, is to customers who need to choose partners to serve them.

Travel agents have to maintain a continuous, cordial relationship with the following suppliers:

a) Airlines
b) Tourist transport operators
c) Accommodation suppliers
d) Travel agents and tour operators
e) Conference/convention facility providers
f) All other individuals or groups who are directly or indirectly involved in tourism activity.

Travel agents and tour operators enter into long term contracts with all the above suppliers for supply of bulk travel services. These services are then assembled into a package tour which is then marketed to the general public through travel agents. Travel agents are therefore principals and responsible to consumers for services in a package. Therefore it becomes all the more important for travel agents to handle their suppliers tactfully.

The traditional and the modern linkages between travel agents and their principal suppliers is very important. It is necessary to study the traditional relationship between travel agencies and principal suppliers like airlines, hotel companies, tourist transport companies, conference and convention facility providers and all other individuals or groups who are directly or indirectly involved in the tourism industry. In this chapter the relationship of travel agents with some of the key suppliers is being explained.

## RELATIONSHIP WITH AIR TRAVEL PROVIDERS (AIRLINES)

Air travel is broadly divided into three categories, viz., domestic, international and charter, representing three related but different markets. Cargo is excluded because it is generally not provided by tour operators. All players offer almost parallel services and aim to create strategic competitive advantages through the development of software application and customer loyalty programmes like Frequent Flyer Programme (FFP),

In marketing terms, airlines have two priorities, the retention and growth of market share and distribution cost reduction. The market share of any airline largely depends upon its distribution network. Distribution cost reduction obviously increases the competitive position and profitability of the airlines.

The channel of distribution network receives commissions from the airlines for the services provided. The rate of commissions paid is negotiated and agreed upon between the airlines and agents. Thus, one agent may receive more commission from one airline than the other. In the present day context, however, some of the airlines have stopped giving commission for sale of their services.

Increasingly airlines and travel agents are using information technology to improve their competitive position. As a result, for agents, the handling of their principal supplier has also become difficult due to the forces of globalisation which are transforming the way our corporate customers conduct their business, i.e. through internet, as a perfect medium for the sale of distributed products with instantaneous delivery. The internet is here to stay. Booking and ticketing processes will get more automated.

In recent times the travel industry has undergone immense environment changes. The most contributing supplier airlines have seen significant macro-economic changes which are often volatile. These are:
- Frequent changes in ATF prices
- Dropping ATF prices reflecting on tickets
- Recession resulting in economic downturn
- Deregulation
- Demographic changes

**Travel agents can handle air service suppliers by the following practices:**

There can be a number of different fares and conditions offered for the same itinerary for overseas travel. Fares for international travel are market driven and can see changes daily, different conditions or numbers of stopovers may apply. Thus, as a travel agent one should obtain the best options for one's clients.

If certain international routes are used frequently, the travel agent should ask for special route fares from the carrier; discounts and rebates in the case of domestic air travel can also be negotiated as in the case of international air travel.

## Point of sales discounts;

- Discount for different types of payments, e.g., direct debiting, EFT or credit cards, etc.
- Special discounts for using preferred carriers on individual bookings
- Rebates for achieving a percentage usage of a particular (preferred) carrier
- Discounts for group bookings
- Discounts for travellers travelling in off-season; and
- Percentage discount on certain non-trunk international routes

On the other hand, when travel agents are booking for their customers, they must convince their customers, that if the bookings are made earlier better discounts would be available. Thus, the objective shall be to make the buyer's overall cost of travel attractive rather than just offering good discounts.

While handling an airline as suppliers it would be advisable to base the above-mentioned discounts on the lowest logical fare. In practice one must know that there can be only three exceptions from taking lowest logical fares:

(i) When application of discounts on another fare is cheaper

(ii) When discounted full economy fare which offers flexibility to achieve a comparable cost and
(iii) Where the overall costs of a fare and associated management cost is comparable when one is purchasing a higher cost fare.

**Customer Centric**

The travel agent is employed by the customer rather than by the airlines since he makes all the travel arrangements for him. Thus, a travel agent would charge the customer the net cost plus an additional fee for the services provided. The process therefore would change from payment to travel agent by the airline to payment by the customer. When the travel agent passes this payment to airlines on or before the settlement date, commission is then passed on to the agent, and in return, the agent passes on part of the commission to his customer.

The international air travel market is an open market with diverse and flexible fare structures. International airlines have alliances, which are reflected in special fare offers, code sharing and incentive schemes like Frequent Flyer Programme (FFP). Besides there is a wide range of fares, an international air traveller selects from a wide variety of itineraries, accommodation type and other services.

International air travel and its suppliers are governed by the following elements:

- There are many suppliers in the international market and supply and demand have a great influence on pricing. During off season, prices go down and demand increases, and during holidays even when holidays are sold at premium, demand remains unchanged;
- Airlines which align their operations often compete in the international market group by offering special deals.
- Consolidators buy airline tickets in bulk and then wholesale to agents, holiday groups, etc. This can naturally influence the availability of tickets especially during holiday seasons.
- International air travel market is influenced more by changes in fuel price or fluctuation in currency value rather than the domestic air travel market.

**Co-operative Approach**

Air carriers are the principal suppliers and therefore assume great importance in total package operations. Travel agents have to adopt a co-operative approach. The co-operating air carriers may function as tour operators and be subject to some theories of liability. (Exp. The air carrier may own/or control TA as a captive TA or the air carrier may be a partner or a joint venture and thereby help in financing organising, operating, or marketing the tour to the general public).

It is therefore important to obtain the best possible rates from airlines, the benefit of which then could then be passed to the clients. In addition obtain the best option of stopovers, for the clients. Special route fares for the frequent fliers and discounts and rebates are yet another area which are to be negotiated in dealing with the air carriers, both international and domestic.

**The travel agent should ensure:**

- Selected suppliers will provide component travel services, which make up the package tour. The travel agent should investigate the reliability and willingness of suppliers to deliver safe and reliable package tour services
- The supplier's financial position
- The existence of insurance and compliance to all applicable licensing and safety regulation (both domestic and foreign)

## THE RELATIONSHIP WITH TOURIST TRANSPORT SUPPLIERS

The relationship between transport and tourism development is a vital area of tourism studies. For development of any destination, adequate and efficient transportation infrastructure and access to generating markets is one of the most important aspects.

According to Burkart and Medlik transportation can be defined as "the means to reach the destination and also the means of movement at the destination".

### Dynamically Changing Needs and Means

In the ancient times the mode of transport used by travellers was a horse, a horse carriage, a hand-driven carriage or a boat. This was followed by a ship. It was, however, in the nineteenth century that mechanised transport was invented beginning with the introduction of railways, motorcar and thereafter the aeroplane, all of which revolutionised transport all over the world.

Developments of road transport in the post-World War I period and air transport in the post-World War II period were the major factors which were responsible and continue to be so for the great support in modern tourism. For the greater part of contemporary tourism, transport means airlines and private cars.

As a broad generalisation, it can be said that holiday makers travelling away from home to another country spend a major portion of their total holiday budget on transport. Transport costs as much as 30-40 percent of the total long-haul holiday expenditure. This fact has been brought about by a number of studies undertaken by various organisations.

The war necessitated innovations in the fields of motor and air transports for the purpose of initially using them for the war itself. After the war was over they were utilized as modes of transport for travel.

Many road systems and airports which were initially built for transporting men and material for use in the war were subsequently utilized for transporting passengers for the purpose of travel and tourism.

There are different modes of transport which have been evolved over the years. Technological developments have revolutionised various modes of transport and there is a continuous research to upgrade them.

Each technological advance in a travel mode affects the other modes. Railways replaced the horse, the private ownership of automobile and public bus system replaced the railways and the airplane replaced the transoceanic ship and long-distance rail travel.

Transport therefore is fundamental to tourism. Indeed, in its strictest sense tourism can be as good as transport allows it to be, i.e., tourism without transport only becomes local leisure. Technology plays an important role in deciding the capacity, volume, segments, value and characteristic of tourism in a given destination. The principal supplier for tourist transport products are broadly:

   (i) Private taxi and airport shuttle operators
   (ii) Private bus line operators
   (iii) Operators of mass transit systems and their patrons
   (iv) Independent operators of commercial vehicles
   (v) Commercial fleet operators
   (vi) Emergency Service providers and
   (vii) Regional and state government transport undertakings

While dealing with suppliers it is important to ensure the following:
- Proper linkage
- Co-ordination
- Payment schedules
- Proper planning
- Maintenance of vehicle
- Training for personnel safety

## (i) Private Taxi and Airport Shuttle Operators

When an independent tourist or group arrives in our country, as a travel agent your first job is to arrange the transfer of the same. In other words, travel agents need the service of private taxi or airport shuttle operators. In countries like Singapore, Malaysia and Thailand and also in India, tourists are issued pre-paid vouchers by overseas operators to use airports shuttle services. Hence, travel agents have to maintain linkages with these frontline service providers.

## (ii) Private Bus Line Operators

This segment of suppliers assumes importance when travel agents are dealing with overseas groups, i.e., when in one season travel agents are sure of bookings for 15-20 groups each consisting of 50-70 passengers. Travel agents would always require the services of these private bus line operators since travel agents will have to move their groups form one tourist centre to another. For example, most of the foreign tourists want to have the Golden Triangle of Delhi-Agra-Jaipur on their itinerary. This circuit is normally covered by road. Thus, to have smooth operations of the group, travel agents shall have good linkages with them. Sometimes travel agents do not handle their groups, rather assign them to some other person located at a different place. Thus, travel agents shall establish healthy linkages with these private tour operators so that they give priority to their assignments and take care of his groups.

### (iii) Operators of Mass Transit Systems

Mass Transit Systems are advanced public transport systems that provide fast and efficient transport to the tourists. The objective for introducing such a system would be to enhance customer service in general, service reliability schedule, information accuracy and on time performance while reducing cost in particular.

## RELATIONSHIP WITH ACCOMMODATION SUPPLIERS

Among important partners in travel agency operations, accommodation plays a crucial role simply because today it is not just a place to stay but it has become a destination in itself. Most of the group movements of foreign tourists in India are done in star category hotels. The product quality or availability of product options varies according to different categories of hotels. In India, for instance, Department of Tourism, along with Federation of Hotels and Restaurants Association of India, (FHRAI) classify hotels in five star categories as follows:

- 5 Star Deluxe Hotels
- 5 Star Hotels
- 4 Star Hotels
- 3 Star Hotels
- 2 Star Hotels
- 1 Star Hotels
- Heritage Hotels

Among these classified hotels, there are various working codes which are used in packages designed for consumers. These are:

## Category of Rooms

- Normal
- Deluxe
- Executive
- Suite
- Deluxe Suite
- Presidential Suite
- Air Conditioned or Non-Air Conditioned Room, and facing particular view-sea, pool, garden, monument, river, etc.

**Plan of Hotels:** Packages also reflect the type of meal plan being requested by the guest and whether this meal plan appears in the list of the hotel's meal plan:

- European Plan (EP) – Only room basis
- Continental Plan (CP) – Only room and breakfast
- Modified American Plan (MAP) – Room, breakfast, lunch and dinner

**Tariffs of Hotels:** It is important to know this because it will help while negotiating the final rates and commissions.

Hotels have normally:

- FIT (Free Independent Traveller) Tariffs, and
- GIT (Group Inclusive Tours) Tariffs.

Hotels tariffs also vary according to season, normally termed as seasonal tariffs and off-season tariffs.

While including any hotel property as part of the package, one should also take care of other aspects like:
- Additional charges (taxes) being charged by the hotel
- Whether the hotel is an independent unit or a single hotel unit or a chain of hotels
- Whether the hotel is a part of the global reservation system or not, to provide instant reservations and
- Whether the hotel property is a partner in global accounting standards to ensure better accounting standards and credit facilities globally.

As a travel agent, one needs to establish linkages with the accommodation providers because you require to block rooms in a large number for a particular season or for mega events, which you plan to organise. It happens many a times that so many tour operators, in absence of availability of rooms fail to book groups for a particular destination consequently, leading to loss of revenue to the agency. It also happens that in the absence of a cordial and healthy relationship between travel agents and hotels, guests are allocated room in a less preferred location which results in dissatisfaction of guests or sometimes the guests are made to wait in the lobby for booking/allocation of rooms in the hotels.

## Managing Accommodation Supplier Relationships

## Important Steps
### a. Technology

Having the right technology can make managing supplier relationships easier. Hotels that focus on both qualitative and quantitative supplier data analysis will be able to easily identify weak spots, risks and opportunities. SRM technology provides with visibility into supplier base, giving a detailed picture of supply chain and making it easy to reduce risks. Because hospitality is a unique industry, it pays to research a few SRM software providers and find one that can integrate well with other systems.

Larger hotels will want to have a system that allows viewing all of suppliers and an analyzation of risk factors. Smaller hotels may decide that they do not need a complete system for SRM, or quite the same level of analysis, but should still consider how to best track suppliers over time.
Involve Other Departments

In a hotel, finding suppliers isn't just about the best deal for the best product. Everything in a hotel, from internet service to towels to the kinds of pens and shampoo have in, can be used to help or hurt marketing and customer loyalty efforts. Internet review sites mean that even the smallest detail of a guest's stay is now open for commentary. It's important that those in procurement work closely with those in marketing and customer relations to make sure they understand the needs and wishes of the guest.

### b. Keep Buying Centralized

Although it's important to make sure all departments in hotel are working together, for SRM to work one department needs to retain some form of control over the process. A standardized form of building relationships and creating contracts reduces supply chain risk, reduces mistakes and simplifies contracting.

### c. Do Your Research

Before you go to a meeting with a supplier, make sure you understand what their process is, what kinds of profit margins they expect and what their pain points are. The more information have, the more confident you'll appear in negotiations, which will help you broker a better deal. Researching the individuals involved in the negotiation can also be helpful. Forming a personal connection to someone often eases a business situation. As stated above, internal research to ensure you fully understand your own needs and limits will also help keep meetings and deals smooth.

### d. Collaborate

Negotiations are often thought of as situations where one side wins and the other loses. But it doesn't always have to be that way. There may be ways that you can work with your supplier to save you both time and money. For example, you may be able to utilize your networks to help each other find additional customers. You may be reluctant to provide another hotel with access to your suppliers, but perhaps you know someone in a related field. Even if it does not save you money, creating more ties and better relationships between you and your supplier can yield benefits such as favourable treatment during difficult times.

The biggest key to Supplier Relationship Management is remembering the word "relationship." Business relationships can be hard work and they don't develop in one day. Relationships need nurturing, care, and consideration to be kept healthy. The good news is just as they aren't built in one day, relationships rarely disintegrate in one day, either. So, if you have relationships in need of strengthening, there's still time.

## RELATIONSHIP BETWEEN TRAVEL AGENTS AND TOUR OPERATORS

Ever since the travel trade has come into existence, travel agents have enjoyed a healthy relationship with tour operators. This relationship is based on the mutual benefit for both the trade partners. If tour operators want to sell their products/services they need retailers and the travel agents fill this gap by acting as their intermediaries. However, today this relationship is facing natural challenges from market conditions, i.e., travel agents are forced to act as tour operator to sustain themselves in the trade. As a result, there exists a thin line between their function and a huge gap in their relationship.

In recent times, tour operators have started reaching to their customers directly due to cut throat competition and price wars. Even big tour operators have started advertising their special tour packages designed for all sections of the society be it up market or budget market.

### CHALLENGES IN RELATIONSHIP

If we look at the whole ambit of the relationship between agents and principal suppliers from this changing perspective, we see that the competition has intensified in the travel market forcing down the margins. Airlines have stopped commissions and accelerated the availability of net fares in the hope of driving down their distribution costs.

For agents, the handling of principal suppliers has also become difficult due to the forces of globalisation, which are transforming the way the corporate customers conduct their business, i.e., through the Internet as a preferred medium for the sale of products with instantaneous delivery. This change is sweeping throughout the industry and there can be no going back. Airlines are not going to restore commission to the levels of the past. The Internet is here to stay. Booking and ticketing processes will get more and more automated.

With the rise of the web and the development of call centres, airlines have the chance to take direct control of their passengers. This has reinforced new phenomena, i.e., internet travel agents such as e-bookers or Expedia. In part this is because airlines are under pressure to sell a product with a limited lifespan.

## Proper Co-ordination

Travel agents, in order to be able to function in the travel industry have to depend a great deal on the suppliers of various services and for this there is a great dependency and coordination with the suppliers. The function of a travel agency is greatly linked with the services being supplied to them in the form of hotel rooms, airline tickets, ground arrangements, etc. It is therefore of utmost importance that the travel agent has a cordial working relationship for getting uninterrupted supply of travel services.

Suppliers are implementing more alternatives to normal booking channels in order to reduce their distribution costs. Competition has intensified a lot in the travel market, forcing down margins. In addition, airlines have reduced or cut commissions altogether and accelerated the availability of net fares to cut distribution costs.

For agents, therefore, handling of principal suppliers has become difficult due to forces of globalisation. The internet is a perfect medium of sale with instantaneous delivery. Booking and ticketing processes are getting more and more automated. With the rise of the web and the development of call centres, airlines have the chance to take back direct control of the passengers. This has reinforced a new phenomenon – the internet travel agents.

In view of all the recent developments a travel agent has not only to maintain linkages with different suppliers with utmost caution and must also handle them in such a manner that they provide satisfactory services for his clients.

It is therefore important to obtain the best possible rates from airlines, the benefit of which could then be passed on to the clients. In addition try to obtain the best option of stopovers for your clients. Special route fares for your frequent fliers and discounts and rebates are yet another area which is to be negotiated in dealing with the air carriers, both international and domestic.

## The Travel Agent should ensure:

- Selected suppliers will provide component travel services which make up the package tour. One should investigate the reliability and willingness of suppliers to deliver safe travel services.

- The suppliers financial position
- The existence of insurance and compliance to all applicable licensing and safety regulation (both domestic and foreign)

Travel agencies and their suppliers should work in collaboration to improve their service delivery to customers by sharing information on product development, marketing and promotional strategies as well as future distribution initiatives. It is also important that both travel agencies and their suppliers should believe in the long term value of establishing a relationship with each other. It is for this reason that trust and commitment are prerequisites for the establishment of such a relationship.

# 9
# TRAVEL TRADE ASSOCIATIONS

> **Chapter Objectives**
>
> After reading this chapter the reader should be able to:
> - Know about the need and importance of forming travel trade associations.
> - Identify different forms of travel trade associations.
> - Understand the role and functions of major international travel associations.
> - Identify the main travel trade associations, worldwide.
> - Compare the functions and objectives of some major associations like UFTAA, ASTA, WATA.
> - Understand the role and functions of TAAI.

Formation of associations by independent firms in a particular trade or a group of industries is primarily done with a view to protecting the interests of its members. Trade organisations are voluntary bodies formed by individual firms belonging to a particular trade, not only to protect but also to advance the common interests of their members. The main objective of forming an association by independent firms is to get strong representations which act as channels of communication with the government and other organised groups to further the interests of their members. In almost all disciplines, members in some way or other have formed organisations/associations.

The ever-increasing importance of the tourism sector and the increase in the growth in its volume over the years, have resulted in the formation of associations in this sector. Secondly, the ever-increasing international character of modern day tourism and the growing influence of international agencies in various fields have also influenced the growth of international co-operation in the field of tourism. All these developments in turn have brought together members of the travel associations at national, regional and international levels collectively, to further their trade interests. Different producers and sellers of various tourist services like tour operators, travel agents, hotel companies, airline companies, ground operators, etc., have formed associations of their members.

The scope of discussion in this chapter is limited to the associations of travel agents and tour operators. These associations today have assumed great importance and provide a platform to their members, where ideas are exchanged and topics of mutual interest discussed and solutions arrived at. They provide services like information, assistance and advice in the conduct of their business to their members. The various associations in the field of tourism can take different forms.

## Forms of Travel Associations

Broadly the following five forms can be identified:

(i) *Those based on the education and training needs of the industry.* These may include professional bodies like Hotel and Catering Management Association, Travel and Tourism Management Association which are primarily concerned with the training and educational standards of personnel working in hotels and travel agencies.

(ii) *Those which are concerned with the sectoral interests of their members.* They include the National Associations of Travel Agents and Tour Operators. Each country has such associations. For instance, the American Society of Travel Agents (ASTA), the Australian Federation of Travel Agents (AFTA), the Associations of British Travel Agents (ABTA), the Japan Association of Travel Agents (JATA), the Indian Association of Travel Agents (IATA), the Swiss Travel Agents Associations (FSAV), the German Travel Agencies Association (DRVS), etc.

(iii) *Those which are responsible for developing, promoting and facilitating tourism in a particular region.* These regional organisations draw their membership from public or private sector organisations, dealing with tourism and sharing a common interest in the promotion and development or marketing of a specific, tourism, geographical area or a region. This area may represent a region, a state, a country or a resort. The membership is opened to groups or organisations, both in public and private sectors, rather than individuals, such as Pacific Area Travel Association (PATA)

(iv) *Those which are concerned with the promotion and development of tourism globally.* These organisations deal with all the aspects of tourism. The rapid expansion in tourism activity globally was responsible for creating a need for world bodies to deal with tourism issues at the government level. The UN-World Tourism Organisation (WTO) is one such global tourism organisation representing public sector tourism from most countries of the world.

(v) *Those which are responsible for promoting and furthering interests of specific trade groups in the travel industry.* This would include travel agents, and tour operators at the global level. Unlike the sectoral trade association of travel agents and tour operators, these have international impact. They play an important role in representing the common interests of travel agents and tour operators worldwide in crucial international issues like negotiation of travel agency commission rates with International Air transport Association (IATA). Universal Federation of Travel Agents Association (UFTAA) and the World Association of Travel Agencies (WATA) are such associations. Both UFTAA and WATA play an important role in representing the interests of travel agents worldwide.

## Major International Travel Associations

Over the years, a large number of world Travel Associations have been formed to advise their members about the latest happenings in the area of travel and tourism. These associations are in fact doing pioneering work in their respective areas and through the annual conferences and meetings, provide a platform to members to discuss the current scenario and future plans.

Following are some of the major travel trade associations at regional and global levels:

1. Pacific Asia Travel Association - http://www.pata.org/ PATA - a non-profit travel trade association serving government tourist offices, airlines, hotels and other travel-related companies throughout the Pacific Asia region.
2. International Air Transport Association - http://www.iata.org/ IATA - a trade association representing and serving the airline industry world-wide.
3. World Tourism Organization - http://www.unwto.org WTO - an intergovernmental organisation that serves as a global forum for tourism policy and issues.
4. World Travel and Tourism Council - http://www.wttc.org/ WTTC - an international organisation of travel industry executives promoting travel and tourism worldwide.
5. The Travel Industry Association of America - http://www.tia.org/ TIA - a non-profit, national association that represents and speaks for the common interests and concerns of all components of the U.S. travel industry.
6. Association for Tourism and Leisure Education - http://www.atlas-euro.org-ATLAS is a global network of universities with research and education interests in tourism and leisure. It conducts research in cultural tourism, sustainable tourism, ICT, human resources, and SMEs.
7. United States Tour Operators Association - http://www.ustoa.com/ USTOA - a professional association representing the tour operator industry, composed of tour companies who conduct business in the U.S.
8. Travel and Tourism Research Association - http://www.ttra.com/ TTRA - an international professional organisation comprising providers and users of travel and tourism research.
9. Airports Council International - http://www.airports.org/ The international association of the world's airports. ACI fosters

cooperation among its member airports and with other partners in world aviation, including governmental, airline and aircraft manufacturing organisations.

10. International Association of Convention and Visitor Bureaus - http://www.iacvb.org/IACVB - promotes professional practices in the solicitation and servicing of meetings and conventions.

11. International Council of Cruise Lines - http://www.iccl.org/ICCL - a trade organization that participates in the regulatory and policy development process to ensure a safe, secure and healthy cruise ship environment.

12. Society for Accessible Travel and Hospitality (SATH) - http://www.sath.org-a non-profit agency offering assistance and information for travellers with disabilities. Includes information for travel agents, resources, and a calendar of events.

13. Cruise Lines International Association - http://www.cruising.org/CLIA - the official trade organisation of the cruise industry of North America. It offers support and training for the travel agent community, including the Cruise Counsellor Certification Program.

14. The Federation of International Youth Travel Organisations - http://www.fiyto.org/FIYTO - an open, world-wide, non-political and non-sectarian travel trade association advocating the special identity of young travellers, and their right to flexible, affordable travel and travel-related services.

15. International Federation for Information Technology and Tourism - http://www.ifitt.org/IFITT - an international organisation that promotes discussion about information technologies in the field of tourism.

16. African Travel and Tourism Association - http://www.atta.co.uk/ATTA promotes the tourism products of members with destinations within Africa and the Indian Ocean Islands.

17. European Regions Airline Association - http://www.eraa.org/ERAA - the representative body for regional air transport throughout Europe. It currently represents 78 airlines and 49 airports.

18. Adventure Travel Trade Association - http://www.adventuretravel.biz/Global membership organization dedicated to promoting and growing the adventure travel market.

19. Association of Corporate Travel Executives - http://www.acte.org/ACTE - a professional association representing corporate travel managers and travel service providers in 29 countries.

20. National Business Travel Association - http://www.nbta.org/The NBTA represents the interests of corporate travel managers and travel service providers in the U.S.

21. OpenTravel Alliance - http://www.opentravel.org/OTA - a trade group developing a common standard for the exchange of information within the travel industry.

22. The International Bureau of Social Tourism - http://www.bits-int.org/ BITS - promotes the right of all to leisure, holidays and tourism.
23. Airlines Reporting Corporation - http://www.arccorp.com/ ARC handles airline ticket distribution, control and settlement and controls accreditation of travel agencies that issue airline tickets.
24. Regional Airline Association - http://www.raa.org/ The RAA represents U.S. regional airlines and the suppliers of products and services that support the industry, before federal and state agencies.
25. International Association of Tour Managers Ltd - http://www.iatm.co.uk/IATM - a professional Association of experienced tour managers and travel guides.
26. Central European Countries Travel Association - http://www.cecta.org/CECTA - a trade organization promoting the Central European region's travel and tourist destinations and services.
27. International Society of Travel and Tourism Educators - http://www.istte.org/ISTTE - an international organisation of educators in travel, tourism, and related fields representing all levels of educational institutions.
28. North West CruiseShip Association - http://nwcruiseship.org/ NWSA - a not-for-profit association working on behalf of the nine member lines to build positive relationships with communities and government agencies and to develop strong partnerships with communities and businesses in Canada, Alaska and the Pacific North West.
29. Passenger Vessel Association - http://www.passengervessel.com/ PVA - a national association representing the interests of owners and operators of dinner cruise vessels, sightseeing and excursion vessels, gaming boats, car and passenger ferries, private charter vessels, and overnight cruise ships under U.S., state, or Canadian regulations.
30. The Association of Car Rental Industry Systems Standards - http://www.acriss.org/ACRISS is a European economic interests group, which has been setting display standards for the car rental industry via global distribution systems since 1989.
31. Small Business Hospitality Association - http://hospitality-1st.com/sbha/SBHA is dedicated to networking and professionalism throughout the small business hospitality industry.
32. Travel Technology Initiative - http://www.tti.org/ TTI facilitates the development of open standards for the exchange of electronic data between tour operators, airlines, ferries, hotels and rail operators.
33. Society Of Government Travel Professionals - http://www.government-travel.org/SGTP - a national, non-profit association for Government travel/finance managers, suppliers and travel agents in the U.S. travel market.

34. Interactive Travel Services Association - http://www.interactivetravel.org/ITSA - an online travel industry trade group devoted to eliminating barriers to growth and protecting consumers.
35. Association of Travel Marketing Executives - http://www.atme.org/ ATME - a professional, non-profit association of executives with vital responsibilities in the marketing of tourism and travel worldwide.
36. Tourism Industry Conference in British Columbia - http://www.bctourismindustryconference.ca/Program and online registration for this conference to be held subsequent years.
37. Society of Incentive and Travel Executives - http://www.site-intl.org/ SITE - a worldwide organization of business professionals dedicated to the recognition and development of motivational and performance improvement strategies of which travel is a key component.
38. Airports Council International North America - http://www.aci-na.org/ ACI-NA represents local, regional and state governing bodies that own and operate commercial airports in the United States and Canada.
39. Student and Youth Travel Association - http://www.syta.org/ SYTA - a non-profit, professional trade association that promotes student and youth travel.

## UNIVERSAL FEDERATION OF TRAVEL AGENTS ASSOCIATION (UFTAA)

Universal Federation of Travel Agents Association (UFTAA) was created in the year 1996 by the merger of the International Federation of Travel Agencies Association (IFTAA) and Universal Organization of Travel Agents Association (UOTAA). Today, Universal Federation of Travel Agents Association forms the only global federation of travel agents and represents through out the world.

The Association with Head Quarters in Monaco, is the International Organisation of the National Travel Agents' Associations. More than 100 Travel Agents' Associations are members of the UFTAA. UFTAA enjoys consultant status with the United Nations, is an affiliate member of the UN-WTO and has relations with the International Civil Aviation Organisation (ICAO).

## Membership Criteria

UFTAA membership is made up of National Travel Agent Association or Organizations from every country in the world. In other words, National Travel Agent Association of every country is eligible for the membership. At present UFTAA has over 35,000 Travel Agencies. National Travel Agents Associations or Organizations are full-time members of UFTAA. Besides the full-time members the Secretary General of UFTAA may register individually any travel agency which fulfils the following criteria:

- A member of a National Association which has membership of UFTAA.
- A member of a National Association in a country which does not have UFTAA membership.
- Located in a country where there is no national association.
- Any individual firm, company or other legal entities such as airlines, hotels or car-rental operators where activities are aligned to those of

travel agent, may obtain registration on the same terms laid down for registered agents.

## The Aims of the Federation

The following are the main aims of the federation:
(i) To act as the negotiating body with the various branches of tourism and travel industry on behalf of its members and also in the interest of the public
(ii) To ensure for all travel agents, through their national associations the maximum degree of cohesion and understanding, prestige and public recognition, advancement of the member's interest and protection from legislation and legal points of view
(iii) To offer to its members all the necessary professional and technical advice and assistance in matters concerning their trade.

UFTAA provides several advantages to its members which include
(i) the right to reproduce the symbol on the stationery
(ii) information service on all matters of legal or professional nature
(iii) free of charge assistance by its legal department for the recovery of outstanding debts
(iv) arbitration services for litigations between a member agency and a hotel company in different countries, etc.

The Annual General Assembly of UFTAA is the policy making body. The assembly decides on the general policy of the federation and makes recommendations on any matter within its competence. The board of directors, consisting of directors elected from candidates proposed by national member associations handle the routine business of the Federation. The executive committee is responsible for handling day-to-day activities and also urgent matters.

The UFTAA world congress, which normally takes place annually, is the advisory body of the federation. The world congress is open to UFTAA registered agents and enterprises, UFTAA individual members, suppliers of services and regional, national and international public authorities.

UFTAA claims to have a series of achievements since its inception in the year 1966. Prominent among its achievements is its collaboration with the International Rail Union resulting in obtaining increased commission on several railway networks, creation of professional training courses and introduction of railway inclusive tours. With regard to air transport, the cooperation between the Federation and IATA over a number of years has resulted in the raising of commission, introduction of an overriding commission, 50 percent reduction for the spouses of travel agents and creation of international correspondence courses for the training of agency sales staff. In the sphere of the hotel industry, the federation following negotiations with the International Hotel Association has created an international convention, setting down regulations for booking, and cancellation fees. A court of arbitration to settle disputes between hotels and travel agents located in different countries, has also been created.

## AMERICAN SOCIETY OF TRAVEL AGENTS (ASTA)

ASTA, short for the American Society of Travel Agents, is the world's largest association of travel professionals. The members include travel agents and the companies whose products they sell such as tours, cruises, hotels, car rentals, etc. The society is the leading advocate for travel agents, the travel industry and the travelling public.

ASTA, the world's largest travel trade association, commemorated its 75th anniversary in 2006. Since its founding on April 20, 1931 as the American Steamship and Tourist Agents Association, ASTA has remained true to the mission outlined by its founding members.

## ASTA History

In 1931, more than 60 agents joined an association that promised to protect and promote

- the mutual interests of its members
- maintain a dignified code of ethics
- combat unfair competition
- stimulate the public's desire to travel
- promote the use of ASTA members' services.

In the 1930s, when agents were booking 80 percent to 90 percent of all steamship travel, ASTA was urging shipping lines to adopt agent-friendly policies and trying to persuade hotels and railroads to pay agent commissions. When the war in the '40s curtailed all but essential travel, ASTA members fought for the survival of their association. In 1946, one year after its formation, the International Air Transport Association (IATA) cut agent commissions to 5 percent from 7.5 percent. ASTA was there to fight for its members. Around the same time, the society changed its name to the American Society of Travel Agents.

### The 1950s

In the 1950s, ASTA won a 27-year battle for rail commissions. It was in the '50s that the society broke new ground by introducing a home study course, the industry's first basic training tool. In the 1960s, ASTA made a lot of progress in education, holding its first School at Sea and opening seven travel schools. In 1968, when President Johnson restricted travel outside of the United States, ASTA waged the largest grass roots campaign of its history.

### The 1970s

In the 1970s, ASTA formed several institutions that continue to benefit members today. ASTA Marketing Services, Inc. (AMSI), was established as a subsidiary of ASTA designed to help ASTA member agents get high quality products and services at discounted prices. The ASTA Political Action Committee (ASTAPAC) was formed to lead the fight for agents' interests in the political arena. The '70s also saw the formation of ASTA's Chapter Presidents' Council. The decade that saw the first rise in air commissions in 25 years, from 5 percent to 7 percent, closed with the deregulation of airlines.

## The 1980s
In the '80s, the Society continued its emphasis on education, holding Training fest, School on Rails, School at Sea and School on the Road.

## The 1990s
In the 1990s, ASTA published the Travel Agent Manual. In 1995, seven major airlines capped agency commissions at $50 on domestic tickets. ASTA filed an anti-trust lawsuit that was settled out of court for $86 million. Before the end of the decade, commissions were cut or capped five more times. In 1999, ASTA secured a Justice Department investigation of five carriers' plan to launch a joint-web site. ASTA published the Air Travellers Bill of Rights and secured Congressional endorsement of the key principles of the bill, as well as gaining passage and funding of the Consumer Access to Travel Information Act.

## Present Day Activities
In the first years of the new millennium, ASTA has continued its efforts to support travel agents and to fight for the travelling public in the legal and legislative arenas, at the state and federal level. Several ASTA-endorsed pieces of legislation to protect passenger rights and end airline preemption went to Congress. Of late, ASTA scored several major victories at the state level in defeating regulations that would prove harmful to travel agents. In Texas, ASTA succeeded in passing a technical corrections bill that will potentially save Texas travel agents thousands of dollars in taxes.

The society has kept up its efforts in the area of supplier relations. ASTA is also continually enhances its member communications and provides members tools to launch or improve their own advertising and public relations campaigns. Educationally, ASTA offers a variety of online and home-study courses for its members to use in furthering their expertise. In 2006, ASTA launched its International Destination Expo, an annual meeting held in a different international location each year that offers a new approach to destination training.

## Membership
There are two basic classifications of membership:
(i) Active
(ii) Allied

Active members are year-round travel agents or tour operators. Allied members include airlines and steamship companies, railroad, bus lines, car rental firms, hotels, resorts, government tourist offices and other organisations regularly engaged in the travel industry or associated industries.

ASTA has over 2,500 travel agency members outside the USA and Canada. All are engaged in travel agency operations on a year-round basis and have been in business for at least three consecutive years. The international roster has its own elected governors and actively participates in all phases of society meetings. International members come from Algeria, Bolivia, Sri Lanka, Denmark, Ethiopia, Fiji Island, Ghana, India, Iran, Japan, the Netherlands, Portugal, South Africa and Sweden.

## ASTA World Travel Congress

The year's foremost meeting place is the ASTA World Travel Congress. The congress is the single most important meeting held annually in the travel industry and the programme includes workshops, seminars, business meetings, film presentations, and social events. Members from throughout the world travel industry participate, give talks, lead discussions groups and conduct sessions. The ASTA World Travel Congress has been the platform for launching many important and beneficial education programmes for agents. The congress grants Travel hall of Fame awards, an honour given to those whose careers have made long-standing impact on the development and expansion of the travel industry and tourism. The awards are given every year to outstanding members.

ASTA consists of the following departments:
- policy implementation
- administration
- industry relations
- membership relations
- communication
- training

The members of the society derive various advantages which include education and training. ASTA has a comprehensive list of travel courses and seminars which are attended by its members. The society also offers professional training courses to senior travel agency personnel. Various research papers and newsletters are brought out from the society's headquarters for use of its members.

## ASTA Chapters

The society has 28 chapters in the United States of America and Canada and another 28 chapters overseas. Each chapter has elected officers and appointed committees. There is a National Board of Directors, which establishes policies of the society. Every two years a new President and Chairman of the Board are elected by active members. Day-to-day activities of the society are looked after by a professional staff, which works under the guidance of an Executive Vice – President who, in fact, is the Chief Operating Officer of the society and makes recommendations on policy matters to the Board and Executive Board. The Vice President directs the headquarters staff in providing a broad programme of services and facilities of ASTA's membership and carrying on the day-to-day business of the Society. ASTA world headquarters are located in New York City, USA.

## WORLD ASSOCIATION OF TRAVEL AGENCIES (WATA)

On May 5th, 1949, 8 professional travel agents from France, Italy, Belgium and Switzerland met in Geneva to create an international body to improve and rationalise the organization of the international tourism. Under the leadership of their first President, Mr. Daniel V. Dedina from Paris, they started to legalise the trademark WATA, World Association of Travel Agencies, on a global basis. The network worked, business exchanges and enjoyed an excellent and growing reputation.

## Structure of the Association

WATA maintains a permanent secretariat at its headquarters in Nyon, Switzerland - to cover the association's administrative needs.

The Executive Committee is responsible for the administration and direction of the Association, its relationship with members and third parties, the fulfilling of the aims of the Association, compliance with the Articles of Association and Rules, resolutions of the General Assembly and ensures the legal representation of the Association.

The General Assembly is the supreme authority of the Association and is convened regularly every year. Each full member disposes of one vote. The WATA Executive Committee consists of:
- President
- Vice President
- Secretary
- Treasurer

## Mission Statement:

The World Association of Travel Agencies (WATA) is a worldwide organisation of selected travel agencies dedicated to the enhancement of the professionalism and profitability of member agents through mutual cooperation and global networking. Its members are committed to the highest standards of business ethics and quality of service to clients.

## Code of Conduct:

The aim of WATA is to be a worldwide network of agencies of which the quality is indisputable. This level of quality must be the characteristic of all WATA members. To reach this level of quality, all WATA members should adhere to the rules mentioned in the Code of Conduct. General rules applicable for transactions between WATA members, as well as between WATA members and non WATA members include the following:

a) The services rendered by WATA members must be the most competitive in price for better, or at least equal, quality than that of their local competitors.

b) Replies to any request must be made without any delay. The new technologies, such as e-mails or faxes are to be used for immediate response.

c) All payments must be effected according to the usual practice of the trade or within the period agreed upon.

d) Payments outside the country of residence of the WATA members must be effected in the currency agreed upon by the parties concerned.

e) In case of exchange regulations applicable to intentional payments, it is the responsibility of the WATA member located in a country with such regulations to undertake all necessary steps to be able to meet the payment deadline agreed upon.

Special rules applicable to WATA members in their dealings with other WATA members include the following:

(a) When a WATA member has business for a certain destination, the WATA member of this destination must be given the opportunity to quote for such business. If this quotation is not accepted, the reasons for the refusal must be communicated, if requested.

b) WATA members must give priority to the services offered by other WATA members in their business dealings provided that such services are similar in price and contents to those of local competitors.

c) Terms of payment between WATA members should be fixed by agreement. However WATA members should benefit from the best facilities offered by the WATA members on the market. Pre-payments should only be asked for when the amount involved in the transaction is in excess of the WATA guarantee or when the servicing agency has to pay a deposit to secure the transaction.

**Relations between the WATA members and the WATA headquarters are specified as follows:**

a) Each WATA member must inform the entire staff about WATA and one or two persons should be designated in each office as WATA contacts.

b) The invoices sent by the headquarters must be paid within 30 days. In case of currency regulations applicable to international payments, if such regulations impose a longer delay, the proof that the transfer has been requested immediately must be submitted to the headquarters.

c) Information of any nature requested by the headquarters must be supplied without delay.

To achieve the desired promotion of the WATA name, each member must:

- Print the WATA logo on his letter-head, vouchers, tariffs, e-mails and visiting cards.
- Include WATA logo and link to WATA website on his personal websites, clearly display the WATA emblem in his office
- Promote on any occasion WATA and in particular with all partners of the travel trade of his city or region.

## WORLD TRAVEL & TOURISM COUNCIL

The World Travel & Tourism Council (WTTC) is the body which represents the Travel & Tourism private sector globally. The WTTC works to raise awareness of Travel & Tourism as one of the world's largest economic sectors, supporting one in 10 jobs (313 million) worldwide and generating 10.4% of world GDP. WTTC conducts research on the Economic Impact of Travel & Tourism in 185 countries for over 30 years. In 2017, the Travel & Tourism industry experienced 4.6% growth, compared to the global economy (3%). One in five new jobs were created by the industry, and is such WTTC is the best partner for governments to create jobs. WTTC priorities are:

(i) Security & Travel Facilitation
(ii) Crisis Preparedness

(ii) Management & Recovery
(iv) Sustainable Growth.

WTTC is the only global body that brings together all major players in the Travel & Tourism sector (airlines, hotels, cruise, car rental, travel agencies, tour operators, GDS, and technology), enabling them to speak with One Voice to governments and international bodies. It is important that WTTC has the broadest geographical representation and includes all aspects of the sector, including organisations that provide vital services to Travel & Tourism. With Chief Executives of over 170 of the world's leading Travel & Tourism companies as its members, WTTC has a unique mandate and overview on all matters related to Travel & Tourism. WTTC works to raise awareness of Travel & Tourism as one of the world's largest sectors, supporting millions of jobs and generating 10.4% of global GDP. WTTC advocates partnership between the public and private sectors, delivering results that match the needs of economies, local and regional authorities, and local communities, with those of business, based on:

- Governments recognising Travel & Tourism as a top priority
- Business balancing economics with people, culture and environment
- A shared pursuit of long-term growth and prosperity

## Members

WTTC is the only global body representing the Travel &Tourism private sector. The Council's Members are the Chairmen or Chief Executives of leading global Travel & Tourism companies, from all geographies and industries, including hotels, airlines, airports, tour operators, cruise, car rental, travel agents, rail, and the emergent sharing economy, enabling them to speak with One Voice to governments and international bodies. Over 170 companies are now represented on the Council.
Following are the key decision makers of WTTC:

- Chairman WTTC
- Vice Chairmen WTTC
- Executive Committee WTTC
- Global Members WTTC
- Regional Members WTTC
- Ambassadors Past Chairmen & Honorary Members

## EUROPEAN TRAVEL COMMISSION

The European Travel Commission (ETC) is an international organisation responsible for the promotion of Europe as a tourist destination. Its members are the national tourism organisations (NTOs) of thirty-three Members, including EU member states, as well as, Iceland, Monaco, Montenegro, Norway, San Marino, Serbia, Switzerland and Turkey. The national tourism organizations of all sovereign states in Europe are eligible for full membership of the European Travel Commission. Regional cross-border organizations and tourism-related bodies may join as associate members. The European Travel Commission is neither part of the European Commission nor an institution of the European Union.

## History

ETC was established in 1948 in Norway. Between World War I and World War II, Europe became aware of the importance of tourism.

### 1925

The establishment of national tourism organizations rapidly led to the creation of the "International Union of Official Tourist Publicity Organizations": its first mission was the launch of a joint publicity campaign named "Europe Calling".

### 1947

This union became the International Union of Official Travel Organisations (IUOTO), which is today known as the World Tourism Organization, WTO.

### 1948

In its first General Assembly, the IUOTO adopted the principle of Regional Commissions: 19 European countries were represented and those countries decided to establish the first such Commission. Since its creation, ETC, has been a results-oriented organisation working closely with government agencies and all segments of the industry to achieve practical objectives. First priority was given to making governments aware of the importance of tourism in their national economies, which had been deeply disturbed by World War II. That is why ETC has always supported an international co-operation, a collective action and the building of a European solidarity.

## Membership

In 1948, the original membership of the European Travel Commission was 19 countries. At that time Eastern European countries, members of IUOTO were invited to participate. None of these countries accepted, apparently due to political reasons. Germany, Yugoslavia, Malta and Cyprus joined the Commission a few years later.

## Mission

ETC sees itself as a virtual organisation marketing Europe as a tourist destination in global markets, primarily by means of the internet. The three principal focuses of the Commission's work are electronic marketing, market intelligence and operational excellence. ETC seeks to provide added value to members by encouraging exchange of information and management expertise and promoting awareness about the role played by national tourism organisations.

## Organisation and budget

The members elect a President, three Vice-Presidents, a Board of Directors, a Chairman of the Market Intelligence Group and a Chairman of the e-Marketing Network for revolving two years terms.

ETC is entirely financed by Members' contributions, calculated according to a set of agreed criteria. Additional financial support for specific campaigns is raised overseas. Long-standing local industry support for ETC's activities is proof of its credibility in the field.

ETC is registered in Belgium as an 'association internationale sans but lucratif' - a non-profit making international association.

## Overseas

The representatives of the overseas offices of the European national tourism organisations operating in the various long-haul markets join together to form an ETC Operations Group and elect a Chairman. They decide on a programme of joint activities for the promotion of Europe for the year ahead, propose a budget, and seek local industry support.

## In Europe

This programme is submitted for approval to ETC's Members in Europe, who meet twice a year (in Spring and Autumn) for a General Meeting.

## Activities

ETC currently promotes and markets "Destination Europe" around the world through its operations groups in the United States, Canada, Asia (China) and Latin America (Brazil). ETC also plans to extend its activities to other emerging markets such as India and Russia.

Vital to ETC activities are its Market Intelligence Group and e-Marketing Network. The Market Intelligence Group commissions and produces market intelligence studies, handbooks on methodologies and best practice, and facilitates the exchange of European tourism statistics on "TourMIS". The e-Marketing Network provides information and expertise about the use of digital media by national tourism organisations, produces the "ETC Digital", and organises an e-Business Academy once a year. The work of all operations groups is carried out by experts from member NTOs.

The official website of the European Travel Commission (ETC). ETC markets Europe as tourist destination on behalf of its 33 member countries. Under a pair of soaring wings, a symbol of travel and discovery deeply rooted in Europe's myths and history, visiteurope.com brings the excitement of a European vacation to potential guests around the world with localised versions in a number of major languages. The content of visiteurope.com is brought jointly by ETC and the national tourism organisations.

# THE INTERNATIONAL AIR TRANSPORT ASSOCIATION (IATA)

IATA is a trade association of the world's airlines. Consisting of 290 airlines, primarily major carriers, representing 117 countries, the IATA's member airlines account for carrying approximately 82% of total Available Seat Miles air traffic.[2] IATA supports airline activity and helps formulate industry policy and standards. It is headquartered in Montreal, Quebec, Canada with Executive Offices in Geneva, Switzerland.

## History

IATA was formed in April 1945 in Havana, Cuba and is the successor to the International Air Traffic Association, which was formed in 1919 at The Hague, Netherlands. At its founding, IATA consisted of 57 airlines from 31 countries. Much of IATA's early work was technical and it provided input to the newly created International Civil Aviation Organization(ICAO), which was reflected in the annexes of the Chicago Convention, the international treaty that still governs the conduct of international air transport today.

The Chicago Convention couldn't resolve the issue of who flies where, however, and this has resulted in the thousands of bilateral air transport agreements in existence today. The benchmark standard for the early bilaterals was the 1946 United States-United Kingdom Bermuda Agreement.

At a time when many airlines were government owned and loss-making, IATA operated as a cartel, charged by the governments with setting a fixed fare structure that avoided price competition. The first Traffic Conference was held in 1947 in Rio de Janeiro and reached unanimous agreement on some 400 resolutions.

Aviation grew rapidly over the following decades and IATA's work duly expanded.

## Priorities

## Following are the Priorities of the Association

### (i) Safety

Safety is the number one priority for IATA. The main instrument for safety is the IATA Operational Safety Audit (IOSA). IOSA has also been mandated at the state level by several countries. In 2017, aviation posted its safest year ever, surpassing the previous record set in 2012. The new global Western-built jet accident rate became the equivalent of one accident every 7.36 million flights. Future improvements will be founded on data sharing with a database fed by a multitude of sources and housed by the Global Safety Information Center. In June 2014 the IATA set up a special panel to study measures to track aircraft in flight in real time. The move was in response to the disappearance without trace of Malaysia Airlines Flight 370 on 8 March 2014.

### (ii) Security

Security has become increasingly important following the September 11 attacks in 2001. Following a series of uncoordinated rules by different countries, the industry has developed a Checkpoint of the Future, which is based on risk assessment and passenger differentiation.

### Simplifying the Business

Launched in 2004, This initiative has introduced a number of crucial concepts to passenger travel, including the electronic ticket and the bar coded boarding pass. Many other innovations are being established as part of the Fast Travel initiative, including a range of self-service baggage options.

An innovative program, launched in 2012 is New Distribution Capability. This will replace the pre-Internet EDIFACT messaging standard that is still the basis of the global distribution system / travel agent channel and replace it with an XML standard. This will enable the same choices to be offered to high street travel shoppers as are offered to those who book directly through airline websites. A filing with the US Department of Transportation brought over 400 comments.

### (iii) Environment

IATA members and all industry stakeholders have agreed to three sequential environmental goals:

An average improvement in fuel efficiency of 1.5% per annum from 2009 through 2020

A cap on net carbon emissions from aviation from 2020 (carbon-neutral growth)

A 50% reduction in net aviation carbon emissions by 2050 relative to 2005 levels.

At the 69th IATA annual general meeting in Cape Town, South Africa, members overwhelmingly endorsed a resolution on "Implementation of the Aviation Carbon-Neutral Growth (CNG2020) Strategy."

The resolution provides governments with a set of principles on how governments could:

Establish procedures for a single market-based measure (MBM)

Integrate a single MBM as part of an overall package of measures to achieve CNG2020

IATA member airlines agreed that a single mandatory carbon offsetting scheme would be the simplest and most effective option for an MBM.

## Services

IATA provides consulting and training services in many areas crucial to aviation.

Travel Agent accreditation is available for travel professionals. Full accreditation allows agents to sell tickets on behalf of all IATA member airlines.

Cargo Agent accreditation is a similar program.

IATA also runs the Billing and Settlement Plan, which is a $300 billion-plus financial system that looks after airline money.

And it provides a number of business intelligence publications and services.

Training covers all aspects of aviation and ranges from beginner courses through to senior management courses.

IATA manages the Ticket Tax Box Service (TTBS), a database of taxes for airlines.

## Strategic partners

IATA's Strategic Partners are aviation solution providers who, through their work with various IATA work groups, help build and maintain relationships with key industry stakeholders and work with IATA in serving the air transport industry.

## INTERNATIONAL CIVIL AVIATION ORGANIZATION (ICAO)

The International Civil Aviation Organization (ICAO), is a specialized agency of the United Nations. It codifies the principles and techniques of international air navigation and fosters the planning and development of international air transport to ensure safe and orderly growth. Its headquarters is located in the Quartier International of Montreal, Quebec, Canada.

The ICAO Council adopts standards and recommended practices concerning air navigation, its infrastructure, flight inspection, prevention of unlawful interference, and facilitation of border-crossing procedures for international civil aviation. ICAO defines the protocols for air accident investigation followed by transport safety authorities in countries signatory to the Chicago Convention on International Civil Aviation.

The Air Navigation Commission (ANC) is the technical body within ICAO. The Commission is composed of 19 Commissioners, nominated by the ICAO's contracting states, and appointed by the ICAO Council.[3] Commissioners serve as independent experts, who although nominated by their states, do not serve as state or political representatives. The development of international Standards And Recommended Practices is done under the direction of the ANC through the formal process of ICAO Panels. Once approved by the Commission, standards are sent to the Council, the political body of ICAO, for consultation and coordination with the Member States before final adoption.

ICAO is distinct from other international air transport organizations, the International Air Transport Association (IATA), a trade association representing airlines; the Civil Air Navigation Services Organization (CANSO), an organization for Air navigation service providers (ANSPs); and the Airports Council International, a trade association of airport authorities.

*Standardizes machine-readable passports worldwide.* Such passports have an area where some of the information otherwise written in textual form is written as strings of alphanumeric characters, printed in a manner suitable for optical character recognition. This enables border controllers and other law enforcement agents to process such passports quickly, without having to enter the information manually into a computer. ICAO publishes Document 9303 Machine Readable Travel Documents, the technical standard for machine-readable passports. A more recent standard is for biometric passports. These contain biometrics to authenticate the identity of travellers. The passport's critical information is stored on a tiny RFID computer chip, much like information stored on smart cards. Like some smart cards, the passport book design calls for an embedded contactless chip that is able to hold digital signature data to ensure the integrity of the passport and the biometric data.

ICAO is active in infrastructure management, including Communication, navigation and surveillance / Air Traffic Management (CNS/ATM) systems, which employ digital technologies (like satellite systems with various levels of automation) in order to maintain a seamless global air traffic management system.

## History

The forerunner to ICAO was the International Commission for Air Navigation (ICAN). It held its first convention in 1903 in Berlin, Germany, but no agreements were reached among the eight countries that attended. At the second convention in 1906, also held in Berlin, 27 countries attended. The third convention, held in London in 1912 allocated the first radio call signs for use by aircraft. ICAN continued to operate until 1945.

Fifty-two countries signed the Chicago Convention on International Civil Aviation, also known as the Chicago Convention, in Chicago, Illinois, on 7 December 1944. Under its terms, a Provisional International Civil Aviation Organization (PICAO) was to be established, to be replaced in turn by a permanent organization when 26 countries ratified the convention. Accordingly, PICAO began operating on 6 June 1945, replacing ICAN. The 26th country ratified the Convention on 5 March 1947 and, consequently PICAO was disestablished on 4 April 1947 and replaced by ICAO, which began operations the same day. In October 1947, ICAO became an agency of the United Nations linked to the United Nations Economic and Social Council (ECOSOC).

In April 2013 Qatar offered to serve as the new permanent seat of the Organization. Qatar promised to construct a massive new headquarters for ICAO and cover all moving expenses, stating that Montreal "was too far from Europe and Asia", "had cold winters," was hard to attend due to the refusal of the Canadian government to provide visas in a timely manner, and that the taxes imposed on ICAO by Canada were too high. According to The Globe and Mail, Qatar's move was at least partly motivated by the pro-Israel foreign policy of Canadian Prime Minister Stephen Harper. Approximately one month later, Qatar withdrew its bid after a separate proposal to the ICAO's governing council to move the ICAO triennial conference to Doha was defeated.

## Statute

The 9th edition of the Convention on International Civil Aviation includes modifications from 1948 up to year 2006. ICAO refers to its current edition of the Convention as the Statute, and designates it as ICAO Document 7300/9. The Convention has 19 Annexes that are listed by title in the article Convention on International Civil Aviation.

## Membership

As of November 2017, there are 192 ICAO members, consisting of 191 of the 193 UN members (all but Dominica, Liechtenstein), plus the Cook Islands. Liechtenstein has delegated Switzerland to implement the treaty to make it applicable in the territory of Liechtenstein. The Republic of China was a founding member of ICAO but was replaced by People's Republic of China as the legal representative of China in 1971.

## Council

The Council of ICAO is elected by the Assembly every 3 years and consists of 36 members elected in 3 categories. The present Council was elected on 4 October 2016 at the 39th Assembly of ICAO at Montreal. The structure of the present Council is as follows:

PART I – (States of chief importance in air transport) – Australia, Brazil, Canada, China, France, Germany, Italy, Japan, Russian Federation, United Kingdom, and the United States.

PART II – (States which make the largest contribution to the provision of facilities for international civil air navigation) – Argentina, Colombia, Egypt, India, Ireland, Mexico, Nigeria, Saudi Arabia, Singapore, South Africa, Spain and Sweden.

PART III– (States ensuring geographic representation)- Algeria, Cape Verde, Congo, Cuba, Ecuador, Kenya, Malaysia, Panama, Republic of Korea, Turkey, United Arab Emirates, United Republic of Tanzania, and Uruguay.

### Standards

ICAO also standardizes certain functions for use in the airline industry, such as the Aeronautical Message Handling System (AMHS). This makes it a standards organization.

Each country should have an accessible Aeronautical Information Publication (AIP), based on standards defined by ICAO, containing information essential to air navigation. Countries are required to update their AIP manuals every 28 days and so provide definitive regulations, procedures and information for each country about airspace and airports. ICAO's standards also dictate that temporary hazards to aircraft are regularly published using NOTAMs.

ICAO defines an International Standard Atmosphere (also known as ICAO Standard Atmosphere), a model of the standard variation of pressure, temperature, density, and viscosity with altitude in the Earth's atmosphere. This is useful in calibrating instruments and designing aircraft.

## ORGANISATION FOR ECONOMIC CO-OPERATION AND DEVELOPMENT (OECD)

The Organisation for Economic Co-operation and Development (OECD) is an intergovernmental economic organisation with 36 member countries, founded in 1961 to stimulate economic progress and world trade. It is a forum of countries describing themselves as committed to democracy and the market economy, providing a platform to compare policy experiences, seeking answers to common problems, identify good practices and coordinate domestic and international policies of its members. Most OECD members are high-income economies with a very high Human Development Index (HDI) and are regarded as developed countries. In 1948, the OECD originated as the Organisation for European Economic Co-operation (OEEC).

In 1961, the OEEC was reformed into the Organisation for Economic Co-operation and Development by the Convention on the Organisation for Economic Co-operation and Development and membership was extended to non-European states. The OECD's headquarters are at the Château de la Muette in Paris, France. The OECD is funded by contributions from member states at varying rates and had a total budget of €374 million in 2017.

## PACIFIC ASIA TRAVEL ASSOCIATION

The association's constitution was "To encourage and assist in the development of the travel industries throughout the Pacific area". While marketing activities were its primary goal, the delegates of the first conference also envisioned the association as one that could work with both government and private business in developing travel.

The Pacific Asia Travel Association (PATA) is a membership association working to promote the responsible development of travel and tourism in the Asia Pacific region.

One of PATA's main accomplishments in its first year was to publicise itself to the international travel community. The association's first executive director Sam Mercer noted that the first conference "focused the attention of the entire travel world on an awakening of tourism in the Pacific". News articles and press releases were sent to, and subsequently published in, numerous publications – including both specialist travel press and general audience newspapers. A particularly effective vehicle for PITA's self-promotion was its quarterly newspaper, PITA News Bulletin, which by the end of its first year was being sent to over 500 addresses throughout the world.

## Pata Today

Founded in 1951, the Pacific Asia Travel Association (PATA) is a not-for profit association that is internationally acclaimed for acting as a catalyst for the responsible development of travel and tourism to, from and within the Asia Pacific region. The Association provides aligned advocacy, insightful research and innovative events to its member organisations, comprising 95 government, state and city tourism bodies, 25 international airlines and airports, 108 hospitality organisations, 72 educational institutions, and hundreds of travel industry companies in Asia Pacific and beyond. Thousands of travel professionals belong to the 36 local PATA chapters worldwide. The chapters organise travel industry training and business development events. Their grassroots activism underpins PATA's membership in Uniting Travel, a coalition of the world's major Travel & Tourism organisations dedicated to ensuring that the sector speaks with one voice and acts in unison on the major issues and includes ACI, CLIA, IATA, ICAO, WEF, UNWTO and the WTTC.

Since 1951 PATA has led from the front as the leading voice and authority on travel and tourism in the Asia Pacific region

In partnership with private and public sector members, PATA enhances the sustainable growth, value and quality of travel and tourism to-from-and-within, the region.

The Association provides leadership and counsel on an individual and collective basis to its member organisations, comprising 95 government, state and city tourism bodies, 25 international airlines and airports, 108 hospitality organisations, 72 educational institutions, and hundreds of travel industry companies in Asia Pacific and beyond.

PATA's Strategic Intelligence Centre (SIC) offers unrivalled data and insights including Asia Pacific inbound and outbound statistics, analyses and forecasts as well as in-depth reports on strategic tourism markets

PATA's events create millions of dollars of new business each year for its members

Thousands of travel professionals belong to 36 active PATA chapters worldwide and participate in a wide range of PATA and industry events.

The PATA Foundation contributes to the sustainable and responsible development of travel and tourism in Asia Pacific through the protection of the environment, the conservation of heritage and support for education.

## TRAVEL AGENTS ASSOCIATION OF INDIA (TAAI)

The Travel Agents Association of India (TAAI) was formed towards the end of 1951 by a group of the 12 leading agents who felt the need to create an association to regulate the travel industry in India along organised lines, in accordance with sound business principles.

The association's membership steadily increased from the original 12 to over 1500 members consisting of Active, Associate, Allied, Government and Non-Resident members. The Travel Agents Association of India is a professional coordinating body of different segments of travel and tourism industry. The association is a non-political, non-commercial & non-profit making organisation. It is recognized as the main representative body of the travel and tourism industry and is also recognised by the world body of Tourism-UFTAA.

### Aims and Objectives

TAAI aims at the development of the travel and tourism industry in the country by constantly improving the standards of service and professionalism in the industry so as to cater to the needs of tourists and within India and overseas. TAAI is also engaged in providing mutual cooperation among the different segments of the travel and tourism industry and among TAAI members by contributing to the progress and growth of the industry as a whole. The principle objective is to safeguard the interest of the travelling public and to maintain high ethical standards within the travel trade.

### Activities

Following are the major activities of TAAI:
- To function as a powerful platform for exchange of ideas, thoughts and experiences
- To help promote, maintain and stimulate the growth of travel and tourism in the country
- To educate and equip the members to meet the challenges of tomorrow through conventions and seminars
- To maintain close contact with world bodies and represent matters affecting travel and tourism of the country
- To draw the attention of controlling and regulating authorities in the country and discuss with them the problems of the industry and work towards the betterment of its members
- To gather useful information on travel and tourism and disseminate it to its members for their guidance and finally to help foster better understanding between the different segments of the travel and tourism industry and bring them into its fold by offering membership under different categories.

### Membership Criteria

1. Active member

(IATA approved Head Office location of a travel agent providing comprehensive services) criteria to become an active member:

- The applicant must be an IATA agent having their location situated in a city or town.
- The applicant should not be a GSA or PSA of any airline.
- The applicant shall not have interests in ownership/management/profit of such GSA/PSA or any interests in the ownership/management/profit of such GSA/PSA to influence the commercial policy and/or management decisions of such GSA/PSA and vice versa.
- The applicant must be located in an easily accessible area and must have professionally trained staff with a certificate issued by IATA/UFTAA or any IATA carrier. Such staff must be in the organisation at least for a period of two years at the time of inspection.
- The paid up capital of the applicant in metros/mini cities whether limited, private limited, partnership or proprietorship should be minimum of Rs. 5 lakhs.
- The proposer and the seconder of the applicant should both be accredited representatives of active members from the same region/chapter for a period of minimum two years respectively. Not more than 3 applicants can be proposed/seconded by a single member.

2. Associate members

(IATA approved Branch Office location of active member) criteria to become an associate member:

- Applicant's registered office or their head office must be an active member of the Association.
- The applicant organisation must be located in an easily accessible area and must have professionally trained staff with a certificate issued by IATA/UFTAA or any IATA carrier. Such staff must be in the organisation at least for a period of one year at the time of inspection.
- The paid up capital of the applicants head office should be a minimum Rs. 5 lakhs in metro cities.
- The proposer must be an accredited representative of an "active" location while the seconder may be an active or associate accredited member. They must be from the same region/chapter and should be members of TAAI for a minimum period of two years.

3. Allied member

(Organisations engaged in allied business, i.e., various segments of travel and tourism industry such as excursion agents, tour operators, hoteliers, airlines, GSA etc.)

## Allied Member:

## Tour Operators:

The applicant must have recognition from the Department of Tourism, Government of India.

### Excursion Agents:
The applicant must have recognition from the Department of Tourism, Government of India or from the respective State Tourism Department.

### Hotels:
The applicant with existing running property, must be members of the Federation of Hotels and Restaurant Association of India or Hotel and Restaurant Association of the respective region.

### Airline Companies:
The Applicant must be an IATA member or operating scheduled airlines.

### General Sales Agents (GSAs)
The applicant must be a GSA of an IATA member airline which is an allied member of TAAI.

The office of the GSA shall only be located in a town/city where the airline does not have its operational office and only undertake such work that the airlines would have itself undertaken in its normal functioning.
or

The applicant must be a GSA of an IATA recognised CRS company which is already an allied member.

### Agents Providing Travel Related Services
The applicant must have a proven record of 5 years, but not as a ticketing agent for any airline/agent/GSA.

### Courier Companies
The applicant must have a proven record of 5 years.

### Travel Related Educational institutions
The applicant must have a proven record if 5 years.

### Banks
The applicant must be nationalised or have a similar standing.

### Government Members (Central and State Government Departments and Public Sector Tourism Organisations.) Criteria to become a Government Member:
Department of Tourism–Government of India, State tourism departments, tourism development corporations of various states and any other travel and tourism related government undertakings are eligible in this category.

There is no separate application form for this category. Only a letter of request from the head of the department, requesting for membership is needed and this should be sent directly to TAAI Secretariat, Mumbai.

## Non Resident Member

**Overseas Travel Agents, Tour Operators and Hotels etc. are eligible in this category criteria to become a non resident member:**

**Active:** The applicant must be an IATA Agent and a member of the respective National Travel Agents Association.
**Allied:** Airline: Must be a scheduled airline.
Hotel: Must have recognition from their National Hotel Association.

The Association is headed by a president who is elected by the members during the annual convention. The president is assisted in his work by Vice-President, Honorary Secretary General, Honorary Treasurer, Chief Honorary Representative and Executive Secretary.

**Administrative Set-Up**

The registered office of the Association is located in Mumbai at:
2-D, Lawrence and Mayo House,
276, DR. D. N. Road,
Fort, Mumbai – 400 001
Email: travels@bom2.vsnl.net.in

The TAAI functions with regional/chapter centres in the following states and Union Territories:

1. Western Region         : Mumbai
2. Northern Region        : Delhi
3. Eastern Region         : Kolkata
4. Southern Region        : Chennai
5. Gujarat Chapter        : Ahmedabad
6. Karnataka Chapter      : Bengaluru
7. Kerala Chapter         : Cochin
8. Andhra Pradesh Chapter : Hyderabad
9. City Committee         : Pune
10. Punjab Chapter        : Jalandhar

For becoming a TAAI member all application forms are to be properly completed, signed by the Head of the organisation duly proposed and seconded, together with entrance and membership fee by way of demand drafts payable at Mumbai, in favour of "The Travel Agents Association of India", is to be sent directly to their respective regions and chapters.

One of the major events of TAAI is their annual convention. The annual convention is attended by a large number of representatives from the travel trade, both government & non-government. Matters concerning all aspects of working of travel agents are put forward to the concerned authorities present at the convention. In addition, important matters related with promotion of product are also discussed during this convention.

Travel Agents Association of India (TAAI) is also represented at various important fora both official and non-official. TAAI is also represented in the Hotel and Restaurant Approval Classification Committee, Reserve Bank of India Advisory Board, National Railway User Consultative Council and Indian Institute of Travel and Tourism Management.

# 10
# TRANSPORT AND ACCOMMODATION SECTORS

### Chapter Objectives

**After reading this chapter the reader should be able to:**
- Understand the importance of the transport sector as a part of the tourist industry.
- Know different forms of transport.
- Understand role of air transport in promoting international tourism.
- Explain the importance of the transport network to tourism.
- Identify various types of accommodation units.
- Know restaurants services and cuisines.
- Importence of supplementary accommodation.
- To know about various form of supplementary accommodation.

## TRANSPORT SECTOR

Transportation will include movement from a destination to the country to be visited as also the local transportation while in the country. The local transportation will include different modes of travel like air, railways, surface transport, taxis and motoring. It is important for travel agents to provide all the necessary information on all the modes of transport within the country, which may include the schedules of both domestic air carriers and railways especially to major tourist centres. As far as rail travel is concerned, it is important for a travel agent to give detailed information about the tourist trains on railways, and other trains connecting metros. In addition information about in rail pass for the foreigners, is to be given. The procedure for booking and reservation is also to be explained to the tourists.

## Bus Travel

The basic features of bus travel is its diversity throughout the world. No single information source is valid for a continent, sometimes not even for a country. The variety of options is very extensive, and this requires a lot of work on the part of the travel agent.

Bus travel is used mostly by low-budget tourists. There are many reasons for preferring a bus to other means of transport. Although long return trips take place as well, there are journeys from one point to another, sometimes with stops in between. Longer return trips require no additional information-gathering for the travel agent:

Buses are usually used for urban and suburban schedules travel where the level of comfort is not expected to be high and where at peak hours passengers might even have to stand. Coaches, on the other hand, are usually much more comfortable and used for regional or cross-country journeys.

Buses and coaches are not bound to rails, so they have the advantage that tourists can go to more destinations than on trains. They reach even the most remote villages in Asia, South America, Africa, and elsewhere. Usually, the main bus stations are situated in the centre of large cities near hotels and restaurants. Several countries offer the choice of express, long-distance or local, slow connections. Often seat reservation is possible or even necessary on busy lines. Long-distance coach journeys require an adequate preparation; for example: documentation, clothing, food and drink.

## Rail Travel

The organised rail transport came in the year 1841.

### Reasons why people prefer rail travel:

- Remains the cheapest means of travel universally
- Introduction of new technology on railways
- Offers a wide range of tourist services
- Recently has become more market oriented
- Product innovation
- High speed, comfortable trains
- Growing market on long transcontinental routes
- Modern rail system spread over the Europe covers densely populated areas in Western Europe

A tourist can travel throughout Europe in fast comfortable trains with all the modern facilities.

Rail transport has developed very fast in Europe.

### Reasons:

- Environmental friendly
- High cost of air travel
- Safety
- Connectivity

- Decongested route ways
- Arrival at destination rested
- Ability to move around the coach
- Personal comfort
- Couchette (sleeper accommodation) at night

## Euro Rail System

Twenty-five European countries have joined together to offer foreign tourists unlimited first class comfortable travel at a reduced rate. Euro rail pass, valid for a period of two weeks to three months, can take tourists to most of the major countries in western and eastern Europe.

Eurail trains are high-tech, fast and user-friendly. They are also the most efficient and safest way of going from one city (or country) to the other. One need not worry about driving in strange cars, paying high fuel costs, reaching airports and taking flights, etc.

Eurail offers a unique and flexible travel experience that allows stopping anywhere, anytime one likes. During the day you can enjoy stunning scenery while travelling. When travelling during the night one can save the costs of hotel accommodation and have a full day to enjoy upon arrival.

On top of that, travelling by train is an excellent way to meet the locals as many people in Europe travel by train on a daily basis. They will be happy to share their travel experience, as well as their pride for their country!

Each Eurail adventure starts at a railway station and each station has its own personality. Most of them are located in picturesque buildings in the middle of the town, close to taxi, tram or subway connections. Many offer great services like restaurants, coffee bars, toilet facilities, reservation offices, bookstores, foreign exchange offices and gift shops. Railway stations form an integral part of the lives of most Europeans. And therefore they are an excellent location to meet fellow travellers.

With a Eurail pass a tourist can explore Europe for thousands of miles running across the European continent connecting one breathtaking scenery to another, and one exciting city to the other. All one needs to do is board a train, sit back, relax and enjoy unlimited travel in an elegant, quiet and comfortable way. The pass can be used from Scandinavia and up through Italy and Iberian Peninsula, Greece and Ireland and also part of Russia.

The system works through over 100 Euro city trains- high standard long distance providing premium, international travel, between European city centres. The Euro rail system is the largest co-operative association sponsored by the major European railways.

## Railways in the System

Austria, Belgium, Croatia, Czech Republic, Denmark, Finland, France, Germany, Hungary, Greece, Norway, Ireland, Italy, Luxembourg, Montenegro, Netherlands, Poland, Portugal, Romania, Spain, Sweden, Switzerland, Bulgaria.

## Validity of the Pass

Eurail passes are available for a minimum period of 15 days and maximum three months. In addition the passes are also available for a period of 21 days, one month and two months. The pass cannot be used for travel until the first and after the last day of validity.

Eurail passes are good for travel in the countries in which the specific pass is valid. As a rule the traveller's pass is valid in the countries mentioned on their pass. If no countries are mentioned, this would means your client has a Eurail Global Pass, valid in the following 18 countries: Austria (including Liechtenstein), Belgium, Denmark, Finland, France (including Monaco), Germany, Hungary, Greece, Norway, Ireland (Republic), Italy, Luxembourg, the Netherlands, Portugal, Romania, Spain, Sweden, Switzerland.

If the pass shows validity for BENELUX, it is valid in Belgium, the Netherlands and Luxembourg.

## Different Products on Euro Rail

### Saver passes

Saver passes are intended for 2 or more people travelling together and offer a discount of approximately 15% per person (compared to the price for 1 person).

The saver pass ticket consists of the actual ticket and a so-called control voucher. This control vouchers bears the names and passport numbers of all travellers and must be kept together with the ticket at all times. You can issue a saver pass for a maximum of 5 travellers per ticket. If you want to sell a saver pass for 6 persons, you could, for example, issue 2 passes for 3 travellers.

### Child Discount

Children aged 4, up to and including 11 pay half the adult fare. This also applies to saver passes. Children under 4 years of age travel for free, unless a reservation for a separate seat/bed is required. Note that Eurail national passes may have different rules concerning child discounts.

### Senior Travellers

Eurail recently introduced special rates for senior travellers choosing a Eurail national pass. These special rates are not available for all national passes. Senior passes are intended for travellers aged 60 and above.

### Youth Passes

With the exception of a few Eurail regional and national passes all Eurail youth passes are in 2nd class and offer a discount of approximately 35% on the 1st class pass. Youth passes are available for travellers under 26 years of age. The travellers must be under 26 on the first day of validity of the pass. There is no special reduction on the youth pass for children.

### 1st and 2nd class
As a rule, Eurail passes are available for 1st class travel, with the youth passes being valid in 2nd class only. However, some Eurail regional and national passes offer 2nd class passes for adults and 1st class passes for youth.

### Tour passes
Eurail tour passes are available for tour operators only and may be sold as part of a package.

### Sleeping Accommodation
Facilities vary depending on availability. Many trains have couchette-coaches having retractable seats unfolding into coaches for night travel. There is no segregation of sexes.

### Reservation
While reservations aren't compulsory on all European trains, they are highly recommended for long-distance trains, during peak travel periods and if one absolutely must reach one's destination by a certain day and time. Advance booking is highly recommended, as the number of seats available is limited. Having a Eurail pass does not guarantee a seat. The costs for a reservation are not included in a Eurail pass and may vary widely depending on the country, type of train, as well as the date of purchase and or travel. On domestic trains with compulsory reservations in Romania, Poland and Austria, seat reservations are free of charge for 1st class pass holders (in Poland also for 2nd class pass holders). Travellers can only obtain these free reservations at a local ticket window.

### Compulsory seat reservations
The Eurail timetable sometimes shows trains marked with the [R] symbol. These trains require passengers to have a seat reservation. Railway companies are using the reservations system to better serve the wishes of clients with regards to seating (window, non-smoking smoking, etc). The compulsory reservations also avoid trains being overcrowded and having corridors packed with travellers. On night trains reservations are compulsory for travel in sleepers, couchette, (reclining) seats.

### Refund

#### General refund rules
Application for refund of a Eurail pass must be presented by the clients to the agency where the pass was purchased. This has to be done within the fixed times indicated hereafter, otherwise no refund can be given.
- At all times the original documents (pass in cover) must be submitted.
- The travel agency must forward the application to the issuing office indicated on the Eurail pass

- There is a 15% cancellation charge
- Neither a lost nor stolen Eurail pass, nor any ticket purchased in replacement of such a Eurail pass, can be refunded or replaced.

## British Rail

Similar to Euro rail passes, British rail passes entitle the holder to unlimited rail travel in England, Scotland and Wales. It is valid on more than 1,600 British trains serving 2,000 railway stations throughout UK.

- Valid for 7, 14, 21 days or one month.
- The pass must be purchased prior to the trip through BA Offices, British Tourist Offices, and Airline Computer Reservation System.
- Cannot be purchased anywhere in UK.
- Advance reservation mandatory on some trains.
- Sleeping berths on some trains at extra cost.
- Children between 5-13 years travel at half rates.
- Senior citizen passes.
- Special Brit rail packages includes tour program rail + hotel accommodation car rental.

## Swiss Rail

It offers the world's most extensive network of rail-cum-public bus transportation. It has the first airport railway station in the world, fully integrated into the national and international train network. The system is the cleanest, safest and most punctual in the world. It offers fast and easy transfers from airport into the heart of the city. Each train offers scenic highlights. There are several possibilities of catering abroad.

## Swiss Pass

Offers unlimited travel through town and country for a period of 4 days to a month.

## Car Rentals

Renting an automobile at hourly, daily, weekly or monthly rates.

Many air travellers prefer to rent an automobile at their destinations rather than use public transport. Some important rental companies are:
- AVIS
- Europe
- Hertz

## Car Rental Reservation Checklist:

- Where is the car rental company located? (Example: airport; downtown; at the hotel.)
- What are its hours of operation?
- Is there a shuttle service available?
- The car categories available (Example: compact, economy, mid-size,

full-size, luxury.)
- Will the car rental company honour special requests? (Example: non-smoking, four-door, car phone, particular model.)
- What types of insurance coverage are available for car rental?
- Does the client's insurance or credit card cover rental car damage due to vehicle theft or collision?
- What are the different rates offered by the company?
- Are per mile costs assessed or does the car come with unlimited mileage?
- Are there any additional charges?
- Are there any other requirements or restrictions?
- What are the requirements to rent and operate the rental car?

Making land arrangements for a client who is visiting a destination is very crucial for successful organisation of a travel. The travel agent has to be an expert and must be familiar with all aspects of land arrangement to be made for a client. The major areas for land arrangements would refer to making proper reservations, organising sightseeing tours, local transport, reservation of accommodations etc.

Travel agents need to be familiar with the details of information concerning sightseeing and excursion tours and selecting accommodation.

## Sightseeing/Excursions/Tours

The advantage of arranging sightseeing in advance is that your client does not have to waste his time, queuing up in the local agency. Also, a balance can be established in advance between leisure time and sightseeing as well as for tours of the city and countryside.

**Motor coach tours:** Apart form the economic viewpoint, there is the advantage of meeting other travellers, but clients have to arrange their own transportation to meeting points, as pick-up is very seldom done on motorcoach tours.

**Private car tours:** Your client is picked up at the hotel, has the choice of time of departure and can stop wherever he like, but this is the most expensive solution. In some places there are regular private car tours, or else sightseeing can be done on a seat-in-car basis.

## Hire of Private Car with Chauffeur

**City Hire:** must be recommended to deluxe clients, whose time is limited between trains, boats or planes or who already know the city and want to see only special places or go shopping. Since very often the chauffeur cannot act as a guide, a private guide will be needed for sightseeing.

**Touring Hire:** if a private car is used for travelling from one city to another, local guides in each place will be sufficient. Distance covered daily should not exceed 250 km. The client's attention has to be drawn to the fact that he will have to pay for the empty run of the car (return to point of departure). The full daily basis charge is due, even if the vehicle is picked up in the evening.

**Motor launch tours/boats trips:** The same applies as for motor coach tours. Deluxe clients will be picked up at the hotel by private car and driven to embarkation pier.

**Self-driven cars** can also be provided when clients fill the necessary conditions and, if required, a local guide can be placed.

Clients must be told that advance reservations is necessary for musical festivals, theatre and concert tickets. Confirmation of requested tickets cannot be guaranteed and tickets are not refundable unless they can be resold.

## Land Arrangements

The details furnished by your clients, will enable you to make an estimate of the land arrangements.

## Selecting Accommodation*

There are numerous types of hotels available all over the world. Various types of hotels available are:
- International hotels where services have been standardised and usually range from 1-star to 5-star deluxe categories.
- Famous hotel chains with similar kind of flavour all over the world.
- Budget category hotels which are cheap with the only basics.
- Family run uniquely styled cosy and comfortable boutique hotels.
- Apartment hotels for longer stays.
- Resort hotels with that unique taste of natural themes.
- Floating hotels and house boats.
- Business hotels with everything that a business traveller might require.
- Heritage hotel that's normally an old building with heritage value attached to it.

Apart from these if the agent is looking for an unusual holiday experience he must choose some form of supplementary accommodations available all over the world. It can be:
- **Bed and breakfast** unit where clients stay with locals and enjoy local hospitality, witness real culture and cuisine.
- **Motel** which are specifically meant for a highway traveller with all related facilities.
- **Circuit house** normally at remote locations.
- **Country homes** which are far away from the maddening crowds of the city.
- **Outdoor camps** that not only offer the client union with nature but also soft and hard adventure options for the more daring and adventurous ones.
- **Youth hostels** which provide decent accommodation with basic comforts for young travellers.
- **Accommodation Units** provide the client stay based on meal plan patterns which are uniformly observed all over the world; These are.

- **EP:** European Plan: Only accommodation (i.e., no meals have been booked when stay in a hotel on EP basis).
- **CP:** Continental plan: Stay along with continental breakfast (can be a mix of various cuisine when served in buffet system).
- **MAP:** Modified American Plan: Stay with breakfast and one major meal of the day i.e. either lunch or dinner.
- **AP:** American Plan: Stay and all meals (breakfast, lunch, dinner) of a day booked at a hotel.

### Selecting Sight Seeing Places at Destinations

A major problem for many visitors to strange cities is how to select a sightseeing tour. They may abhor the idea of being herded about like sheep, yet few would disagree that a good tour can greatly help to overcome the feeling of insecurity, even intimidation, that often accompanies arrival in a metropolis where one has no friends and where the prevalent language is not one's own.

For a tourist, a half-day coach tour, taken as soon as possible after arrival, puts things in order. It gives him a feel of the pulse of a city and a grasp of how it is laid out. He may dislike the tour pace - too long at one sight, too little at another, too much getting on and off the bus and too much time stalled in traffic or waiting at a stop for stragglers. But almost always he will leave the tour with the confidence that he has learned how to cope with the city, to find the best shops, restaurants and entertainment and to know what museums, parks or historic sights or interesting neighbourhoods to revisit at leisure.

Organised sightseeing has become so competitive in many cities, however, and so many options are sometimes available, that it often is difficult to select the best. How does one find it? In telephone interviews, this question was put to a variety of people who ought to know: travel agents, tourism officials and tour operators themselves. Almost all agreed that the best recommendation is word of mouth from someone you trust, but this isn't always available.

Many travellers don't realise it, but a lot of foreign sightseeing - even a two-hour tour - can be arranged through travel agents before leaving home.

### Booking Flights

Having studied the city-to-city flight schedule information in the OAG flight guide, your passenger should be in a position to select the most suitable flights.

The next step for the agent is to check seat availability on behalf of the intended passengers. The agent does this by telephoning the selected airline and asking the reservation staff to check seat numbers in the airline's computer database.

Automated travel agents can check seat availability themselves by typing an availability command into the computerised reservation system, (CRS).

The various CRSs are used by travel agents to access information about schedules, availability, fares, and other travel formalities. A CRS is a means for the automated agency to communicate directly with the airlines, through which reservations can be made and tickets and itineraries issued.

Each flight must be checked in turn. If the appropriate seats are available the agent will ask the airline's reservations clerk to reserve flights. Alternatively, if using a CRS, the agent reserves flights by creating a PNR in the name of the passenger(s).

## Computerised Travel Agency Systems

Computerised travel reservation has become a norm today as travel agencies extensively use this system. There are several commands, which are to be learned by the reservation executive. The examples of the types of commands show a Galileo CRS availability request, and its response. Other CRS systems include Sabre, Worldspan, Apollo, and Marsha. All these are Global Distribution Systems, whose computer reservation systems (CRS) are used by travel agencies throughout the world. Computer formats or commands are similar across all systems, i.e. they all include a specific date and route. This information is mandatory.

Other information, however is optional, such as departure/arrival time, preferred carrier, and preferred connecting city.

A CRS allocates a unique booking reference to each new reservation, and is a way of tracking and opening the reservation at another time. If the booking reference is not known, the information can also be traced by using a passenger's name and possibly a departure date. Obviously, it may take longer to trace the booking this way since a name, unlike a booking number is not necessarily unique.

## Hotel Reservation

Dialogue with the customer to determine destination, dates, purpose of trip (business, leisure or combination), room type, bedding type, meal plan, any particular services or facilities required, client's frequent guest programme memberships, any hotel preferences.

### Cross match room type with rate category:

Contact the hotel to check availability for requested dates and room rates. If the hotel requested is not available through your CRS, call the reservation centre or property, directly. CRS has recent information but often, it is not up to the minute. Sometimes the hotel actually has a room available even if the CRS shows it as full. It is therefore best to phone.

If rooms are available, try to book over the phone, using a credit card whenever possible for guarantee. Most hotels today take credit cards for guarantee and the client pays on site at the time of check-out. Some resorts and smaller hotels may require cash or check payment however and will require a deposit issued on your agency's check. For this you would follow your agency's policies.

Be sure to get the name of the reservation agent and a confirmation number. Sometimes hotels will request a fax in order to confirm the reservation. Send the fax and request that they advise rates, guarantee and cancellation policy by return fax. Invoice hotel for tracking purposes so your agency can be sure it gets its commission. If you book through the CRS, remember to get a confirmation number. It is important to have a guarantee, as without it you are leaving your clients vulnerable to not having a room waiting for them. Always remember to advise your clients of cancellation policies.

If the preferred hotel is not available at all, you should begin a search for an alternate, first through the reservation system and then by calling properties on the phone. Sometimes hotels are sold out for conferences or special events in select cities. Nevertheless, you may still find available rooms through local tourist bureax or local wholesalers.

## Car Rental Reservation

Before you call the car rental company's "toll-free" number or you access the CRS/GDS, request from the customer, the following information, which will also be used for the voucher should he obtained:

- Customers membership number (if applicable)
- Corporate agreement number (if applicable)
- Family name and given name of renter
- Rental location
- Return date
- Rental length expressed in days
- Return location
- Special remarks (for instance, baby seat)
- Car group
- Your IATA or Travel Agent Identification number
  You also need to enquire how the payment will be made:
  (i) customer's credit card (you then need a referral to receive your commission)
  (ii) you pay for the rental (you need a voucher)

## Reserve the Car

- Make the reservation with the car rental company through the CRS/GDS or a phone call to the specific "toll-free" number
- Issue the voucher
- Fill-in the voucher, hand it over to the client and have him pay the appropriate value
- You are now responsible for all car rental fees for up to 30 days of rental, if you establish a full value voucher for your customer
- There are various types of voucher values

## Tour Package Reservation

Once a client has been qualified and informed and is ready to purchase a tour, you will need to make a reservation. Depending on your location and that of the tour operator, reservations can be made either directly with the tour operator or with a sales agent for the tour operator. In either case the actual transaction will normally occur over the telephone or through your agency's computer reservations system. Increasingly, the Internet is providing another reservation channel. Whatever methods you use, the same basic information will be exchanged with the tour operator.

Making tour reservations for a client is not extremely difficult, but as with most aspects of the travel business, developing a system and sticking to the system can greatly improve your efficiency and accuracy as a travel agent. Accuracy is important because it will help reduce errors. Errors can be embarrassing and costly both in financial terms and in terms of your professional reputation. The following is a list of details you should cover with a tour operator and/or the tour operator's sales agent when you make a reservation for a client:

- Your full name and the name of your agency or organisation. Many tour operators will maintain your name and that of your agency in their computer systems, thereby facilitating this part of the process
- The name and availability of the tour that your client wants to take
- The dates of the proposed tour.
- The full names, addresses and any other relevant contact information, such as phone and fax numbers, of the tour participants.
- Air transfer information; this information should include the clients' gateway city, which is the city from which they will depart, and also details of the city from which they will return at the conclusion of the tour.
- Any special requests or situations. Special requests and situations would include special meal preferences, medical or health conditions, allergies, physical disabilities or challenges. It could also include anniversary, birthday or matrimony plans as well as any other important positive information.

Because your time with the tour operator or tour agent will be limited, if you are using the telephone, it is important to take detailed notes about the matters discussed during your conversation. It is also very important to get the name of the representative with whom you spoke and set up the reservations. This will facilitate any changes and eliminate guesswork if any problems arise during the reservation and ticketing process.

## Ferry Reservation

Ferry reservation procedures differ depending on the region of the world and types of services offered. There are, however, important similarities when making reservations. Consider the following points when making reservations:

- Get the name of the reservation agent with whom you are speaking, in the event that you lose the phone connection or receive inaccurate information, you will know with whom you spoke.

- Provide the reservation agent with full and correctly spelled name of your client. Ask the reservation agent to read back the name to you and to verify the spelling.
- Provide the reservation agent with the date, time, and class of service needed.
- Provide the reservation agent with the form of payment.
- Get a confirmation number for the reservation.
- Get a written confirmation and ticket and send these to your client.

When making a ferry reservation via telephone, it is important to establish a process for timely delivery of the tickets. It is best to have the tickets, or at least written confirmation of the tickets, sent to you for verification, this allows you to maintain control of the process

If working with an automated system such as a fax or computer, be sure to have a process for getting the reservation entered accurately. Every system should have a procedure for providing written confirmation to your clients.

Moving people from one place to another for holidays and business reasons is the key role of travel and tourism. The development of public and private transport made mass-market tourism possible. As the discretionary incomes of more people in developed countries increased, their propensity and ability to buy more tourism products grew. However, transport systems are not created to serve tourism needs only. They also serve other markets which owe nothing to tourism. Indeed most systems do not depend heavily on the demand for transport for tourism purposes. The latter is an important element but is not necessarily the predominant one, except in undeveloped countries whose economies are heavily dependant on tourism. With the seasonality of tourism demand, many transport systems would find problems of staffing, idle resources and negative cash flows if solely dependant on tourist traffic.

Transportation can be defined as "the means to reach the destination and also the means of movement at the destination" (Burkart and Medlik). The pattern of the geographical distribution of world travellers as well as distribution of travellers within their own country, is greatly influenced by the transport systems and services that enable the travellers to get from home to the tourist destination. Transport systems link the tourist generating regions with the attractions tourists wish to visit (i.e. their destination). In general, transport routes and systems enable tourist movements to take place.

Some transport experts believe that providing facilities for tourists can complicate the task of supplying the other services which form the backbone of the business. Some of these other services may play a bigger part in developing transport systems. An example is the carriage of mail. The granting of a licence to carry mail helped considerably the development of facilities whose viability would otherwise have been in doubt.

Carefully planned and controlled transport systems, designed to serve all types of travellers can be profitable. However, they are capital intensive.

Railways have to lay tracks and purchase substantial amounts of rolling stock. With road transport, there is the cost of purchasing vehicles of different capacities and maintaining and replacing them. Central and local governments have to meet the high cost of building road systems. With air transport, airlines have to purchase and maintain increasingly costly aircraft of different sizes. Bigger and better airports have to be built for the larger sophisticated planes.

## Key Issues

The design of transport systems requires careful consideration of a number of factors. These include the rolling stock, track and terminals needed, the estimated total demand and the competitive position. The latter includes competition within individual modes of transport and between modes. The instability of demand and increasing international competition aggravate the problems.

Thus, there is a very wide choice open to tourism operators for the transport element of their packages. However, the mode of travel, timing and duration of journeys that are acceptable, will depend on the attitudes and preferences of the target markets (consumers) for which the packages are intended. It is not just a question of cost. With airlines, the standard and quality of the flight schedules and in-flight services and customers' views of their safety record play an important part in establishing ready acceptance of the holiday packages on offer. With coaches and trains, the punctuality and quality of the service and to a lesser extent, safety records, should be taken into account. For sea trips, the reputation and image of the shipping line and the inherent luxury of the ships, as well as the on-board entertainments, are important considerations. Therefore, operators have to consider many things before sound decisions can be made on the transport services that will be used.

## Basic Component

For development of any destination, adequate and efficient transportation infrastructure and access to generating markets is one of the most important aspects. The destinations which can be reached by efficient transport systems are the ones which receive the maximum number of tourists. Within the country, efficient modes of transport are vital for movements of domestic tourists. Transport, therefore, is one of the basic components of tourism. A tourist in order to get to his destination, has to travel and, therefore, some mode of transport is necessary to make possible this travel. In fact, transport is the necessary pre-condition of travel.

## Modes of Transport

Technological developments have revolutionized various modes of transport and there is continuous research to upgrade them. Each technological advance in a travel mode affects the other modes. Railways replaced the horse, the private ownership of automobile and public bus system replaced the railways and the airplane replaced the transoceanic ship and long-distance rail travel. There are four major modes of transport. These are:

(i) Surface Transport
(ii) Air Transport
(iii) Rail Transport
(iv) Sea Transport

**(i) Surface Transport**

The invention of the new transport medium, travel by a private car and coach received its first impetus in the ten years which preceded World War I. The entire shape of the tourist industry was therefore transformed by the invention of this new transport medium. The growth of the private car may be identified as a major cause for the decline of the railways. In both *USA* and the *United Kingdom*, passenger rail traffic almost halved in the first ten years or so after the First World War. The motor car gradually came to be the alternative means of transport for both short and medium range journeys. Subsequently, with the growth of a fine network of fast and superfast national and international highway systems, long journeys were also performed by motor car and motor coach.

Although the first motor car had come into operation by the end of the 19th century, by the time of the First World War; their numbers jumped manifold. It became increasingly important in the pursuit of leisure and tourism. The actual number of holiday makers travelling by road increased tremendously as more and more people took holidays away from home. The provision of good motor roads and road services were important factors in the development of both domestic and international tourism. With the tremendous increase in road traffic, improved roads and dual carriageways were introduced after 1930. In 1930s, Germans pioneered the development of motorways with their autobahn. Improvements in road transport facilities stimulated tourism in many European countries such as *France*, *Spain* and *Germany*. Mention may be made of the great progress made in the *USA* in building highways, expressways and superhighways. In many other countries of the world newer and faster roads were built which made movement of traffic by road faster and more comfortable.

The motor car has provided actual mobility and people are no longer anchored to a particular holiday centre as they tended to be when they mostly travelled by train. Speed is yet another important factor which makes it possible for people with a limited amount of time to travel to distant places. People with even one week of holiday considered it sufficient to travel. The gradual spread of the network of roads, opened up many new areas and made many places hitherto not very accessible, easy to get to. The railways, on the other hand, tended rather to concentrate and restrict movement to particular destinations.

## Car Ownership

In the subsequent years, road transport made striking advances. Soon after 1950, there were rapid developments in transport; whereas the car ownership multiplied, the motor coach appeared in increasing numbers and the coach tour became popular. Greater use of motor cars and coaches is being made at present for the purpose of tourism. A great majority of people travel by the above modes. Increasing use of this mode of transport is being made in USA and Canada as also in other major tourist countries. The construction of motorways in many countries has made speedy travel over long distances by car and the coach easy and has made many remote places more accessible. The development of *'motorail'*, the carrying of cars and coaches over extended distances by train, is making it possible for holiday makers to use motor cars in holiday areas. Several countries are continuing to build motorways and highways and new road systems to cater to the increasing volume of road transport, including tourist transport. There are large-scale highway programmes in the pipeline at present in different regions of the world. When completed, these will cater to the ever-increasing demands of the tourists. Some of the large highways programmes in the pipeline in different regions of the world are:

(i) The Trans-African Highway
(ii) The Trans-West African Highway
(iii) The Trans-East African Highway
(iv) The Trans-Europe North-South Motorway
(v) The Pan-American Highway
(vi) The Asian Highway
(vii) The Silk Route Highway

## (ii) Air Transport

Air transport has been the most rapidly expanding transport sector over the past fifty years and now is the main form of long distance travel. It has certainly been a key factor in the growth of international tourism. Although commercial air travel took place before the Second World War, air transport for the masses has essentially been a post-war phenomenon. The main period of growth was during the 1960s, when overseas holiday became a symptomatic benefit of a society experiencing rising living standards.

Although international air travel was born at the end of World War I and slowly grew between the two wars, it was only at the end of World War II that it made a tremendous breakthrough. It emerged into a practical mode of transport over long distances only in the late forties when the aircraft industry in America applied the technical and manufacturing resources it had developed during the war. This period saw the development of large pressurised civil aircraft like the Douglas DC-6s and the Lockheed Constellations followed by the DC-7s and the superconstellations operating at twice the speed and flying altitudes of their predecessor war planes.

In the year 1952 the two-class travel was introduced which was made possible by the larger capacity of the new aircrafts, which also resulted in lower airfares. The steady fall in the real cost of flying has been chiefly productive in traffic across the Atlantic and within the USA, stimulated by the introduction of tourist fares in the year 1952. This period also saw the first post-war attempt to build a *"package holiday"* around air transport, the model for most of today's global tourism. The growing willingness of tourists to use to air travel during this period was responsible for the annual flood of North Americans across the Atlantic to Europe. This trend continues even today. Within Europe, there has been the spectacular explosion of the Mediterranean resorts.

The commercial jet air travel, however, was pioneered by Great Britain in the year 1952 with the inauguration of jet flights, by BOAC. Thereafter, Pan American introduced the Boeing 707 service between *Paris* and *New York* in the year 1958. By the year 1968 most of the European carriers had converted totally to jet aircraft. As a result of the introduction of jet air services, there was a tremendous boost to air travel from the year 1958. The most decisive development during this period was, however, the development of the concept of *'inclusive tours'* in which travellers were carried on charter flights at rates substantially lower than those on normal scheduled services. Air transport can be considered to be responsible for the introduction of cheaper travel, especially long distance, enabling a large majority of potential travellers to think of visiting far off countries for the purposes of holiday.

## Introduction of Jets

The introduction of 'Jumbo Jets' in the year 1970 heralded the phenomenon of mass, market, international tourism as well as business tourism. Jumbo jets – the Boeing 747s, DC-10s and L-101s made air travel convenient, comfortable and luxurious. Luxury air travel was made possible for business as well as non-business travellers as the big size of jets gave the airlines space enough to partition off a section of the plane for executives who were willing to pay extra for the luxury. Pan Am and the Japan Air Lines (JAL) were among the first carriers to offer passengers what came to be known as business class travel. The seats in this class were wider, giving more space to stretch and relax in comfort, making the long distance travel less wearisome.

As an outcome of the success of business class, yet another class known as *'Executive Class'* was introduced. It was once again Japan Air Lines which in the year 1975 started an 'Executive Service' lounge in the Imperial Hotel in Tokyo, complete with conference rooms, having all the facilities for meetings. Lufthansa opened a lounge at Frankfurt and SAS at Copenhagen airports. Many other airlines such as TWA with Ambassador Club, Singapore with Silver Kris Lounges, Pan Am with Clipper Club, Air France with Le Club, Cathay Pacific with Marco Polo, British Airways with Supper Club, and airlines like Qantas, Air India, Air Canada, Singapore Airlines, Swissair, etc., offer additional on-ground facilities to their clients. These include special check-in-counters, priority baggage handling and clearance, free transport to and from airport, free drinks, etc. The membership is open to those who pay a nominal fee or is offered free to travellers who have travelled frequently on the carrier.

The improved fuel efficiency of the later models of jet engines combined with ingenuity and marketing expertise of airlines, travel agencies and tour operators have made air travel accessible to an increasing number of people. This is also illustrated by the North Atlantic route – the so-called golden route of traffic, which saw the successive introduction of excursion fares in 1948, coach fares in 1952, family fares in 1955, group inclusive tour fares in 1967, youth fares in 1972 and apex fares in 1975. As a result of these innovations in air travel, fares per seat mile declined in real terms, between 1962 and 1975.

## Advances in Air Travel

Great advances have been made in air travel in the recent years, more particularly for overseas holiday making. Tourism in turn has had a significant impact on the aircraft industry and on the carriers. Factors like comfort, speed, and safety influence the tourist' choice of mode of transport. Now wide bodied jets such as Boeing 747, the McDonnel-Douglas DC 10, the Airbus A 300, A 320 and Lockheed Tristar L-1011 are all part of the response to the requirements of the ever growing travel market. The technical brilliance of the supersonic aircraft like the Concorde and of the Tupolev 144 were remarkable landmarks in aviation history.

Ongoing advances in the aerodynamics and engine technology will inevitably push the range of new generation aircraft towards a capability of non-stop flights anywhere on the planet. With airport and airspace already at a premium, the only solution is larger aeroplanes. Both the world's biggest aircraft manufacturers Europe's, Airbus Industries and Boeing in the United States have started manufacturing new-generation aircrafts. Airbus industries have already launched its 600-800 seater double decker A380, while Boeing is going ahead with its project of stretched variants of its increasingly popular and successful B747 "Jumbo Jet". A number of airlines have already placed orders for the purchase of this new-generation aircraft. Another major company McDonnel-Douglas is also planning a new generation aircraft, the MD-12 four-jet double-deck aircraft, with capacity between those of the Airbus and Boeing projects (over 500 seats).

The air-transport industry has a bright future in spite of rising fuel costs and inflation. As far as, long distance air travel is concerned the large majority of the aircrafts used will continue to be of the wide-bodied generation. Air transport, thus is a single key factor which has been primarily responsible for the spurt in growth of tourism especially long-haul tourism. The future of air transport is bright and the airlines would continue to play a vital role in the growth and development of tourism in the coming decades of the present century.

## (iii) Rail Transport

The newly completed railway track between Liverpool and Manchester in England featured special provisions for carrying passengers in addition to freight. However, the birth of organised rail travel came in the year 1841. A Baptist preacher of Derbyshire, England, was on his way to a temperance meeting in Leicester when he was inspired with the idea of engaging a special train to carry the friends of Temperance society from Leicester to Loughborough and back to attend a quarterly delegate meeting. The man behind this was Thomas Cook. He broached his idea to his friends. A few weeks later, 570 passengers made the journey by the Midland Countries Railway at a specially reduced fare. This venture was followed by various excursions to beauty spots. In the year 1843, 3,000 school children were taken on a trip from Leicester to *Derby*. From 1848 to 1863 Thomas Cook conducted circular tours of Scotland, with 5,000 tourists a season.

The Liverpool and Manchester railway, opened in the year 1830. This encouraged many other countries in Europe to open railway lines. Railway tracks were laid in France, Austria and in Switzerland. Across the Atlantic the tracks were laid in America. This revolution in rail transport technology produced an immediate expansion in European tourism. In the year 1881 the railways carried over 600 million passengers over lines operated by one hundred odd companies. The railways were now keen to stimulate travel and to improve the system. There was also an element of competition and the various railways were now keen to stimulate travel and to improve the system. In the early 1870s, first class railway travel was introduced by an American, G.M. Pullman, who developed the Pullman coaches with their luxury furnishing and dining facilities. Long distance travel could now be undertaken in comfort and pleasure. The Pullman cars manufactured in America were imported by some railway companies in England and other countries in Europe. The cars which were very comfortable for long journeys were first introduced in America. The longer distances in America necessitated the ensuring of great comfort for passengers. By the year 1872 the Pullman Company had 700 cars working over 30,000 miles of railway under contract with other 150 different companies.

## Rapid Expansion in Europe

Europe was one continent where rail transport developed very fast. In Europe the expansion of rail networks linking different countries within Europe as also outside Europe expanded rapidly. The urge and the motivation to travel within Europe was responsible for the introduction of several new railway lines which were responsible for the introduction of great trains, both for short and long distances. These trains and train journeys even today are remembered with nostalgia.

The great Inter-European Express, the Nord Express connecting Paris with Vienna in Austria, the Orient Express from Paris to Vienna and Constantinople, the Trans-Siberian, the Ostend-Vienna and Ostend-Warsaw services, and those from Berlin and Vienna to the Riviera and Italy, are all creations of early twentieth century. There were several other services like between Entente countries, the Calais-Brindisi, the express from the Channel ports and Paris to Switzerland and Italy through Basle and Lausanne by the Lotschberg and Simplon, the Paris-Rome-Palermo, the Sud Express from Paris to Madrid, Lisbon, Seville, and even the fast services from Paris to Riviera, Nice and Genoa in Italy.

## Factors Responsible for Growth

The compelling influence of mass individual, as well as organised travel in the subsequent years brought in great development in the rail transport not only in Europe but in many other continents. It was, however, in

Europe that revolutionary experiments were made and are continued to be made in the area of high speed luxury trains.

The energy crisis in 1974 which resulted in widespread recession and galloping inflation had adversely affected travel by air and by private car. It was becoming increasingly expensive to travel by air and private car and coach. The fuel consumption per passenger per kilometre was two to four times more in automobiles and ten times more in aeroplanes as compared to trains.

The factor of increase in oil prices was responsible for the remarkable achievement in the growth of faster and cheaper rail transport. Besides the cost factor, the railways also had an advantage over the airlines in that the terminal stations were often located in the heart of the cities and train timings are generally more convenient. To add to this, the growing congestion on highways and airports had given a further impetus to this trend. All the above factors coupled with advanced technology and increasing needs for mobility, were leading to a renaissance of the rail transport.

The railways which were pioneers in the growth and development of early mass travel and were relegated to a secondary place with the introduction of motor and air transport, were once again assuming an important role. In almost all the European countries, the United States of America, Asia and elsewhere, revolutionary ideas for achieving higher speeds and comfort were being conceived and put into practice.

The trend however, was discernible in the year 1960. The British Railways electrified its London-Manchester line, a very busy line to achieve the speed of 160 kilometres per hour. The new high-speed trains on this line reduced the running time by a full one hour from the former three hours forty minutes trip. Passenger traffic almost doubled in five years. In Germany, a new intercity system introduced in 1971 provided a rapid train service at two-hour intervals between major cities in the country and brought over 30 per cent more passengers in the first twelve months. Passengers were provided with extra conveniences like telephones, secretariat services, latest stock quotations and 'a la carte' dining-car service round the clock. Similarly, in France, the 160 kilometres per hour turbine train service, which began in 1970 between Paris and Caen in Northern France cut travel time by almost one-fifth. Passenger loads went up by 25 per cent in the first year. High-speed train services elsewhere in Europe connect Paris and Lyons in France, Rome and Milan in Italy and Moscow and Leningrad in Russia.

## High-Speed Trains

It was Japan which took the epoch-making decision to use the latest technology and convert the rail line between Tokyo and Osaka, covering a distance of 515 kilometres into a high-speed track. This ambitious project was completed in the year 1964. The superfast train known as Hikari Express – 'bullet train' – running on the new Tokaido line at a speed of 210 kilometres per hour, cutting the journey time to less than three hours against six and a half hours taken earlier–was a revolution in high-speed trains. Encouraged by the success of its bold venture, Japan went further and built the new Sanyo line, 565 kilometres in length on which trains travelled even faster at a maximum speed of 260 kilometres per hour. Elsewhere in Asia, new and faster rail tracks were introduced as the number of passengers carried by rail has been increasing in Malaysia, the Philippines and Thailand.

## European High Speed Trains

The single most significant development in the future of European public railways took place in the year 1989 when the community of European Railways (representing the 12 members of the European community plus Austria and Switzerland) announced plans for a trans-continental high speed comfortable and state-of-art rail network, covering most of the countries in Europe. The £100 billion project, by the year 2015 would cover over 20,000 miles of new track capable of handling trains travelling at a speed of over 350 km per hour. The French TGV (Train à Grande Vitesse) and German ICE (Inter-city Express) network have already led the way.

In France, a world record of speed was broken in the year 1981 when a new high speed train owned by state-run SNCF railroad company shattered the 26 year old world record for rail speed by clocking 380 kilometres per hour (236 miles). The record breaking time was achieved near the central French city of Tonnerre during the test run of the French manufactured 'Train a Grande Vitesse' (TGV). It broke the previous record of 331 kilometres per hour (205 miles) that was set earlier. The commercial operations of this high-speed train began in 1981 between Paris and Lyon. The fastest train in the world, TGV, was launched in September 1981 covering the 560 kilometres distance between Paris and Lyon in one hour and 48 minutes. In comfortable, sound-proofed cars the only noise heard is the quiet hiss of air conditioning. The later version, the 'TGV Atlantique', reduced an hour off journeys from Paris to main cities in the West of France from Brest to Bordeaux. By mid-1990 the French started running TGVs along half their long distance routes, to bring London, Bordeaux, Rotterdam and Cologne within 3.5 hours from Paris. The 320 mph (515 km/h) TGV Atlantique today holds the world record in speed.

Several other new rail projects were announced in the European countries. The Italian State Railways inaugurated highspeed trains between Rome and Milan. The non-stop train makes the 393 miles (638 kilometres) trip in four hours and 20 minutes, about an hour less than the standard runs. Sweden improved its four major lines to reduce the travel time between its major cities in the year 1994.

## The Eurostar

Eurostar is a high-speed railway service connecting London with Amsterdam, Avignon, Brussels, Bourg-Saint-Maurice, Disneyland Paris, Lille, Lyon, Marseille, Paris, and Rotterdam. All its trains traverse the Channel Tunnel between the United Kingdom and France, owned and operated separately by Getlink.

The London terminus is St Pancras International, the other British calling points being Ebbsfleet International and Ashford Internationalin Kent.

The service is operated by eighteen-car Class 373/1 trains and sixteen-car Class 374 trains which run at up to 320 kilometers per hour (199 mph) on a network of high-speed lines. The LGV Nord line in France opened before Eurostar services began in 1994, and newer lines enabling faster journeys were added later—HSL 1 in Belgium and High Speed 1 in southern England. The French and Belgian parts of the network are shared with Paris–Brussels Thalys services and also with TGV trains. In the United Kingdom the two-stage Channel Tunnel Rail Link project was completed on 14 November 2007 and renamed High Speed 1, when the London terminus of Eurostar changed from Waterloo International to St Pancras International.

Until 2010, Eurostar was operated jointly by the national railway companies of France and Belgium, SNCF and SNCB/NMBS, and Eurostar (UK) Ltd (EUKL), a subsidiary of London and Continental Railways (LCR), which also owned the high-speed infrastructure and stations on the British side. Eurostar has become the dominant operator on the routes that it operates, carrying more passengers than all airlines combined. Other operators have expressed an interest in starting competing services following deregulation in 2010. On 1 September 2010, Eurostar was incorporated as a single corporate entity called Eurostar International Limited (EIL), replacing the joint operation between EUKL, SNCF and SNCB/NMBS.

## Launch of service

On 14 November 1994, Eurostar services began between Waterloo International station in London, Gare du Nord in Paris and Brussels-South railway station in Brussels. The train service started with a limited Discovery service; the full daily service started from 28 May 1995.

In 1995, Eurostar was achieving an average end-to-end speed of 171.5 km/h (106.6 mph) between London and Paris. On 8 January 1996, Eurostar launched services from a second UK railway station when Ashford International was opened.

On 23 September 2003, passenger services began running on the first completed section of High Speed 1. Following a high-profile glamorous opening ceremony and a large advertising campaign, on 14 November 2007, Eurostar services in London transferred from Waterloo to the extended and extensively refurbished St Pancras International.

## Channel Tunnel

The Channel Tunnel is a crucial part of the route as it is the only rail connection between Great Britain and the European mainland. It joins LGV Nord in France with High Speed One in Britain. Tunnelling began in 1988, and the 50.5-kilometre (31.4 mi) tunnel was officially opened by British sovereign Queen Elizabeth II and the French President François Mitterrand at a ceremony in Calais on 6 May 1994. It is owned by Getlink, which charges a significant toll to Eurostar for its use. In 1996, the American Society of Civil Engineers named the tunnel as one of the Seven Wonders of the Modern World. Along the current route of the Eurostar service, line speeds are 300 kilometres per hour (186 mph) except within the Channel

Tunnel, where a reduced speed of 160 kilometres per hour (100 mph) applies for safety reasons. Since the launch of Eurostar services, severe disruptions and cancellations have been caused by fires breaking out within the Channel Tunnel, such as in 1996, 2006 (minor), 2008 and 2015.

## High Speed 1

High Speed 1 (HS1), formerly known as the Channel Tunnel Rail Link (CTRL), is a 108-kilometre (67 mi) high-speed railway line running from London through Kent to the British end of the Channel Tunnel. It was built in two stages. The first section between the tunnel and Fawkham Junction in north Kent opened in September 2003, cutting London–Paris journey times by 21 minutes to 2 hours 35 minutes, and London–Brussels to 2 hours 20 minutes. On 14 November 2007, commercial services began over the whole of the new HS1 line. The redeveloped St Pancras International station became the new London terminus for all Eurostar services. The completion of High Speed 1 has brought the British part of Eurostar's route up to the same standards as the French and Belgian high-speed lines. Non-stop journey times were reduced by a further 20 minutes to 2 hours 15 minutes for London–Paris and 1 hour 51 minutes for London–Brussels.

## Super-High Speed Trains

After more than 25 years of research, the world of railways is on the verge of entering an exciting super high-speed era. Magnetic levitation (Maglev) technology will enable trains to run at supersonic speeds within the next decade. Soon commercial passenger trains will run at more than 550 kilometres per hour floating frictionless a few centimetres above the rails. It was Japan which first started working on Maglev in the late sixties. A milestone was achieved in 1999 April, on the new Yamanashi Maglev Test Line when a manned Maglev train clocked a record 552 kilometers per hour.

Independent of wheel and rail friction super high-speed trains have been a long-standing dream of researchers. With Maglev, the train is magnetically-levitated (not supported by wheels) and is propelled by a linear induction motor instead of conventional rotary electric motor. The levitation method utilised ordinary direct-current electromagnets that are attached to the bottom of the vehicle. Their magnetic field lifts the train. An electronic circuit amplifier controls the current to the electromagnets in order to maintain the gap between rail and magnetic cores. The gap is measured by a sensor. Barring the air-conditioning system, Maglevs have no moving parts and therefore there is very little wear, no noise or vibration and low energy consumption.

In Asia, in many countries, new and faster rail tracks are being introduced. The new rail services are even giving airlines and the coach transport their greatest competition.

## Trains in USA

In the United States of America, the railways are coming back into the scene in recent years. Increasing number of railway lines are being built, to carry a large number of passengers not only within the suburbs, but also long distances. There is a great spurt in the urban rail system construction all over the United States. It is increasingly being felt that as a mass transit system, it can reduce automobile pollution. Long distance trains running on the Amtrak system between New York and San Francisco have been modernised. The Amtrak has also added new double Pullman coaches on the system with a view to encourage more rail travel. High-speed train services now connect highly populated Washington-Baltimore-Philadelphia-New York-Boston 'Corridor' in the United States.

The concept of high-speed trains has come to USA as well. Amtrak has recently selected the Canadian firm to build its first high-speed train to link Washington and Boston at speeds up to 150 mph. The national passenger railroad Amtrak is planning to procure train sets composed of six cars each, as well as leading and trailing locomotives. Another famous company, GEC-Alsthom NV of France, the maker of the world-famous French high speed train TGV (Train a Grande Vitesse) is also joining to modernise the rail system in USA.

The day is not far off when trains will cruise at the speeds of 600 kilometres per hour. The new technology aims at dispensing with conventional rails. It aims at providing an air-cushion to replace the conventional run on a track. The projected aero-trains will not only be fast but also sleek looking, noise free, low pollutant, and above all, will cause no wear and tear on the track because they never touch it. Glimpses of such trains are already available in France, Germany and Japan where many experiments have already been performed successfully.

## (iv) Sea Transport

While railways were responsible for inland travel, especially in Europe, the steamship crossed the boundaries and made strides in inter-continental travel. Shipping technology made a number of innovations in the nineteenth century. In America, a number of sailing ships were built which were considered to be superior to those built in England or elsewhere. The English felt a great need for improved communications across the Atlantic with America for the purpose of trade and passenger transportation. As a result of this there were great strides in the development of deep sea shipping. The history of the Cunard Steamship Company in England demonstrates important features in the growth of North Atlantic Shipping. A subsidy in the form of an award of the mail contract represented a recurring theme in the development of passenger transportation. With the passage of time, toward the last quarter of the nineteenth century, emigrant traffic became an important factor in North Atlantic travel. America was considered at this time the 'new world' full of opportunities and fortunes for people in Europe. A great number of people from the continent started going to America in search of fortune. First Great Britain, and later Germany, along with other countries, became the principal generators of emigrants to the new world. Many travelled as tourists to see the new world. The opening of the Suez Canal in 1869 brought about the possibility of a much shortened route between the West and the East and in turn stimulated the introduction of better steamship carriage to the Far-East.

## Deep Sea Travel

Ships in the cruising fashion for the charter and operation of cruises on a limited scale, dates from the mid-nineteenth century. One of the earliest cruises, perhaps, was that described by Mark Twain in his first book, The Innocents Abroad, published in 1869. Cruising, however, did not play a significant part in the world of shipping until the beginning of the twentieth century. The period just before the First World War can be considered the heyday of liner passenger service. It was an era of large comfortable and fast ships operated by a relatively small number of companies in various countries. The glamour of the deep-sea travel was, however, reserved for the wealthy Europeans and Americans. In the luxury liners, a big space reserved for the not too wealthy was used by the emigrant traffic. In fact, the biggest volume of trans-Atlantic passenger transport was the emigrant traffic. In the recent past, one of the most important developments in sea traffic has, in fact, been that of holiday sea cruises, especially in the Mediterranean and Caribbean and also in South-East Asia.

## Holiday Sea Cruises

In the recent past one of the most important developments in the sea traffic has in fact been that of increase in holiday sea cruises, especially in the Mediterranean and Caribbean as also in South-East Asia. Sea transportation can be divided into the following two categories:

(i) cruise and ocean-going ships
(ii) ferries.

The main shipping lines which organise cruises or ocean-going passenger routes have established two conferences to represent their interests in the tourist industry. These are the International Passenger Ship Associates (IPSA) and the Trans Pacific Passenger Conference (TPPC) which represent the Pacific and Atlantic shipping companies.

Until the 1930s steamships provided the only means of long distance transport between the major continents and the growth of air travel, especially of inclusive air tours, has had a severe impact on the shipping lines. In the post-war years they were faced with increasing competition from the airlines, rising operating costs and growing obsolescence in their shipping fleets and very high rebuilding/refitting costs. Most companies chose to diversify into other areas of activity and those that remain have turned increasingly to the **cruise line business.** This is the luxury end of the tourist market. For example, only 4% is repeat business. The tourists on a cruise ship are not just buying a trip from A to B, they are buying a stay at a floating resort, with a level of service and accommodation comparable to the best five star deluxe resorts and hotels.

## Fly Cruise

The appeal of the cruise is that it is an all-inclusive package, with accommodation, meals and entertainment all included in the price of a ticket. In the past 10 years cruise lines have introduced innovations and special interest packages to appeal to a wider clientele. Most cruise lines offer a fly-cruise deal for example where passengers fly out to the Caribbean before joining the cruise ship in the West Indies. The most prestigious was probably the Cunard package which involved flying out of Britain to the United States on the Concorde and returning on the QE2. The appeal to passengers of these fly cruise packages, is that in the past when cruises started at Southampton or New York, it took several days of sailing through cold waters and possibly rough seas before warmer waters were reached. Now tropical sunshine and warm waters are just several hours travel away.

In order to appeal to a younger clientele many cruises now offer full spa and fitness facilities as well as a wide range of sporting activities. For example, the Norwegian Caribbean Lines offer snorkelling and scuba diving lessons on board by qualified instructors; golf and tennis clinics are available on many ships. Some companies offer unique cruises for example, the Sun Line have an Amazon River Cruise that includes a performance at the Opera House Manaus and their Transatlantic Grand Cruise begins in Athens and ends in Fort Lauderdale, with stops in the eastern and western Mediterranean and the Caribbean.

## Cruise Market

The three main centres for cruise trips are the Caribbean, the Mediterranean and the Far East. The cruise market is dominated by United States tourists, who account for 80% of all cruise passengers, although the headquarters of the main cruise line companies are based in Europe. For Caribbean sailings many lines now fly passengers to San Juan, Puerto Rico, Jamaica, Barbados or cruises begin at the Florida ports. The west coast cities of Los Angeles, San Francisco and San Diego are attracting more cruise lines and are beginning to rival the Florida based lines, especially for Mexico and Panama cruises. In the Pacific more cruise lines are offering seven day cruises from Hong Kong and the ships of the Holland America, Cunard, Royal Viking and P&O Lines offer larger cruises calling in at Hawaii, Tahiti, Malaysia, Singapore, New Zealand, Australia and Japan.

Cruise ships are very labour intensive and average about one crew member for every two passengers. In other words a ship carrying 800 passengers should have about 400 crew members. Cruise ships vary in size from the relatively small ship carrying 100 passengers to the luxury liner carrying 900 to plus 2000 passengers, with cinemas, swimming pools and a wide range of onboard entertainment facilities. The food on any ship is extremely important. Whereas land restaurants do not need to change their menus every day - they simply change customers - cruise ships with their captive clientele, must constantly change their menus and offer consistently high-quality food to a number varying from five hundred to more than two thousand passengers per meal. Understandably, food along with labour and fuel, is one of the high operating costs of the cruise business.

Cruises are classified in four general categories:

   (i) volume cruises
   (ii) premium cruises
   (iii) luxury cruises
   (iv) speciality cruises.

**Volume cruises,** also called mass-market cruises, account for approximately 60% of all cruise revenues. Cruise lines in this category offer three types of cruises: short cruises of 2 to 5 days, standard-length cruises of 7 days, and longer cruises of 9 to 14 days. Accommodation and service are comparable to most standard hotels. Volume cruise lines emphasise short itineraries and quick turnover. Turnover refers to the number of times that new passengers are brought on board. Fast turnover means the cruise line conducts more cruises over a shorter period of time and, thus, generates more revenues. Carnival Cruise Lines, Kloster Cruise Limited and Cunard Cruise Lines are examples of successful mass market cruise lines.

**Premium cruises,** also known as upscale cruises, represent the second largest segment of the cruise industry. Cruises in this category account for about 30% of all cruise revenues. Premium cruises range from one-week sailings to longer voyages of two to three months. A typical premium cruise offers accommodation, facilities, meal service and entertainment equivalent to the facilities of a first-class resort hotel. Royal Viking Cruises and Cunard Cruise Lines, which also operate mass-market cruises, are two of many premium cruise companies.

**Luxury cruises** constitute about 18% of the market. Cruises in this category offer a high level of elegance and comfort and are also the most expensive type of cruise. The ships that conduct luxury cruises are referred to as luxury liners. Whereas mass-market ships emphasise quick turnover, luxury liners feature long itineraries and exotic destinations. For example, the Seabourn Pride, which has a capacity of only 212 passengers, sails from New York to Europe, West Africa, the Caribbean and South America all in one itinerary. A typical luxury cruise liner may take from 6 to 12 months to complete its journey. Besides Seabourn Cruises, other luxury cruise lines include Crystal Cruises, Renaissance Cruises and Oceanic Cruises.

**Speciality cruises** include **whale-catching**, **scuba diving**, **archaeology** and **biology** cruises. This type of cruise accounts for 4% of cruise revenues. The ships used for such cruises are specially equipped passenger vessels with only basic food and beverage service. This segment of the cruise industry is particularly popular among well-educated single travellers and couples without children. Examples of speciality itineraries include cruises to Antarctica, the Amazon River.

Although the main feature of most cruises is the ship itself, exotic ports of call remain a highlight of the cruise experience. The destination and the length of the stay are determined by the type of cruise, local attractions, availability of shopping and other factors. A typical mass-market cruise stops for a relatively short time at each port of call, allowing passengers enough time to make brief tours and shop for souvenirs. Premium and speciality cruises tend to stay longer at each destination and sometimes offer optional land arrangements, such as hotel accommodation or guided tours.

## Varied Activities

Cruise passengers have the option of signing up for guided tours or arranging local transportation for private sightseeing. Before arriving at a port, most ships schedule a lecture, film or slide show, describing the region. Land-based tours are generally economical and of high quality. Often, a shore excursion or ground tour may be booked in advance, through a tour operator, the cruise line or with the purser on board ship.

Since the beginning of the 1960s, passenger shipping industry has gradually shifted its emphasis from the voyage services to cruises. More and more rich and elderly people initially promoted the cruise as they wanted a holiday in a completely relaxed atmosphere.

Cruises became increasingly popular to motivate top producers as more incentive winners wanted to enjoy the delights of life on the high seas. Cruise lines aim to please as cruises offer everything which is a five-star luxury like gourmet dining, top class entertainment, and excellent service. In addition, they offer fascinating shore visits with unusual shopping opportunities and enough activities to keep most athletic and energetic individuals satisfied.

Sea transport for the tourist, however, has not made much progress as compared to rail-road and air transport. Because of the advances in air transport technologies resulting in reduced airfares on most of the routes, and especially across the Atlantic, most of the shipping lines were unable to compete, resulting in a decline in their services. Coupled with this, the higher labour costs, prohibitive cost of replacement of older and outdated vessels, operating costs, etc., resulted in many companies closing their business, especially after the early sixties. During 1960s and 1970s most of the major shipping companies either reduced their services or discontinued their long-established routes.

The passenger liners, could not withstand the competition with airlines. Cruising on the other hand did manage to come up to a point where it was necessary to diversify the product and change the marketing strategy in order to survive. On the other hand, short sea voyages or ferry services have managed to withstand competition and are doing well in many areas. Channel crossing between some European countries and England by ferry service or hovercraft has been a profitable business for many ferry companies. This could be attributed to the general growth of tourism in the region. Lower prices are due to competition and also shorter journey time. Increase in the private car ownership in the region is another very important factor in the success of short sea voyages.

## EASY ACCESSIBILITY A KEY FACTOR

Mass tourism, as it is known internationally could not have existed without inexpensive and easily accessible transportation. Almost all the destinations in the world depend a great deal on efficient means of transportation being made available to tourists. The choice of a particular mode of transport, however, depends on several factors. Many theories have been put forward on the mode selection decision processes. The choice of selection of mode of transport is affected by the following factors:

- Distance and time
- Comfort
- Safety and utility
- Availability and frequency
- Comparative cost
- Ground services
- Status and prestige
- Geographical position and isolation
- Departure/arrival times
- Level of competition between services

The relative importance of the above factors, selection of different modes will, however, vary from one visitor type to another.

## CASE STUDY-1

### The Royal Orient Express

The weekend train, The Royal Orient Express takes the passengers back in time through India's most culturally fascinating state, Gujarat. The train perhaps is the world's most exotic train.

Travel by night and taking day trips to fascinating tourist places along the route, the Royal Orient journeys to palaces and forts steeped in legends of heroism and chivalry. One can feel the spirituality of an ancient Jain temple and soak the feet in warm waters of Arabian Sea as also laze on the beach. Safari in jungles to see the only lions outside Africa and shopping for exquisite handicrafts as old as history are other royal attractions.

The Royal Orient Train has been provided with personalised service that only the royalty was privileged with. A joint venture of Gujarat State Tourism and the Indian Railways, the train is equipped with all the modern amenities like experienced in a first class hotel. Air-conditioned ambience that keeps the temperature down to 15 degrees. The watering hole, bar with all the favourite drinks, is available for the passengers. Running hot and cold water, spacious baths, clean and comfortable cabins provide comfort like any five star deluxe hotel.

There are multi-cuisine restaurants to suit the taste buds of connoisseurs of good food. There is provision of a library for those looking for a quiet and laid back time.

The Royal Orient Train offers two packages: Corporate package and Honeymoon package. Both these packages are for six nights and seven days..

## CASE STUDY-2

*Super Cruise*

The Queen Elizabeth 2, often called "the QE2," is the flagship of the Cunard Line from 1969. The QE2 is considered the last of the great transatlantic ocean liners and is the last oil-run passenger steamship. The QE2 travelled all over the world, but now operates as a cruise ship based out of Southampton, England.

The ship weighs 70,327 tons and is 963 feet (294 m) long. The highest speed on board is 60 km/h. This makes it one of the largest and fastest passenger vessels. She is larger than the Titanic, but smaller than her successor RMS Queen Mary 2. The "2" in the name is to honor Queen Elizabeth, the wife of King George VI of the United Kingdom, who launched her in 1969.

The QE2 was built by the John Brown Shipyard in Scotland.

**Facilities**

The major facilities available on board are as follows:

- 5 restaurants and 2 cafes
- 3 swimming pools
- A pub, night-club and several bars
- 481 seat cinema
- Casino
- Shopping promenade and a branch of world famous department store called Harrod's
- Health Club
- Beauty Salon
- Library
- Hospital
- Computer Learning Centre

**Typical Itinerary**

A typical one year itinerary for the QE2 will include:

- A world cruise lasting about 80 days
- 30 Atlantic crossings
- Numerous cruises out of Southampton and New York
- Several party cruises
- One or more 'theme' cruises

**Capacity**

Passengers: 1,900

Crew: 1,015

Total: 2,915

## CASE STUDY-3

### Airbus A380

The world's biggest-ever passenger plane, the Airbus A380, was introduced to the world near the southern French city of Toulouse, in January 2005 in the presence of four European leaders and 5,000 invited guests.

The A380 super jumbo has been made by the European company Airbus involving France, Britain, Germany and Spain. All these countries have invested heavily in the 10-year, €10-billion-plus (U.S. $13-billion-plus) programme to make the world's most modern and largest passenger plane.

Hailed as a "European success story" by the European Union, the massive plane can seat up to 840 passengers on its two full decks, and its size easily eclipses the Boeing 747, the biggest plane to rule the commercial skies for decades.

Companies have already placed firm orders for 149 of the aircraft, which comes with a catalogue price of between U.S. $263 and $286 million. Airbus has already booked orders from several leading airlines like Singapore, Gulf, American for the A380.

The plane has three-class seating configuration -- first, business and economy. These will transport 555 passengers. This number is 139 more than a Boeing 747. The cost of the tickets is expected to be 20 per cent lesser than 747. The airbus offers unprecedented luxuries like deluxe bedrooms, gyms, bars and spacious lounges.

**Key highlights of Airbus A380:**

- **Width:** Wingspan is 80m, enough room on wings to park 70 cars.
- **Height:** Tail is as high as a seven storey building.
- **Length:** As long as eight London buses parked end-to-end.
- **Power:** At take-off, A380's four Rolls-Royce engines will generate thrust equal to 3,500 cars.
- **Capacity:** 555 seats in first class, business, economy. An all economy A380 can seat 840.

  With an all economy arrangement and no leg stretching extras, the A380 packs in 840 passengers. In an all-freight configuration, it will hold 150 tons of cargo

- **Add ons:** A380 can house bars, billiard rooms, showers, libraries and sleeping quarters for staff.

# CASE STUDY-4

## *Palace-On-Wheels*

Palace-On-Wheels is rated among the 10 most luxurious train journeys in the world and is one of the best ways to travel in royal Rajasthan. The train starts from Delhi and covers 14 tourist spots of Rajasthan. Some important destinations covered by the Palace on Wheels include Jaipur, Chittaurgarh, Udaipur, Sawai Madhopur, Jaisalmer and Jodhpur.

The Palace-on-Wheels comprises 14 fully air-conditioned deluxe saloons, equipped with world-class amenities to enhance the pleasure of travelling. The 14 coaches are made up of 104 passenger berths in double bedded cabins, each with channel music, intercom, attached toilet, running hot and cold water and a shower.

The coaches are named after former Rajput states matching the aesthetics and interiors of the royal past. Each saloon has a mini pantry and a lounge to ensure availability of hot and cold beverages and refreshment and a place to relax and get together. The train has two lavish restaurants "The Maharaja" and "The Maharani" with a Rajasthani ambience, serving palate tickling Continental, Indian and Rajasthani cuisine. The train also boasts of a well-stocked bar offering the choicest of spirits of Indian and International brands. Each coach also offers a good collection of books to choose from.

In 1991, the Palace-on-Wheels has been refurbished to a great extent. The decor in the saloons and bar lounge has been changed, keeping in mind the traditional aesthetic yet modern. The toilets have been redone and are maintained sparkling clean. Each saloon lounge has been equipped with a colour television and a CD player. A satellite phone is provided to communicate anywhere in the world from the train.

**Individual facilities available on board include the following:**

**Accommodation**

14 fully air-conditioned deluxe saloons, each a combination of a 4 twin bedded chamber with channel music, intercom, toilets, running hot and cold water, shower, wall to wall carpeting and other amenities.

**For Disabled Persons**

Special assistance is available in the form of wheel chairs, and a special attendant for manual assistance.

**Luggage Collection**

Luggage is picked up and taken to respective saloons.

**Arrival Kit**

Each guest is provided with an arrival kit consisting of stationery items, brochures, cards, etc. Anything additional can be asked for, from the attendant. The attendant or 'Khidmatgar' is always available at service, to take care of all travel needs.

**Meals**
An exotic array of dishes to choose from the Continental, Indian and Rajasthani cuisine are available on the Palace-on-Wheels.

**Mineral Water**
Mineral water is made available all through the journey.

**Newspapers/Magazines**
The leading dailies and newspapers and a large collection of magazines is available on the train.

**Security**
Adequate safety arrangements are made in the train itself.

**Toiletries**
All essential toiletries like soaps, shampoos, moisturisers, etc., are provided in the train.

**Wine/Beer**
A complimentary bottle of wine/beer, courtesy Palace-on-Wheels for royal guests.

**Common facilities on board**
**Bar**
A well stocked bar serves wine, liquor and spirits of Indian and International brands, to keep 'high spirits'.

**Group Photograph**
To cherish the special moments of glory and to remind one of the good times, a group photograph is given to passengers as a souvenir.

**Lounge**
A lounge for relaxing, interacting, making friends, getting together and indulging in games.

**Mail Box**
A mail box is provided on board, which discharges mail with utmost care and efficiency.

**Medical Aid**
First aid is available on the train, whereas a doctor can be arranged on call at the very next station.

**Restaurants**
Two lavish and beautifully done-up restaurants; "The Maharaja" and "The Maharani" serve mouth-watering Continental, Indian and Rajasthani cuisine.

**Shopping**
Certain handicrafts and other special items of Rajasthani origin can be bought while visiting the places covered by the Palace-on-Wheels and a catalogue of typical Rajasthani items is also available on board.

**Smoking**
The Palace-on-Wheels is a no-smoking train.

# Review

Transport—major impact on the growth and direction of tourism development • Basic component of tourism • A necessary pre-condition of travel

## Definition

"The means to reach the destination and also the means of movement at the destination".

## I. Modes of Transport

- Air - Schedule or charter
- Rail - Local or international
- Water - Sea, ferries, cruises, inland water ways
- Surface - Coach, car

## II. Choice of Mode

Choice of mode is affected by following factors:
- Distance and time factor
- Safety and utility
- Status and comfort
- Comparative price and service offered
- Geographical position and isolation
- Range of services offered
- Level of competition between services
- Remains the cheapest means of travel universally
- Introduction of new technology on railways
- Offer wide range of tourist services
- Recently have become more market oriented
- Product innovation
- High speed, and comfort
- Growing market on long distance, transcontinental routes

## III. Rail

- Schedule rail services
- Private hire services
- Tour and excursion operations

**Reasons for travel by train**

1. Safety
2. Facility to move around
3. Personal comfort and privacy
4. Ability to look out and enjoy the scenery enroute
5. Arriving at destination, rested and relaxed

6. Decongested route ways
7. Savings in hotel charges

## Major Railway Systems

### Euro Rail
- Largest cooperative association sponsored by major European railways.
- Unlimited first class, comfortable travel in 28 European countries.
- Passes valid for a period of 2 weeks to 3 months.
- The system works through over 120 Euro city trains.
- Availability of sleeping accommodation.
- Euro rail youth pass.
- General Sales Agents (GSAs)

### British Rail
- Limited rail travel in England, Scotland and Wales.
- Validity from 1 week to 4 weeks.
- Availability of sleeping berths on some trains.
- Special British rail packages (Rail + Hotel accommodation + Car rentals)
- General Sales Agents (GSAs)

### Swiss Pass
- Unlimited travel through town and country side.
- Validity from 4 days to 1 month.
- The first airport-railway station in the world fully integrated into national and international train network.
- Several possibilities of catering on board.
- Private charter trains.
- Special services for groups.
- General Sales Agents (GSAs)

### Amtrak System
- All long distance trains in USA operated by the system.
- Coach accommodation.
- Private accommodation.
- Car-train packages.
- Discounted hotels and sight-seeing packages.
- Heritage trains.
- General Sales Agents (GSAs)

## IV. Road Transport

Increase in the private car ownership in Europe, USA and elsewhere has done more to change travel habits than any other factor in tourism.

- Gave families a new freedom of movement.
- Control of routes and stops enroute.
- Privacy.
- The ability to use the vehicle for accommodation (caravans).
- The ability to carry baggage and equipment easily.
- Point to point travel.
- Reduced transportation costs (in case of families).
- Control on departure times.
- Freedom to use the automobiles once the destination is reached.
- Greater freedom and flexibility.

## Coach Services
- Intercity schedule bus services.
- Charter coach tours (Cosmos, Greyhound)
- Coach tours
- Inter-country bus services (scheduled)
- Inter-country bus (chartered)
- Airport services

## Car Rentals
Renting an automobile at hourly, daily, weekly or monthly rates.
- Many air travellers prefer to rent an automobile at their destinations rather than use public transport.
- AVIS, Europe, Hertz
- Reservation agents
- Customer service counters
- Rental agents

## V. Water Transport
- Immigration, trade and war were the principal reasons for undertaking water transport.
- First cruise in 1844.
- Gradually American ports, Mediterranean, Greece, Norway, Baltic Sea became popular.
- Ferry Transportation - Large Ferries provide coastal transportation.
- Channel tunnel.
- Decline in ocean liner shipping since 1950 signified the development of cruise industry as most shipping liners diversified into cruising.
- About 70% of the cruise passengers originate in Canada and USA.
- A cruise ship is like a floating resort with all the facilities of a five star hotel.
- Cruise market caters to all segments now.
- Fly cruise.

Transportation is a concern of every traveller, whether he is planning how to reach a destination or trying to hail a taxi. Numerous transportation options exist, ranging from one-way trips in a first-class jet to budget accommodation on a freighter. It is very important that various transport systems available for the traveller, whether he is on a business trip or on a leisure holiday, should make the journey comfortable and hassle free. Carefully planned and controlled transport systems, designed to serve all types of travellers can be profitable.

## ACCOMMODATION SEGMENT

An accommodation facility constitutes a vital and fundamental part of tourist supply. Among the important inputs, which flow into the tourist system, is tourist accommodation, which caters to international tourists forming a vital component of the tourism superstructure and an important feature of the total tourist image of the country. An adequate supply of accommodation suitably tailored to the requirements of the tourist market is one of the basic conditions of tourism development. The provision of accommodation facilities and their growth should, at the same time, be regarded in a much broader context as they make an important contribution to the economy as a whole, by stimulating economic development, social contacts and commercial activities.

Of all the constituents of the tourism industry, the accommodation sector constitutes the most important segments. Tourism is, to a great extent dependant on the type, quality and quantity of accommodation available in a particular country. It is an important part of the tourism infrastructure and the expansion of tourism inevitably brings about the development of accommodation. It is rather the core of the tourist industry.

Many countries have recognised the vital importance of the accommodation industry in relation to tourism and their governments have coordinated their activities with the industry by providing big incentives and concession to hoteliers, which has resulted in the building of a large number of hotels and other type of accommodations. For example, availability of hotel sites on liberal repayment terms, special concessions in the form of long term loans, liberal import licenses and taxation relief, contribution to the equity capital, cash grants for construction and renovation of buildings, and similar other concessions are provided to the industry. Many countries in the world offer most of these incentives.

## Hotel Accommodation

The basic unit of accommodation is the 'hotel'. Although the earliest hotels date to the 18th century, their growth on any scale occurred only in the following century when the different modes of transport especially the railways created sufficiently large markets to help make large hotels possible. During this period a number of hotels were put up at important destinations. In most of the cases, especially in Europe, the hotels were developed along the main railway and highway routes in major cities and towns. In many other countries within and outside Europe the number of hotels also increased catering to the increasing volume of traffic.

Hotels provide accommodation, meals and refreshments for irregular periods of time for those who may reserve their accommodation either in advance or on the premises. In broad terms hotels provide facilities to meet the needs of the modern traveller. The dictionaries define hotel in several ways: 'a place which supplies board and lodging', 'large city house of distinction', and 'a public building'.

Over the years the concept and the format of hotels, have changed a great deal. There are various types of hotels catering to the increasing demands of tourists. The size, the façade, architectural features and the facilities and amenities provided differ from one establishment to another. In addition, the landscape in a particular destination area also greatly influences the architectural features of a hotel.

Accommodation can be divided into two main categories i.e serviced or self-catering.

Hotels providing service accommodation, mean that there is a staff employed by the hotel to provide meals, refreshments and perhaps a bar service. Rooms are cleaned daily, and beds changed. Guests may have their clothes laundered or dry cleaned, request meals in their rooms, buy newspapers, souvenirs and perhaps picture postcards. Some large hotels also have shops, which sell gifts, clothes and other items. There may be hairdressing and beauty saloons on the premises, as well as a swimming pool (indoor or outdoor), gymnasium or fitness club. Depending upon the location, a hotel may have a disco or a nightclub available to guests and a public restaurant/bar. City centre hotels may provide secretarial and office facilities for business travellers in the form of a business centre. Conference rooms of varying sizes may also be found in hotels.

## Forms of Hotel Accommodation

- International hotels
- Commercial hotels
- Residential hotels
- Resort hotels
- Floating hotels
- Airport hotels

## International Hotels

Modern and western style hotels are located in all metros and other large cities as well as principle tourist centres. These are luxury hotels are classified on the basis of internationally accepted system of classification. These are five such categories ranging from 1-star to 5-stars. International chains own a large number of such hotels.

## Resort Hotels:

These cater to the needs of the holiday-maker. These are located near the sea, mountain regions and other areas of natural beauty. In these hotels rest, relaxation and entertainment are the key factors and the atmosphere is informal. The emphasis is on entertainment, recreation and sports, both

indoor and outdoor. This type of accommodation rarely attracts commercial patronage. The duration of stay in these hotels is longer.
Types of resorts:
- Summer resorts
- Winter resorts
- Hill resorts
- Health resorts
- All Season resorts

Most of the resort hotels are seasonal establishments.

## Commercial Hotels

These direct their appeal primarily to the individual traveller. Most hotels which receive business guests are located in important commercial and industrial centres of large towns and cities. These are generally run by owners.

## Residential Hotels

Also known as apartment houses with complete hotel services tariff here is charged is on monthly/yearly basis. The accommodation provided is both furnished and unfurnished. No meals are provided for the guests. Apartment hotels are popular in the United States and Western Europe and are coming up in many other countries.

## Floating Hotels

These are located on the surface of the water. All facilities and services of a hotel are provided. The atmosphere is exclusive and exotic. In some countries, old luxury ships have been converted into floating hotels.

## Airport Hotels

Airport hotels are located near airports and cater to the needs of transit passengers, airport crew and passengers of delayed or cancelled flights. All services provided are of a 5-star hotel category. There is a provision of shuttle services between the hotel and airport.

## Hotel Reservation Checklist

It is important for a travel agent to know:
(i) where is the hotel located? Downtown? Near the airport? Near historical sites?
(ii) the type of rooms available in the hotel (Example: single, double, smoking/non-smoking.)
(iii) what are the room rates? Does the hotel offer any special or promotional rates? (Example: advance purchase discounts, weekend specials, rates which include breakfast and/or other amenities, corporate rates.)
(iv) what taxes are involved in the hotel stay? (Example: room occupancy tax; state tax, departure taxes, surcharges.)

(v)   can the client's reservations be guaranteed if held with a credit card?
(vi)  does the hotel issue a confirmation number? Can the client receive a copy of the hotel confirmation in writing?
(vii) the hotel's address and phone/fax numbers.
(viii) the hotel's parking facilities.
(ix)  what are the hotel's cancellation policies? Is there a penalty levied if the client cancels?
(x)   what special features does the hotel offer? (Example: restaurants, pools, on-site recreation, etc.)
(xi)  is the hotel accessible to the disabled?
(xii) what are the hotel's check-in and check-out times?

## Restaurant Services and Cuisines

The food is served on (i) "a la carte" ordered and charged on the basis of selection from the menu and (ii) fixed menu offering 1/2/3 choices only with a fixed charge.

Dining rooms are mostly used for the tourist groups and/or in smaller places. The dining rooms are also used as multipurpose halls for parties, meeting and social get together. There are important sources of additional revenue for the management.

Restaurants: General or Specially (Chinese, Thai, Japanese, Continental European, Tandoori, etc.) The service can be for limited hours.

24 hours service with a limited menu, the accent is on fast service and the meals served, are confirmed to certain hours:

Breakfast 0700 – 1000 hrs
Lunch     1200 – 1500 hrs
Dinner    1900 – 2330 hrs

## Room Service

Food is ordered by the guest from their rooms and is served in guest's room. The menu and service is limited to specific hours and is selected. The charges are slightly higher than in coffee shops/restaurants

## Meal Plans

EP - European Plan: Room only
CP - Continental Plan: Continental breakfast (Juice/Fruit, Toast, Tea, Coffee)
AP - American Plan: Breakfast, lunch, dinner
MAP - Modified American Plan: Breakfast, lunch/dinner

## Supplementary Accommodation

The accommodation industry offers a wide range of products. Most people are familiar with hotels but do not realise how many other types of facilities there are to choose from. This section cannot list them all but should set you thinking about the many creative alternatives that can be offered in the form of supplementary accommodation to the clients who cannot afford to stay in a hotel offering full service.

Supplementary accommodation offers accommodation only. In some cases, however, a limited service may also be provided. The services provided are minimal, which include overnight stay and some meals. The standards of comfort are, however, modest since the accommodation itself is moderately priced. The atmosphere in supplementary units is rather informal. Following are the main forms of supplementary accommodation:

(i) motels
(ii) youth hostels
(iii) camping sites
(iv) bed and breakfast establishments
(v) tourist holiday villages
(vi) apartments
(vii) farm houses
(viii) guest houses

### Motels

Primarily designed to serve the needs of motorists, motels always exclusively meet the demand for transit accommodation. They serve the function of a transit hotel except that they are geared to accommodate motor travelling guests for an overnight stay. The important services provided include accommodation, parking, garage facilities, restaurant facilities, catering and recreational facilities. All the motels are also equipped with petrol filling stations, repair services, garage, etc. Motels are of different types. Some motels provide just the minimum services while others are well furnished with comfortable accommodation and excellent facilities. The accommodation provided in a motel is of Chalet type, which is furnished, has a dining hall with a fixed menu. Shopping facilities for the travelling public are also provided for in a motel.

### Youth Hostels

Youth hostels can be defined as a building, which offers clean, moderate and inexpensive shelter to young people exploring their own country or other countries and travelling, independently or in groups, on holiday or for educational purposes. It is a place where young people of different social backgrounds and nationalities meet and come to know each other. The youth hostels are equipped to accommodate young men and women, who travel on foot, by bicycle or other means of locomotion and who, at very little cost, are provided with a place to sleep, eat or to make their own meals. The services provided include accommodation, meals and also recreation. The accommodation provided in the hostels is for a limited number of days.

### Caravan and Camping Sites

Caravan and camping sites constitute a significant accommodation category in many holiday areas. These are very popular in some European countries as also in the United States of America. These are also known as open-air hostels, tourist camps or camping grounds. Camping, originally practiced by hikers on foot, is increasingly giving way to car camping. The sites are usually located within the large cities in open spaces. Equipped to receive mobile accommodation in the form of caravans, the camping sites provide facilities for parking, tent pitching, water, electricity and toilets. Though the services provided generally include restaurants, recreational rooms, toilets and at certain places a grocer's shop, the type of services often vary from place to place. Some countries have enacted legislation establishing the minimum standards of facilities, that must be provided which include health and sanitation standards and prices to be charged for parking and use of various services and facilities.

## Bed and Breakfast Establishments

Also known in some countries as apartment hotels and hotel garnis, they represent a growing form of accommodation units catering for holiday as well as business travellers. These establishments provide only accommodation and breakfast and not the principal meals. These are usually located in large towns and cities along commercial and holiday routes and also resort areas and are used by en-route travellers. Some of these establishments are very popular with holidaymakers.

## Tourist Holiday Villages

Tourist villages were established in some of the European countries in the fifties. These villages are situated at warm sea sides and in the region, which offer certain facilities for the tourists. The villages are mostly promoted by important clubs, social organisations and also by tourist organisations. The village complex is a centre of accommodation providing extensive sports and recreation facilities, riding, swimming, tennis, volleyball, football, sauna, mini-golf, badminton, table tennis and yoga. These provide both board and lodging. The atmosphere in these villages is kept as informal as possible. Telephone, radios, newspapers and TV are not provided unless there is an emergency. The accommodation provided is usually in multiple units and may provide for self-catering. The furnishing provided in the rooms is minimal.

The holiday villages are usually based on family units, each providing a convertible living room, bath/shower and sometimes kitchen. The villages are self-sufficient, providing almost all necessities required by the residents. There is a small shopping complex where one can buy articles of daily need. The services of doctors are also available in the village.

## Apartments

In the past, it was necessary to sign a lease for a lengthy period of 6 months or more, in order to enjoy the comfort of an apartment. Now, in many cities, apartments are available for a periods of one week, or in some cases, on a day-to-day basis. London is one city that has a very well developed programme for renting apartments to travellers. This is a good option for families. In an apartment, there is more space and the kitchen allows food preparation according to the taste of the family.

## Farmhouses

In many countries, government tourism officials have attempted to disperse tourism revenue into the countryside and away from concentrated urban centres by encouraging the development of farmhouse accommodation. Farmhouse owners who wish to be approved for participation in these programmes must ensure that certain standards of comfort and hygiene are met, before their houses can be listed and promoted. Staying in farmhouses is an good option for independent travellers who wish to meet "real" people, make friends and experience the life and culture of a country. This type of accommodation is very well-developed in Ireland and is growing rapidly in many other countries such as Italy, where it is promoted under the name "Agritourism".

## Guesthouses

There are two types of guesthouses. Some are large, old houses that have been renovated and brought up to high standards of comfort and luxury. They operate like small, personalised hotels. These can be quite expensive. People who like personal attention and enjoy notable architecture or interesting locations will enjoy this type of guesthouse. This category is developing rapidly in the USA. In many European countries similar properties are available at fairly reasonable prices, are called "pensions".

The order style of guesthouse is an actually a family home that has extra rooms available for overnight guests. Also called a "Bed and Breakfast," this is not at all like a hotel. Guests eat with the family and often share the living room, the TV and the bathroom too. As with farmhouse stays, this is an excellent way to meet "real "people. Children can make friends and play with the children of the house and their friends in the neighbourhood. This accommodation is well developed in Britain, Ireland, and other countries. In German-speaking countries, it is called a "Gastehaus".

# 11
# COMMUNICATION WITH THE CLIENT

### Chapter Objectives

**After reading this chapter the reader should be able to:**
- Understand the need and importance of customer service in the travel industry with special reference to travel executive.
- Analyse the nature of client complaints and tips for handling complaints.
- Define the concept of communication skills.
- List key points to better communication skills.
- Understand the difference between positive and negative language.
- Understand practicle tips for handling complaints.
- Define listening skills.
- Understand barriers to communications.

Customer service is of vital importance to all organisations in the travel and tourism sector. Excellent customer service results in a high level of satisfaction and encourages customers to return and to recommend the organisation to others. Many organisations in the travel and tourism sector offer the same or similar products and services, and it is often the quality of the customer service which distinguishes one from another. Travel and tourism organisations realise that consistently high standards of customer service will ensure customer loyalty and improve business performance.

The skills needed by an employee of a travel and tourism organisation are of vital importance. Aspects such as personal presentation, teamwork and communication skills are all exceptionally important to the provision of excellent service. Travel and tourism organisations are in the business of providing information and selling products and services, and learners will have the opportunity to develop and demonstrate these skills with customers in real or simulated situations across different industries within the sector.

In effective customer service plays a key role in retaining the clients. An organisation has to be very careful in trying to understand the customer needs and requirements while on a tour and should ensure that he is satisfied all the time and has no cause to complain. However, during his stay he has to come in touch with many functionaries starting from his arrival at the airport until he returns. A travel executive should ensure that any complaint made must be properly attended to and resolved to the satisfaction of the clients.

Tracking consumer trends is a crucial way to understand what consumers are doing now and may be doing next which ideally should inspire you to dream up new goods, services and experiences for and with your customer, to meet and anticipate their needs.

### The Issue

**Does what you deliver match with what your customers want?**
**If they have made adjustments, is it time for you to do the same?**
Build customer loyalty. Why does it matter?

- It's cheaper to retain customers than to find new ones
- Loyal customers spend more and are less likely to demand discounts
- They recommend you to their friends
- If they book with you they are not booking with your competitors

### Customer loyalty and Travel Agents

- Low repeat levels
- Hotels, carriers tour operators are retaining your customers
- So start by measuring it
- Then target ways to improve it.

### Ways to Increase your Customers Loyalty

- Regular contact: pre-departure courtesy call offering (extras), post holding follow-up call
- Relationship pricing: price incentive for repeat business, perceived added values
- Tailored product: first pick of product, recognising individual needs
- Reinforcing promotions: loyalty schemes, tailored direct marketing

### Summing Up

- Understand your customer and be alert to their changing needs
- Give them good reason to stay loyal
- Share costs with partners
- Spread your message online at low cost

### Definitions

#### Role of Customer Service

**Client** – is profit, rest are overheads
**Service** – more of intellect and less of materials

**Reliability** – delivery of experience, every time

**Relationship** – trust, trust and trust and then, add value by properly managing the relationship with a client.

**Complaint** – valuable feedback

## Delivering Reliable Service
- Quality doesn't have to be defined, you understand and feel it without definition
- Delivery of experience
- Break obsession with process
- Bring clients into the process and make them co-conspirators in the creation of adventure.
- Clients are influenced in the manner they are handled.

## Maintaining Client Relationship
- Did I deliver the promise that I made when I sold the tour?
- Do I know what the client wants, do I know each one of them by name, their interests and requirements during the tour?
- Do I know who the decision influencers are?
- Am I able to measure my achievements through my clients' objectives.

## Client Complaint

The complaints of the clients are a valuable feedback and should be taken seriously. The travel executive who is dealing with the clients should not only listen to the complaints properly but should also appreciate the clients for bringing the same to the notice. Most of the complaints of the clients may be sorted out with foresight and proper decision making. Given below are some valuable tips:
- Paying proper attention to the complaint
- One has to be quick in resolving the complaint, otherwise damage will already have been done
- Proper attitude is extremely important
- Communication – that we have addressed it proactively
- Log it – both complaints and commendations

Following practical tips will help resolve the complaints in the best possible manner:

**Practical Tips for Handling Complaints**

- Receive the client making a complaint with a smile
- The travel executive must pay proper attention while listening/recording the complaint, as it gives reassurance to the client
- Remain calm and confident
- Do not argue with the client
- Use positive body language
- Establish and maintain eye contact

- Do not raise your voice or shout. Remember clients look forward to you as a guide and a friend
- Observe and listen carefully and allow the client to speak
- Apologize for the situation and thank the client for bringing the matter to you
- Do not blame colleagues in front of the clients
- Take responsibility for solving the problem
- Reassure the client
- Ask questions to find out more details
- Do not reach a conclusion before you have sufficient information
- Summarise information to check mutual understanding of the problem
- Do not personalise the situation. Do present alternative solutions
- Carry out the agreed solutions
- Check if the client is satisfied with the final outcome
- Refer the problem to senior authorities, if necessary, or if the client insists

## Communication skills

Communication is a process of exchange of thoughts, feelings, opinions, ideas and information through verbal or non-verbal means between two or more individuals. The backbone of the communication process is knowledge. Having adequate knowledge helps in answering everyone's queries. In the service industry having a deep knowledge about products and understanding the customers' needs and desires, helps in serving them better and delighting them. It is a dialogue and not a monologue. This process involves a speaker and a listener. The speaker initiates the conversation while the listener responds to it and the conversation goes on.

There are many definitions of the word 'communication'. The most comprehensive is:

**'The interchange of thoughts, opinions, ideas or information by speech, writing or signs'. It is also the exchange of feelings and attitudes.**

We communicate mainly through verbal and non-verbal ways. However, our interactions with others are not always the way we want them to be. It is important for the communicator to know various barriers, which stand in way of effective communication and also how to overcome these. Unless the barriers are overcome, the message communicated is distorted and not complete.

Sound knowledge of the foundation gives rise to the thought process, if the thoughts are clear then it further stimulates the speech process clearly with fluency and without fumbling. And therefore for communication to become a skill, it should be blended well with proper pronunciation, fluency, grammar and effective listening.

Communication in travel and tourism takes place face-to-face, by means of telephone, in writing and electronically (e-mail and fax). It is important to use the appropriate method of communication for a given situation. If a customer wants a quick reply, e-mail or fax are very useful ways of transmitting information speedily. Written communication, perhaps a letter or internal memo, tends to be more formal than face-to-face communication, which is why it is often used to confirm decisions that were agreed verbally.

Face-to-face communication - There are many occasions in travel and tourism when staff deal directly with customers face-to-face, either individually or in a group situation, e.g. tourist information centre staff directing a party of overseas visitors to nearby attractions, a hotel receptionist welcoming a guest or a travel agent advising a client on the benefits of a particular holiday.

Important rules when dealing with customers face-to-face include:
1. Always smile when you greet the customer;
2. Keep a reasonable distance from the customer -
3. Not too close but not too far away;
4. Listen to what the customer is saying;
5. Always thank the customer when appropriate.
6. Make eye contact but don't stare;
7. Make sure that you look interested (even if you're not!)
8. Address the customer by name
9. Don't interrupt the customer

## Effective Listening

**There are three levels of listening:**
(i) **Attentive** – Listening for important information.
(ii) **Empathetic** – Listening to appreciate the other's attitudes, feelings and emotions.
(iii) **Casual** – Listening to an informal discussion and for pleasure.

Attentive listening is a 'hygiene factor' to communication. This means that when two people are talking to each other they need to be attentive and not distracted or else it will be a very dissatisfying experience for both parties.

In business, every situation demands a complete understanding of the customer. Be it negotiating or while resolving a query, we need to know what the customer is feelings and thinking and how he is perceiving the situation.

After we understand the customer only then we can address his needs and satisfy him. Empathetic listening helps us do this effectively. However, the hardest level of listening is empathetic listening. We can listen empathetically by making a conscious effort at reading the non-verbal signs during the interaction with the customer.

- Preparing in advance
- Prepare remarks and questions in advance. When possible free your mind for listening.
- Limit your own talking
- You can't talk and listen at the same time.
- Think like the other person.

**Keys to Effective Listening**

- Their problems and needs are important, and you will understand and retain them better if you keep their point of view in mind.

### Ask questions

- If you don't understand something or feel you have missed a point, clear it right away.

### Don't interrupt

A pause, even a long pause, doesn't always mean they have finished saying everything they wanted to say.

### Take notes

This will help you remember important points. But be selective. Trying to note down everything they say can result in being left far behind or in retaining irrelevant details.

- Listen for ideas, not just words.
  You want to get the whole picture, not just isolated bits and pieces.

- Pay attention.
  Be open-eared and open-minded. The other person wants your attention and wants to be listened to.

  Fight off distractions. Only in this way can you stay with the other person's conversation.

- Make encouraging responses.
  An occasional 'Yes', 'I see', etc., shows the customer you're still with them but don't overdo or use meaningless comments.

- Turn off your words.
  This isn't easy, but personal fears, worries, and problems not connected with the contact form a kind of "static" that can blank out your message.

- React to ideas, not the person
  Don't become irritated at the things other may say or their manner in presenting them to you.

## Barriers to Effective Communication

We have seen what we mean by the process of communication. But, at times even after taking care of every other detail some misunderstandings arise. So, to eliminate these misunderstandings, we have to understand the most common barriers to effective communication.

The process of communication has multiple barriers. The intended communiqué will often be disturbed and distorted leading to a condition of misunderstanding and failure of communication. The Barriers to effective communication could be of many types like:

(i) linguistic
(ii) psychological
(iii) emotional
(iv) physical

(v) cultural
(vi) Organisational Structure Barriers:
(vii) Attitude Barriers:
(viii) Perception Barriers:
(ix) Physiological Barriers:
(x) Technological & Socio-religious Barriers:

## (i) Linguistic Barriers:

The language barrier is one of the main barriers that limit effective communication. Language is the most commonly employed tool of communication. The fact that each major region has its own language is one of the Barriers to effective communication. Sometimes even a thick dialect may render the communication ineffective.

As per some estimates, the dialects of every two regions changes within a few kilometers. Even in the same workplace, different employees will have different linguistic skills. As a result, the communication channels that span across the organization would be affected by this.

Thus keeping this barrier in mind, different considerations have to be made for different employees. Some of them are very proficient in a certain language and others will be okay with these languages.

## (ii) Psychological Barriers:

There are various mental and psychological issues that may be barriers to effective communication. Some people have stage fear, speech disorders, phobia, depression etc. All of these conditions are very difficult to manage sometimes and will most certainly limit the ease of communication.

## (iii) Emotional Barriers:

The emotional IQ of a person determines the ease and comfort with which they can communicate. A person who is emotionally mature will be able to communicate effectively. On the other hand, people who let their emotions take over will face certain difficulties.

A perfect mixture of emotions and facts is necessary for effective communication. Emotions like anger, frustration, humour, can blur the decision-making capacities of a person and thus limit the effectiveness of their communication.

## (iv) Physical Barriers:

They are the most obvious barriers to effective communication. These barriers are mostly easily removable in principle at least. They include barriers like noise, closed doors, faulty equipment used for communication, closed cabins, etc. Sometimes, in a large office, the physical separation between various employees combined with faulty equipment may result in severe barriers to effective communication.

### (v) Cultural Barriers:

As the world is getting more and more globalized, any large office may have people from several parts of the world. Different cultures have a different meaning for several basic values of society. Dressing, Religions or lack of them, food, drinks, pets, and the general behaviour will change drastically from one culture to another. Hence it is a must that we must take these different cultures into account while communication. This is what we call being culturally appropriate. In many multinational companies, special courses are offered at the orientation stages that let people know about other cultures and how to be courteous and tolerant of others.

### (vi) Organisational Structure Barriers:

There are many methods of communication at an organisational level. Each of these methods has its own problems and constraints that may become barriers to effective communication. Most of these barriers arise because of misinformation or lack of appropriate transparency available to the employees.

### (vii) Attitude Barriers:

Certain people like to be left alone. They are the introverts or just people who are not very social. Others like to be social or sometimes extra clingy. Both these cases could become a barrier to communication. Some people have attitude issues, like inflated ego and inconsiderate behaviours.

These employees can cause severe strains in the communication channels that they are present in. Certain personality traits like shyness, anger, social anxiety may be removable through courses and proper training. However, problems like egocentric behaviour and selfishness may not be correctable.

### (viii) Perception Barriers:

Different people perceive the same things differently. This is a fact which we must consider during the communication process. Knowledge of the perception levels of the audience is crucial to effective communication. All the messages or communiqué must be easy and clear. There shouldn't be any room for a diversified interpretational set.

### (ix) Physiological Barriers:

Certain disorders or diseases or other limitations could also prevent effective communication between the various channels of an organization. The shrillness of voice, dyslexia, etc are some examples of physiological barriers to effective communication. However, these are not crucial because they can easily be compensated and removed.

### (x) Technological & Socio-religious Barriers:

Most of the organizations will not be able to afford a decent tech for the purpose of communication. Hence, this becomes a very crucial barrier. Other barriers are socio-religious barriers. In a patriarchal society, a woman or a transgender may face many difficulties and barriers while communicating.

## Communication Styles

People have different styles or a combination styles for communicating. We can broadly classify them into the following three styles:

### (i) Aggressive

Aggressive behaviour is shown by putting forward your own needs, ideas and feelings, while at the same time ignoring or putting down those of other people.

**It involves:**
- Blaming others for problems and mistakes.
- Using sarcasm, adopting a patronising attitude or verbal hostility.
- 'Telling' others to do what you want.

**Reasons:**
- Concerned with achieving one's own goals and having little or no concern for the goals of others.
- Concerned with 'beating' others down to look better than or 'superior' to the others.

### (ii) Submissive

Submissive behaviour is when you are not putting forward your own needs, ideas, feelings, ignoring or running yourself down to others.

**Involves:**
- Giving into other people's requests and putting pressure on oneself.
- Apologetic attitude.
- Saying 'Yes' when one wants to say 'No'.
- Verbal statements such as 'Sorry to take up your valuable time, but..."
- "It's only my opinion, but..."
- "If you say so, we will..."
- Non-verbal signals such as hesitant, quiet voice, little eye contact.
- Nervous movements, arms crossed in protection, hand wringing.

**Reasons:**
- Trying to avoid hurting or upsetting others.
- Trying to gain the approval of others.

### Assertive

The benefits of being assertive is that it improves self esteem of the person who uses this behaviour. Assertive people also recognise responsibility for their own feelings and thoughts and blame others less and make fewer excuses for themselves.

They also spend less time worrying about offending others or scheming on how to beat others down. This increases personal performance and they are more likely to be recognised and rewarded.

**Involves statements such as:**
- "I believe that... What do you think?"
- "I would like to tackle the task in this way. How does that affect you?"

- Non-verbal signals such as a steady, medium-pitched voice, even pace.
- Steady gaze but not a dominating glare, relaxed and open facial expression and body posture.

**Reasons**
- Concerned with interacting in a manner that develops one's self-assurance and confidence and that of others too.
- Concerned with working effectively coupled with respecting other people's rights.

For the travel executive it is of paramount importance that they listen to the needs and requirements of the passengers attentively, otherwise there may be some misunderstanding. Whenever any client speaks to a travel executive, it is important that full attention is paid to the spoken word and understood properly. Many a times there could be a problem if the travel executive is not attentive to the requirements of the clients who may have cause for complaint. Listening is a five part process and includes hearing, attending, understanding, responding, and remembering. If this process is followed properly there could be no cause for any complaints and the clients will be fully satisfied.

## Ways to Better Communication

People communicate in various ways to express their thoughts. Every person has a different style of communication and the same is influenced by various factors. A person may be aggressive in asserting his reason for a particular issue. Another person may be submissive in his behaviour and yet another assertive to prove his point. For all these three different types of styles, there are reasons, which compel a person to use one of these three styles. What is important is that a person has to be balanced in order to be able to communicate a point in a manner so that the other is clear about the contents of the message.

Some of the important points to keep in mind while communicating are:
- Use a positive tone of voice
- Be persuasive by enthusiasm
- Present your ideas in an orderly manner
- Use the "you" appeal
- Be stimulating
- Be conscious of bias
- Be a mirror of your message
- Watch your body language
- Empathise all the time

## Listening Skills

We use listening skills more than any other communication skill but listening is rarely taught. Listening effectively requires that you maintain a considerable amount of self-control and concentration. One may be hearing, that is the physical part, where the brain absorbs and perceives the sounds, but not listening. In listening one has to understand and react to whatever has been spoken.

Listening is a five part process and includes:
- Hearing
- Attending
- Understanding
- Responding
- Remembering

In today's high-tech, high-speed, high-stress world, communication is more important then ever, yet we seem to devote less and less time to really listening to one another. Genuine listening has become a rare gift—the gift of time. It helps build relationships, solve problems, ensure understanding, resolve conflicts, and improve accuracy. At work, effective listening means fewer errors and less wasted time.

There are 10 tips to help you develop effective listening skills.

Step 1: Face the speaker and maintain eye contact.
Step 2: Be attentive, but relaxed.
Step 3: Keep an open mind.
Step 4: Listen to the words and try to picture what the speaker is saying.
Step 5: Don't interrupt and don't impose your "solutions."
Step 6: Wait for the speaker to pause to ask clarifying questions.
Step 7: Ask questions only to ensure understanding.
Step 8: Try to feel what the speaker is feeling.
Step 9: Give the speaker regular feedback.
Step 10: Pay attention to what isn't said—to nonverbal cues.

## Body Language

Body language is the unspoken communication that goes on in every face-to-face encounter with another human being. It tells you their true feelings towards you and how well your words are being received and vice-versa where they perceive your reaction to them. Between 60-80% of our message is communicated through our body language. Only 7-10% is attributable to the actual words of a conversation.

As a travel executive, your body language should convey the following to the customer:
- He/she is special
- The client is very important to the company
- Every request from the client will always be attended to
- The travel executive is always there whenever the clients need him/her.

It is always good to practice positive body language, as this is necessary to maintain a good rapport with the clients. Even in day-to-day life this works wonders in interpersonal communication and maintaining harmony. Negative body language can cause unwanted harm and misunderstanding.

A few examples of both positive and negative body language are given below:

|       | POSITIVE | NEGATIVE |
|-------|----------|----------|
| Eyes  | Direct eye contact | Frown<br>Shifting eyes, looking away<br>Looking down |
| Mouth | Smiling | Straight, sulky<br>Drooping |
| Head  | Tilted, straight, nodding | Lowered, tilted back |
| Arms  | By your side | Crossed, crossed behind back |
| Body  | Leaning forward, straight | Leaning back |
| Legs  | Straight | Crossed, shifting feet, crossing legs, tapping feet |

## Other Individual Examples are:

| NONVERBAL BEHAVIOR | INTERPRETATION |
|--------------------|----------------|
| Brisk, erect walk | Confidence |
| Standing with hands on hips | Readiness, aggression |
| Sitting with legs crossed, foot kicking slightly | Boredom |
| Sitting, legs apart | Open, relaxed |
| Arms crossed on chest | Defensiveness |
| Walking with hands in pockets, shoulders hunched | Dejection |
| Hand to cheek | Evaluation, thinking |
| Touching, slightly rubbing nose | Rejection, doubt, lying |
| Rubbing the eyes | Doubt, disbelief |
| Hands clasped behind back | Anger, frustration, apprehension |
| Locked ankles | Apprehension |
| Head resting in hand, eyes downcast | Boredom |
| Rubbing hands | Anticipation |
| Sitting with hands clasped behind head, legs crossed | Confidence, superiority |

| | |
|---|---|
| Open palm | Sincerity, openness, innocence |
| Pinching bridge of nose, eyes closed | Negative evaluation |
| Tapping or drumming fingers | Impatience |
| Steeping fingers | Authoritative |
| Patting/fondling hair | Lack of self-confidence; insecurity |
| Tilted head | Interest |
| Stroking chin | Trying to make a decision |
| Looking down, face turned away | Disbelief |
| Biting nails | Insecurity, nervousness |
| Pulling or tugging at ear | Indecision |

## Language Usage

Language is an exceedingly powerful tool. Whether you communicate orally or in written form, the way you express yourself will affect whether your message is received positively or negatively. Even when you are conveying unpleasant news, the impact can be softened by the use of what we call positive language. You can use positive language to project a helpful, positive image rather than a destructive, negative one.

**Negative language often has the following characteristics:**
- Tells the recipient what cannot be done.
- Has a subtle tone of blame.
- Includes words like 'can't,' 'won't', 'unable to', that tell the recipient what the travel executive cannot do or allow.
- Does not stress positive actions that would be appropriate, or positive consequences.

**Positive language has the following qualities**
- Tells the recipient what can be done
- Suggests alternatives and choices available to the recipient
- Sounds helpful and encouraging rather than bureaucratic
- Stresses positive actions and positive consequences that can be anticipated.

The tone of the voice is also very important. Speaking in a soft evenly modulated voice helps in getting the message through to the client faster than a harsh voice. This is because when a client hears an angry or gruff tone, he concentrates more on the tone than on the words being conveyed to him. A few examples of positive language are:

| WORDS TO BE USED WITH CARE | POSITIVE WORDS |
|---|---|
| BUT – shows difference of opinion with the client, aggressive behaviour a belligerence, never use as a conjunction | HOWEVER- less aggressive and sounds conciliatory |
| TRY – usage in the wrong place will make the client unsure of the end result of his query/request | ENSURE – a positive word that gives the client confidence in the travel executive |
| PROBLEM – sends up a signal of an unhelpful scenario | SITUATION – a feeling that a solution for every 'situation' is always there! |
| BUSY – 'no time to attend to a client'- reaction | WILL – the effort is being put in to look into the situation-"I will look into this ………." |
| PLEASE – used at the end of a statement sounds like a command | PLEASE – at the beginning of a statement sounds like a request |
| "I'LL TRY" – gives the feeling that the request will not be carried through | "I CAN" - positive statement |
| "I DON'T KNOW"- Can't do anything further | "I'LL SEE IF I CAN FIND OUT" – leaves a positive outlook |
| "CAN I"- you are not giving much choice to the other person | "MAY I" – sounds softer to the ears. |
| "I THINK…"- my mind is made up | "I BELIEVE…."- I can be convinced otherwise |
| "YOU MUST………."- insistence | "IF YOU CAN…….."- A plea. |
| "YOU SHOULD………."-Inflexibility | "YOU COULD TRY………….."- An option is being given. |
| "YOU HAVE TO…….." | "MAY I SUGGEST THAT…" |

## Interview Preparation

There is a competition these days for the job of a travel agency/airline employee in the industry. There are many applications for a handful of vacancies. One needs to be thoroughly prepared to get the job.

Majority of the travel agencies/airline look at the following parameters for employment:

**Basic Qualifications** - Educational qualifications, passport, age, height/weight, etc, are verified by the documentary evidence one provides.

**Capability** - This involves identifying the right personal qualities in an applicant. The minimum requirement is a sincere, dependable and hard working individual who can provide service in a friendly way, interact well with people, work as part of a team and cope with difficult or emergency situations.

**Specific Wants** - These requirements are tailored to the travel agency/airline needs. Some require the knowledge of a foreign language. Others need a work experience in the hospitality trade.

## The Selection Process

A candidate first has to fill up the application form as this helps to screen out the candidates. Messy, illegible or badly completed application forms demonstrate poor standards of presentation, and suggest a lack of commitment. This also helps to 'screen out' unsuitable candidates. They provide a useful overview of the candidate and the same information is used to question the candidate in the personal interview. This information offers selectors a clear view into the candidate's awareness and sensitivity and can sometimes be used to add to the observations made at the interview. The general standard of writing also indicates the language proficiency.

Many companies ask for recent photographs - this may be the first stage in the personal selection, so it is important to make a good impression.

Interviews are the norms. Most of the companies have one/two rounds of interviews. Once the preliminary sessions are over, there will usually be a pause whilst selectors gather and mull over their observations. After this some candidates may be sent home, leaving those who have proved most suitable to continue the selection process. Alternatively, all candidates may be sent home to await further communication, with suitable ones being invited back at a later date.

Many may also have an English language or an isometric/logic, general knowledge written test included between two rounds of interviews.

Public speaking, group discussion and presentations are all included in one or more of the interview rounds. The confidence and ability to stand up and talk in front of a group of people tells a lot about an individual and helps in the selection process.

## Appearance for an Interview

The way that you look and the way that you act determines what people think about you. If you smile – people think that you are pleasant; if you wear wrinkled clothing people think that you do not care. How you feel about yourself on the inside should show on the outside. Some of us know this; some of us do not. The first and foremost rule is that you must be the centre of attention during a job interview, not your clothes. To do this, be conscious of your total appearance. Determine if your appearance is suitable for you and appropriate for getting the job that you want.

It only takes five seconds to form the first impression, so the way you dress can determine whether or not you get initial consideration. Resist the temptation to dress casually, as the opinion of travel companies is that if you can't look professional at an interview, you may have trouble maintaining the travel agency's image at work!

## Group Discussions

This is a method often adopted by many travel agencies today after the initial interview round. Candidates should be alert and articulate in these discussions to leave an impression on the interviewers.

In order to succeed at any unstructured group discussion, you must define what your objective in the group is. A good definition of your objective is - to be seen to have contributed meaningfully in an attempt to put forth your views. In other words you must ensure that you are heard by the group. If the group hears you, so will the evaluator. If you are not a very assertive person, you will have to simply learn to be assertive for those 15 minutes. You have to make your chances.

The second important implication is that making just any sort of contribution is not enough. Your contribution has to be meaningful. A meaningful contribution suggests that you have a good knowledge base, are able to structure arguments logically and are a good communicator. These are qualities that are desired by all evaluators.

A few tips for group discussions include:
- Hear the topic clearly.
- Try starting the discussion. This always carries extra weight.
- Don't sound loud and overbearing.
- Give the others a chance to speak once you have got your point through.
- Always look at the other participants. Don't look elsewhere. Look interested.
- Try not to repeat points already made by others.
- Do not gesticulate too much while putting a point forth.
- Speak in a clear, crisp tone and sentences.
- If you couldn't start the discussion, try rounding it off once you feel that the interviewer is planning to stop it.

Many group discussion participants feel that the way to succeed in a GD is by speaking frequently, for a long time and loudly. This is not true. The quality of what you say is more important than the quantity.

# 12
# TRAVEL TECHNOLOGY

### Chapter Objectives

**After reading this chapter the reader should be able to:**
- Understand the importance of technology in travel.
- Identify various areas where technology is being used.
- Explain how the technology has facilitated the working of travel agents.

Travel technology (also called tourism technology, and hospitality automation) is the application of Information Technology (IT) or Information and Communications Technology(ICT) in the travel, tourism and hospitality industry. Some forms of travel technology are flight tracking, Trip Planning journey planner, Booking Price Tracking and more.

The use of technologies in the field of travel and tourism has revolutionised various systems and is responsible for cost-reduction, time saving and enhanced and quick services, thereby contributing to the profitability of the agency. If we compare the travel industry of today with that of 25 years ago, we find a world of difference in its functioning. The industry today wears a different look, as it is mostly automated and high-tech.

The entry of technology in the travel business has revolutionised the way the travel industry functions. In this modern world, a travel agent has to be up to date with the application of various technologies available to receive and provide information on time. It is also important for a travel manager to assume prime responsibility to ensure the availability of required infrastructure and support system for the adoption of technological advancement to manage the business profitability.

Information Technology has played an important role in the hospitality and tourism industry over the last decade. Technology has helped reduce costs, enhance operational efficiency, and improve services and customer experience. Both customers and businesses can benefit from improved communication, reservations, and guest service systems.

Technology has helped tourism and hospitality industries replace expensive human labor with technological labor. This helps reduce labor costs, but also helps avoid customer service issues.

Since travel implies locomotion, travel technology was originally associated with the computer reservations system (CRS) of the airlines industry, but now is used more inclusively, incorporating the broader tourism sector as well as its subset the hospitality industry. While travel technology includes the computer reservations system, it also represents a much broader range of applications, in fact increasingly so. Travel technology includes virtual tourism in the form of virtual tour technologies. Travel technology may also be referred to as e-travel / etravel or e-tourism / etourism (eTourism), in reference to "electronic travel" or "electronic tourism".

e-Tourism can be defined as the analysis, design, implementation and application of IT and e-commerce solutions in the travel &tourism industry; as well as the analysis of the respective economic processes and market structures and customer relationship management.

From a communication science perspective, eTourism can be also defined as every application of Information and Communication Technologies (ICTs) within both the hospitality and tourism industry, as well as within the tourism experience.

The advent of technology is fostering a change in the travel and tourism industry regarding how companies interact with customers. Consequently, travel companies are adopting various technologies to improve operational efficiencies and meet customers' expectations, according to leading data and analytics company, Global Data.

### Important areas where technologies can be applied:
  i. For making reservations
  ii. Transmitting information to the clients
  iii. Confirmation
  iv. Receiving information
  v. Retrieving information
  vi. Requesting information
  vii. Up to date destination information
  viii. Ticketing
  ix. Purchase procedures
  x. Maintaining inventory records
  xi. Dealing with principal supplier
  xii. Sales and marketing

The travel industry has come a long way; a wide variety of transport system networks have made connectivity easy and simple. The transport network has made the world a small place and with the development of science and automation, new ways of travel are constantly being evolved to satisfy man's urge for simple, hassle free and peaceful travel.

## Multiple use of Technology

There are multiple uses of technology in tourism activities. Obviously, the spreading of multimedia computers connected to the internet into the houses of numerous people, has dramatically changed the way tourism consumers define their destinations, the itineraries, the mode of transportation, the choices of hotels and the lodging establishment, the extent of leisure they want to gain access to.

The uses of technology are numerous. How consumers make their reservations have changed significantly over the last 15 years or so. Many companies have already explored the diverse uses of information and information technologies including, web based services offerings.

## Trends in Industry

1. Being a competitive industry with entrance of new global players coming from abroad.
2. Continuous change in customer demands.
3. Expectations of a tourist have increased and they look for more convenience and value.
4. Tourists are getting knowledgeable.
5. There is a need of automated technologies.

Information Technology (IT) enabled tourism is called 'e–tourism'. Online tourism is at a platform that enables direct booking, easy payment for the end-user, business-to-business trading for product providers, travel agents and resellers. All the websites and portals launched by the government as well as private organisations offer a wide range of tourism products and services like airlines, hotels, restaurants, car rentals, camp-sites, tours, activity centres, concerts, festivities, shopping and many more with choicest assortments of services. Tours can be planned online through the agents' websites. Reservation or shopping of facilities for train, airlines, cruise, hotels, resorts, motels, car rentals and adventure tours can be done online.

Following are the various segments where computer technology is extensively used today:

## 1. Air Transportation:

Travel by air is the fastest mode of travel today. The world has become one large market; it has come on one platform because of easy air connectivity. Travel by this mode has grown tremendously today because it is easy and saves time. The technological advancement in this mode of travel is commendable.

The tourism industry has derived maximum benefit from it. There were days when travel by air was a fantasy and an elite market product. The service providers relied only on the telephones and used to telex messages to the airlines for making and confirming booking. Fares were manually calculated and tickets manually made. This was the most tedious and cumbersome task for the airline. The reliability factor was also low. The customers at the airports had to undergo a long painful procedure, which took a long time. Travel by air was an expensive affair. Subsequently came the fax machines, which simplified work and flow of information in the right manner. The application of technology in the airline industry brought in a sea of change.

## Reservation Systems

Today the reservation systems are computerised and are globally connected. The airline industry today offers the following services at the click of a button:
- A whole wide range of flight schedules and reservation.
- Access to unlimited city fares anywhere in the world.
- Update on the current domestic and international schedule for all major carriers.
- Construct difficult itinerary schedules automatically.
- Calculate minimum connecting times at airports automatically.
- Schedule display with complete flight information on aircraft type, flight number, seating display, meal codes, operating days and number of stops enroute.
- Access to unlimited fares with current and accurate pricing and updated restrictions on a particular fare selected.
- Obtain special fare quotes for groups, promotional travel and excursion fares.
- Obtain flexible automatic ticketing.
- E-ticketing
- E-mail and SMS of itinerary to the passengers.
- When hotel bookings to be made as per the client's requirements, it gives one a list of good, star category hotels. The client can view the hotel property, can check the tariff list and kinds of rooms and facilities available in the hotel, how to reach the hotel, its address, different rates of the hotel rooms, booking and cancellation policy.
- Car bookings as per the client's requirements, it gives the client the car rental company list with the fleet of cars available, the rate chart, booking and cancellation policy.

### The Internet Usage

Increased penetration of the internet has made a great dent in the profitability of travel agents globally, coupled with the zero commission policy of the world airlines, it has further squeezed travel agencies which need to do some hard work to stay back in the business. The days of commission simply for issuing a ticket by the travel agent are over. On top of it, customers are increasingly resorting to online search, to do their own shopping for the tickets, hotels and car hire. Cutting out the agencies as middleman altogether, travel agencies are going to have to provide high quality services to the customers to be around in the business.

## Travel Sites

With general public access to the internet, many airlines and other travel companies began to sell directly to the passengers. As a consequence, airlines no longer needed to pay the commissions to travel agents on each ticket sold. Since 1997, travel agencies have gradually been disintermediated, by the reduction in costs caused by removing layers from the package holiday distribution network.

Many travel agencies have developed an internet presence of their own by posting a website, with detailed travel information. Full travel booking sites are often complex and require the assistance of outside travel technology solutions providers such as Travelocity. These companies use travel service distribution companies which operate Global Distribution Systems (GDS), such as Sabre Holdings, Amadeus IT Group, Galileo CRS and Worldspan (now Travelport GDS), to provide up to the minute, detailed information on tens of thousands of flights, hotels and car rentals.

Some online travel sites allow visitors to compare hotel and flight rates with multiple companies for free. They often allow visitors to sort the travel packages by amenities, price, and proximity to a city or landmark.

Travel agents have applied dynamic packaging tools to provide fully bonded (full financial protection) travel at prices equal to or lower than a member of the public can book online. As such, the agencies' financial assets are protected in addition to professional travel agency advice.

All travel sites that sell hotels online work together with GDS, suppliers and hotels directly to search for room inventory. Once the travel site sells a hotel, the site will try to get a confirmation for this hotel. Once confirmed or not, the customer is contacted with the result. This means that booking a hotel on a travel website will not necessarily result in an instant answer. Only some hotels on a travel website can be confirmed instantly (which is normally marked as such on each site). As different travel websites work with different suppliers, each site has different hotels that it can confirm instantly. Some examples of such online travel websites that sell hotel rooms are Expedia and Orbitz.

The comparison sites, such as Kayak.com, TripAdvisor, and SideStep search the resellers site all at once to save time searching. None of these sites actually sell hotel rooms.

Often tour operators have hotel contracts, allottments and free sell agreements which allow for the immediate confirmation of hotel rooms for vacation bookings.

Mainline service providers are those that actually produce the direct service, like various hotels chains or airlines that have a website for online bookings. Portals will serve consolidators of various airlines and hotels on the internet. They work on a commission from these hotels and airlines. Often, they provide cheaper rates than the mainline service providers as these sites get bulk deals from the service providers. A metasearch engine on the other hand, simply culls data from the internet in real time rates for various search queries and diverts traffic to the mainline service providers for an online booking. These websites usually do not have their own booking engine.

## 2. Rail Transportation

Travel by rail is readily available in most parts of the world and combined air-rail and air-bus travel has become frequent. The technology today provides instant connectivity. Many airports are connected by direct rail links to a town terminal and the main railway station from where passengers can catch fast trains arriving at their city of destination in comfort and peace for example 'Amtrak' in USA, 'Via Rail Canada' in North America, 'Orient Express' and 'Euro Rail' in Europe and 'Queensland' in Australia.

To enhance the comfort levels of leisure travellers, the technology of today has came out with luxury trains for tourists who want to travel long distances, without the worry of packing and unpacking, getting up early to a catch train. Generally superior, first class service is offered throughout the trip. These are air-conditioned trains with comfortable reclining seats and sleeping cars. In such trains all provisions for the traveller's eating, sleeping and bathing is made in star category style. They offer high level of passenger service, technical efficiency and computerised booking worldwide.

Hence, the technology today has facilitated movement of people who are in pursuit of good times.

## 3. Surface Transportation

Travel on land gives one a choice to travel by rail or road. Road transport offers a variety of modes to travel by car, bus, coaches and caravans. This service is readily available in all parts of the world. Automation in the automobile industry has been commendable and it is the travel industry, which has benefited most. The technology has transformed this mode of transport completely.

Today, one finds coaches centrally air conditioned with comfortable reclining seats, safety belts, curtains, music and video systems, glass holders, magazine holders and toilet facilities. The latest updation in coach transport is the limousine service. The star category hotels provide this service to their esteemed guests for drop to and pickup from the airport.

Coach tours, which are normally group tours, are conducted by travel agencies and hotels for sightseeing in the city and take passengers to places of their interest surrounding the city, such group tours have given tremendous growth to tourism where travellers can visit a place with all the comforts. Some of these include escorted motor coach tours and hotel packages.

If one does not intend to travel in a group then, today technological growth gives one the option of travelling by car. There are several worldwide reputed car rental companies which provide cars on rent for people who want to travel alone like, Avis Rent-a-Car, Eurocar and Hertz. These companies provide transport services in two categories:

(i) self driven cars and
(ii) chauffeur driven cars

## 4. Car Rental Companies

The car rental companies provide a wide variety of car models to suit the customer's taste and pocket. These cars are of the latest models with the latest automobile techniques to lure the customers', ensuring their safety. Automation has helped them to provide the following services:

Rental locations at the airports, railway stations and major city centres.

Rent at one place and leave the car at another i.e., one-way rentals.

Free world wide reservation service with verification of guarantee and deposit information.

The car segment portion of the passenger itinerary print out can be obtained.

Thus, the service provided through car rentals is very convenient for people who want to make their own discoveries. Technology today has made it possible to have an access to car rental companies from anywhere in the world. The computerised network ensures foolproof safety of the bookings.

## 5. Water Transportation

There are a variety of water transports available from ferries to cruises. The indigenous application of technology in water transport has made cruises the biggest desire for leisure travellers. These huge sailing ships have all the modern standards of living, swimming pools, rest rooms, squash courts, gymnasium, billiards, shopping malls, restaurants to name a few. They cater to all the pleasure needs of a customer thereby bringing in huge revenue to the service providers. Tourism of today has got a major thrust from this field, thanks to technology, from traditional cruises to fly cruises.

For people who travel short distances, water transport is the most efficient mode available in the form of a Hovercraft. It is a cross between a ship and an aircraft which rides on a cushion of air about two meters above the surface of the water. It can ferry cars and passengers over short distances at upto 110 km an hour.

## 6. Hotel Industry

Like with the airlines, computer technology has entered the hotel industry in a big way. A hotel's most crucial internal resources are information and with the use of computers the information is available in a way that saves labour and ultimately increases the profits.

Although computers in the hotel industry started being used as far back as the late 1960s, it was only in the 1970s that the advances in computer technology made it possible for the right combination of compactness and versatility for different sizes of hotels. The lower cost encouraged many individual hotels to install the system. Today, computers are installed in large numbers and are widely accepted in the hotel industry. One of the most important factors for its large-scale acceptance in the industry has been its reliability. The computer system has been found to be very reliable in the dissemination of the right kind of information, at the push of a button.

Today, the hotel industry is a major market for the computer manufacturers and the software vendors. It has been increasingly realised that the hotel computer systems achieve better internal and external control and, through the use of analysis methods, provide the opportunity to improve the overall profitability of the unit. Like in the airlines, the computers offer substantial advantages for reservation systems in terms of speed and accuracy. The errors are almost negligible.

All over the world hotel systems have traditionally been divided into the following two main areas:
(i) front office application
(ii) back office application

Following are the application areas in each of the above:
**Front office:**

- Reservations
- Registration
- Guest accounting
- Night auditing
- Communication operations (telephones, telex, fax)

**Back office:**
- Financial management
- Inventory control systems accounts
- Profit/loss accounts
- General ledger
- Credit and verifications.

## In-room terminals

The hotels have introduced "in-room terminals" which are hooked by television and telephone into a data system that includes official airline guides, news agencies, stock market agencies, weather bureaus, shopping services, travel clubs, entertainment guide and electronic games. The hotels have developed a "contact software" to streamline information flow in and outside the hotel.

Computer usage has helped hotels in having an efficient and sound information system, providing up-to-date accurate information of the guests on one hand and product (hotel) information on the other. The guest can have an easy access to the required information. Voice-mails and room faxes with automatic bill settlement facility have become a standard practice. Interactive TVs are introduced to facilitate message reading and viewing of bills. Television gives a host of information on the hotel facilities. They also enable internet browsing. All the systems in the hotel are integrated with both front office and back office.

The computer technology after the internet has given "intranet". Today all the hotels are looking at extending their intranets to what is commonly known as extranet. The hotel can extend their intranet to companies or to organisations that do a lot of business on a regular basis with that hotel, so that they can have immediate access to book online.

**Customer Relationship Management (CRM).** This is the new technology for hotel companies. It signifies the ability to know and understand guests' histories in order to be able to market more effectively to them.

The hotel companies that are creating targeted marketing programmes such as loyalty programmes and e-marketing strategies, are benefited with this automated crm systems. It acts as an all compass customer database, which helps to have more personalised communications and enhance the guest's experiences. The 'guestware system' tracks the guest's preferences and past requests.

Technology has given a major thrust to the hotel industry. Hotels have been able to serve their guests efficiently, improve guest relations and in turn grow their top lines, increase return patronage and profits for the company. Future trends to watch out for in travel and tourism industry in 2018:

1. Augmented and Virtual Reality (AR and VR): The past few years have seen an increase in AR or VR popularity among travel and tourism companies, and the trend is set to continue. These technologies are being used either for content marketing or to enhance the customers' experiences. For example, airlines have started using VR technology to show travellers the cabins in advance, in order to increase ticket or ancillary services sales.
2. Artificial Intelligence (AI): AI is behind many evolving technologies and innovations in the travel and tourism sector. The ways in which it helps the industry can be classified into three major categories: Machine Learning, ChatBots or TravelBots, and Robots. Thanks to AI, operations which usually require human intervention and a lot of time to learn new skills, can be automated, thus speeding up processes, while improving quality and performance, and decreasing costs.
3. Internet of Things (IoT): IoT has a lot of potential to shape the future of the travel and tourism industry, and companies have started to realize that. An example can be of an industry player using IoT to reduce anxiety and stress levels associated with lost bags. Passengers can track their baggage via a link found on their mobile boarding pass in the airline applications.
4. Voice Technology: Voice technology is another digital novelty that is beginning to disrupt the travel and tourism sector, as more and more customers switch from typed-in search to voice interactions. More and more hotels have started experimenting with voice-activated devices. Among them are: W Austin of Marriott International, Kimpton Alexis Hotel, and Westin Buffalo.
5. Wi-Fi connectivity: When travelling, people want to always be connected, either to get destination ideas, options regarding places to visit or eat, find directions to points of interest, or share their experience with friends via social media or other connectivity platforms. As a result, investing in network services helps companies offer a more seamless and highly personalized experience to customers, boosts operational efficiency, real-time decision making, strengthens the physical (via CCTV) and the cybersecurity, along with data privacy.
6. Wearable devices: Despite a sluggish start, travel and tourism companies are gradually using this technology to offer customers a more personalized and united experience. For instance, the Walt Disney Company deployed a wearable, customizable, RFID-equipped MagicBand, which connects to the theme park infrastructure, to reduce waiting times and track guests' locations and activities.

We observe that technology has played a vital and productive role in every travel activity. It has made travel simple, easy and cost effective for every individual. Tourism industry has benefited immensely as technology has provided enormous data on all air carriers, rail, road, resorts, car rental companies, tour packages, accommodation, pricing and promotions. Computer systems have streamlined the functioning of all the above products in the travel and tourism set-up. It has helped in the smooth functioning of airlines, tourist transport companies, and accommodation units including hotels and has increased the efficiency of the people working in these areas.

# 13
# BUSINESS TRAVEL

> **Chapter Objectives**
>
> After reading this chapter the reader should be able to:
> - Understand the MICE business and the various segments it covers
> - Identify various travel trade fairs and exhibitions and the travel agent's role.
> - Define conferences and conventions and how travel agents can handle the organisers in making arrangements for accommodation, transport, etc.
> - Describe incentive and corporate travel and role of travel agents in organising incentive travel for the winners.
> - Understand various steps required for organising an event
> - Use of technology in event planning.

MICE refers to Meetings, Incentives, Conferences and Exhibitions. The acronym MICE is applied internationally with the "E" sometimes referring to as events and "C" sometimes referring to conventions, MICE refers to a particular type of tourism in which large groups, usually planned well in advance, are brought together for some particular purpose. The MICE market refers to a specialized niche of group tourism dedicated to planning, booking, and facilitating conferences, seminars, and other events, which is a big segment in the travel industry with considerable profit.

Within MICE, incentive tourism is the fast growth segment and is usually a type of employee reward by a company or institution for targets, achieved or exceeded or a job well done. Unlike the other types of MICE tourism, incentive tourism is usually conducted purely for entertainment, with a bit of professional or educational purpose being included.

## Components of MICE Travel

MICE travel involves a number of components, and the agents provide a full range of travel and conference services for large and small groups and events of shorter and longer duration. Personnel and businesses involved in the MICE market include corporate meeting planners, meetings and convention departments of hotels, conference centres or cruise ships, food and beverage managers, logistics firms, private tour operators and transfer companies, incentive houses, professional trade organizations, tourism boards, tourism trade associations, and travel-selling professionals.

Because of the organization and planning involved, MICE travel agencies are usually affiliated with large corporations. Destinations often market themselves as MICE locations and bid for events through their convention and visitor bureaus. They might be able to offer subsidies to attract large events because of the increased revenue the visitors provide through their economic impact on the host location.

## Types of MICE Travel

a. **Meetings**
b. **Conference**
c. **Incentive**
d. **Exhibition**

To understand which type of MICE travel you'll be booking with your agent, it's important to understand the different terms that comprise the acronym. While meeting and conference travel may sound similar, for instance, the slight differences between them will be important when explaining your needs to agent.

The International Association of Professional Congress Organizers defines a meeting as any number of people coming together in one place for a particular activity, which can be a one-time event or recur regularly. Simply put, meeting travel refers to organizing any number of people for such a meeting, which means it could also include a company sporting trip.

On the other hand, a conference is similar to a meeting in that it is a gathering of people coming together in one place, but conferences usually have specific objectives and exchanges of information. Therefore, conference travel involves organizing itineraries, meetings, and events for people from the same profession or field.

Incentive travel may be one of the harder components of MICE travel to understand since it doesn't necessarily deal with group events. Instead, incentive travel is typically given to employees as a reward. Incentive travel doesn't usually have a business or explicit educational component but instead is more of a non-business vacation with the aim of continued motivation for performance.

At an exhibition, products or services are displayed, and they might be the primary focus of the event, which means that exhibition travel agents are those who organize such showcases. Exhibitions are often included in other conferences and meetings, though, meaning that there is often overlap between agents in these industries. Businesses court new clients and debut their latest offerings at these events.

## Role of the Travel Agent

The Meetings, Incentives, Conventions and Exhibitions (Events) (MICE) is large in size and rapidly changing. In most countries around the world, the Mice industry (or as it is now named under the auspices of the united Nations World Tourism Organisation (UNWTO)-" The Meetings Industry" is recognised as a high-yield component of the tourism industry with direct connections with other key areas such as trade, education, science, training and communication. In many countries, particularly within the Asia Pacific region, it has great potential for future expansion.

The travel industry has to play an important role, not only in upgrading the MICE industry, but also enhancing the trained, technical personnel to handle various facets of the industry. It is important for travel agents to be actively involved in the MICE industry and help it grow. With their knowledge about the travel industry, travel agents are increasing being involved is the MICE business.

A large percentage of the travel agent's business consists of business clients and they seek advice on choosing hotels, ground arrangements and also sightseeing when say attending a conference, meeting or exhibition. Travel agents also are responsible for arranging hotel accommodation, transport, pre and post tours and also transport for a large number of delegates attending conferences and conventions. In addition, travel agents are helping many corporates in organising incentive trips for the winners.

The present chapter explains in brief what the MICE business involves and various concepts which travel agents should comprehend before handling any of the MICE components.

## TRAVEL INDUSTRY FAIRS AND EXHIBITIONS

Travel industry fairs and exhibitions are the major marketing vehicles in today's highly competitive market place. In the rapidly changing world and with a view to keeping pace with new innovations in products, travel fairs and exhibitions have a special significance and importance. Today, no country, howsoever advanced and developed in technology, can afford to keep itself aloof from participating in travel fairs and exhibitions. These are considered an effective way to facilitate contacts, for exchange of information and ideas and to initiate sales in many industries.

In the present world, no country can be self-sufficient in any field in spite of technological advancements. Rapid innovations in various fields make it difficult for any country to keep pace unless, the knowledge and experience is shared on a common platform. Almost all the countries in the world organise travel fairs and exhibitions of one kind or another on a small, medium or large scale. Several countries have put up permanent exhibition grounds, complexes equipped with state-of-art facilities to accommodate as many exhibitors as possible or just to participate. The scale of participation is constantly on the rise especially in well-known travel fairs. Sometimes it is not possible for several exhibitors to get the space because of an increase in the number of participating countries wanting to display their products. In several cases the booking for the space is to be done well in advance of the event dates.

### Participation Advantages

International trade fairs and exhibitions give an opportunity to the exhibitors of participating countries to meet a large number of buyers and exhibitors from different countries at one place, to study the market trends and to compare the price and quality of similar products. In addition, participation in trade fairs and exhibitions also provides a common platform to participating countries to come together under one roof and exchange technical knowhow and personnel as well as help promote joint ventures between two countries. Apart from the presentation of exhibits, the fairs also provide a platform for exchange of knowledge and information through a medium of seminars, workshops, symposia on related exhibition, by experts from participating countries.

Participation in trade fairs also provides an opportunity to the exhibitors from participating countries to assess their own progress vis-a-vis that of the exhibitors from other countries and the steps necessary to achieve better performance and results. The importance of the fairs can also be assessed by the fact that they are organised not only by different trade bodies or chambers, but also by semi-government and government bodies which assist in organising such fairs and send their official representatives to participate directly or indirectly.

Following are the advantages to the exhibitors:

a) transfer of technology and knowhow between countries;

b) exchange of information and technical knowhow under one roof;

c) assessing the progress vis-a-vis that of the other country and steps necessary to achieve better performance;

d) creating better conditions for two-way communications among international partners in the market;

e) creating proper surroundings or encounters and dialogues between suppliers and customers.

## Important Action Areas for Participation

Certain important action areas, which are to be taken care of by the prospective participants in order to get maximum mileage from the fair, need particular mention. The following observations are considered to be of practical importance for those who are planning to participate in the trade fairs and exhibitions:

a) Visitors to trade fairs are normally senior and high-ranking executives with decision-making power

b) Transaction of actual business may not come through and this should not disappoint the exhibitor. It is not unusual for some period of time to lapse before business deals are concluded. The participation in the fair should primarily be utilised to establish as many contacts as possible and to initiate discussion with prospective business partners

c) Systematic collection of data on visitors is very important as it will help in follow-up action. A business opportunity should not be missed on account of a delayed follow-up or due to failure to give the required information immediately on the spot

d) No opportunity should be missed to cultivate the media. Through this contact, the product will receive the required publicity

e) The importance of the type of publicity material prepared for the exhibition can hardly be overemphasised. This gives an opportunity to the visitors to go through the contents at his leisure.

f) Use of audio-visual media with emphasis on the product will greatly help the visitor identify the product.

g) The representation at the stand needs to be of a high level so that discussion with the visitors is meaningful. First impressions are extremely crucial and help a great deal in transacting business.

h) Opportunities to hold business discussions with the customers should not be missed. In addition to transacting business with existing clients, it is necessary to contact new clients.

i) Competing products should be examined with a view to updating one's own product. Trends in pricing, design, packaging, distribution, etc., should always be studied with a view to achieving better results in the competitive market.

j) Exhibition authorities bring out comprehensive catalogues of all the exhibitors. It is necessary that the exhibitor gives complete information to fair authorities about the firm and its products for inclusion in the catalogue. The catalogue is used quite often as a reference book even after the fair is over.

## The Beginning

It was in the late 1950s that the first attempts were made to establish and organise fairs. The main objective of fairs for the tourist industry from the very beginning was twofold:

1. As "public fairs" the purpose is to enable travel agents and tour operators, hoteliers, carriers and national tourist offices to establish contact with their markets, especially with the travelling public, and thus to promote their programmes and services.

2. As "trade fairs" in the more specific sense, their aim is to create opportunities for contact and business discussion, contract negotiations and exchange information within the industry itself.

In relation with the first of these two objectives, tourist fairs are often combined with exhibitions organised by manufactures of sports equipment, both water and snow, camping and caravan or by leisure industries. Since the emphasis is on the consumer, the fair gives greater importance to their requirements. In many of these exhibitions, there is a direct sale. On the trade side, the trade fairs are mostly for professionals and the emphasis is purely on transacting business. During the trade fairs, conventions and annual assemblies of trade associations are sometimes held in conjunction with the fair. In major travel generating as well as receiving countries, the organisation of travel trade fairs has become a regular annual event.

The first such travel trade fair known as the International Tourism Borse (ITB) was held in the year 1967 in *Berlin*. Since then, there have been a number of other countries which organise travel trade fairs regularly.

The enthusiastic participation in these travel trade fairs is a result of the ever-expanding travel trade industry. A large number of exhibitors participate in these fairs representing all segments of the travel industry and include travel agents, tour operators, hoteliers, airline companies, shipping companies, national tourist organisations, etc. In addition, travel trade media is also present.

Over the years there has been a steady growth in the number as well as participation in the travel trade fairs. Not only this, the organisers have been increasing the number of participants. New exhibition complexes are being constructed to give the travel trade fairs a modern look. The reasons for the spurt in the travel trade fairs can be attributed to the involvement of tourism organisations in the marketing of tourism, particularly international tourism. It has been increasingly felt in the travel trade circles, especially those responsible for marketing, that the medium of travel trade fairs is a cost-effective way of communicating. Exhibitions by their very nature enjoy economies and advantages of lower costs because of the scale. The sheer size of the exhibition also makes it a great attraction, both for buyers and sellers of tourist products.

Participation in travel trade fairs have several inherent advantages which are responsible for the growth in their numbers over the years and also the participation. Some of these advantages of participating in the travel trade fairs are as follows:

a) Opportunity to both buyers and sellers of tourism services to meet under one roof and transact business;
b) Lower cost of participation because of the advantage of scale
c) Effective vehicle of communication with clients
d) Better quality of attendance
e) Single platform to introduce the product (in the form of a brochure)
f) Easy access to travel trade media
g) Cultivating new information about the travel product
h) Acquiring new information about the travel product
i) Opportunity for effective public relations.

## Making a Choice

There has been an appreciable growth, both in the number of people looking for convenient places to display their products as well as consumers, to inspect and get an opportunity to buy these products. The travel trade fairs are the most convenient places for this to happen.

Every organisation which has to do something with the tourism business feels it necessary to participate in these fairs either as an exhibitor or as a visitor. Participation in the travel trade fairs in fact has been a very important issue. The advantages of such a participation have been amply recognised. However, the question arises as to where to participate. Each travel firm would like to get maximum advantage with minimum cost from participation in a trade fair. Because of the multiplicity of events, making a choice has become rather difficult. Besides, there are various types of fairs available in different countries where participation is possible. There are the international fairs, both trade and consumer, the regional fairs and the national fairs.

Although international fairs like World Trade Mart *(WTM)*, International Tourism Borse *(ITB)*, International Tourism Exchange (BTE), International Brussels Trade Fair *(BTF)* are very popular with the travel trade, there are some other fairs also where participation is quite significant. The two most important international trade fairs, however, are WTM in London and ITB in Berlin. Almost everybody who is somebody in the travel business likes to be seen in these two prestigious travel marts. Attendance as well as interest in these two fairs have been extremely high ever since these fairs have been organised.

## UFTAA Survey

Market research section of the Universal Federation of Travel Agents' Association *(UFTAA)* conducted a survey with the objective of determining as to who are the people who attend several of these fairs and what they hope to gain by participating. The UFTAA survey was first used at the annual congress of UFTAA in Vienna and then at the International Brussels Trade Fair (BTF) in Brussels and the World Travel Market (WTM) in London. The sample of the survey consisted of over 100 participants at each of the above events. Each participant was asked 70 questions, of which 15, allowed an "open response". The major findings of the survey showed that travel industry trade fairs, though competitive, attract many of the same travel professionals and that an overwhelming percentage of those attending participated in the trade fair because they expected to gain business at each of these fairs.

### Major Findings

The following were the main findings of the survey:
- (i) 80-95 per cent of participants at the above three events expected "positive practical benefits" from their attendance
- (ii) three main motives for attending the trade fair were: forming of new business contacts, acquiring new information and promoting their own services
- (iii) about half the participants at both the fairs were travel agents or tour operators
- (iv) the suppliers of services like hotel companies and airlines were the next largest group
- (v) the average age of participants at BTF in Brussels was over 40 years in case of 70 per cent of the participants as compared to under 40 in case of 64 percent at WTM in London
- (vi) more than half of the participants at the two trade fairs were from outside the country where the fair was located (58% in the case of WTM). Most of the foreign visitors, however, were from receiving countries rather than from buying countries

(vii) advance publicity for BTF was received largely through direct mailing (42%) and only through trade press (24%) and national associations (17%); on the other hand publicity on WTM was received largely through the trade press (49%) rather than direct mail (29%) or national associations (16%)

(viii) regarding importance of press coverage for the event, 43 per cent of those interviewed at BTF said that the same was important as compared to 96 per cent at WTM who believed that the fair was an important event

(ix) ITB and WTM in that order are the most important trade fairs in the industry according to participants at both trade fairs

(x) comparative attendance at other trade fairs shows that many participants at WTM also go to ITB (43%), but few attend any other trade fairs (11% go to ASTA, but fewer attend all the others). Participants at BTF, on the other hand, participate extensively in other trade fairs

(xi) the most stimulating themes for seminars and workshops according to the participants were topics on travel agents versus direct sale, automation, incentive travel, licence regulation, insurance issues, marketing, commissions, and sales through videotex

## Marketing for New Products

In addition to ceremonial and official events, the programme at trade fairs includes a series of seminars and workshops, discussion panels and presentations by private firms and official organisations including national tourist organisations active in tourism. The seminar programmes include half/full day sessions on important subjects such as international conferences and conventions, marketing and promotion, modern information techniques, prospects and forecasts for international tourism.

Travel trade fairs provide an opportunity to travel agents and tour operators of acquainting themselves with the latest trends in the travel and tourism world under one roof with every sector of the industry represented, Each contact made during the fairs gives a certain return on the company's marketing investment to travel agents and tour operators. Trade fairs provide an efficient and cost effective international business environment where new products and services can be presented and negotiations on future contracts made.

Travel trade shows provide an opportunity to a tour operator to introduce his products in the form of a travel brochure and put the same in front of a buyer as travel show networking proves more valuable for individual operators because many buyers go to a travel trade show already holding established contracts with other sellers. Travel agents look forward to these shows to receive new products and negotiate future deals.

Worldwide, there are several travel industry fairs held at regular intervals which are frequented by the members of travel trade. These are held throughout the year. Some of them like ITB, WTM have, however become quite popular with the trade and attract very large attendance as compared to others. In fact, these two events claim to be the largest, attracting a large number of both buyers and sellers from around the world and can be called international events of the travel industry.

## International Tourism Borse (ITB)

The ITB, as it is popularly known in the travel trade world, was held for the first time in the year 1967. The ITB's story commenced way back in the sixties. In the year 1966, Messer Berlin provided space for nine exhibitors from the world of tourism at the Overseas Imports Fair and also staged a two-day convention in the Berlin Congress Hall. It was these two events that gave birth to the world's largest travel and tourism trade fair.

The publicity and the marketing of the fair by the organisers made it very popular in the subsequent years. In the year 1972 the fair attracted over 1,30,000 visitors from over 60 countries. The ITB organisers in the year 1973 included annual convention of the active members of the ASTA subsequently held its 1975 full convention in Berlin coinciding with ITB of that year.

From its inception in the year 1967, ITB today claims to be the world's largest travel trade fair. In the year 2005, about 6350 exhibitors representing 170 regions and countries of the world attended the fair. More than 50,000 trade visitors and over 70,000 private travellers transacted business. The trade visitors attending ITB 2005 included 22 per cent from outside Germany.

### ITB Survey

Based on a survey conducted by an independent trade fair market research institute and reported in Messer Berlin Press Release in March 1995, 42 per cent of exhibitors were able to finalise deals at the ITB 1995. They reported signing contracts in the following sectors of the market:

- Holiday and recreational travel (64%)
- Business travel (32%)
- Incentive travel (26%)
- Educational and study trips (23%)
- Conferences and congress travel (19%)
- Sports travel (15%)
- Adventure tours (13%)
- Travel to health resorts and for health reasons (7%) and
- Other contracts signed (18%).

Based on their numerous contacts with the international tourism industry, 34 per cent expected follow-up business to be good, and further 48 per cent expected that it would be satisfactory.

Among the general public visiting the fair, 89 per cent intend to take at least one holiday and 70 per cent of them have already decided on their destination. Among those who have made their decision, more than half have already made their bookings. Altogether 81 per cent of general interest visitors stated that they would be booking a trip based on information and ideas obtained at ITB 95.

One in four trade visitors (24%) was able to sign contracts during ITB. The sector in which the most business was conducted was that of holiday and recreational travel, with (52%). Other contracts were signed in the following sectors: business travel (18%), adventure tours (14%), incentive travel (12%), educational and study trips (12%), conference and congress travel (11%), sports travel (9%), travel to health resorts and for health reasons (5%), and travel for other purposes (8%). Trade visitors signed contracts with exhibitors from the following countries/regions: Germany (43%), European Union (26%), Central and Eastern Europe (18%), North America (18%), Central America/Caribbean (15%), South America (14%), East Asia (14%), Africa (14%), Australia/New Zealand/Oceania (10 per cent) and Western and Central Asia (8%).

Trade visitors in ITB '95 represented the following sectors of the tourism industry: travel agents (24%), tour operators (18%), carrier (15%), hotel companies (14%), institutes (11%), tourism offices and associations (8%) and national tourism organisations (7%). Twenty-nine per cent of the trade visitors attending the ITB '95 came from outside Germany, the majority of them from Austria, Poland, Italy, Switzerland, France, Spain, the United Kingdom, Belgium, Greece and Russia.

## Range of Programmes

The international tourism exchange also includes a series of extensive supporting programmes. These include seminars and workshops, discussion panels and presentations by private firms and official organisations including national tourist organisations active in tourism promotions. The seminar programmes include sessions on international conference and conventions, marketing and promotion, modern information techniques, prospects and forecasts for international tourism and a host of other important topics. Over the years the scope of the fair is being widened to incorporate more areas of interest in the field of tourism. For instance, the congress "Electronics in Tourism" has been introduced with a view to updating the travel trade in the latest technology concerning use of electronics in various tourist trade fields. ITB has also become an annual venue for several regional meetings of travel agents and hotel chains.

Originally being held for a period of seven days, it is now held for period of six days. During ITB '95 a travel visitor's day was devoted entirely to business contacts. No general public is allowed on the exclusive trade visitors' day. The travel fair is normally held in the month of March each year. The total available space for exhibitors is around 163,000 square metres.

**World Travel Market (WTM)**

World Travel Mart is another, important event meant exclusively for travel and tourism professionals. Popularly known as WTM, the World Travel Mart is an annual event held in London (England) every year in the month of November. WTM was first organised in the year 1980, as an international forum where the world's travel industry members meet to exchange ideas, establish new contacts, launch new products, and develop new business.

WTM attracts several thousand industry professionals every year from a number of countries. Similarly, the number of industry visitors is also increasing each year. According to organisers, WTM was attended by over 30,000 industry visitors in the year 2000 from over 138 countries. The industry visitors included tour operators, retail travel agents, hotel companies, inclusive organisers, group travel organisers, business travel agents and tourist transport companies. Almost 50 per cent of the total industry visitors, however, were tour operators and travel agents.

## Meridian Club Membership

WTM has evolved a unique feature since the last few years whereby the exhibitors can meet the leading buyers with prior arranged appointments. This feature is the membership of the Meridian Club. Meridian Club is a business club for industry buyers, open only to those buyers nominated by the exhibitors. Main stand holders (exhibitors) are entitled to nominate for buyers per square metre of contracted stand space. For example an exhibitor with 25 square metre stand can nominate 100 buyers. The companies which are sharing space with main exhibitors, are each able to nominate 20 buyers. Meridian Club benefits to the exhibitors include exclusive two Meridian Days during the Mart, to meet only the industry's leading buyers, access to Meridian Club and pre-arranged appointments. The club membership gives a range of other advantages which include:

(i) pre-registration and advance event information
(ii) advance exhibitor list to enable members to pre-arrange business appointments
(iii) express entry and a complimentary welcome business pack which includes the event catalogue.

Meridian Club membership includes senior managers of the companies having decision-making powers to transact business deals on behalf to their companies.

## Database Driven Web-site

World Travel Market has recently launched a new high-tech "database driven" web-site that delivers personalised information and various services designed to make participation more effective. The most interesting new feature is the "meeting scheduler" a tailor-made appointment booking service which enables Meridian Club members to request meetings with main or space sharing exhibitors. Meridian Club members select who they wish to meet, view their available time slots and request a meeting. A summary of e-mails is sent to each exhibitor, each week detailing any new accepted or declined meetings. This new technology at WTM, according to the organisers, will help buyers and sellers to make the most of their time at World Travel Market.

World Travel Market provides an opportunity to the exhibitors to present their products and services and negotiate future business contracts. By providing a system of prearranged appointments with prospective new clients as well as existing ones, the forum provides an opportunity for generating additional sales. It also helps to maintain high visibility among the international travel media.

## International Brussels Travel Fair (BTF)

Popularly known as BTF the International Brussels Travel Fair is held every year in the month of November in the city of Brussels in Belgium. The city of Brussels has the unique advantage of being the capital of the European community. Its geographical location in the centre of Western Europe gives it an advantage over other cities in organising the travel trade fair, with increasing international participation. The three-day event is held between Thursday and Saturday. Started in the year 1975, the fair was held in four halls with an exhibition space of 12,000 square metres (gross) and 8,000 square metres (net). Since the last two years the fair venue has been moved to Hysel Exhibition complex with more exhibition space and modern facilities.

The BTF is more a technical than a promotional event. It may be described as a workshop. All the three days of the duration of the fair are for professionals and they are, therefore, of great interest to operators, hoteliers and travel agents. The Brussels event is said to have proved consistently profitable for its organisers during its 36 years operation.

## Salon Mondial du Tourism et Voyages (SMTV)

Popularly known as SMTV, the Salon Mondial du Tourism et Voyages is held in Paris every year in the month of February. The fair is held for a period of six days, of which the first two days are kept exclusively for the trade visitors. Travel mart is planned for subsequent days. Trade attendance at the mart is quite impressive. The fair organisers organise a buyers' and sellers' mart during the trade days.

The SMTV had its first fair in Paris in the year 1975, in a spacious exhibition complex covering a gross area of 24,000 square metres (net 12,000 square metres). The venue of the fair has since been shifted to the most modern exhibition complex in La Defense, located at the west end of the city of Paris.

## Feria International Tourismo (FITUR)

Spain has a special significance in the field of tourism. Few other countries in the world receive as many tourists as Spain does, in one year. The total tourist arrivals outnumber even the total population of the country. Spain also holds the key to the Spanish-speaking markets. Tourism being a major industry, the holding of a trade fair in the country was therefore considered to be crucial. Spain's International Tourism Fair (FITUR) was first started in the year 1980. The fair is organised each year in the month of January in a spacious exhibition complex of Madrid's 1,800 hectare Casa de Campo. The total exhibition area consists of about 15,000 square metres. The fair is held for a period of six days, out of which the first three days are exclusively devoted to trade. The fair in Madrid places major emphasis on the Spanish–speaking markets. This is because participation in the fair promotes tour programmes in Latin America as well as in Spain itself.

### Travel Trade Workshop (TTW)

A travel trade fair on a smaller scale but with a stronger orientation towards the public in general is the Tourism Trade Fair 'Salon International Tourism' held regularly in early spring each year in Montreux, Switzerland. The Swiss lakeside resort of Montreux provides an excellent, picturesque setting for the first of the season's major travel events. The trade fair is held for a duration of three days in the month of October each year. The event is meant for professionals only.

Started in the year 1975, the Tourism Trade Fair is a leading event of its kind in Switzerland. Special trains and buses are utilised to bring in professionals from other parts of the country. The total exhibition space covers 10,200 square metres of the Montreux Congress Centre.

### European Incentive and Business Travel and Meetings (EIBTM)

The meeting and incentives exhibition, known as the European Incentive and Business Travel and Meetings Exhibition, is a buyer-seller meet in the area of incentive and business travel. The major objective of the EIBTM is to encourage the expansion and development of the incentive travel industry through a programme. Carefully selected international buyers travel to the event and stay free, a concept pioneered by EIBTM as a major initiative to guarantee attendance by leading buyers. Held for the first time in the year 1988 at Palxpo Exhibition Centre, Geneva, EIBTM is classed as a 'world ranking' event in the area of incentives and conferences. A new visitor promotion campaign for the exhibition includes:

 i) increased target for hosting quality buyers
 ii) new meeting and incentives consultancy service to offer free service to participating buyers
 iii) regular market bulletins to keep industry contacts up-to-date with what buyers perceive to be business trends
 iv) a computerised 'World Who's Who in Business Tourism' is prepared for the exclusive use of buyers which enables them to pinpoint key suppliers from over 100 countries.

The EIBTM is held every year for a period of three days in the month of May. The display area is over 12,500 square metres.

In addition to the major travel trade fairs, there are some more important events drawing a good number of exhibitors and professional visitors.

### Swedish International Tourism and Travel Fair (TUR)

Started in the year 1982, the fair is held every year in the month of March in Gottenburg, Sweden. The gross area of the TUR is 20,000 square metres, (14,200 square metres net). A separate area is set aside for camping.

### Dutch Travel Trade Exhibition Tour

Started in the year 1981, the fair is held every year in the month of

December. It covers a gross area of 14,850 square metres. The fair is held in a spacious RAI Exhibition Centre in Amsterdam and is a very well organised fair.

Among the trade fairs discussed it is recognised by travel trade that only two, i.e., the ITB and WTM, are truly of international character. The global character of these two trade fairs can be judged by the fact that a large percentage of exhibitors as well as visitors are from overseas. Although organisers of most of the other fairs also claim these to be of an international character, these are only the national exhibitions with the participation of some overseas clients.

In between the few international exhibitions and scores of national exhibitions, another interesting range of regional exhibitions, have also surfaced. These regional exhibitions are normally organised by one or the other of the regional tourism organisations such as Pacific Asia Travel Association, etc. These associations specialise in setting up regional shows in prime target markets abroad. One such regional exhibition is the PATA Mart.

## PATA Travel Mart

PATA Travel Mart organised by Pacific Asia Travel Association needs special mention. The Travel Mart is geared to bring worldwide buyers of Pacific Asia Travel product services to meet with PATA member supplier organisations. The core of the Travel Mart concept is the appointments system whereby meetings are held during private, scheduled business appointments. This enables buyers and sellers of Asia/Pacific travel products and services to meet in pre scheduled, private business sessions to discuss and contract business for the coming years.

PATA makes efforts to secure the participation of tour wholesalers, conference and incentive planners, tour operators, corporate travel buyers and leading travel agents from around the world to meet with representatives from member hotels, airlines, cruise lines, government tourist offices, auto rental companies, ground operators and other suppliers. The names and business profiles of these participating buyers are furnished in an "Advance Guide to Buyers" and mailed to all registered booth contacts. The contacts are then requested to review the Appointment Guide and discuss with their staff the types of buyers they would like to meet during the Travel Mart. This information is then passed on to PATA via the Appointments Request Form. Buyers are also asked to review the Appointment Guide of Sellers and advise PATA of sellers' representatives with whom they would like to have appointments during the Mart. The information is put into a computer and schedules appointments for both contacts and buyers according to the following priority system:

1) Buyer and seller wish to meet each other
2) Buyer wishes to meet seller

Appointments are not scheduled based on requests by sellers only. An on-site appointment scheduling session is held immediately prior to the start of the Mart to enable the sellers to book additional meetings during unscheduled periods of the Travel Mart schedules. Seller requests are provided to the buyers to inform them of the sellers' interest in seeing them during the Travel Mart.

## Computer Appointment Scheduling

After the computer scheduling has been completed, one receives a copy of his appointment schedule approximately two weeks prior to the Mart. Every buyer receives a copy of his organisation and forwards copies to all his Travel Mart delegates. A secondary appointment schedule, reflecting cancellations that occurred subsequent to the appointment scheduling, are given to all delegates during registration at the Travel Mart site.

Participation in the Travel Mart is, however, limited. Among the buyers, the eligibility is restricted to only the delegates whose organisation has received an invitation to participate. The buyers are to be from organisations which are either doing business in the Asia/Pacific or have the ability to develop programmes and send their clients to PATA areas. Among the sellers, only delegates from PATA member organisations, who have registered as a booth-holder or co-exhibitor for the PATA Travel Mart, are eligible. The delegate category includes sales and marketing representatives of carriers, hotels, ground transport companies, auto rental companies, and destination promotion organisations.

The number of travel industry fairs has increased since the first travel trade fair known as the International Tourism Borse. This is a result of the ever-expanding travel trade industry. More and more industry fairs are being added in the list of existing events. Earlier in the chapter some important established travel trade fairs have been discussed. Some recent additions include the following:

1. International Tourism Trade Fair (ITTF) Zagreb, Croatia
2. British Travel Trade Fair (BTTF), Birmingham, England
3. Moscow International Travel and Tourism Exhibition (MITT) Moscow, Russian Federation
4. International Travel Expo (ITE) Hong Kong
5. International Tourism Asia, (ITA) Hong Kong
6. Feira International de Lisboa (BTL) Lisbon, Portugal
7. International Mediterranean Tourism Market (IMTM) Tel Aviv, Israel
8. Swedish International Travel and Tourism Trade Fair, (TUR), Gothenburg, Sweden
9. International Travel Exhibition, Copenhagen, Denmark
10. Arabian Travel Mart, (ATM) Dubai, *UAE*
11. India International Tourism Expo and Mart (IITEM), New Delhi, India

Participation in travel industry fairs is a costly affair for the exhibitors because of the rising cost of renting space. In addition, to the high cost of a stand, the exhibitor has to spend a considerable amount of money on decorating the stand, travel, publicity material, receptions, etc. Any exhibitor, therefore, has to take into account the relevant advantages which will be available to him vis-a-vis the cost of participating. In order to achieve maximum benefits from the participation, certain basic norms are to be taken into consideration with a view to achieving maximum mileage.

These would include the status of the fair, whether it is of international or national status, expectations from each fair, in order to determine its value, type of competing exhibitors, quality and the attendance of buyers, timings of the fair, etc. Careful planning will go a long way in obtaining the best results from the participation in the travel trade fairs and exhibitions.

## Conferences and Conventions Segment

The recent growth in the international co-operation in the field of business and industry has resulted in the development of a meeting ground where people representing a particular discipline come together for deliberations, exchange of ideas etc. in other words a conference, a business meeting is organised where all the above activities take place. This has been happening everywhere in the world, as there are no barriers between east and west, north and south. Business in the widest context is taking place everywhere. The business travel sector is in the forefront these days and is rapidly growing into a very important segment of tourism.

Attending conferences and conventions related to one's profession or trade, industry or commerce has become very important. Many countries with a view to attracting more tourists have established modern convention complexes where all types of latest facilities are provided for business meetings, seminars, workshops, etc. In large hotels modern conference and convention facilities are provided for the persons who travel for professional and business purposes. Conferences and conventions associated with various disciplines are increasingly being held in various parts of the world.

Business tourism can be divided into several categories. Each of these categories may however, cover a range of different activities. The categories are:
(i) business trips
(ii) attending a corporate meeting, conference or a training programme,
(iii) attending an associate conference,
(iv) organising or visiting exhibitions and trade fairs relating to one's field,
(v) using travel as an incentive or reward for performance,

However, the most important business activity is attending conferences and conventions. The conference and convention business has become a very organised sector requiring special skills. This sector has achieved phenomenal growth during last fifty years. With the increase in the number of conferences and conventions worldwide more and more countries are looking towards getting the major share of this segment. However, the size and the volume of obtaining the share of this segment is determined by certain factors most important among these perhaps is the geographical factor.

## Geographical Factors

The factors which determine the geographical distribution of international conferences and conventions, include the following:
- Location of main subsidiary offices of convention organising associations;

- Availability of sufficient facilities and organization arrangements for holding conventions;
- Cost factors like hiring of a convention centre, hotel accommodation transport, etc.
- Accessibility to the convention centre;
- Location of convention venue in relation to potential participants.
- Availability of tourist attractions of the prospective convention venue;
- Importance of convention venue in relation to the convention field;
- Effective marketing and promotional functions of the organisers.

At the national level, convention marketing is generally undertaken through convention and visitors bureau within the National Tourist Organisations of various countries. A large number of NTOs, however, do not have convention bureaus functioning within their premises. In the absence of convention bureaus, the overseas tourist office can assume the additional responsibility for soliciting congress and convention business. This is possible only if the tourist offices are in a position to give priority to this activity. In a majority of cases because of the skeleton staff and various other promotional activities, tourist offices are not in a position to give undivided attention to convention business.

The major marketing objectives of NTO are:
- To include international associations to choose meeting sites in the NTOs country
- To convince national affiliates to extend invitations to their 'parent' associations to meet in NTOs country
- To assist worldwide promotion of attendance of congresses realized through the above efforts and also for other congress booked for NTOs country
- To update and upgrade from time to time the facilities at various congress and convention centres.

## The Structure of the Market

There are two major categories of bodies of both international and domestic nature representing convention market. These are:
(i) **Global Conventions**
- International Governmental Organisations.
- International Non-governmental Organisations.
- Multinational Corporations.

(ii) **Domestic Conventions**
- Domestic Governmental Organisations.
- Domestic Non-governmental Organisations.
- National Institutions, Associations and Companies.

## The Conference Bidding Process

The bidding for a conference involves various logical steps which if followed properly help a great deal in winning a bid. Any local organisation, a local chapter of an international organisation, an independent association, or a government body wishing to assume the role of an international conference host may initiate a bid. A group of common interest agencies can also jointly cooperate and launch a bid. The following are the steps in the bidding process:

(i) **Preparatory Stage**
   - Identification of bid prospects
   - Conducting a preliminary study; evaluation of the bid project:
   - Congress hosting requirements
   - Traditional congress finding sources
   - Cost benefit analysis
   - Congress site selection process
   - Organisational structure/decision makers
   - Knowing competitors

(ii) **Drawing up bid proposal:**
   - Preparing bid paper and support material
   - Formal letter of invitation/proposal to host the congress indicating hosting capability; usually includes a convention package Convention package: a listing of facilities and services which will be made available to the delegates, together with corresponding rates
   - Endorsements from concerned government agencies
   - Information/promotional materials

(iii) **Bid Presentation**
   - Presentation of the bid to the international body: executive committee, site selection committee, and or general membership assembly.

(iv) **Follow through until bid is won.**

(v) **Post-bidding Stage**
   - Upon winning: drawing up of memorandum of agreement defining respective areas of responsibilities between the local association and the international organization; or
   - Upon losing: evaluation of rebidding possibilities and revision of bid proposal.

## International Congress and Convention Association (ICCA)

Founded in the year 1963, the International Congress and Convention Association is responsible for promoting congress and convention travel at the international level. The Association serves as the essential link and clearing house between ICCA members, international organisations and the congress industry at large. Spread over all the continents and operating in over 100 countries, ICCA members are joined in one strong organisation with its headquarters in Amsterdam, Holland as the principal link. The association is headed by an executive director and a full time staff of eight persons. The main responsibility of the full time staff is to implement the policies of the organisation set by the board of directors.

It has over 1,000 members in over 90 different countries. The members are divided by the type of the company into different sectors which include: destination marketing, meetings management, meetings support, transport, venues and honorary members. The member companies and organisations situated in the same geographical area are divided into chapters. The divided chapters include: African, Asia Pacific, Central European, France-BeneLux, Iberian, Latin American, Mediterranean, Middle East, North American, Scandinavian and UK/Ireland Chapter. The purpose of dividing the members into sectors and chapters is to enable networking between those members which have certain aspects in common in order to enhance their business activities in the industry.

ICCA has two departments, which share the responsibilities and activities of the organisation between them. The two departments are:

(i) The secretariat
(ii) The information department

The secretariat department is responsible for looking after the following matters:

- Membership
- Finances
- Publicity and public relations
- Administration of operations for ICCA General Assemblies.

The Secretariat is also charged with administrative support for marketing plans, education programmes, liaison with international professional organisations such as the Joint Industrial Council, the American Society of Association Executives and the Council of International Organisations of Medical Sciences, documentation for meetings of the Board of Directors and General Assemblies.

The information department on the other hand is responsible for looking after the following matters:

- To bring out important publication material including congress bulletins.
- To bring out questionnaires and a bi-annual congress calendar containing over 2,500 events.
- To process and evaluate continuously professional publications and commercial calendars.

The information department centres around ICCA's computerised data bank. It is through the data bank that all information about international meetings is systematically gathered from all ICCA members throughout the world from international organisations and researched by a team of researchers. Together, the secretariat and the information department form the Head Office team, which serves as the essential link and clearing house between ICCA members, international organisations and the congress industry at large. Over the years the association has served and established its position as a source of reliable and valuable information, advice and documentation to its executives and meeting planners.

## Membership

Membership is divided into the following nine categories:
a. Congress travel agents
b. Airlines
c. Professional congress, convention and exhibition organisers.
d. Statutory Bodies of Tourist and Convention Bureaus.
e. Transportation companies (other than those mentioned under B)
f. Hotels
g. Congress, convention and exhibition centres.
h. Ancillary services.
i. Honorary membership

## India Convention Promotion Bureau (ICPB)

National Tourism Administration in every country can play a key role in the development and promotion of the convention market. A large number of countries that host international conferences and conventions have set up convention bureaus to promote and assist in the organisation of conventions. These bureaus could either be a department of the National Tourism Organisation or outside it, comprising the public and private sectors concerned with convention market. With a view to promoting international conventions and conferences the NTOs in several countries have formed an international-level body known as the Convention Promotion Bureau enlisting the government, public and private sectors of the tourism industry. A full-time marketing director heads the bureau.

## Aims and Objectives

- To promote the country as a venue for international conferences and conventions
- To launch an awareness programme within the country and overseas:
- To gather data of international conferences and prepare a data bank of National Associations/Institutions and to carry out continuous research on the international conference market
- To launch regular advertising and publicity programmes in suitable domestic and international media
- To encourage professionalism in the conference industry
- To provide necessary guidance to the central and regional governments in the development of conference infrastructure
- To conduct seminars/workshops as part of an awareness programme and marketing
- To seek affiliation with world bodies
- To help the association bid for the conference by way of providing assistance with an introduction letter
- To conduct research and gather information to create the largest information centre in the country on conferences
- Educate associations on the need to bid for international conferences and procedures for joining world bodies

- Advise the government on the need for growth of the conference infrastructure and help with the existing plans for expansion
- Train conference personnel towards a more professional approach to conference management
- Organise workshops for associations

## Membership

(i) Category A
(ii) Category B
(iii) Category C
(iv) Honorary

Category 'A' membership comprises: the Department of Tourism NTO, National Air Carriers, Hoteliers, Travel Agencies, Tour Operators, International Congress Centres and any other organisations duly approved by the country's NTO.

Category 'B' membership comprises: regional/local tourism development corporations, airport authorities, trade fair authority, centres of education and learning, surface transport companies, air Cargo agents, ancillary services such as interpreters, photographers, audiovisual and other suppliers, restaurants, banks, central and regional government, advertising agencies, newspapers/magazines, trade journals, sports authority, national sport bodies, merchants/traders, Federation of Indian chambers of commerce and industry, rent-a-car companies, authorised foreign exchange dealers, duty-free shops and other organisations duly approved by the relevant government authority and as described by the governing body.

Category 'C' membership comprises: travel agents associations, tour operators, federation of hotels and restaurant association duly approved by the government and as decided by the governing body.

Honorary membership category comprises: distinguished individuals/organisations duly approved by relevant government authority and as decided by the governing body.

## INCENTIVE AND CORPORATE TRAVEL

Incentive travel, very broadly defined, is the lure a travel trip to motivate employees, distributors and customers to achieve business goals and objectives. Incentive travel has become increasingly popular with lot of corporations in the last few years and is used by large and small corporations. Incentive travel has become a huge market for the industry and is considered one of the most effective marketing and motivational tools available today. It is a reward for those special endeavours or efforts to achieve production targets.

### Definitions:

"An incentive is something which encourages people to act on stimulus to increase the output".

"An incentive is a motivational force that creates a desire to excel".

The Society for Incentive Travel Executives (SITE) defines incentive travel as a modern, management tool, used to achieve extra-ordinary goals by participants or a travel prize upon attainment of their share of the uncommon goal.

In economics, an incentive is any factor (financial or non-financial) that enables or motivates a particular course of action or counts as a reason for preferring one choice to the alternatives. The study of incentive structures is central to the study of all economic activity (both in terms of individual decision-making and in terms of co-operation and competition within a larger institutional structure). Economic analysis, of the differences between societies (and between different organisations within a society) largely amounts to characterising the differences in incentive structures faced by individuals involved in these collective efforts. Eventually, the incentives' aim is providing value for money and contributing to organisational success.

## Categories

Incentives can be classified according to the different ways in which they motivate agents to take a particular course of action. One common and useful classification divides incentives into three broad classes:

### (i) Remunerative incentives

(Remunerative incentives or financial incentives) are said to exist where an agent can expect some form of material reward, especially money in exchange for acting in a particular way.

### (ii) Moral incentives

Moral incentives are said to exist where a particular choice is widely regarded as the right thing to do or as particularly admirable or where the failure to act in a certain way is condemned as indecent. A person acting on a moral incentive can expect a sense of self-esteem, and approval or even admiration from his community.

### (iii) Travel as an incentive

Travel as an incentive, however, is of recent origin. Today, it is scored over all other incentives. It is considered as a highly visible honour and recognition. The experience of the incentive winner creates an unforgettable memory which scores over cash or material awards.

Travel incentives are a way for companies to promote their business and increase sales by offering a free or discounted travel package to their employees and customers. Many companies offer these incentives as a bonus for making a purchase, such as a cruise with the purchase of a new car. Other uses include rewarding individuals for business referrals and generating business leads.

However, if programmes are to be effective, all the factors that affect behaviour must be recognised, including: motivation, skills, recognition, an understanding of the goals, and the ability to measure progress.

**Effective Incentive Programme**

Many companies mistakenly assume that what works for one organisation will work well for all organisations. Companies often attempt to create incentive programmes without thinking in detail about how each program feature will best suit their targeted audience.

To facilitate the creation of a profitable incentive programme, every feature must be tailored to the participants' interests. A successful incentive programmes requires clearly defined rules, suitable rewards, efficient communication strategies, and measurable success metrics. By adapting each element of the programmes to fit the target audience, companies are better able to engage program participants and enhance the overall programme effectiveness.

An incentive programme represents a substantial investment to most organisations. Receiving a sufficient return on that investment requires the full participation of the programme participants. Incentive programmes are based upon the concept that effort increases as people perceive themselves progressing towards their goal.

An Incentive Industry Primer," the Incentive Marketing Association ties incentive programmes to the psychological equation:

$$Ability \times Motivation = Performance.$$

In order to properly motivate, programmes must be designed to offer a variation of products and services to programmes participants based on their unique interests and diverse needs. Successful programmes need to carefully develop their reward methods to keep participants eager to approach a new goal once they have achieved a reward.

## Incentive Programme Design and Implementation

In order to create an effective program, organisations must keep the overall objective in mind when considering programme design and implementation.

Objectives should be formed based on the organisation's overall goals and should be straightforward and specific so participants clearly understand the expectations.

Program objectives can vary depending on the needs of each individual organisation. They should be challenging, yet achievable. If objectives are viewed as unattainable, the program will be destined for failure. Objectives may include:
- Motivating employees,
- Recognising performance,
- Persuading customers to make a purchase, or
- Reinforcing a marketing message.

Once the programme goals have been determined, every aspect of the program must be measured against this goal in order to ensure the program's success in goal achievement. If successful, objectives should provide measurable results allowing the organisation to track performance and measure the overall success of the programme.

## Types of Incentive Programmes

### 1. Points Program:

Points-based incentive programs are a type of programme where participants collect and redeem points for awards. Depending on the programme type and the organisational objectives, points can be awarded on a number of criteria including:
- Positive employee behaviour,
- The demonstration of organisational values,
- Repeat customer purchases,
- The sale of new products, increased overall sales,
- The use of proper safety precautions

In addition to point awarding, the levels at which points can be redeemed can be customised by the organisation and set at virtually any level. Points programmes are a way for organisations to motivate behaviour over time while improving the organisations' overall performance.

### 2. Employee

Employee incentive programmes are programmes used to increase overall employee performance. Employee programmes are often used:
- To reduce turnover
- Boost morale and loyalty
- Improve employee wellness
- Increase retention
- And drive daily employee performance

### 3. Consumer

Consumer incentive programmes are programmes targeting the customers and consumers of an organisation. In a study researchers found that a simple 5% increase in a company's customer retention rates will increase the average lifetime profits per customer. Consumer programmes are becoming more widely used as more companies realise that existing customers cost less to reach, cost less to sell, are less vulnerable to attacks from the competition, and buy more over the long term.

### 4. Dealer/Channel

Dealer incentive programmes are used to improve performance for dealer and channel resellers using sales incentive programs. These programs help companies:
- Capture market share,
- Launch new products,
- Reduce cost of sales,
- Increase product adoption,
- Drive sales.

## 5. Sales

Sales incentive programs (also termed sales incentive plans or SIPs) are used to motivate salespeople to achieve sales goals over a period of time. These programmes are primarily used to:
- Drive sales,
- Reduce sales costs,
- Increase profitability,
- Develop new territory,
- And enhance margins.

Sales incentive programmes have the clearest connection directly to outcomes.

## Online Programs

When first emerging in 1996, the use of online incentive programmes was extremely rare. According to the Online Incentive Council (OIC), since its emergence, the number of online programmes has almost doubled in size every year. At present, nearly every traditional incentive company offers an online component in programmes including employee motivation and recognition, sales performance, channel programmes, and consumer promotions. Companies that run their programmes online experience efficient communication, reporting, and awards fulfilment. Online incentive programmes pose an attractive alternative to traditional offline programmes since online programmes save money and time and allow organisations to have much greater control.

## Incentive Rewards

While there are many important factors to consider when creating an incentive programmes, selecting the appropriate rewards is vital to any programme's success. The goal in choosing rewards is to select items that will spark the participant's interest or feelings, and support the programme's objectives. Effective rewards will both motivate short-term behaviour and provide motivation over time. While rewards come in a variety of shapes and sizes, some of the common types are as follows:

### (i) Cash

While incentive programmes participants often state that they prefer cash to non-cash rewards, research has shown that cash is a poor motivator due to its lack of "trophy value." In a recent study conducted by the Centre for Concept Development, three of five respondents agree that a cash payment is perceived to be part of an employee's total compensation package and not as part of an incentive programme. Additionally, cash is quickly forgotten as many participants tend to spend it on everyday items or use it to pay bills. Given that most people don't generally talk about cash awards, cash programme do little to generate the interest required to create an effective incentive programme.

### (ii) Non-cash rewards

Merchandise and other non-cash rewards are more often perceived as separate from compensation. Accordingly, non-cash rewards tend to stand out as rewards for performance, which enhances their long-term effect. Branded merchandise and other non-cash rewards have high trophy value, bringing greater recognition to the recipient at the time of the award and possessing a long-term lasting effect that can result in increased engagement in the organisations goals.

### (iii) Gift cards/certificates

Gift cards/certificates are prepaid retail cards or certificates which are redeemed at a later time at checkout. In general, they are available in two types:
a) cards which carry a major credit card brand and are redeemable at all merchants accepting the credit card brand and
b) retailer-specific cards, issued by well-known merchants, redeemable only through the issuing retailer.

### (iv) Merchandise

Merchandise rewards can range anywhere from small branded key chains to high-end electronics.

### (v) Experiential

Experiential rewards are rewards which provide program participants with an experience. This form of reward gives organisations the ability to offer their employees and customers innovative, rewarding "life experiences" as incentives. Examples of experiential rewards include a seaplane flight and lunch, a two hour horse ride on the beach, a day of sailing for two, a "meet and greet" with a star athlete, or even the use of a party planner for an occasion of one's choice. Experiential rewards allow participants to share their experiences with others and reinforce the reward and the behaviour that led to the giving of the reward.

### (vi) Non-monetary rewards

Non-monetary incentives are used to reward participants for excellent behaviour through opportunities. Non-monetary incentives may include flexible work hours, payroll or premium contributions, training, health savings or reimbursement accounts, or even paid sabbaticals. If it comes to environmental behaviour, often labelling and recognition certificates are used. This may include stickers, T-shirts with banner logo, etc.

### (vii) Travel as an incentive

Travel as an incentive, however, is of recent origin. Today, it is scored over all other incentives. It is considered as highly visible honour and recognition. The experience of incentive winner creates an unforgettable memory which scores over cash or material awards.

Travel incentives are a way for companies to promote their business and increase sales by offering a free or discounted travel package to their employees and customers. Many companies offer these incentives as a bonus for making a purchase, such as a cruise with the purchase of a new car. Other uses include rewarding individuals for business referrals and generating business leads.

## Reasons for Offering Incentives

The companies offering their employees, possibility of an incentive trip are motivated by one or more of the following direct reasons:
- Increasing sales volume and/or employee productivity.
- Selling new accounts and/or slow moving items.
- Introducing new products.
- Pushing low season sales.
- Over taking competition.
- Indirect benefits to the firm.
- Improving employee morale and goodwill.
- Improving employee attendance.
- Getting demoted employees to perform better.

The concept of incentive is that it should be self-liquidating to the company. The incentive programme should pay for itself through increased sales or reduced company cost.

## Types of Incentive Organizations

A full service organisation that specialises in incentive travel is able to offer client assistance in developing and managing the incentive programme within the client's company and in organising, planning and directing travel.

Travel agencies have established special incentive travel departments. These firms may or may not be able to offer a client, professional assistance in the incentive planning portion.

## Profile of Incentive Winner

An incentive winner is informed, educated and motivated. He has an important role in the choice of destination. He would require a programme out of ordinary.

## Main Users of Incentive Travel

Today, almost every industry uses some incentive travel programme. These are the industries with complex marketing systems involving layers of sales people, dealers and distributors. Following are the main users of the incentive travel programme.
- Insurance
- Automobiles
- Electronics and electrical appliances
- Office equipment
- Personal computers

- Consumer product companies
- Cosmetics
- Furniture and household goods
- Airlines
- Mobile service provideers

## EVENT MANAGEMENT

An event is an actual or contemplated occurrence, (especially important) happening item or programme. It is something that happens. It could also be a public or a social occasion as also each of several contests making up a sports competition.

Event management is the application of the management practice of project management to the creation and development of festivals and events.

Event management involves studying the intricacies of the brand, identifying the target audience, devising the event concept, planning the logistics and coordinating the technical aspects before actually executing the modalities of the proposed event.

The recent growth of festivals and events as an industry around the world means that the management can no longer be ad hoc. Events and festivals, have a large impact on their communities and, in some cases, the whole country.

The industry now includes events of all sizes from the Olympics down to a breakfast meeting for ten business people. Every industry, charity, society and group will hold events of some type/size in order to market themselves, build business relationships, raise money or celebrate.

### Basics

- To understand the reason behind the event being organised.
- The community at which the event is aimed.
- Parallel complementary issues/activities within that community.

## Decision Making Process

To decide on:
- Topic/theme
- Whether it should be a joint event with another agency
- Duration
- Location
- Accommodation
- Timing
- Mix vision with practical reality
- For large events balance speakers from within the community with those from without.
- Funding

### Venue
- One with a reasonable access (rail, air and road access).
- Adequate parking space.

### Planning Team
- Keep it small
- Ensure inclusion of at least one person who has previous experience in event management.
- Assign responsibility for complete components of activity to individuals.

### Programme
- Do not have a welcome only by a dignitary.
- Make a welcome speech into a proper presentation.
- Do not overcrowd – build in gaps – for refreshment, etc.
- Consider interactivity.
- For multi-day events, consider a social programme.

### Budget
- Identify fixed and variable costs.
- Calculate a breakeven/delegate number/fee balance.
- Round up and add contingency.
- Consider the market price and adjust parameters (especially costs).
- Consider risks – establish decision dates for any cancellation and consider sharing risks with partner organisations.

### Sponsorship
**Consider sponsorship of:**
- The event
- Some component of the event
- Gifts

### Promotion
- Well enough in advance.
- Crucial to the success of any event that is advertised and promoted.
- For mega event advertising PR.

### Booking
- Make it easy.
- Set the booking deadline in line with cancellation arrangements.

### At the Event
- Make sure the delegate see welcoming faces.
- Make sure the signage is effective and easy to follow.
- Make sure the equipment and the delegates' belongings are secure.

## Post Event
- Evaluation.

## Categories of Events
Events can be classified into four broad categories based on their purpose and objective:
  (i) Leisure events, e.g., leisure sport, music, recreation
  (ii) Cultural events, e.g., ceremonial, religious, art, heritage, and folklore
  (iii) Personal events, e.g., weddings, birthdays, anniversaries
  (iv) Organisational events, e.g., commercial, political, charitable, sales, product launch

## Event Planning
Event planning is the process of planning a festival, ceremony, competition, party or convention.
Event planning includes:
- Budgeting
- Establishing dates and alternate dates
- Selecting and reserving the event site
- Acquiring permits and
- Coordinating transportation and parking

Event planning also includes some or all of the following, depending on the event:
- Developing a theme or motif for the event
- Arranging for speakers and alternate speakers
- Coordinating location support (such as electricity and other utilities)
- Arranging decor, tables, chairs, tents
- Event support and security, police, fire, portable toilets
- Parking, signage
- Emergency plans
- Health care professionals, and
- Cleanup

Event planning is a relatively new career field. There is now training that helps one trying to break into the career field. There must be training for an event planner to handle all the pressure and work efficiently. This career deals with a lot of communication and organisation aspects. There are many different names for an event planner such as a conference coordinator, a convention planner, a special event coordinator and a meeting manager.

## Steps to Planning an Event
The first step to planning an event is determining its purpose, whether it is for a wedding, company, birthday, festival, graduation or something else. From this, the event planner needs to choose entertainment, location,

guest list, speakers, and content. The location for events is endless, but with event planning they would likely be held at hotels, convention centres, reception halls or outdoors depending on the event. Once the location is set the coordinator/planner needs to prepare the event with staff, set up the entertainment, and keep contact with the client. After all this is set, the event planner has all the smaller details to address like set up of the event such as food, drinks, music, guest list, budget, advertising and marketing, decorations, all this preparation is what is needed for an event to run smoothly. An event planner needs to be able to manage the time wisely for the event, and the length of preparation needed for each event so it is a success.

## Services of Event Management Company

Event management companies and organisations service a variety of areas including:
- Corporate events (product launches)
- Press conferences
- Corporate meetings and conferences
- Marketing programs (road shows, grand opening events)
- Special corporate hospitality events like concerts
- Award ceremonies, film premieres
- Launch/release parties
- Fashion shows
- Commercial events
- Private (personal) events such as weddings.

Clients hire event management companies to handle a specific scope of services for the given event, which at its maximum may include all creative, technical and logistical elements of the event. (Or just a subset of these, depending on the client's needs, expertise and budget).

## Sustainability

Sustainable event management (also known as event greening) is the process used to produce an event with particular concern for environmental, economic, and social issues. Sustainability in event management incorporates socially and environmentally responsible decision making into the planning, organization and implementation of, and participation in, an event. It involves including sustainable development principles and practices in all levels of event organization, and aims to ensure that an event is hosted responsibly. It represents the total package of interventions at an event, and needs to be done in an integrated manner. Event greening should start at the inception of the project, and should involve all the key role players, such as clients, organizers, venues, sub-contractors, and suppliers.

## Technology

Event management software companies provide event planning with software tools to handle many common activities such as delegate registration, hotel booking, travel booking, or allocation of exhibition floorspace.

A recent trend in event technology is the use of mobile apps for events. Event mobile apps have a range of uses. They can be used to hold relatively static information such as the agenda, speaker biographies, and general FAQs. They can also encourage audience participation and engagement through interactive tools such as live voting/polling, submitting questions to speakers during Q&A, or building live interactive "word clouds". Mobile event apps can also be used by event organisers as a means of communication. Organisers can communicate with participants through the use of alerts, notifications, and push messages. They can also be used to collect feedback from the participants through the use of surveys in application. Some mobile event applications can help participants to engage with each other, with sponsors, and with the organisers with built-in networking functionality.

# Glossary of Travel Agency and Airlines Terms

### AGENTS, RETAIL
An agent who sells his individual travel services, e.g., accommodation, transportation, insurance, etc., to the visitors.

### AIRLINES, REGIONAL
Feeder airlines whose role is to bring passengers to the major hubs, where they will connect for longer distance flights on larger aircraft.

### AFFINITY GROUP
A group bound together by common interest or affinity. Where charters are concerned, this common bond makes the concerned members eligible for charter flights. The group must travel together on the departure and return flights but can travel independently where ground arrangements are concerned.

### ARRANGEMENTS, LAND
All services provided for the traveller by his tour operator after the traveller reaches his first foreign destination. Also referred to as ground arrangements.

### ACCOUNTS, KEY
The most important accounts by sales volume/margin.

### ATTRACTIONS
Natural or built features of a destination which singly or collectively create the appeal of a country.

### APEX
Advance Purchase Excursion. This fare has to be purchased, from 14 days to two months in advance. It is generally available on return basis only with minimum and maximum stay requirements. No stopovers are allowed and there are cancellation charges.

### AIRPORT CODE
The three letter code given to each airport. Used in all airline schedules, manuals, and on baggage tags.

### AIRLINE
Any air transport enterprise offering or operating a scheduled international, domestic or regional service.

## AREA, BAGGAGE CLAIM
An area of an airport where arriving passengers can collect their baggage brought with them in the flight.

## AIRWAY BILL
Equivalent to the term "air consignment note" meaning the document entitled airway bill consignment note made out by or on behalf of the shipper which evidences contract between the shipper and carrier(s) for carriage of goods over routes of the carrier(s).

## ADVERTISING SPECIALITIES
Useful articles imprinted with an advertiser's name given as gifts to consumers.

## AIR TRAFFIC CONTROL
The air navigation service that involves managing the airport movements of all airside vehicles and all aircraft, both on the ground and in the air.

## AIR CARGO
Also known as air freight, consist of goods shipped by air, including letters, packages, cars, horses and construction equipment.

## AIRPORT
Location where aircrafts take-off and land, as well as load and unload passengers and cargo. Many of the larger airports have their own fire and law enforcement departments, customs, immigration and medical facilities along with retail and hotel establishments.

## ARRIVALS
Passengers enter this area as they leave the aircraft where they will encounter immigration, customs and baggage claim.

## AERODROME CONTROL
Directs the pilot in the vicinity of the airport and gives permission to land.

## AGENTS
An accredited passenger sales agent, selling tickets and travel services on behalf of its principals i.e., carriers both domestic and international and other travel service providers.

## ATTRACTIONS AND AMENITIES
Services needed by the tourists at the destination or resort. These are usually built and might be a stately home, an activity centre, a theme park or even a catering facility such as taste food outlet or five-star restaurant.

## AVIATION
The science and practice of flight and airplanes. Aviation is grouped into three broad classes: Commercial, General and Military.

## AUTOMATED TICKET/BOARDING PASS (ATB)
Form of automated ticket and boarding pass. It is a single copy non-carbonized ticket (normally on card stock) with each coupon imprinted separately. Each coupon used for air transport comprises a flight coupon

and a detachable passenger coupon and boarding pass for a specific flight. One coupon is issued as the passenger receipt which together with all passenger coupons and boarding passes builds up the passenger copy of the passenger ticket and baggage check.

## ADVERTISING
Any paid form of non-personal presentation and promotion of ideas, goods, or services by an identified sponsor.

## AIRPORT TAX (DEPARTURE TAX)
Charge levied by a city, state or country at the time of the passenger's departure.

## ALLIANCE
A formal agreement establishing an association between airlines to achieve a particular aim. This can allow companies to remain as separate entities, yet increase their efficiencies. Alliance allows for increased customer service with minimal increased cost to individual airlines.

## AVAILABLE SEAT KILOMETRE (ASK)
A measure of capacity available. The ASK is calculated by multiplying the number of seats available on a flight leg by the number of kilometers flown during that flight leg.

## AVAILABLE SEAT KILOMETRE (ASK) COST
Operating cost to fly one aircraft seat one kilometre.

## BIOMETRIC VISA
It requires statistical analyses of biological observations and phenomenon. The process takes finger scans and a digital photograph as part of the visa application process. The process is to proof and protect customers from identity theft. The unauthorised persons will not be able to access the biometric data and the data will not be used inappropriately.

## BREAKFAST, ENGLISH
This type of breakfast is generally served in Great Britain. It usually includes hot or cold cereal, bacon or ham and eggs, toast, butter, jam or marmalade and beverage (though not juice).

## BAGGAGE
Personal property of passenger or crew carried on an aircraft by agreement with the operator.

## BAGGAGE ACCOMPANIED
The baggage carried on the same aircraft as that on which the passenger is carried.

## BERTH
1. Dock or pier. 2. The bed or beds within the passenger cabins.

## BAGGAGE CHECK
Means those portions of the tickets, which relate to the carriage of the passenger's checked-baggage.

## BAGGAGE, EXCESS
A passenger's baggage presented at check-in counter of an airline that is in excess (either in terms of weight or dimensions) of the free allowance, on which charges are to be paid.

## BAGGAGE, UNACCOMPANIED
The baggage not carried on the same aircraft as that on which the passenger is carried.

## BUSINESS TRAVEL
Business travel is the act of travelling for purposes which are related to their work, like to meetings, conferences and conventions on behalf of the corporate entity or business at its expense. Business travel is that category of tourism in which travellers visit distant destination within their own country or outside the country to conduct their business activities. This could involve attending meetings, participating in seminars; conferences and conventions as also trade fairs and exhibitions.

## BUCKET SHOP
An unlicensed retailer, bound by no trade association, buys seats in bulk from airlines at a massive discount and sells them individually to the public.

## BOOKING FORM
A form completed by a travel agent when a booking is created. The form records details of the customer's name, contact address and telephone number, itinerary, payment details and booking conditions.

## BRAND IMAGE
The set of beliefs consumers hold about a particular branded product.

## BREAKFAST, CONTINENTAL
This generally consists of a beverage (coffee, tea, cocoa or milk, rolls, butter or jam or marmalade. It includes tea, coffee and juices, toast, butter, jam and pastry and perhaps fresh seasonal fruit as part of room tariff.

## BOOKINGS, GROUP
A set of rooms set-aside for groups of ten or more people and negotiated at special price. This negotiated price is lower than the normal price.

## CHARGE, CANCELLATION
Means the service charge made by reason of failure of a passenger to use reserved accommodation without having cancelled such accommodation prior to the latest appropriate time for cancellation specified by the carrier.

## CUSTOMER SERVICE
All customer-provider interactions other than proactive selling and the core product delivery that facilitate the organisation's relationship with its customers.

## CIRCLE TRIP FOR NORMAL FARES
Travel from and to the same point by a continuous, circuitous air route which may have two or more fare components which do not meet the round trip definition.

### CIRCLE TRIPS FOR SPECIAL FARES
Travel from and to the same point by a continuous, circuitous air route, comprising two international fare components which do not meet the conditions of the round trip definitions.

### COUCHETTES
Sleeping accommodation provided by some European railroads, consisting of a day compartment which may be converted into bunks for four (1st class) or six (2nd class) passengers. Pillows and blankets are provided.

### CHECK, BAGGAGE
Means those portions of the tickets, which relate to the carriage of the passenger's checked baggage.

### CARGO
Equivalent to the word 'goods' meaning anything carried or to be carried in an aircraft other than mail or baggage moving under an airway bill is also cargo.

### COMMISSION
Amount of money earned by agents from sale of flight and other services like insurance, hotel rooms, etc. Commission is usually a percentage of the sale price.

### CATEGORIES, RATE
Rate categories indicate the amount of money hotels charge for a room and the various discounts available within the initially quoted price.

### CODE SHARE
The term is popularly used in the airline industry. A single flight on which space is shared and sold by two airlines. A ticket may be issued under the code of either airline and the flight may have two flight numbers.

### CARGO TRANSFER
Cargo arriving at a point by one flight and continuing its journey by another flight of the same carrier.

### CLASS, BUSINESS
Referred to as "C" or "J". Several airlines have their own terminology. The fare for this class is higher than that of economy class commensurate with the comfort and services offered.

### CUSTOMS
Authority in a country responsible for collecting taxes on imported merchandise or merchandise brought in from outside that country. This authority is also responsible for processing the flow or people, animals and goods including personal property and hazardous materials in and out of their country. They work to prevent smuggling and prevent forbidden goods from entering or leaving the country.

### CONDUCTOR, TOUR
Person employed to escort members of a tourist group for the entire journey. Also called leader, escort or courier.

## COSTS, FIXED
All expenses that will remain the same no matter how many clients take a tour.

## COSTS, VARIABLE
All expenses that change according to the number of clients who take a tour.

## CHECK IN (HOTEL)
System of registration upon arrival in a hotel. The check-in time in classified hotels across the world is 1200 noon.

## CHECK OUT
System of payment upon departure from the hotel. The check out time in classified hotels across the world is 1200 noon.

## CONSOLIDATOR
Selected travel agents who receive an allocation of discounted tickets from the airlines, then farm them out to other travel agents. It includes a wholesaler of discounted tickets.

## CONCIERGE
A staff member who provides assistance to guests such as help in obtaining theatre and other entertainment tickets, renting a car, arranging sight seeing, also known as hall porter.

## CONFIRMATION
Written acknowledgement of reservation often indicated by a number or code.

## COMPLEMENTARY SERVICES
Services that accompany a core product and support its acquisition usage and/or disposition.

## COUPON, PASSENGER
For carbonised documents: that portion of the passenger ticket and baggage check that constitutes the passenger's written evidence of the contract of carriage.

## CARRIAGE
Equivalent to term 'transportation' means carriage of passengers and/or baggage by air gratuitously or for hire.

## CODE, AIRPORT
The three letter code given to each airport. Used in all airline schedules, manuals and on baggage tags.

## CHECK IN
Various formalities in connection with flights undertaken by a passenger at an airport before departure. These formalities include the checking of passenger documents, allocation of seats and issue of boarding cards and baggage tags.

### CHARTER, TOURIST
A flight booked exclusively for the use of a specific group of tourists who generally belong to the same organisation or who are being 'treated' to the flight by a single host.

### COUPON, FLIGHT
That part of an airline ticket, which contains details of the flight, reserved for a passenger.

### CRUISE
An all expense prepaid tour pre-arranged by a luxury ship to a specific port.

### CONDITIONS OF CARRIAGE
Means the terms and conditions established by a carrier in respect to its carriage.

### COUPONS
Documents issued by tour operators in exchange for which travellers receive prepaid accommodation, meals, sightseeing trips, etc. Also referred to as vouchers.

### CANCELLATION FEE
Penalty levied by airlines when a passenger fails to use a reservation.

### CHARTER (FLIGHTS)
To contract for the complete and exclusive use of an aircraft. The term often refers to flights operated by tour companies to resorts or popular holiday destinations during high season.

### CLIENT
A person to whom you provide a product and/or service.

### CLOSING
Any process involving getting the prospect to commit to paying for your product or service.

### CONVENTION
A speciality market requiring extensive meeting facilities. It is usually the annual meeting of an association and includes general sessions, committee meetings, and special-interest sessions.

### CARRIER
A public transportation company such as air or steamship line, railroad, bus, etc.

### COUNSELLING
Counselling involves advising management about public issues and company positions and image.

### CUSTOMER SATISFACTION
Customer satisfaction with a purchase depends up the product's performance relative to a buyer's expectations. If performance matches expectations, the customer is satisfied.

## CLASS, ECONOMY
Symbolised by "Y". This is difficult to classify except when used for excursion fares. Sometimes referred to a full fair, particularly when business class facilities are not available.

## CONDITIONS OF CONTRACT
The term and conditions shown on the passenger ticket and baggage check.

## CONFIGURATION
The seating arrangements of the aircraft.

## CONFIRMED RESERVATION
Oral or written statement by a supplier that the request for a reservation has been received and will be honoured.

## CARRIAGE, INTERNATIONAL
Carriage in which according to the contract of carriage, the place of departure, and any place of landing are situated in more than one nation. As used in this definition, the term national includes all territory subject to the sovereignty, mandate, authority or trust ship thereof.

## CHARTER, FLIGHTS
Non-scheduled flights typically for travellers who want to hire a plane to fly to a specific place at a specific time. A charter airline operates these flights that take place outside normal schedules through hiring arrangements with a particular customer.

## CIVIL AVIATION
The broad segment of aviation that includes commercial and private aviation, as well as general aviation but excludes military aviation.

## CARRIAGE, DOMESTIC
Carriage in which according to the contract of carriage, the place of departure, the place of destination or stopover and the entire transportation are within one nation or its territories.

## CODE-SHARING
This enables a passengers to fly a segment of their trip on an airline other than the airline that sold the ticket for the flight.

## CONSTRUCTED FARE
Unspecified through fares created by the use of add-on amounts or two or more fares shown as a single amount in a fare calculation.

## COUPON, ELECTRONIC
An electronic flight coupon or other value document held in carrier's database.

## DESK, FRONT
Reception area in a hotel where guests check in and check out. This is the first contact point of guests with hotel employees.

### DESTINATIONS
The place at which travellers terminate their journey. It may also mean ultimate stopping place according to contract of carriage. It may also mean places with some form of actual or perceived boundaries such as physical boundary of an island, political boundaries or even market created boundaries.

### DESTINATIONAL TOURIST
A tourist who terminates his journey at a particular country for the purpose of making a tour, travelling from place to place for pleasure in that country.

### DESTINATIONAL TRAFFIC
Persons (tourists) carried by transportation lines and terminating their journey at one particular place.

### DELUXE ROOM
A regular size sleeping room in a hotel. This type of room would offer the best location, the best view and the highest level of comfort, furnishings, amenities and décor. Bedding usually includes a queen size or king size bed with comfortable mattresses.

### DISTRIBUTION CHANNEL
A set of independent organisations involved in the process of making a product or service available for use or consumption by a consumer or business user.

### DISEMBARKATION
The leaving of an aircraft after landing, except by crew or passengers continuing on the next stage of the same through flight.

### DIRECT ROUTE
The shortest all year route operated by an TC member in both directions between ticketed points at which it exercises traffic rights.

### DIRECT ROUTE FARE
The fare over the direct route between two points.

### DIRECT FARE
For fare construction purposes, a fare between two points without the application of construction calculation.

### DIRECT FLIGHT
A flight which does not require passengers to change the aircraft between starting point and destination. For example one can directly fly from Singapore to Los Angeles without changing an aircraft.

### DOMESTIC INDEPENDENT TRAVEL
A tour constructed to meet the specific desire of a client within a single country.

### DOUBLE
Room in a hotel with a double bed that can be used for either one or two people. It could also be a bed designed for two people.

## DUTY FREE
Goods sold at ports or airports that are free of government taxes and customs duties. Some countries have allowances of how much duty free merchandise a person may bring back into their country. These restrictions usually apply to liquor, wine, tobacco, perfume, jewellery and other gifts and souvenirs.

## DATE LINE, INTERNATIONAL
Imaginary line at approximately 180° latitude in the Pacific Ocean where, by international agreement, the earth's day begins.

## ENROUTE
Along the way to a destination.

## ESTIMATED FLIGHT TIME
The overall general flight time between two points (the point of departure and the point of arrival).

## ESTIMATED TIME OF ARRIVAL (ETA)
The time at which a flight is expected to arrive at the destination.

## ESTIMATED TIME OF DEPARTURE (ETD)
The time at which a flight is projected to depart from a particular city.

## EMBARKATION
The boarding of an aircraft for the purpose of commencing a flight, except by such crew or passengers as have embarked at a previous stage on the same through flight.

## ELECTRONIC COUPON
An electronic flight coupon or other value document held in carrier's database.

## ELECTRONIC MISCELLANEOUS DOCUMENT (EMD)
An electronic record issued by a carrier or its authorised agent, in accordance with applicable tariffs, for the issuance of the MCO or tour order.

## E-TICKET
Electronic ticket is a digital form of a reservation. A passenger is issued a receipt from a machine or via email that contains a record locator or reservation number that confirms a booking or reservation. This information is available on the computer at the check-in counter and the passenger presents this confirmation number upon check in and is issued a boarding pass. It eliminates the need for a paper ticket. E-tickets offer greater flexibility for airlines by eliminating manual tasks to process and account for paper tickets.

## EUROPEAN PLAN
Hotel accommodation with no meals whatsoever included in the cost of the tariff of the room.

## EXCHANGE ORDER
A documents issued by a carrier or its agents requesting issue of an appropriate ticket or provision of services to the person named in such document.

## EXCHANGE VOUCHER
A document issued by a carrier or its agents requesting issue of an appropriate passenger ticket and baggage check or provision of services to the person named in such document.

## EXCURSION FARES
These fares are priced midway between APEX and full fare economy class. There are no advance booking requirements, but often a minimum stay abroad is mandatory. The passenger can change his booking and also stopover without surcharge. Different airlines however, have conditions on this.

## EXCURSIONIST
A temporary visitor staying less than twenty four hours in the country visited.

## ENDORSEMENT
An authority from a carrier to transfer a transportation (document like ticket or flight coupons) to another carrier.

## ESCORT
A professional tour escort often called tour manager or courier.

## ESCORT TOUR
A tour accompanied by a professional tour escort also called tour manager.

## EUROPEAN UNION (EU)
European Union is a family of democratic European countries, committed to working together for peace and prosperity. It is not a state intended to replace existing states, but it is more than any other international organisation. The EU is, in fact, unique. Its member states have set up common institutions to which they delegate some of their sovereignty so that decisions on specific matters of joint interest can be made democratically at European level.

There are 25 members of EU including Austria, Belgium, Cyprus, Czech Republic, Denmark, Estonia, Finland, France, Greece, Hungary, Ireland, Italy, Latvia, Lithuania, Luxembourg, Malta, Poland, Portugal, Slovakia, Slovenia, Spain, Sweden, the Netherlands and the United Kingdom.

## EXCHANGE
The act of obtaining a desired object from someone by offering in return.

## ELECTRONIC TICKETING (ET)
A new means of issuing tickets through electronic means (i.e., through the Internet and the use of self-service kiosks).

## FARE, ADULT
The fare for a person who has attained his twelfth birthday.

## FARE, INFANT
The fare for a person who has not attained his second birthday.

## FARE, SPECIAL
A fare other than the normal fare.

## FARE COMPONENT
A portion of an itinerary between two consecutive fare construction points.

## FARE CONSTRUCTION POINTS
The terminal points of a fare component (these are also termed fare break points).

## FARE, CABOTAGE
Special reduced fares known as "Cabotage Fares" are available but only to the nationals of the territories qualifying as cabotage traffic.

## FIRST CLASS
Symbolized by "F" in most airlines. Passengers travelling in this class are seated in a separate section with superior seating, a la carte menu and complimentary drinks. Passengers also get extra baggage allowance, unlimited stopovers and there are no cancellation charges.

## FLIGHT, CONNECTING
A flight which transfers a passenger to another aircraft in another city. It also means a flight that requires the passenger to change aircraft as part of the itinerary. An example would be of a passenger travelling from New Delhi to New York via London. The passenger in this case will be required to change the aircraft at London to proceed to New York.

## FLIGHT TIME, ESTIMATED
The overall general flight time between two points (the point of departure and the point of arrival).

## FLIGHT NUMBER
An alphanumeric code, made up of a 2-character airline code plus between 1 and 4 numbers, assigned to a particular route.

## FIRST CLASS HOTEL
This establishment is of superior category where rooms are provided with telephone, private bathrooms and toilet. Restaurant and laundry services are available.

## FIXED CONVERSION RATE (FCR)
Irrevocable fixed exchange rate between the euro and the legacy currencies of EMU countries.

## FULL BOARD
Daily hotel rates which include guest accommodation plus three meals.

## FLY/CRUISE TOUR
A travel plan wherein the travellers fly to a port of embarkation and then board a cruise ship for most of the tour. Fly cruises are generally part of the tour package.

### FLY/DRIVE TOUR
An independent tour that allows travellers to visit multiple destinations during their trip and usually includes air transport, a car rental and lodging at several hotels.

### FRANCHISE
A contractual association between a service organisation (a franchiser) and independent business people (franchisees) who buy the right to own and operate one or more units in the franchise system.

### FACILITATION
The act of assisting progress or helping to move forward. To make easier or less difficult. Promoting any measures which will facilitate international travel with main emphasis on achieving minimum entry and exit formalities for temporary visitor.

### FARE, TOUR BASING
A reduced round trip fare available on specified dates, and between specified times, only to those passengers who purchase pre-planned, pre-paid tour arrangements from an agent prior to their departure.

### FOREIGN INDEPENDENT TOUR (FIT)
This type of tour offered by travel agent/tour operators refers to custom designed tour taking into consideration the requirement of the tourist.

### FORWARDING CARRIER
Means the carrier responsible for the condition which creates a need for involuntary change in the passenger's journey; on missed connections the carrier on whose flight a passenger is originally ticketed to be carried to a connection point.

### FARE, CONSTRUCTED
Unspecified through fares created by the use of add-on amounts, or two or more fares shown as a single amount in a fare calculation.

### FLIGHTS, SCHEDULED
Typically take place using predetermined routes according to a planned timetable.

### FLIGHT COUPON
That part of an airline ticket which contains details of the flight reserved for a passenger.

### FARES, EXCURSION
These fares are priced midway between APEX and full fare economy class. There are no advance booking requirements, but often a minimum stay abroad is mandatory. The passenger can change his booking and also stopover without surcharge. Different airlines however, have conditions on this.

### FLIGHT CREW
Term referring to pilots.

## FARE, APPLICABLE
For fare construction purposes, a fare which is established after the application of all fare construction calculations, e.g., excess mileage fare, higher intermediate fare, etc.

## FLIGHT SCHEDULE
The timetable showing all flights of an airline, and their scheduled departure and arrival times.

## FARE, SPECIAL
Any fare other than a normal fare.

## GROUP BOOKINGS
A set of rooms set-aside for groups of ten or more people and negotiated at special price. This negotiated price is lower than the normal price.

## GROUP, ASPIRATIONAL
A group to which a person wishes to belong.

## GUARANTEE
Hold status of reservation, prepaid either by a cash deposit or credit/debit card number.

## GATEWAY
First point of arrival/last point of departure in a country/area.

## GLOBAL DISTRIBUTION SYSTEM (GDS)
The mean by which airlines offer for sale (distribute) their seats through computer terminals situated in travel and other airline offices throughout the world. Often referred to as computer reservation systems. Users may access a number of intermediary host systems to reserve airline seats, book car hire, or hotel accommodation. Several airlines have grouped together to form the host systems such as Amadeus, Galileo, Sabre, Apollo and Worldspan.

## GATEWAY CITY
City airport serving the passenger as an entry or departure point in a foreign country.

## GV 10
This is a group ticket for 10 people travelling together. A discount fare originally created for tour operators. It is now widely used by airlines to conceal discounting to individuals.

## GROUND ARRANGEMENTS
All services for the traveller by the tour operator after the traveller reaches his first foreign destination. Also referred to as land arrangements.

## GRATUITIES
The passenger's personal expression of thanks (tips) to the ship's service personnel for services received.

## GROUP INCLUSIVE TOUR (GIT)
A tour which includes air and ground arrangements for a minimum of

15 persons. They may or may not stay together as a group for both the land and air portion of the trip.

**GO-SHOW**
A passenger who shows up for a flight without a reservation.

**GUARANTEED TOUR**
A tour which is guaranteed to operate unless cancelled 60 days prior to departure. In the event of cancellation within 60 days of the departure date, full commission is paid to agents of sold clients.

**GUIDE**
A person who is licensed to take paying guests on local sightseeing excursions.

**GUIDED TOUR**
A tour conducted only by local city guilds.

**GUARANTEED PAYMENT RESERVATION**
Payment for a room is guaranteed and will be paid for by a company or organization whether it is used or not.

**GLOBAL POSITIONING SYSTEM (GPS)**
The use of satellites to convey the positions of airplanes to air traffic controllers.

**HOSTED TOUR**
A tour where participants have an opportunity to travel independently, but also to receive guidance and assistance from a host at each of the tour's destinations.

**HALF BOARD**
Includes two full meals per day; also known as MAP (Modified American Plan) as part of the price of a hotel room.

**HIGH SEASON**
Time of year when tourist traffic and rates are usually the highest because demand is highest. Horizontal diversification strategy. A product growth strategy whereby a company looks for new products that could appeal to current customers, which are technologically unrelated to its current line.

**IATA RATE OF EXCHANGE (OR IROE)**
Rates of exchange notified by IATA to convert local currency fare to NUC and to convert total NUC amounts to the currency of the country of commencement of transportation.

**ITX**
"Independent Inclusive Tour Excursion" fares. This is available to the public ostensibly, only as a component of holiday package which also includes hotel accommodation and/or car hire.

**INDEPENDENT TOUR**
A tour where participants travel independently without an accompanying group or tour guide.

## ITINERARY
Pertaining to journey. A tourist itinerary is a composition of series of operations that are a result of the study of the market. A tourist itinerary follows a set pattern and there is no scope for deviation. A paper document issued to customers with flight reservations and all booked flight details.

## INTERNATIONAL, CARRIAGE
Carriage in which according to the contract of carriage, the place of departure, and any place of landing are situated in more than one nation. As used in this definition, the term national includes all territory subject to the sovereignty, mandate, authority or trust ship thereof.

## INDEPENDENT TRAVEL, DOMESTIC
A tour constructed to meet the specific desire of a client within a single country.

## INDIRECT ROUTE
Any scheduled continuous air route other than a direct route.

## INDUSTRY RATES
Rate for employees within the travel industry including those of airlines, hotels, travel agencies, tour operators, wholesale packagers.

## INCENTIVE TRAVEL
A reward participants receive for achieving or exceeding a goal.

## ITINERARY, SUGGESTED
A preliminary itinerary provided by tour operations for the travellers consideration. This itinerary generally shows routing and approximate times as well as recommended hotels and suggested sight-seeing excursions, and spells out the conditions under which these services will be provided.

## INBOUND TOURISM
From the point of view of a destination, this describes the tourists who arrive from another country. It is therefore, a form of international tourism contributing to the economy of the receiving nation.

## INCENTIVE TRAVEL
Travel and tourism products such as all-inclusive holidays given as reward to the employees for achievement or incentive to reach targets in business.

## ISSUING AIRLINE
TC Member whose tickets are issued to the passengers.

## ISSUING CARRIER
Airline whose ticket is issued or in whose name a ticket is issued.

## IMMIGRATION
Official point of entry to a country, where the visas and passports of crew and passengers are checked.

## IMMIGRATION AUTHORITY
Agency that monitors persons entering or leaving the country by validating appropriate documentation to allow entry to the country or to forbid

entry to the country. The immigration authority has the right to forbid entry into the country because of missing documentation or because the person is a possible threat. In some countries, immigration is a separate agency from customs.

### INTERLINE
When a passenger travels and connects to a different airline to reach a destination.

### INTERLINE TRANSFER
Transfer from the service of one carrier to the service of another carrier.

### LOST DOCUMENT
An Accountable Traffic Document which is no longer in the possession of its lawful custodian without having been identified as stolen.

### LOWER BED
A single bed placed at the conventional height from the floor.

### LEISURE TOURISM
Tourism or travel for pleasure and relaxation as opposed to business. It can take place at home (domestic) or abroad (international) and for a variety of reasons.

### LEAKAGES
Money that leaves the local economy because it is used for taxation or the purchase of goods and services from outside the region. Leakages are used in calculations of the tourism income multiplier effect.

### LINERS
Regular scheduled voyages on a set route on the sea or called 'Line voyages' and vessels (passenger or cargo) trading on these routes to a timetable are called liners. In older usages 'liner' also referred to ships of the line, i.e., line of-battle ship. This usage is now rare. Today, the term refers to a ship that is constructed to higher standard then a normal cruise ship, enabling it to cross oceans such as Atlantic and Pacific with passengers, in inclement weather conditions.

### LANDING
When an aircraft touches down on the runway after a flight or returns to the ground.

### LAYOVER
To a passenger this term refers to the time between flights at an airport. To an airline cabin crew this term refers to the time they are off duty at a city other than their domicile. With regard to crew, a layover period is the amount of time that separates two on-duty periods within a pattern or assignment. The layover station or city refers to the actual location of where the crew is off-duty for their rest period. For example, if a cabin crew arrives in Paris at 1800 and departs the next day at 2100, the layover period is 27 hours and the layover station is Paris.

## MISCELLANEOUS CHARGE ORDER (MCO)

A voucher exchange with any IATA airline for flights, excess baggage etc. Instead of issuing an executive with a first class ticket, a company issues him with an MCO for the equivalent value. He flies to his business appointment economy class and later uses the remaining value of his vouchers to pay his holiday flights. MCO is a document issued by a travel agent for collecting money for the services which are related to air travel but of a nature which cannot be covered by an air ticket.

## MAXIMUM PERMITTED MILEAGE

This refers to the full fare paying passenger's right not to proceed directly from his place of origin to his destination but to stop over and vary his route by 20 percent of the minimum mileage without any surcharge.

## MANIFEST

A list or invoice of a ship's passengers, crew and cargo.

## MOTORCOACH TOUR

A tour that utilises motor coaches or buses to move tourists from one destination to another and to visit sightseeing attractions along the way. This type of tour gives ample opportunity for observing country/city sights.

## NO SHOW

The status of reservation when the guest does not arrive by the check in deadline. Also a passenger holding a flight reservation who fails to use it and cancel it prior to the flight departure.

## NON-SCHEDULED FLIGHTS

Typically charter flights for travellers who want to hire a plane to fly to a specific place at a specific time.

## NET RATE

A Wholesale Rate.

## NEUTRAL TICKET

The form of ticket for use by travel agents not bearing any preprinted individual airline identity.

## NEW RECEIVING CARRIER

Means a new carrying airlines selected for onward carriage by the forwarding carrier from the point where involuntary change of routing becomes necessary.

## NORMAL FARE

A fare established for intermediate, first or economy class service and any other fare denominated and published as a normal fare (e.g. C2, F2, Y2). Children's fares and infants' fares which are established as a percentage of the fares referred to above, are also considered to be normal fares.

## NEUTRAL UNIT OF CONSTRUCTION (NUC)

Unit of common international value, such as a currency, established by IATA to calculate international air fares and charges.

## OCCUPANCY
Room occupancy from the agents perspective, is the rate charged per person. It may be charged as a single or double (e.g., single occupancy, double occupancy, etc.). From the hotels' perspective, occupancy means the number of guests the hotel is accommodating on any given night (e.g., 80% occupancy of a 400 room hotel would be 320 rooms sold).

## ONE WAY SUBJOURNEY
Part of a journey wherein travel from one country does not return to such country and for which the fare is assessed as a single pricing unit using a one way fare.

## ON REQUEST
Refers to the status of a seat request. (i.e., not yet confirmed).

## OVERBOOKING
The practice of booking more rooms than the hotel's capacity of rooms by a hotel in anticipation of cancellations or no shows.

## OUTBOUND TOURISM
International tourism seen from the point of view of the originating country. Outbound tourism is a form of importation of services from abroad and has a negative effect on that country's tourism account.

## OPEN TICKET
A ticket which has been issued for a particular journey but on which a specific date has yet to be entered.

## OCCUPANCY, SINGLE
Sole occupancy of a cabin that is designed to accommodate two or more passengers, in which instance a premium is ordinarily charged.

## OPEN SEATING
Free access to unoccupied tables in the ship's dining room, as opposed to specific table assignments.

## ONLINE TRANSFER
Transfer from the service of one carrier to another service of the same carrier.

## ORDER, EXCHANGE
A document issued by a carrier or its agents requesting issue of an appropriate ticket or provision of services to the person named in such document.

## POINT-TO-POINT
Favoured by the trans-Atlantic carriers and those on the Hongkong/ London and Australia rates. It offers a discount on the full fare return for the passenger sacrificing rights to stop over and utilise the maximum permitted mileage.

## PASSENGER, NON REVENUE
A person travelling on a free or service charge only ticket. Airline employees travelling as part of their benefits are referred to as non-revs or pass riders

## PASSENGER
Any person, except members of the crew, carried or to be carried in an aircraft with the consent of the carrier.

## PASSENGER TRANSFER
A passenger arriving on a flight and continuing his journey on another.

## PASSENGER TRANSIT
A passenger continuing his journey in the same through flight.

## PASSENGER NAME RECORD (PNR)
A record of each passenger's travel requirements which contain all information necessary to enable reservations to be processed and controlled by the booking airline and the airline(s) participating in the carriage.

## PASSENGER (PAX)
Person travelling is often referred to, in shortened form, as PAX.

## PASSENGER LOAD
Total number of passengers on the aircraft.

## PREPAID TICKET ADVISE (PTA)
PTA is the name given to the document asking a carrier to issue a ticket in favour of a person beginning his journey in a place other than that where payment was made.

## PARTICIPATING CARRIER
Means a carrier over whose routes one or more sections of carriage under the ticket is undertaken or performed

## PLAN, CONTINENTAL
Daily hotel rate which includes accommodation and breakfast.

## PACKAGE
An inclusive set of products or services designed to attract the leisure traveller. It normally includes all the elements of travel like transport, accommodation, meals, sightseeing etc.

## PACKAGE RATES
Negotiated with wholesalers who book large volume business.

## PASSPORT
A formal document issued by a government, that identifies the holder as a national or citizen of that country. This document allows the holder to enter and pass through other countries at the request of the issuing country. It allows for legal protection abroad and the right to enter the person's country of nationality. It contains the holder's photograph, signature, date of birth and nationality. Over time, the League of Nations, United Nations and ICAO have issued guidelines of standardisation for the layouts and the features of passports. These are seen in the passports of today.

## PURSER
The person who is in charge of the cabin crew. Some airlines refer to this position as Lead or 1 or Senior Flight Attendant. The purser is responsible

for coordinating the crew and their duties, completion of paperwork and international customs documents. Often this position requires additional training or qualification by an airline including service, conflict resolution and company procedures and other management skills.

## PARTICIPATING CARRIER
The carrier over whose routes one or more sections of carriage under the airway bill or ticket is undertaken or performed.

## PASS, BOARDING
Boarding pass or a boarding card indicates the name, class, flight number, seat number allocated to a passenger. This is normally issued at the check-in counter in exchange for passenger ticket coupon.

## RE-BOOKING
Change of reservation or other changes which do not require ticket reissuance.

## REFUND
The repayment to the purchaser of all or portion of a fare or change for unused carriage or service.

## RATE, CORPORATE
Rates typically offered to the business travellers ranging from 20-30% off rack rate.

## RESORT RATES
These rates can fluctuate based on advance payment, deposits, season or individual property agreements.

## REROUTING
With respect to a passenger, means a change of route, fare, carrier, type of aircraft, class of service, flight or validity from that originally provided in the appropriate transportation document.

## ROUND TRIP
A Round trip (RT) is travel entirely by air from a point to another point and return to the point of origin comprising two half round trip fare components only, for which the applicable half round trip for each component, measured from the point of unit origin is the same for the routing travelled.

## ROUND THE WORLD
Travel from a point and return thereto which involves only one crossing of the Atlantic Ocean and only one crossing of the Pacific Ocean.

## ROOM BLOCK
A group of rooms or meeting space usually reserved through travel agents or wholesalers. These are held with a deposit.

## ROOM NIGHT
One overnight stay per person per room, i.e., two persons in one room for one night = two room nights.

## ROOM SERVICE
Food and beverages served in the sleeping rooms of the guests.

## REVALIDATION
Authorised stamping or writing upon the passenger ticket evidencing that it has been officially altered by the carrier.

## RETURN SUBJOURNEY
Part of a journey wherein travel is from a point/country and return thereto and for which the fare is assessed as a single pricing unit, using half-RT fares: RT/CT/NOJ and special fare OJ returning to the same or another country.

## SPECIAL FARE
Any fare other than a normal fare.

## SEASONAL RATES
Variations in prices for the same service, depending upon the time of the year.

## SHOULDER SEASON
Time of the year between the high and off-season during which intermediate fares are applied.

## SEASON
A consistent pattern of sales movements within the year.

## SINGLE ROOM
A room designed for one person; some rooms will have only one single bed while most will have twin beds.

## SITA
A global communication network set up to handle interairline message transmission in Europe; the USA system is known as the AIRINC network.

## STAND-BY
A passenger who does not hold a confirmed reservation, but waits at the airport ready to undertake a journey, if a seat may be made available at the last minute.

## SUGGESTED ITINERARY
A preliminary itinerary provided by tour operations for the travellers' consideration. This itinerary generally shows routing and approximate times as well as recommended hotels and suggested sight seeing excursions, and spells out the conditions under which these services will be provided.

## SCHENGEN VISA
The word Schengan originates from a small town in Luxembourg. In the year 1985, Seven European Union Countries signed a treaty to end internal border check points and controls. Later, more countries joined and currently there are 24. Alphabetically Austria, Belgium, Czech Republic, Denmark, Estonia, Finland, France, Greece, Hungary, Iceland, Italy, Latvia, Lithuania, Luxembourg, Malta, Netherlands, Norway, Poland, Portugal,

Slovakia, Slovenia, Spain, Sweden. All the countries except Norway and Iceland are members of European Union.

## SUITE
Consists of two or more rooms, typically a living and sleeping room. A suite may have more than one bedroom or extra rooms such as kitchenette or conference room.

## SIDELINE CITY
To city in the fares list.

## SIDE TRIP
Travel from and/or to an enroute point of a fare component.

## STAGE, DECLINE
The product-life-cycle stage when a product's sales decline.

## SEGMENTATION, DEMOGRAPHIC
Dividing the market into groups based on demographic variables such as age, gender, family size, family life cycle, income, occupation, education, religion, race, and nationality.

## SCHEDULED FLIGHT
An air transport service that operates according to a pre-planned timetable on a specified licensed routes. The services are to operate regardless of number of passengers booked.

## SERVICES, COMPLIMENTARY
Services that accompany a core product and support its acquisition usage and/or disposition.

## TRANSFER
The service provided to travellers from the time they arrive in a destination until they depart a given city. The service would include - taking them from airport, air terminal, pier, railway station or bus terminal to their hotel and vice versa, generally accompanied by the local representative of the other operator who planned and organise the tour.

## TOURIST VISA
A document issued or endorsed on a passport under the authority of the government to a person visiting a particular country as a tourist.

## TERMINAL
Area at an airport where the formalities for departing and arriving passengers take place.

## TOURIST CENTRE
A village or town with a definite concentration of tourist resources, material base and infrastructure of tourism development.

## TOURIST CHARTER
A flight booked exclusively for the use of a specific group of tourists who generally belong to the same organisation or who are being 'treated' to the flight by a single host.

## TAX
Charge levied on transportation documents or hotel bills.

## THROUGH FARE
A fare applicable for travel between two consecutive fare construction points via an intermediate point(s).

## TICKET ON DEPARTURE (TOD)
A procedure by which a travel agent makes special arrangements for a passenger's ticket to be issued by airlines staff at the departure airport.

## TOURISM ACCOUNT
The way in which a country records the income from tourist arrivals and the expenditure by its own nationals on overseas tourism. The difference between these two accounts is known as the tourism balance.

## TOUR, MOTORCOACH
A tour that utilises motor coaches or buses to move tourists from one destination to another and to visit sight seeing attractions along the way. This type of tour gives ample opportunity for observing country/city sights.

## TOUR, CONDUCTED
A prepaid, prearranged vacation in which a group of people travel together under the guidance of a tour leader who stays with them from the start to the end of the trip. Also referred to as an "escorted tour".

## TRANSFER, CARGO
Cargo arriving at a point by one flight and continuing its journey by another flight of the same or a connecting carrier

## TRAFFIC DOCUMENT
Value documents issued manually, mechanically or electronically for air passenger transportation over the lines of the airline and for related services, whether or not they bear a pre-printed individual airline identification.

## TRANSFER, ONLINE
Transfer from the service of one carrier to another service of the same carrier.

## TRAFFIC DOCUMENT, ACCOUNTABLE
Paper value ticket, a miscellaneous charges order, a multiple purpose document whether issued or blank (excluding electronic formats).

## TRAFFIC DOCUMENT, STANDARD
A neutral BSP ticket, a miscellaneous charges order, a multiple purpose document whether issued or blank.

## TARIFF
The published fares, rates, charges and or related conditions of carriage of a carrier.

## TICKET
A document representing the contract of carriage concluded between the arriver and the passenger as well as the passenger's receipt for the money paid.

### TRANSFER, INTERLINE
Transfer from the service of one carrier to the service of another carrier.

### TICKETED POINT MILEAGE (TPM)
Distance between pairs of points published in the TPM manual using nonstop sector mileage.

### TICKETED POINT
Points shown in the 'good for passage' section of the passenger ticket.

### TOUR BASING FARE
A reduced round trip fare available on specified dates, and between specified times, only to those passengers who purchase preplanned, prepaid tour arrangements from an agent prior to their departure.

### TRANSFERS
Any mode of transport that shuttles participants from their point of arrival, frequently an airport, to their first accommodation, typically a hotel.

### TRANSFER, PASSENGER
A passenger arriving on the flight and continuing his journey on another.

### THROUGH PASSENGER
A person continuing on through an intermediate stop to a further destination.

### TOTAL CUSTOMER COST
The costs to a customer include money, time, energy, and psychic costs.

### TOTAL CUSTOMER VALUE
A customer derives value from the core products, the service delivery system, and the company's image. These components make up total customer value.

### TERMINAL
Part of the airport which is divided into arrival and departure sections. These sections can be superimposed on top of one another, if it is a multi-story terminal, or are located at their ends of the terminal building, if it is not. These are the general public access areas and, in more modern international airports, they also provide amenities such as stores, bars, restaurants, and banks or currency exchange services and travel insurance vendors.

### TERMINAL CONTROL AREA
A block of airspace of cylindrical or irregular shape, located at intersections of several airways, and typically situated at high-density traffic areas near one or more busy airports. The block extends from at least 200 m above the ground to an altitude determined by local traffic conditions and by the airspace structure above it. Its lateral dimensions depend on the amount and density of traffic to be handled.

### UPGRADE
To move up to a higher standard of accommodation at little cost or on a complimentary basis.

## UNACCOMPANIED MINOR (UM)
A child, up to the age of 12, who travels alone, not accompanied by an adult.

## UNIT DESTINATION
The ultimate stopping place of a pricing unit.

## UNIT ORIGIN
The initial starting point of a pricing unit.

## VARIABLE COSTS
All expenses that change according to the number of clients who take a tour.

## VOUCHERS
Documents issued by the tour operators in exchange for which travellers receive pre-paid accommodation meals, sightseeing trips, etc. Also referred to as coupons.

## VISA, TRANSIT
An endorsement on a passport which is issued to a tourist whose destination is somewhere else and is passing through. Such visitors passing through a country en-route to some other destinations are granted transit visa on production of a through ticket for the onward journey.

## VOUCHER, EXCHANGE
A document issued by a carrier or its agents requesting issue of an appropriate passenger ticket and baggage check or provision of services to the person names in such document.

## VISA, TOURIST
A document issued or endorsed on a passport under the authority of the Government to a person visiting a particular country as a tourist.

## VISITOR, TRANSIT
A visitor who is passing over or through a country en route to some other destination. Unlike destination tourist, he spends limited time and visits few places of tourist interest.

## VISITOR
Any person visiting a country other than that in which he has his usual place of residence, for any reason other than following an occupation remunerated from within the country visited.

## VISITOR PLANT
All accommodation, transport, etc., points of interest in a destination area.

## VISA
Visitor's intention to stay abroad. An endorsement on the passport issued by the representative of a government. The endorsement enables a person to travel to a country for which it is issued.

## VISA, ENTRY
An endorsement on passport issued to a person who wishes to visit a country for purposes of business, employment, permanent residence,

profession etc. Initially issued for a period of three months these are extendable to a further period of three months.

### VISA, TOURIST
An endorsement on a passport issued to a person who wishes to visit a country as a tourist. The visa is effective for a period of three months. Tourists must arrive within six months of the date of issue of visa. The tourist can extend his stay for a further period of three months if he applies to the concerned authorities.

### VISITING FRIENDS AND RELATIVE (VFR)
A form of tourism in which the main motivation is those stay with or near one's friends or relatives.

### WHOLESALER
A supplier who sells packages through travel agents. A firm primarily engaged in wholesaling activity.

### WHOLESALING
All activities involved in selling goods and services to those buying for resale or business use.

### YIELD MANAGEMENT
A pricing method using price as a means of matching capacity with demand. The goal of yield management is to optimise the yield or contribution margin.

### YAW
The movement of the plane as its nose turns left or right.

### YIELD
Average revenue received for carrying one passenger one kilometre. To calculate yield for a given flight, divide passenger revenue for that flight by total Revenue Passenger Kilometres (RPKs).

# Hospitality Industry Terms

**À la carté**: A menu from which items are chosen and paid for individually. This type of meal arrangement is hardly ever included in any tour.

**American Plan**: Hotel accommodation with three meals daily included in the price of the room.

Meals are usually "table d'hote".

Sometimes referred to as "full pension", especially in Europe.

**Bungalow**: Individual house or cabin having one or more bedrooms separate from the main building of a resort hotel.

**Commercial Hotel**: Establishment catering to individuals on business and for tourists staying for a short time. This provides a comfortable sleeping accommodation and meal service, ranging from modest rooms and a coffee shop to elegant suites and a first-class speciality restaurant. This also includes additional facilities such as a conference room, a banquet hall, business centre, etc. In big cities these hotels are generally located near the business districts or in the centre of the city.

**Continental Breakfast**: This generally consists of a beverage (coffee, tea, cocoa or milk), plus rolls, butter and jam or marmalade.

**Couchettes**: Sleeping accommodation provided on some European railroads, consisting of a day compartment which may be converted into bunks for 4 (1st class) or 6 (2nd class) passengers. Pillows and blankets are provided.

**Coupons**: Documents issued by tour operator in exchange for which travellers receive pre-paid accommodation, meals, sightseeing trips, excursions, etc. Also referred to as Vouchers or Exchange orders.

**Check-in**: The term refers to registration formalities to be completed by a guest on arrival at the hotel. Guests have to sign a hotel registration card. In some countries guests may have to deposit their passport at the reception. The check-in time generally is, 1200 hours. The check-in deadline is generally 1800 hours.

**Check-out**: These refers to departure formalities before leaving the hotel. The check-out time is the hour at which the room must be vacated by the guest.

**Continental Plan**: Daily hotel rate which includes accommodation and breakfast.

**Day Rate**: This is a special rate for use of hotel rooms during daytime which is approximately from 08.00 to 18.00 hours.

**Deluxe Hotel**: These establishments are of the finest category. The rooms in these establishments are spacious with private bathrooms, toilet, television, telephone. Full service is available including restaurant, bar, laundry, hairdresser, coffee shop etc.

**English Breakfast**: This type of breakfast is generally served in Great Britain. It usually includes hot or cold cereal, bacon or ham and eggs, toast, butter, jam or marmalade and beverage (though not juice).

**European Plan**: Hotel accommodation with no meals whatsoever included in the cost of the room.

**Exchange Orders**: See "Coupons".

**First Class Hotel**: This establishment is of superior category where rooms are provided with telephone, private bathrooms and toilet. Restaurants and laundry services are available.

**Full Board**: Daily hotel rate which includes guest accommodation plus three meals.

**Full Pension**: See "American Plan".

**Garni**: When appended to the name of a hotel, this means that the establishment does not have a restaurant or dining room. Such hotels usually have a breakfast room.

**Garni Hotel**: These are establishments which do not have restaurant facilities. Such hotels, however, serve continental breakfast to their guests.

**Half Board**: Daily hotel rate which includes accommodation plus breakfast and one additional meal (either lunch or breakfast).

**Half Pension**: Hotel accommodation which includes continental breakfast and either table d'hote lunch or dinner in the price of the room. Also referred to as "Modified American Plan".

**Hospitality Suite**: A special room in a hotel used exclusively for entertainment of participants at a business meeting or convention.

**Hotelier**: A person, firm or corporation which provides hotel accommodation and/or meals, refreshments, etc., to visitors.

**Junior Suite**: A large room with a partition separating the bedroom from the sitting room.

**Motel**: A place which provides wayside amenities for tourists travelling by road, by automobile. A motel provides, under one roof, all usual facilities expected by the tourist including attached bath.

**Motorcoach Hire**: A motorcoach hired by a party. The basic conditions of hire are usually the same as for private cars, but take into consideration the seating capacity of the vehicle.

**Optional**: Means that clients have a choice of taking or not taking the service mentioned. If they take it, there is always an additional charge which is not included in the basic tour price.

**Pension**: A French word, widely used in Europe, meaning guest house or boarding house.

**Resort Hotel**: In addition to the facilities provided in the city hotels, resort hotels provide attractions such as swimming pools, private beaches, sport facilities like tennis courts and other outdoor and indoor recreational facilities. These are situated in areas of scenic beauty, sightseeing attractions or in the surroundings, providing entertainment opportunities. These could be of various types like beach resorts, health resorts, winter resorts, etc.

**Service Charges**: These are a percentage of guest hotel bill and are generally between 10 per cent and 15 per cent assessed as tips (gratuities) to the hotel staff for the services.

**Sleepers**: Sleeping cars consisting of a private bedroom with accommodation for one or two persons. Pillow, sheets and blankets are included.

**Suite**: A set of rooms comprising a living room connected to one or more bedrooms. A suite may have more than one entrance.

**Supplementary Accommodation**: Various types of accommodation units other than the conventional hotel type. It includes accommodation for travellers in motels, youth hostels, camping sites, etc.

**Table d'hote**: A complete menu deviations from which involve additional charges. This is the type of meal which will generally be provided when meals have been included in the price of the tour. In Europe, table d'hote menus hardly ever include coffee or tea after the meal (these are considered "Extra").

**Tips**: Gratuities to hotel employees, porters, guides, etc. In a few countries tipping is not allowed.

**Tourist Hotel**: These hotels are in a lower price range. Rooms available are simple and plain. Bathrooms and toilets are common and are usually located on each floor.

**Tourist Lodge**: A small house providing temporary accommodation to a tourist. The accommodation provided is inexpensive as compared to conventional hotel. The lodge also offers meals.

**Transfer**: The service provided for the travellers when they arrive and leave a given city, which takes them from the airport, air terminal, pier or railway station to their hotel and vice versa, accompanied by a representative of the local agency. The cost depends on whether transfers are carried out by a private car or a taxi, and also on the distance between the airport, or air terminal, or station and hotel. Porterage of two pieces of hand luggage is included.

**Vouchers**: See "Coupons".

**Youth Hostel**: A building which offers clean, simple and inexpensive shelter to young people exploring their own country or the world, travelling independently or in groups for a holiday or educational purposes.

# Travel Trade Publications

The travel industry has a wide assortment of publications that are designed to keep travel professionals up-to-date with the news of the industry. There is a large selection of travel trade papers providing invaluable service for the industry. A large number of weekly, monthly and quarterly journals are published all over the world, serving the needs of those working in the tourism industry.

Most of the publications are designed purely for news coverage. They cover topical news both of social and commercial events. Publications such as *Travel Weekly* published in United States, *TTG*, published simultaneously in UK and Asia, and *Pacific Travel News* published in New Zealand are essentially the newspapers to keep travel agents, tour operators and other travel personnel up-to-date on the latest changing travel scene. These publications fulfil the very important function of informing the right kind of people about the latest in travel industry.

On the other hand, there are publications which are designed to bring detailed information on destination areas and the travel opportunities that exist in various destinations. An example of this is PATA's publication, *Pacific Travel News* and *Travel Trade Asia* published from Hong Kong. Both these publications devote most of their pages to well researched feature stories which provide all the information on a particular destination. The information is complete enough to enable a travel agent to use it as an aid in selling to a client going to a destination and also as an aid in planning an itinerary. Specially designed and prepared multicoloured 'pullouts' on various destinations are special features of such a magazine.

In addition to the general interest travel trade publications, there are a good number of special interest travel trade publications such as conventions and conferences, incentive travel, etc. An example of these is *Incentive Travel, International Conference and Convention, Travel and Travel Management Newsletter*. These special interest publications give detailed information about special events and are quite useful for travel planners.

Another type of service performed by the travel industry press comes in the form of 'Directories' such as *Pacific Hotel Directory, IHA International Hotel Guide, Hotels and Restaurants International*, which comes out at regular intervals and lists all the hotels in all the countries of the world. There are other directories available on other types of information such as lists of travel industry personnel in various categories of industry, in airlines, tour operating companies, steamship companies, etc. *The World Directory of Travel Agents* is yet another important publication which lists travel agencies, tour operators, the travel basics for various countries, the world calendar of events, etc. *The WATA Master-Key,* published every year, is yet another example of valuable publication for use by the travel industry.

The other way that the travel industry publications provide information is through the advertisements that they carry. The hotels, tour operators, airlines and shipping companies use the travel industry press to sell their products, and very often the travel agents will receive the first word about a new product by way of the pages of the travel industry publications which he subscribes and reads. Similarly the airlines use the travel magazines to tell about their new equipments of new routes or increased schedule or new services.

In short, travel trade publications provided the travel industry with a means of continuing information, of keeping up with the sales trends in a fast moving and changing industry. In an industry as fast changing as tourism, employees can only update their knowledge of travel products by regularly subscribing and reading the travel trade press. The newspapers complement the work of the training bodies in providing the latest news, and for untrained travel agency staff they may well be the main source of such knowledge as well as being a forum for trade advertising and job opportunities.

## Data Sources for Travel Tourism

The need for identifying the various data sources in the field of tourism has assumed a greater importance in the recent past. The data sources are very crucial as these help the practitioners of the tourism field to properly know at a glance the trends in tourism fashions, the markets and their requirements as also for planning and promotion. Over the past few decades there has been a multiplicity of these sources. The sources of information available today on travel and tourism have mushroomed and continue to grow with the growth in tourism activity all over the world.

Not only have the sources of information multiplied in volume, these have multiplied in range also. The wide range of data incorporate information on accommodation units; travel agencies and tour operations; transportation; recreation; research studies; books, periodicals, journals; tourist statistics; regional tourism developments; employment; marketing trends and projections, etc. In fact, there is hardly a single tourism activity on which information is not available.

Together with the volume and range of information available on travel and tourism, the sources of information have also multiplied. There are a wide range of sources from where the information is made available. These include both private and government sources, travel agencies and tour operators, airline companies, travel trade journals, reports and research studies. International organisations dealing with tourism and allied areas are yet another important source of information. National tourist organisations of various countries contribute a great deal of material. Trade and professional associations are yet another source. Bibliographies, yearbooks and handbooks published regularly are another important source of such information. Added to these are individual authors and writers of books whose compilations are good sources of information.

The range, volume and type of information on travel and tourism are, however, not available at one place. There is a great need for the development of a comprehensive list of volume, the range and sources of information available on tourism so that the same could be gainfully utilised by all concerned. The travel industry executives, officials working both in government and private sectors, international organisations, academicians as also the students of the subject do require the above information and there is, therefore, a great need for providing the same to them. Such information can be gainfully used in not only analysing but also solving travel industry problems.

An attempt has been made in this book to compile a comprehensive list of data sources available on travel and tourism. The list broadly includes the following:

i) travel trade journals and periodicals

ii) bibliographies

iii) trade and professional associations

iv) international tourism organisations

v) research journals.

This list, however, is not comprehensive. There may be some sources which are left out due to non-availability of information. While selecting sources of information, efforts have been made to emphasise on the relevant data. The list has also been kept rather brief to enable the user to use it gainfully rather than discard the same.

# International Tourism Periodicals

*Asia Travel Trade* : Interasia Publications Ltd., 200 Lockhart Road, 13th Floor, Hong Kong.

*Asia Travel News* : American Society of Travel Agents, 488 Madison Avenue, New York, N.Y. 10022, USA.

*Asian Hotelkeeper and Catering Times* : Media Transasia 3/F Sarasin Building 14, Surasat Road, Bangkok, Thailand.

*British Travel News* : British Travel News, 239 Old Marylebone Road, London N.W.I., England.

*Canada Tourism News* : Canadian Govt. Office of Tourism, Ottawa, Canada KIA OH6.

*Canadian Travel Courier* : 481 University Avenue, Toronto, Ontario, Canada.

*Canadian Travel News* : 1450 Don Mills Road, Ontario, Canada.

*Congressi* : Centro International dei Congress Palazzo dei Congressi, Firenze, Italy.

*Digest of Tourist Statistics* : British Tourist Authority, London, England.

*Far East Traveller* : 1350 Avenue of the Americas, New, York, USA.

*Far East Traveller* : 28-4-1, Motoasabu, Minato-ku, Tokyo, Japan.

*Future Tourist* : P. O. Box 138, Balmain, Sydney, Australia 2041.

*Gourmet* : Gourmet Incorporated, 777 Third Avenue, New York, N.Y. 10017, USA.

*Hungarian Travel* : Hungarian Tourism Board, P.O. Box 223 H-1906, Budapest, Hungary.

*In Britain*: British Tourist Authority, 64 St. James' St., London SWIA, England.

*Incentive Travel Manager* : Barrington Publication Inc; 825 South Barrington Avenue, Los Angeles, California 90049 USA.

*Index* : Centro Per La Statistica Aziendale, Via A, Baldes, 20, 50131 Firenze, Italy.

*International Tourist Quarterly* : The Economist Intelligence Unit Ltd., Spencer House, 27 St. James' Place, London SWI, England.

*Journal of Leisure Research* : US Department of Commerce, Washington D.C., USA.

*Journal of Travel Research* : Business Research Division, University of Colorado, Colorado, USA.

*Look East* : Ruang Seang Publishing Ltd. Partnership 987-989- New Road, Bangkok, Thailand.

*Marco Polo* : Cathay Pacific Airways, 17 Thomson Road, 13th Floor Hong Kong.

*National Geographic* : National Geographic Incorporated, (2) Century Plaza, 2049, Century Park East, Los Angeles, California, USA.

*Orientations* : Pacific Magazines Ltd. 13th Floor, 200 Lockhart Road, Hong Kong.

*Pacific* : Fuji Incorporated, Ginza Chuo Building, 1-20, Tsukiji, 4-Chome, Chuo-ku, Tokyo, Japan.

*Pacific Magazine* : Pacific Magazine Emphasis Inc. Central Roppongi Building, 1-4-27 Roppongi, Minato-ku, Tokyo, Japan.

*Pacific Travel* : Pacific Asia Travel Association, 274 Brannan St., San Francisco, California, 94107, USA.

*Pacific Travel News* : Pacific Asia Travel Association, 288 Avenue, San Francisco, California, 94108, USA.

*Recreation and Tourism* : SRI International, 333 Ravenswood Avenue, Melano Park, California, USA.

*Service World International* : Cahnes Publication, 55, Wabash Avenue, Chicago, 911, 60603, USA.

*Singapore Travel News* : Singapore Tourist Promotion Board, 131, Tudor Court, Tanglin Road, Singapore.

*South Asia Travel Review* : Thomson Press Hong Kong Ltd., Media Transasia, 3/F Sarasin Building, 14 Surasak Road, Bangkok, Thailand.

*Sunset* : Lane Publishing Company, 3055 Wilshire Boulevard Los Angeles, California 90010, USA.

*Tourism International* : 136, Gloucester Place, London N.W.I., England.

*Tourism International Air Letter* : Tourism International Press, 154, Cromwell Road, London SW7, England.

*Touristiques Internationale* : 40, rue du Colisee, Paris 75014, France.

*Tourist Review* : Organe official del L'Association International d'Experts Scientifiques du Turisme AIEST Case Potale 2728, 3001, Berne, Switzerland.

*Travel* : Travel Magazine, Inc; Travel Building 5 Floral Park, New York-11001, USA.

*Travel Agent* : World Travel Inc. 730 SW Fifth Avenue, Portland, Oregon, USA.

*Tourism Journal* : Asian Institute of Tourism, University of Philippines, Diliman, Quezon City 3004 Philippines.

*The Travel Agent* : American Traveller Incorporated, 2 West 46th Street, New York, NY 10036 USA.

*Travel Holiday* : Travel Magzine Incorporated, Travel Building, Flora Park, New York 10036 USA.

*Travel Holiday Inc.* P.O. Box 49692 Los Angeles, California 90049, USA.

*Travel and Leisure* : 1750 Avenue of the Americas, New York, USA.

*Travel Asia Pacific* : 306, Temple Chambers, Temple Avenue, Fleet Street, London E.C.4, England.

*Travel Journal* : Moritani Travel Enterprise, Inc., Izumiya Tokoten Building, 1,3-Chome Kojimachi, Chiyoda-Ku, Tokyo 102, Japan.

*Travel Holiday Magazine* : 51 Atlantic Avenue, Floral Park, New York, U.S.A.

*Travel Review* : Media Transasia, 3/F Sarasin Building, 14 Surasak Road,

Bangkok, Thailand.
*Travel News Asia* : Travel News Asia, 1911 Hanglung Centre, Peterson Street, Hong Kong.
*Travel Research Journal* : World Tourism Organisation, Avenida Del Generalisimo, 59, Madrid, Spain.
*Travel Trade Reporter* : Orient Pacific Enterprises Ltd., 526 Ploenchit Road, Bangkok, Thailand.
*Travel Trade Reporter* : Orient Pacific Enterprises, Penthouse Six, Aman Hotel, 526 Ploenchit Road, Bangkok, Thailand.
*Travel Journal International* : Moritani Travel Enterprise, Inc. 1, Kojimachi 3-Chome, Chiyoda-ku, Tokyo 102, Japan.
*Travel Post* : Intergroup Communications, Inc. Katigbak Building, 1000 A Mabini Street, Ermita, Manila, Philippines.
*Travel Trade Le Repertuire Des Voyages* : 40, Rue de Colisee Paris 75008, France.
*Travel Trade* : Box M-204, Sydney Mail Exchange, N.S.W. 2010, Australia.
*Travel Trade* : 605 Fifth Avenue, New York, NY:10017, USA.
*Travel Trade Gazette Europa* : 11, Blot Court, Fleet Street, London, England.
*Travel Trade Gazette* : 30 Calderwood Street, London, England
*Travel Trade Gazette Asia* : 5 B, 5th Floor, 9 Comfort Terrace, Hong Kong.
*Travel Week* : 73, Commonwealth Street, Sydney, Australia.
*Travel Management Daily* : 888 7th Avenue, 29th Floor, New York, USA.
*Travel Weekly* : 1, Park Avenue, New York, U.S.A.
*Viaggi Vacanze* : Via A. Manzoni 37 Milan, Italy.
*Voyages* : 59, Rue du Rocher, Paris 75008, France.
*Vue Touristique* : Centre International de Documentation de la F.I.J.E.T. 1060 Bruxelles, Belgium.
*World Travel* : Shimru Building, 17, Shiba, Nishikubohiramachi, Minato-ku, Tokyo, Japan.
*Hospitality and Tourism*, University of Surrey, Oxford, England.
*Leisure Recreation and Tourism*, Abstract CAB, Oxford, England.

# Travel Industry Journals

*Airlines and Aerospace*: ADPR Consult (M) Sdn Bhd, Suite 10.1 10th Floor, No. 1 Jin Sulaiman, 50000 Kuala Lumpur, Malaysia.

*Asia Travel Trade*: Interasia Publications Ltd., 200 Lokhart Road, 13th Floor, Hong Kong.

*Asta Travel News*: American Society of Travel Agents, 488 Madison Avenue, New York, N.Y.-10022, USA.

*Business Traveller*: Interasia Publications Ltd., 200 Lokhart Road, Hong Kong.

*Canadian Traveller*: Gemini Group, 53 Meadow Street, Garden City, New York-11530.

*CNN Traveller*: WTO and Highbury House Communications PLC. USA.

*Digest of Tourist Statistics*: British Tourist Authority, London, England.

*Traveller*: 1/F Beverly House, 43-107, Lockhart Road, Wanchai, Hong Kong.

*Far East Traveller*: 1350, Avenue of the American, New York, USA.

*Far East Traveller*: 28-4-1, Motoasabu, Minato-Ku, Tokyo, Japan.

*Hotel and Restaurant International*, Hotel Associates, Chaners' Publishing, Chicago, Illinois-606030, USA.

*Holiday and Business Travel*: Lyipereed Ltd., 27, Belsize Lone, Hampstead, London-0003.

*Icao Bulletin*: P.O. Box 400, Palace de L8 L' Aviation International, 1000 Sherbrooke Street, West Montreal, Quebec, Canada H3 2R2.

*Incentive Travel Manager*: Barrington Publications Inc. 825 South Barrington Avenue, Los Angeles, California 90049, USA.

*International Tourist Quarterly*: The Economist Intelligence Unit Ltd., Spencer House, 27 st., James' Place, London SWI, England.

*Journal of Leisure Research*: US Department of Commerce, Washington D.C., USA.

*Journal of Travel Research*: Business Research Division, University of Colorado, USA.

*Leisure World*: P.O. Box 58, Windsor, Ontario, Canada NGA 6N3.

*Pacific Magazine*: Pacific Magazine Emphasis Inc., Central Roppongi Building, 1-4-27 Roppongi, Minato-Ku, Tokyo, Japan.

*Pacific Travel*: Pacific Area Travel Association, 274 Brannan St., San Francisco, California, 94108, USA.

*Pacific Asia Travel News*: American Publishing Company, 4636 East Elwood Street, Suite, 5, Phoenix, USA.

*Pata Travel News Asia/Pacific*: Asian Business Press Pvt. Ltd., 17 Tractor Road, Singapore 2262.

*Recreation and Tourism*: SRI International, 333 Ravenswood Avenue, Melano Park, California, USA.

*South Asia Travel Rewiew*: Thomson Press Hong Kong Ltd., Media Transasia, 3/F Sarasin Building, 14 Surasak Road, Bangkok, Thailand.

*Tourism International*: 136, Gloucestor Place, London, N.W.I. England.

*Travel Trends*: Cross Section Publications Pvt. Ltd., F-47, Bhagat Singh Market, New Delhi-110001, India.

*Tourist Review*: Organe officel del L'Association Internationale d'Experts Scientifiques du Turisme AIEST Case Postale 2728, 3001, Berne, Switzerland.

*Travel Agent*: World Travel Inc., 730 SW Fifth Avenue, Portland, Oregon, USA.

*Travel Courier*: Bexter Publishing, 310 Dupont St. Tornoto, Ontario, Canada M5R1V0.

*Travel Reivew*: Media Transasia, 3/F Sarasin Building, 14 Surasak Road, Bangkok, Thailand.

*Travel News Asia*: Travel News Asia, 1911 Hanglung Centre, Peterson Street, Hong Kong.

*TW*: TW Tagungswirtschaft/Convention Industry, Post Box No. 101528, D-6000 Frankfurt am Maine 1 Germany.

*Traveller*: National Geographic Society, 1145 17th Street, N.W. Washington D.C. 20036, USA.

# Education and Training in Travel and Tourism

## OVERSEAS

**I. Higher Degree in Tourism**

Centre D'Etudes du Tourisme, Universite D'Aix en Provence, 3 Agenue Robert Schuman, 13-l00 Aix en Province, France.
    Doctorate of 3rd Cycle Speciality in Economy and Law of Tourism,
        Duration: 2-3 years.

The Scottish Hotel School, University of Strathclyde, Ross Hall, Crookston Road, Glasgow G 52 3NQ, United Kingdom.
    Master of Science (M.Sc.) in Tourism.
    Duration: One year.

Department of Hotel and Catering Management, University of Surrey, Guildford, Survey, United Kingdom.
    Post Graduate Diploma in Tourism with possible extension to M.Sc.
    Duration: 1-2 years.

Universita delgi Studi di Firenze, via Curtatone, Florence, Italy.
    Higher Diploma Courses
    Duration: 1-2 years.

George Washington University, Washington, D.C., USA.
    Master's Degree in Tourism Administration
    Doctor of Education with a concentration in Tourism.
    Duration : 2-4 years

University of Calgary, Canada.
    Advance Master's Degree in Tourism Administration.
    Duration : 2 years

University of Surrey, Guildford, Surrey England
    Post Graduate Diploma in Tourism.
    Duration : 1 year

University of Simon Bolivar Caracas, Venezuela
    Post graduate Courses in Tourism.
    Duration : 1 year

University of Sorbonne, Paris, France
    Post graduate courses in Tourism.
    Duration : 1 year

University of Zagreb, Yugoslavia.
    Advance Courses in Tourism Administration
    Duration : 2 years

University of Lincolnshire and Humberside UK

Bachelor of Business Administration
B.B.A. Hons. with specialisation in Tourism
Duration : 3 years

Edith Crown University, Perth, Western, Australia, E-mail : business@cowan.edu.au
Degree Course in Tourism Management
Duration : 3 years.

The Netherlands Institute of Tourism and Transport Studies, Sibeliuslaan 13 4837 CA Breda. The Netherlands
Graduate Course in Tourism Management
Duration : 4 years

Centre International De Glion, CH 1823 Glion Sur, Montreux, Switzerland
Graduate course in Hospitality and Tourism Management
Diploma Course in Hospitality and Tourism Management
Duration : 1-3 Years

## II. Diploma and Short Courses in Tourism

Department of Hotel and Catering Management, University of Surrey, Guildford, Surrey, United Kingdom.
University certificate.
Duration: 1 year.

Centre D'Etudes Superieures du Tourisme, Universite de Paris l, 13, Rue de Santeuil, Paris 5e, France.
Higher Diploma,
Duration: 1 year.

Institute Technici per il Tourismo, Via Della Badia dei Roccettini II, San Domenico di Fiesole, Florence, Italy.
Certificate of Profession.
Duration: 1 year.

Scuola International di Scienze Turistiche, Via Cavalier, d'Arpino 5/A 00197 Rome, Italy.
Post Graduate Diploma.
Duration: 1 year

Hochschule Fur Welthandel, Institut Fur Fremdenverkhresforschung, Fraz-Kleingasse 1, 1190 Vienna, Austria.
University Course in Tourism leading to the University Certificate,
Duration: 1 year.

Adelaide College of TAFE Adelaide, South Australia, Australia.
Diploma in Tourism Management,
Advanced Certificate in Tourism.
Duration : 1-2 years

University of Hawaii, School of Travel Industry Management, Honolulu Hawaii,
Advanced Course in Travel and Tourism.
Duration : 2 years

## III. Technical Courses in Tourism

Technical courses in tourism are directed at the development of technical and practical skills in tourism with the direct objective of a career in the industry. The main emphasis in these courses is on vocational orientation. The course contents are suitably structured to equip students with at least the basic techniques of practice in one or other section of the industry. These courses are below University level. In practice however, they attract students with a wide variety of educational background and qualifications.

Institute Professionale Alberghiero, Via di Tor Corbone 53, Rome, Italy.
Courses in specialist training such as agriculture, catering and tourism.
Diploma di Qualifica is awarded on completion.
Duration: Three years.

École Nationale de Commerce, 70 Boulvard Bessiers, 75017 Paris, France.
Diploma Course,
Duration: 2 years.

Lycee Technique D'Hotellerie et de Tourisme, 144 Rue de France, 06048 Nice, France.
Diploma Course
Duration : 2 years

Hosta Hotel and Tourism School, CH-1854 Leysin, Switzerland
Diploma in Travel and Tourism
Duration : 9 months

Lycee Technique D'Hotellerie et de Tourisme, 144 Rue de Lucerne, 67085 Strasbourg, France.
Diploma in Tourism
Duration : 2 years

Instituto Technici per il Turismo, Via delle Terme di Diocleziano 23, Rome, Italy.
State Diploma
Duration: 5 Years.

Provinciaal Institut Voor voedings-industrieen en Toerisme 1070 Brussel-Emile Gryzonlaan l, Anderlecht, Brussels, Belgium.
Graduate in Tourism,
Duration: 2 years.

Coloma Instituut Malines, Belgium
Diploma Course.
Duration: 2 years.

Hoger Technisch Instituut, Spoorwegstreat 12, 8200 Bruges, Belgium.
Diploma Course.
Duration: 2 years.

Institute International de Glion, 1823 Glion-sur-Montreux, Switzerland.
Diploma in Tourism.
Duration: 2 years (Full time).

Durham Technical College, Framwellgate Moor, Durham, United Kingdom.
Diploma in Travel and Tourism.
Duration: 2 years (Full time).

Henley College of Further Education, Coventry; United Kingdom.

Diploma in Tourism Studies.
Duration: 2 years (Full time).

## IV. Business Studies Courses in Tourism

Department of Hotel and Institutional Management, Sheffield Polytechnic, Pond Street Sheffield S/ 1 1 WB, United Kingdom.
Higher National Diploma in Business Studies (Tourism)
Duration: 2 years

School of Hotel Keeping and Catering, Ealing Technical College, St. Mary's Road, Ealing, London W 5 5RF, United Kingdom.
Higher National Diploma in Business Studies (Tourism)
Duration: 2 years

Faculty of Tourism, Catering and Hotel Administration, Bournemouth College of Technology, Landsdowne, Bournemouth BHI 3 JJ, United Kingdom.
Higher National Diploma in Business Studies (Tourism)
Duration: 2 years (Full time).

Fachhochschule Munchen, Studienrichtung Fremdenverkehr, Lothstrasse 34, 8 Munich 2. West Germany.
Management Studies and Business Administration with a tourism option.
Duration: 4 years:

Netherlands Wetenschappelijk Instituut Voor Toerisme en Rekreatie; Haagweg 21, Breda, Holland.
Business and Tourism Studies.
Duration: 3 years.

Blackpool Technical College, Courfled Hornby Road, Lance, United Kingdom.
Courses in Tourism Studies.
Duration: 1-2 years.

Higbury Technical College, Dovercourt Road, Gesham Portsmouth, United Kingdom.
Technical Course in Tourism
Duration: 1-3 years.

## V. Tourism Courses for Students from Developing Countries

International Centre for Advanced Technical and Vocational Training, International Labour Organisation (ILO), Palazzo del Lavore, Corso Unita D'Italia, 10127 Turin, Itlay.
Three Certificate Courses a year.
Duration: 3 months.

Institute of Tourism and Hotel Management, Salzburger Unterrichtsanstalten Fur Fremdenverkehrsberufe, Schloss Klesheim, A 5071 Siezenheim bei Salzburg, Austria.
Diploma Course.
Duration: 8 months (Full time)

Scuola Internazionale Di Scienze Turistiche, Via Cavalier d Arpino 5 A 00197 Rome, Italy.
Post graduate Course.
Duration: 7 months (Full time).

International Centre for Advanced Tourism Studies (CIEST) World Tourism Organisation (WTO) Calle Humboldt, 49, Mexico, D.F. Mexico.
Correspondence Courses on:
(i) Introduction to Tourism
(ii) Tourism Marketing
(iii) Promotion of Tourist Services
(iv) Forecasting, Distribution, Promotion
(v) Distribution and Sales of Tourist Services
Post graduate Certificate Courses.
Duration: 6-9 months.

Bournemouth College of Technology, Lansdowne, Bournemouth BHI, 3 JJ United Kingdom.
Diploma Course.
Duration: 8 months

Commissariat General au Tourisme de Belgique, Central Station, Brussels, Belgium. (The Belgian National Tourist Office).
Certificate Course
Duration: 3 months.

Deutsches Wirtschaftswissenschaftiliches Institut Fur Fremdenverkehr an der Universitat Munchen, HermannSack-Strasse 2, 8 Munich 2 West Germany.
(The courses are under the sponsorship of the German Ministry of Economic Co-operation and are conducted in association with the University of Munich).
Graduate level course.
Duration: 3 years.

**VI. Courses sponsored by the Tourist Industry.**

With a view to improving the technical skills and managerial qualities of the existing staff, the tourist industry in recent years has evolved certain training programmes: A number of courses and seminars are conceived or sponsored by the tourist industry. These include the following:

IATA Aviation Training and Development Institute, 800 Place Victoria. P. O. Box 113, Montreal, Quebec, Canada H4Z IMI E-mail : atdi@iata.org
IATA/UFTAA Courses on :
Senior Management Level Diploma
Management Level Diploma
Consultant Level Certificate
Foundation Level Certificate
The above career development courses in travel and tourism are convenient self teach, home study as also class room courses.
Duration : 3 months to 2 years.

Algemene Vakschool Voor het Reisbureaubedrif, Leidse Dreef 2 Leiderdo Holland: (A.N.V.R. Courses). The Dutch Association of Travel Agents and Tour Operators, the A.N.V.R. started the course for the initial training of prospective travel industry personnel.
Certificate Course.

Duration: 10 months.

American Hotel and Motel Association 1407, South Harrison Road, P. O. Box 1240 East Lansing, Michigan 48826 (Professional Training Courses of 3-6 months)

Universal Federation of Travel Agents Association (UFTAA) 30, Avenue Marnix 1050, Brussels, Belgium.
Professional training courses (Correspondence).
Duration : 6-12 months

American Society of Travel Agents (ASTA) 711 Fifth Avenue, New York, N.Y. 10017, USA.
Professional Training course.
Duration : 3 -12 months

International Union of Official Travel Organisations (IUOTO), Palazzo del Lavero, Corso Unita D'Italia, 10127, Turin, Italy.
General Correspondence Course.
Duration : 9 months

Courses available
- Bachelor's Degree courses
- Diploma courses
- Certificate courses
- PG Degree courses
- PG Diploma courses
- PG Certificate courses

## 1 BACHELOR'S DEGREE COURSES
- BA in Travel and Tourism Management
- BA in Hospitality, Travel and Tourism Management
- B.Sc. in Travel and Tourism Management
- BA Tourism Studies
- B.Sc. in Hospitality and Travel Management
- BBA in Travel and Tourism Management
- BBA in Hospitality and Travel Management
- BBA in Air Travel Management
- Bachelor of Tourism Studies
- Bachelor of Tourism Administration
- B.Com. Travel and Tourism Management
- BA Travel and Tourism

Duration: Bachelor's Degree programs are 3 years long (each).
Eligibility: 10+2 passed in any stream (Science, Commerce or Arts) is the minimum educational qualification required.

## 2 DIPLOMA COURSES
- Diploma in Travel and Tourism Management
- Diploma in Hospitality and Travel Management

- Diploma in Tourism Studies
- Diploma in Aviation Hospitality and Travel Management
- Diploma in Tourist Guide
- Diploma in Tourism and Ticketing
- Diploma in Airfare and Ticketing

Duration: Depending on the institute and the program, course duration could be anywhere between 1- 2 year. Some institutes are also known to offer foundation Diploma course lasting for a period of 6 months.

Eligibility: 10+2 passed in any stream (Science, Commerce or Arts) is the minimum educational qualification required.

3 CERTIFICATE COURSES

- Certificate in Travel and Tourism Management
- Certificate in Travel Management
- Certificate in Tour Guide
- Certificate in Tourism Management

Duration: Depending on the institute and the program, course duration could be anywhere between 6 months to 1 year.

Eligibility: 10th / 12th passed (depending on the criteria set by the institute).

# International Organisations

## UN ORGANISATIONS

Department of Economic and Social Affairs: (Statistical Office, Centre for Housing, Building and Planning) 1 United Nations, New York, N.Y. 10017 U.S.A.

United Nations Conference on Trade and Development (UNCTAD): Palais des Nations 1211 Geneva 10, Switzerland.

United Nations Development Programme (UNDP): 1 United Nations Plaza New York, N.Y. 10017 U.S.A.

United Nations Environment Programme (UNEP): C.P. 30552 Nairobi, Kenya.

## UN ECONOMIC COMMISSIONS

Economic and Social Commission for Asia and the Pacific (ESCAP): United Nations Building, Rajdamern Avenue, Bangkok, Thailand.

Economic Commission for Africa (ECA): P.O. Box 300, Addis Ababa, Ethiopia.

Economic Commission for Europe (ECE): Palais des Nations 1211 Geneva 10, Switzerland.

## SPECIALISED AGENCIES

Food and Agriculture Organisation (FAO): Via delle Terme di Caracalla, 00100, Rome, Italy.

Inter-Governmental Maritime Consultative Organisation (IMCO): 101-104 Picadilly, London, WIY UAE England.

International Bank for Reconstruction and Development (IBRD): 1818 H. Street, N.W. Washington D.C. 20431 U.S.A.

International Civil Aviation Organisation (ICAO) : 1000 Sherbrooke Street, West Montreal Quebec, Canada.

International Development Association (IDA): 1818 H Street, N.W. Washington D.C., 20431 U.S.A.

International Finance Corporation (IFC): 1818 H Street, N.W. Washington D.C., 20431 U.S.A.

International Labour Organisation (ILO): 4, route des Morillons 1211, Geneve 22, Switzerland.

International Monetary Fund (IMF): 700 19th Street, N.W. Washington D.C. 20431 U.S.A.

United Nations Education, Scientific and Cultural Organisation (UNESCO):

7, Place de Fontenoy 75700 Paris, France
World Health Organisation (WHO) : 1211 Geneve, Switzerland.
World Tourism Organisation (WTO) captain Haya, 42, 28020 Madrid, Spain, E-mail:omt@world-tourism.org

## NON-GOVERNMENTAL ORGANISATIONS

American Hotel and Motel Association (AHMA), 888 Seventh Avenue, N.Y. 10010, USA.
American Society of Travel Agents (ASTA) www.asta.com
American Society of Travel Agents (ASTA): 711 Fifth Avenue, New York, N.Y. 10017 USA.
Conference of Government Tourism Organisations and Travel Agencies 01 Litewska 200-581, Warsaw, Poland.
Discover America Travel Organisation (DATO) 1899 L Street N.W-Washington, D.C. 20036, U.S.A.
East Asia Travel Association: 2-10-1 Yurakucho, Chiyodaku Tokyo, Japan.
European Travel Commission (ETC): P.O. Box 536 Dublin, Ireland.
Federation of International Youth Travel Organisations (FIYTO): 81 Islande Brygge 2300, Copenhagen 5, Denmark.
Inter-American Federation of Journalists and Writers in the Tourist Trade, Calle Rivadavia 755, Buenos Aires, Argentina.
International Academy of Tourism 4 Rue des Iris Monte Carlo, Monaco.
International Air Transport Association (IATA): 800 Place Victoria, P.O. Box 113 Montreal, Quebec Canada, H 42 IMI E-mail : atdi@iata.org
International Airline Passenger Association (IAPA) www.iapa.com
International Association of Convention and Visitors Bureaus, 1390 Market Street, San Francisco, California 94102 USA.
International Association of Scientific Experts in Tourism (AIEST) C.P. 2728, 3001 Berne, Switzerland.
International Bureau for Tourism and Youth Exchanges, P.O. Box 147, 1389 Budapest, Hungary.
International Bureau of Social Tourism: 7, Boulevard de I'lmperatrice, Gare Centrale, Bruxelles 1, Belgium.
International Centre for Advanced Tourism Studies (CIEST) Coronel Porfirio Diqz, 50 San Jeronimo Lidice, Mexico 20 D.F. Mexico.
International Centre for Conservation (ICC): 13 Via di San Michele 00153, Rome, Italy.
International Congress and Convention Association (ICCA): 15, Rue de L'Arcade, 75008 Paris, France. www.icca.nl.
International Federation of Camping and Caravaning: Rue d'Arenberg 44-B.P. 955, Brussels, Belgium.
International Federation of Tour Operators (IFTO): Amaliegade 37, 2 TR, 1256, Copenhagen K, Denmark.
International Federation of Tourism Journalists and Writers (IFTJR): Rue de L' Autumne 32, 1050, Brussels, Belgium.
International Federation of Tourist Centres : Schrutkagassell, 1130 Vienna,

Austria.

International Hotel and Restaurant Association (IH&RA) www.Ih-ra.com

International Social Travel Federation, 99-101 rue de la Loi, 1040, Brussells, Belgium.

International Touring Alliance (ITA) 2, Quai Gustave Ador 1207, Geneva, Switzerland.

International Union for Conservation of Nature and Natural Resources 1110 Morges, Switzerland.

International Youth Hostel Federation (IYHF): Midland Bank Chambers, Howardsgate, Welwyn, Garden City, Hertfordshire, England.

Pacific Asia Travel Association (PATA), Unit B1, 28th Floor, Siam Tower 989 Rama 1 Road, pathumwan Bangkok 10330 Thailand E-mail patabkk@patath.org

The Travel Research Association (TRA): P.O. Box 8066 Foothill Station, Salt Lake City, Utah 84108, USA.

Universal Federation of Travel Agents Association (UFTAA): 30, Avenue Marnix, 1050 Bruxelles, Belgium.

Universal Federation of Travel Agent's Association UFTAA www.uftaa.com

World Tourism Organisation (WTO) Calle Captain Haya, 42, Madrid-20, Spain.

World Association for Professional Training in Tourism: 105 rue St Lazare 75009 Paris, France.

World Association of Travel Agencies (WATA): 37 Quai Wilson 1211, Geneva 1, Switzerland.

World Travel and Tourism Council 1.2 Queen Victoria, Sovereign Court, London Elw' 3HA, UK. Email-enquries@wttc.org

# Travel Related Publications of International Organisations

### World Tourism Organisation (UNWTO)

WTO, Publications Section, Calle Captain Haya, 4228020, Madrid, Spain.
- Domestic Tourism
- Economic Review of World Tourism
- Handbook on Tourism Forecasting Methods
- Integrated Planning
- International Travel Statistics
- Marketing of Tourist Products of Developing Countries
- Physical Planning and Area Development
- Testing the Effectiveness of Promotional Campaigns in International Travel Marketing
- Technical Bulletins
- The Impact of International Tourism on the Economic Development of the Developing Countries
- The Role of Tourist Administration Concerning the Environment and Folklore
- The Changing World of Travel Marketing
- Tourism Compendium
- Tourism Latest Trends
- Tourism Surveys and Research
- Tourism Vocational Training in Africa
- Economic Effects of Tourism
- Evaluating Tourism Resources
- Travel Abroad. Frontier Formalities
- Travel Research Journal
- World Travel
- World Travel Statistics

# Travel Related Publications of International Organisations

- WTO: What it is, What it does, How it Functions
- *Aims, Activities and Fields of Competence of National Tourist Organisations*
- *Compendium of Financial and Fiscal Schemes for Development*
- *Economic Review of the World Tourism*
- *International Travel Statistics*
- *Survey of Africa's Tourism Prospects*
- *Relations between the National Tourist Office and the Travel Agencies*
- *Resolutions and Recommendations of the UN Conference on International Travel and Tourism (Rome, 1963)*
- *Study on the Economic Impact of Tourism on National Economics and International Trade*
- *Technical Bulletins*
- *Travel Research Journal*
- *Tourist Bibliography*
- *World Travel and Tourism Review*
- *Compendium of Tourist Statistics*
- *Travel and Tourism Fairs*
- *Shining in the Media Spotlight*
- *What Good Tourism Managers Need to Know*
- *Tourism 2020 Vision-Executive Summary*
- *Role and Structure of National Tourism Administration*
- *Manila Declaration on World Tourism*
- *Economic Effects of Tourism*
- *Physical Planning and Area Development for Tourism in the six WTO Regions*
- *Tourism Forecasting*
- *Development of Leisure Time and Right to Holidays*
- *Determination of the Importance of Tourism as an Economic Activity within the framework of the National Accounting System.*
- *Domestic and International Tourism's Contribution to State Revenue*
- *Study of Tourism's Contribution to State Revenue*
- *Concept, Production and Innovations of the Tourism Product*
- *Tourist Carrying Capacity*

## Organisation for Economic Cooperation and Development (OECD)

OECD-Publications Office, 2 Rue Andre Pascal, 75775 Paris Cedex 16, France.

- *Evolution of Tourism in Mediterranean Countries*
- *International Tourism and Tourism Policy*
- *Measures of Leisure*
- *Equality and Welfare*
- *Tourism Development and Economic Growth*

- Tourism Development and Economic Growth-Estoril Seminar
- Tourism Policy and International Tourism in OECD Member Countries
- Consumer Protection Concerning Air Package Tours
- Tourism Development and Economic Growth
- Impact of Tourism on Environment
- Tourism Policy and International Tourism in OECD Member Countries.
- Case Studies of the Impact of Tourism on the Environment

## International Labour Organisation (ILO)

ILO Publications, International Labour Office CH-1211 Geneva 22 Switzerland

- Activities of the International Labour Organisation in the Field of Tourism
- Careers in Hotel and Tourism Sector
- Study on the Training of Travel Agency Personnel
- Training of Tourist Office Personnel
- Vocational Training for Hotel and Tourist industry

## Pacific Asia Travel Association (PATA)

228 Grant Avenue, San Francisco California 94108, USA www.pata.org.

- Pacific Travel News
- Annual Statistical Report
- Pacific Hotel Directory
- Pacific Area Destination Handbook
- Glossary of Travel and Marketing Terms
- The Pacific: Your Log of Exploration
- Inside PATA
- Meetings Pacific
- Events in the Pacific.

## International Civil Aviation Organisation (ICAO)

P.O. Box 400, Place de L'Aviation Internationale, 1000 Sherbrooke Street West, Montreal, Quebec, Canada H3 A 2 R2.

- ICAO Bulletin
- International Standards and Recommended Practices on Facilitation
- Council Statements
- Digests of Statistics
- Manual Circulars
- Journal of Travel Research
- Tourism Recreation Research
- Annals of Tourism Research
- Cornell Hotel and Restaurant Administration

- *Hospitality Research Journal*
- *Journal of Leisure and Research*
- *Journal of Travel and Tourism Marketing*
- *Travel and Tourism Analysis*

## World Travel and Tourism Council (WTTC)

1-2 Queen Victoria Sovereign Court, London, ElW 3 HA, UK
- *Travel and Tourism in India : The Economic Impact and Potential*
- *South Africa's Travel and Tourism-The Economic Impact of Travel and Tourism*
- *China and Hong Kong: The Economic Impact of Travel and Tourism*
- *Steps to Success – Global Good Practices in Travel and Tourism*

## Business International Limited. The Economic Intelligent Unit (EIU)

P. O. Box 154, 151 Dartford Trade Park Hawley Road, Dartford DAI IQB, Kent United Kingdom
- *Competitive Strategies for the International Hotel Industry.*
- *European Car Hire Industry*
- *The European Long Haul Travel Market*
- *European Railways*
- *Far East and Pacific Travel in the 1990s.*
- *The Japanese Overseas Travel Market in the 1990s.*
- *Tourism in Eastern Europe*
- *The World Cruise Ship Industry*
- *Tourism and the Environment*
- *International Tourism Forecasts to 2005*

# Bibliography

Addison, William, *English Spas* (London: Batsford, 1951).
Aerni, M.J., 'The Social Effects of Tourism'. Current Anthropology, 13 (1972).
AJ. Burkart, *Tourism Past, Present and Future,* (London, Heinemann 1996)
Alastair, M. Morrison, *Hospitality and Travel Marketing* (New York: Delemar 1989).
Aldous, T. *Battle for the Environment* (London: Fontana/Collins, 1972).
Anand, M.M. *Tourism and Hotel Industry in India* (New Delhi: Prentice-Hall of India, 1976).
Andrew, S. Introduction to Tourism and Hospitality Industry *(Tata McGraw, Hill 2007)*
Archer, B.H. 'Tourist Research in the United Kingdom'. Journal of Travel Research. 10; 4 *(March 1972).*
Archer, B.H. *Demand Forecasting in Tourism* (Cardiff : University of Wales Press, 1974).
Archer, B.H. *The Impact of Domestic Tourism* (Cardiff: University of Wales Press, 1973).
Ashworth, G. J. *Marketing in the Tourism Industry* (London : Routledge 1990).
Ashworth, G. *Recreation and Tourism* (London : Bell and Hyman 1984).
Avvill, R. *Man and Environment* (London: Penguin, 1967).
Balsdon, J.P.V.D. *Life and Leisure in Ancient Rome (London: Bodley Head, 1966).*
Beazely, E. *Designed for Recreation* (London: Faber, 1970).
Bernecker, Paul. *Methods and Media of Tourist Publicity* (Vienna: Austrian National Tourist Office, 1961).
Bhatia, A. K. *International Tourism Management* (New Delhi: Sterling, 2019).
Bhatia, A.K. *Tourism Development-Principles and Practices* (New Delhi: Sterling 2019)
Bhatia, A.K. *Tourism in India-History and Development* (New Delhi: Sterling, 1978).
Bhatia, A.K. *Tourism Management and Marketing* (New Delhi: Sterling 2019)
Bhatia, A.K, *Travel Tourism – An Industry Facilitator* (Lotus Press New Delhi 2010)
Boniface, B and Cooper, C. *The Geography of Travel and Tourism* (London: Heinemann, 1987).
Brunner, E. *Holiday Making and the Holiday Trades* (London: Oxford University Press, 1945).
Bryden, John M. *Tourism and Development* (Cambridge: Cambridge University Press, 1973).
Bull, A. *The Economics of Travel and Tourism* (London: Pitman, 1991).
Burkart, A.J. and Medlik, S. *Tourism: Past, Present and Future* (London: Heinemann, 1976).
Burkart, A.J. *The Management of Tourism* (London: Heinemann, 1975).
Burton, R. *Travel Geography* (London : Pitman, 1995).

Burton, T.L. (Ed.) *Recreation Research and Planning* (London: Allen and Unwin, 1970).
Butler, R.W. 'The Social Implication of Tourism Development'; Tourism Research 2, 2 *(1974).*
Calder, N. *The Environment Game* (London: Panther, 1969).
Checchi and Co. *The Future of Tourism in the Far East* ( 1961).
Cherry, G.E. *Town Planning and its Social Context* (London: Hill, 1970).
Christian Gronroos, *Service Management and Marketing* (Lexington, Mass: Lexington Books, 1990)
Chuck, Y. Gee. *The Travel Industry* (New York :Van National Reinhold 1989).
Clare, A. Gunn *Tourism Planning* (Washington DC: Taylor & Francis, 1993).
Clare, Gunn. *Tourism Planning* (New York : Taylor and Francis, 1988).
Clayne, R. Jensen. *Leisure and Recreation-Introduction and Overview* (Philadelphia: Lea and Febiger, 1977).
Cleverdon, Robert. *The Economic and Social Impact of International Tourism on Developing Countries* (London: The Economic Intelligence Unit Ltd., 1979).
Cohen, Eric. 'Towards a Sociology of International Tourism', Social Research 39, 1 (1972).
Colley, G. *International Tourism Today (London: Lloyds Bank Review, 1967).*
Cooper, C. *Tourism Principles and Practices* (London : Pitman, 1993).
Cooper, Chris *Tourism Development* (London, Wiley 1991)
Cosgrove, Isabel and Jackson; R. *The Geography of Recreation and Leisure* (London: Hutchinson, 1972).
Crampon, L.T. *An Analysis of Tourist Markets* (Colorado: University of Colorado Press, 1963).
Crampon, L.T. *The Development of Tourism* (Colorado: University of Colorado Press; 1963).
Critian Gronross, *Service Management and Marketing* (Lexington, Mass, Lexington Books, 1990)
Dale, E. *Management Theory and Practice* (New York: McGraw-Hill, 1973).
Davidson, R. *Business Travel* (London : Pitman, 1994).
Davidson, R. *Tourism in Europe* (London : Pitman, 1992).
Davis, H.D. *Potentials for Tourism of Developing Countries* (London: Finance and Development, 1968).
Donald, E. Hawking (Eds.) *Tourism Planning and Development Issues* (Washington: George Washington University, 1980).
Donald, E. *Tourism Marketing and Management Issues* (Washington: George Washington University, 1980).
Douglas Pearce. *Tourist Development* (Longman, 1989).
Douglas, Pearce. *Tourism Today : A Geographical-Analysis* (New York : Longman, 1987).
Dower, M. *The Challenge of Leisure* (London: Civic Trust, 1965).
Dumazedier, J. *Towards a Society of Leisure* (New York: Free Press, 1967).
Ed Gell, D. L. *International Tourism Policy* (New York : Van Nostrand Reinhold 1990).
Edmunds. *Environmental Administration* (New York: McGraw-Hill, 1973).
Edward, J Mayo. *The Psychology of Leisure Travel* (Boston : CBI Publishing

Company, 1981).

Edwards, Francis, G. *How to Focus Your Marketing Efforts* (London: Louis A. Allen Associates, 1976).

Engel, James F. (Eds). *Market Segmentation: Concepts and applications (New York: Holt, Rinehart and Winston 1962).*

Feiffer, M. *Giving Places* (London : MacMillan, 1985).

Forster, John. *'The Sociological Consequences of Tourism'*, International Journal of Comparative Sociology, *(1964).*

Foster, D. *Travel and Tourism Management* (London : MacMillan, 1985).

Frank, R.E. *Market Segmentation* (New Jersey : Prentice-Hall, Inc; 1972).

Gearing Charles, E. *Planning for Tourism Development* (New York: Praeger Publishers, 1976).

Glasser, R. *Leisure: Penalty or Prize?* (London: Macmillan, 1970).

Gray, H. Peter. *International Travel-International Trade* (Lexington: Health Lexington Books, 1970).

Gregory, A. *The Travel Agent, Dealers in Dreams.* (The Prentice Hall Ltd. USA 1985)

Gunn, C. *Tourism Planning* (New York : Taylor and Francis, 1988).

Hammarskjold, K. *'Economics of Air Transport and Tourism'* (Montreal: I.C.A.O., 1972).

Harison, D, *Tourism and Less Developed countries* (London Wiley 1996)

Heath, E. *Marketing Tourism Destinations* (New York : Wiley 1992).

Hibbert, Christopher, *The Grand Tour* (London: Weidenfel and Nicolson, 1969).

Hiller, Herbet L. *'The Development of Tourism in the Caribbean Region.'* Air Travel and Tourism *(August 1972).*

Hodyson, A. *The Travel and Tourism Industry* (Oxford: Pergamon, 1987).

Hollander, S. *Passenger Transportation* (Michigan: Michigan State University, 1968).

Holloway, J. C. *Marketing for Tourism* (Harlow: Longman, 1995).

Holloway, J.C. *Marketing for Tourism* (London : Pitman 1988).

Howard. *Marketing Made Simple* (London: W.H. Allen, 1972).

Hudson, E. *'Vertical Integration in Travel and Leisure Industry.'* Institute of Air Transport *(Paris, 1972).*

Hunziker, W. *Social Tourism, Its Nature and Problems* (Geneva: Aliance International de Turisme, 1951).

Hurdman, L.E. *Tourism : A Shrinking World (New York : Viley, 1980).*

Ian M. Matley. *The Geography of International Tourism* (Washington : Association of American Geographers, 1976).

Inskeep, E. *Tourism Planning* (New York : Van Nostrand Reinhold, 1991).

Jefferson, A. *Marketing Tourism* (Harlow : Longman, 1988).

Jefferson, A. *Marketing Tourism-A Practical Guide* (Harlow, Longman 1991).

Jenkins C.L *Tourism-The State of the Art,* (London, Wiley 1986)

Jenkins, J. R. Zif, J.J. *Planning the Advertising Campaign (New York : MacMillan, 1973).*

John M. Bryden. *Tourism and Development* (London: Cambridge University

Press, 1973).

John, Lea. *Tourism Development in the Third World* (New York : Routledge 1988).

Joseph, D. Firdgen, *Dimensions of Tourism* (East Lansing, Michigan : American Hotel and Motel Association 1991).

Kaiser, Charles Jr. and Larry E. Helber. *Tourism Planning and Development* (Boston: CBI Publishing Company, Inc., 1978).

Kotler, P. *Introduction to Marketing Management, Analysis, Planning and Control* (London: Prentice-Hall, 1975).

Kernan, J. B. *Promotion* (New York: McGraw-Hill, 1970).

Keyser, H. Tourism Development, (Oxford University Press, Cape Town 2002)

Kerry Godrey and Jackie Clarke. *The Tourism Development Handbook* (London: Cassell, 2000).

Kotler, P. *Marketing for Hospitality and Tourism*, (Pearson Education, Delhi-1996)

Kotler P. *Principles of Marketing* (New York : Prentice-Hall, 1999)

Krippendorf, J. *The Holiday Makers. Understanding the Impact of Leisure and Travel* (Oxford : Heinemann 1987).

Lansing, J.B. Blood, D.M. *The Changing Travel Market* (Michigan: University of Michigan, 1964).

Law, C. *Urban Tourism : Attracting Visitors to Large Cities* (London: Mansell, 1993).

Laws, E.C. *Tourist Destination Management: Issues, Analysis and Policies.* (London : Routledge, 1995).

Laws, Eric, *Tourism Marketing* (Stanley Thorns 1997).

Lawson, Malcom. *Teaching Tourism-Education and Training in Western Europe-A Comparative Study* (London : Tourism International Press, 1975).

Leadley, P. *Leisure Marketing* (Harlow: Longman, 1992).

Lickorish, L. J. *Tourism and International Balance of Payments* (Geneva: International Institute of Scientific Travel Research, 1953).

Lickorish, L. J. *Tourist Promotion and Publicity Media* (Geneva: National Institute of Scientific Travel Research, 1955).

Lickorish, L.J. and Kershaw, A.G. *The Travel Trade* (London Practical Press, 1974).

Loughlin, Carleen. 'Tourism in the Tropics: Lessons from the West Indies' Insight and Opinion. *(1970).*

Lundberg, D.E. *The Tourist Business* (New York : Van Nostrand Rheinold 1990).

Lundberg, Donald. *The Tourist Business* (Boston: Cahners Books, 1974).

Lundberg, *International Travel and Tourism* (New York: Institute of Certified Travel Agents, 1970).

Mathieson, A, *Tourism: Economic, Physical and Social Impacts* (London : Longman, 1982).

McIntosh, R.W. *Tourism Principles, Practices and Philosophies* (Ohio: Grid; 1977).

Medlik, S. and Middleton V.T.C., 'The Tourist Product and its Marketing Implications', International Tourism Quarterly (1973).

Medlik, S. *Dictionary of Travel, Tourism and Hospitality*, (Butterworth-Heinemann, Oxford 1996)

Medlik, S. *Economic Importance of Tourism* (Surrey: University of Surrey, 1972).

Medlik, S. *Higher Education and Research in Tourism in Western Europe* (London: University of Surrey 1966).

Medlik, S. *Profile of the Hotel and Catering Industry* (London: Heinemann, 1972).

Middleton, V. *Sustainable Tourism* (Butterworth-Heinemann, Oxford 1998)

Middleton, V.T.C. *Marketing in Travel and Tourism* (London : Heinemann, 1988).

Middleton, V.T.C. *Marketing in Travel and Tourism* (Oxford : Heinemann, 1993).

Mill, R.C. *The Tourism Business: an Introductory Text* (London : Prentice-Hall, 1985).

Mill, R.C. *The Tourism System* (London : Prentice-Hall International, 1985).

Mill, R.C. *Tourism-The International Business* (New Jersey : Prentice-Hall, 1990).

Mitchell, Frank 'The Value of Tourism in East Africa', East African Economic Review. 2, (June 1970).

Morisson, A. M. *Hospitality and Travel Marketing* (New York : Delmar, 1989).

Murphy, Peter E, *Tourism : A Community Approach* (New York : Methuen 1985).

Neulinger, John. *The Psychology of Leisure* (Springfield: Charles C. Thomas, 1974).

Nicholson, M. *The Environmental Revolution* (London: Penguin, 1972).

Norval, A.J. *The Tourist Industry* (London: Issac Pitman and Sons Ltd., 1936).

Ogilvie, F.W. *The Tourist Movement: An Economic Study* (London: Staples Press, 1933).

Page, S. *Urban Tourism* (London : Routledge, 1995).

Parker, S. *The Future of Work and Leisure* (London: Mac Gibbon and Kee, 1971).

Patmore, J. A. *Land and Leisure* (London: David and Charles, 1970).

Pauline Horner, *Travel Geography for Tourism*, (Stanley Thorns, 1987)

Peaker, A. 'Holiday Spending by the British at Home and Abroad', National Westminster Bank Quarterly Review (August 1973).

Pearce, D. *Tourism Organisations* (Harlow : Longman, 1992).

Pearce, D. *Tourism Today* (Harlow : Longman, 1987).

Pearce, D. *Tourist Development* (Harlow: Longman, 1989).

Pearce, Sales, J. *Travel and Tourism Encyclopedia* (London: Blandford, 1959).

Peters, Michael. *International Tourism: 'The economics and Development of the International Tourist Trade'* (London: Hutchinson, 1969).

Philip Kotler. *Marketing for Hospitality and Tourism* (London: Prentice Hall and Inc. (1999)

Pigram, J. *Outdoor Recreation and Resource Management* (London: Croom Helm 1993).

Pimlott, J.A.R. *The Englishman's Holiday* (London: Faber, 1947).

Poynter, James M. *Tour Design, Marketing and Management,* (Prentice Hall, London 1993)

Pudney, John. *The Thomas Cook Story* (London: Michael Joseph, 1953).

Rae, W.F. *The Business of Travel* (London: Thomas Cook and Son, 1891).

Ram Acharya. *Civil Aviation and Tourism Administration in India* (New Delhi: National Publishing House, 1978).

Ray, Youell, *Leisure and Tourism* (London, Longman 1997)

Raymond, F. *Ecological Principles for Economic Development,* (London: John Wiley, 1978).

Reilly, R. T. *Travel and Tourism Marketing Techniques* (New York: Delmar 1988).

Richards, G. *Tourism and the Economy* (Surrey: University of Surrey, 1972).

Roberts, K. *Leisure* (London: Longman, 1970).

Robinson, G.W.S. 'The Recreation Geography of South Asia,' *Geographical Review* (October 1972).

Robinson. H. *A Geography of Tourism* (London: MacDonald and Evans, 1976).

Rosemary Burton. *Travel Geography* (London, Longman 1989)

Ross, G. F. *The Psychology of Tourism* (Melbourne : Hospitality Press, 1994).

Rothfield, Crampon, Wahab, *Tourism Marketing* (London: Tourism International Press, 1975).

Ryan, C. *Recreational Tourism : A Social Science Perspective* (London : Routledge, 1991).

Schmoll; G:*A Tourism Promotion* (London: Tourism International Press, 1977).

Sessa, Alberto. *Tourism in Developing Countries* (Paris: Reprint from Manual on the Conservation, UNESCO, 1970).

Seth, P.N. *Successful Tourism Planning and Management* (New Delhi: Cross Section Publications, 1978).

Sigaux, G. *History of Tourism* (London: Leisure Arts, 1966).

Smith, S. *Tourism Analysis* (New York: Longman, 1989).

Smith, S.J. *Tourism Analysis* (Harlow : Longman 1995).

Smith, S.L.J. *Recreation Geography* (Harlow : Longman, 1983).

Smith, S.L.J. *Tourism Analysis* (Harlow : Longman, 1989).

Standeven, J. *Sport Tourism,* (Kinetics Publication Illionois, 1999)

Sunetra, Roday, *Tourism-Operations and Management,* (Oxford University Press, New Delhi, 2009)

Susan Horner, *Marketing Tourism Hospitality and Leisure in Europe* (London: International Thomson Business Press, 1996).

Sutton, Geoffrey. *How to Sell Travel* (London: Travel Topics, 1959).

Sutton, W.A. 'Travel and Understanding Notes on the Social Structure of Touring'. *International Journal of Comparative Sociology.* (1967).

Tata, J.R.D. 'The Story of Indian Air Transport'. *Journal of Royal Aeronautical Society* (London: 1961).

Trease, Geoffrey. *The Grand Tour* (London: Heinemann, 1967).

Tull, D.S. *Marketing Research: Measurements and Methods* (London : Prentice-Hall 1993).

Turner, Louis and Ash John. *The Golden Hordes-International Tourism and the Pleasure Periphery* (London: Constable and Company, 1975).

Wahab, Crampon Rothfield. *Tourism Marketing* (London Tourism International Press, 1976).

Wahab, Salah. *Tourism Management* (London: Tourism International Press, 1975).

Wall, G, *Tourism Change, Impacts and Opportunities,* (Prentice Hall, 2000)

Walter, Pasini, *Tourist Health : A New Branch of Public Health* (Rimini : WHO 1988).

Waters, Somerset R. *"The American Tourist"*, Annals of the American Academy of Political and Social Sciences: *(1966).*

Weiler, B, *Special Interest Tourism* (London, wiley (1996).

White, J. *History of Tourism* (London: Leisure Art, 1967).

Yale. *Business of Tour operation*, (London Longman, 1995).

Young, George. *Tourism: Blessing or Blight?* (London: Penguin, 1973).

Yukic, T.S. *Fundamentals of Recreation* (London: Harper Row, 1963).

Zeithaml, V.A. *Services Marketing* (London: McGraw-Hill, 1996).